Working Life

Working Life

A Social Science Contribution to Work Reform

Edited by
Bertil Gardell
and
Gunn Johansson
both of the University of Stockholm, Sweden

JOHN WILEY & SONS
Chichester · New York · Brisbane · Toronto

British Library Cataloguing in Publication Data:

Working life.
 1. Industrial sociology
 2. Psychology, Industrial
 I. Gardell, Bertil
 II. Johansson, Gunn
 331.1   HD6955   80–40289

 ISBN 0 471 27801 7

Photoset by Thomson Press (India) Limited, New Delhi
and printed in the United States of America.

Contents

v

PART 5. THE ROLE OF SOCIAL SCIENCE IN WORKING LIFE POLICY

List of Contributors

ERIK ALLARDT, Ph.D.
Professor of Sociology, Research Group for Comparative Sociology, University of Helsinki, Finland

OSBORNE BARTLEY, M.D.
Professor, Chairman of the Swedish Confederation of Professional Associations

HANS BERGLIND, Ph.D.
Professor of Social Work, Department of Sociology, University of Stockholm, Sweden

DONALD E. BROADBENT, Sc.D.
Department of Experimental Psychology, Oxford University, Great Britain

TORE BROWALDH, D. Eng.
Vice Chairman, Svenska Handelsbanken (Swedish Commercial Bank)

ALBERT B. CHERNS, Ph.D.
Professor of Social Sciences, Department of Social Sciences, University of Loughborough, Great Britain

GUNNAR DAHLSTEN
President, Swedish Match Company, Stockholm, Sweden

EDMUND DAHLSTRÖM
Professor of Sociology, Department of Sociology, University of Gothenburg, Sweden

PETER B. DOERINGER
Regional Institute of Employment Policy Boston University, USA

BARBARA SNELL DOHRENWEND, Ph.D.
Professor of Psychology, City University of New York, USA

BRUCE P. DOHRENWEND, Ph.D.
Professor of Social Science, Social Psychiatry Research Unit, College of Physicians and Surgeons, Columbia University, New York, USA

ix

JAN EDGREN, D. Econ.

Director, Swedish Employers' Confederation

SVEN EKETORP, D. Eng.

Professor of Ferrous Metallurgy, Royal Institute of Technology, Stockholm, Sweden

MARIANNE FRANKENHAEUSER, Ph.D.

Professor of Experimental Psychology, Department of Psychology, University of Stockholm, Sweden

BERTIL GARDELL, Ph.D.

Professor of Work Psychology, Department of Psychology, University of Stockholm, Sweden

BJØRN GUSTAVSEN, Ph.D.

Director, Work Research Institute, Oslo, Norway

DAVID HAMBURG, M.D.

President, Institute of Medicine, National Academy of Sciences, Washington DC, USA

GUNN JOHANSSON, Ph.D.

Senior Researcher, Department of Psychology, University of Stockholm, Sweden

ROBERT L. KAHN, Ph.D.

Professor of Psychology and Program Director, Institute for Social Research, University of Michigan, Ann Arbor, USA

ROBERT A. KARASEK, Ph.D.

Assistant Professor, Department of Industrial and Management Engineering, Columbia University, USA

RITA LILJESTRÖM, Ph.D.

Lecturer, Department of Sociology, University of Gothenburg, Sweden

CARINA NILSSON, Ph.D.

Social Science Adviser to the Swedish Confederation of Trade Unions

STANLEY PARKER, Ph.D.

Office of Population Censuses and Surveys, Social Survey Division, London, Great Britain

ADAM PODGÒRECKI, Ph.D.   *Professor of Sociology, Centre for Socio-Legal Studies, Wolfson College, Oxford, Great Britain*

GÖSTA REHN, D. Econ.   *Professor of Labour Market Policy, Institute for Social Research, University of Stockholm, Sweden*

BENGT G. RUNDBLAD, Ph.D.   *Professor of Labour Market Sociology, Department of Sociology, University of Gothenburg, Sweden*

CARL THAM   *Under Secretary of State, Ministry of Labour, Sweden*

EINAR THORSRUD, Ph.D.   *Professor of Social Psychology, Work Research Institute, Oslo, Norway*

HAROLD L. WILENSKY, Ph.D.   *Professor of Sociology, Department of Sociology, University of California, Berkeley, California, USA*

Preface

During 1978 the Centenary of the University of Stockholm was celebrated and a series of symposia covering a wide range of subjects was arranged. This book is the result of one of them, arranged by the Department of Psychology and financed by a generous grant from the Bank of Sweden Tercentenary Foundation.

The symposium was prepared by an organizing committee with the following members: Hans Berglind, Professor of social work, Gunnar Borg, Professor of applied psychology, Marianne Frankenhaeuser, Professor of experimental psychology, Bertil Gardell, Professor of social psychology of work, Gunn Johansson, Ph.D., David Magnusson, Professor of psychology, and Nils-Eric Svensson, Ph.D., Managing Director of the Bank of Sweden Tercentenary Foundation.

The aim of this symposium was to present and evaluate, at an international level, basic social science research on human conditions at work in industrialized societies. The interdependence of working conditions and general conditions of life were to be emphasized. Influences from technological and economic development were to be considered, as were changing expectations and goals in the surrounding society. The ambition was to reach a wide social science coverage, so that psychological, sociological, sociomedical, and economic aspects of working life would be discussed.

The symposium was structured into five sections, each covering a special aspect of working life. The first session dealt with *psychosocial effects of advanced technology* and touched upon issues like advanced technology and democratic leadership, stress-induced health problems in relation to advanced technological systems, and the role of social science in relation to technological research and development. In a second session, the *time aspect of production systems and relations between work, family and leisure* were considered. Among the topics discussed were perspectives and evaluations related to changing or different forms of production on the one hand, and organization of the reproductive functions of society, the role and vitality of democratic institutions, and the content of leisure on the other. Impact on economic life of change in values and expectations due to more general changes in the larger society were also discussed in this session.

One session concerned *social effects of changes in the labour market* and considered social and human costs of structural and technological change, the effectiveness of societal policies in the field, the role of labour unions in relation to social control of economic and technological change, etc. More general issues were discussed in a session on *quality of life in industrial society*. Relationships between specific features of the economic system, including technology, level of living, life styles, and costs of adaptation for different groups in the industrialized society were considered.

In a final session *research policy in the field of working life* was discussed. The participants discussed present and potential contributions of behavioural science to long-range needs in the industrialized society and to policy making, research organization, and the role of the universities in the process of social change.

Each one of these sessions was planned to include scientific presentations as well as comments from a couple of discussants representing different sectors in society: government, government authorities, trade unions, private enterprise, etc. For this purpose the scientific papers were precirculated to all symposium participants.

The book includes all scientific contributions, most of the discussants' contributions, and a couple of contributions from chairpersons of the various symposium sessions. Apart from the discussants represented in this volume, the following participants made contributions at the symposium: Mr Gunnar Dahlsten, managing director, Swedish Match Company (Session 3 on social effects of a changing labor market), Mr Olof Palme, MP, former Prime Minister of Sweden (Session 4 on quality of life in industrial society), and Ms Anna-Greta Lejon, MP, former Swedish minister of immigration (Session 5 on the role of social science in working life policy).

The joint effort of a large group of people made the symposium, and thereby this volume, possible. We wish to take this opportunity to thank them all. Apart from the speakers and the members of the organizing committee, special thanks are due to Gunnel Björkgren, Ulla Falkenborg, Rolf Å. Gustafsson, and Björn O. Lindström, who did some of the hard work involved.

BERTIL GARDELL
GUNN JOHANSSON

Introduction

Working Life
Edited by B. Gardell and G. Johansson
© 1981 John Wiley & Sons Ltd

Strategies for Reform Programmes on Work Organization and Work Environment

BERTIL GARDELL

PURPOSE OF THE CHAPTER

The volume *Working Life* is built on the belief that scientific knowledge may contribute to an understanding of human costs of productivity, expressed in terms of worker control and worker health and well-being, and that this knowledge may be used in the organization of work in industrialized societies. The purpose of this introductory chapter is to give a general background and contextual setting for the various contributions to this discussion presented in the book. With this purpose in mind I will try to bring out some of the strategies emerging in industrial countries today—with reference especially to the Scandinavian scene—through which work could be better organized from a social and human point of view.

THE PROBLEM

Programmes for work reform and worker participation in decision-making have a long history, seen from an ideological point of view. But it was the late 1960s and early 1970s which really saw growing interest in these matters materialize. The reasons for this are manifold but tied to more general factors in the social and economic development of Western societies, such as increased standard of living, increased years of schooling, increased information through mass media, etc. Signs of worker unrest over bad working environment, tight social control, unchallenging tasks, increased demands for readjustment to change began to crop up in most countries, and there was a growing recognition among management, labour organizations, and politicians that something had to be done. Responses, of course, were different in different countries owing to the economic and political context.

In the Scandinavian countries labour has for a long time been organized into effective, rather centralized unions dealing not only with traditional bargaining issues but also to an increasing extent with more general sociopolitical issues, such as welfare policy, education, labour market policy, etc.

3

Trade unions also have had for many years an established interest in health and safety issues. Up to the mid-1960s, however, industry was regarded by both unions and politicians almost solely as a resource for political reform and for increased private and public consumption. There was no feeling that severe social costs were tied to prevalent means of increasing productivity. At least the social and human costs were felt to be well compensated for by increased standard of living and increased leisure.

During the 1960s a number of studies, as well as more unsystematic but tough practical experience, began to tell another story.

—*Structural change* was shown to mean increased difficulties, especially for elderly people and low-education groups, in keeping within the labour market (Berglind, 1976).
—*Physical and chemical risk factors* in the working environment were felt to be responsible for ill-health, absenteeism, and recruitment difficulties (Bolinder, Englund, and Magnusson, 1976).
—*Monotony and coercion* were felt to be increasing problems leading to low-quality production and to turnover, absenteeism, and recruitment difficulties especially among the young labour, (Gardell, 1971).
—*Mechanization* was felt to lead to increased mental fatigue which meant that increased leisure hours were not used for cultural and social activities as intended (Gardell, 1976b).
—*Shift work*, together with effects of mechanization, not only leads to difficulties in relation to worker health and family life but also to less participation in political, social, and cultural affairs, meaning less integration in the larger society (Magnusson and Nilsson, 1979).

Management in many countries—not least in Sweden—responded early to these signs and introduced programmes for work reorganization at the shop-floor level. Some of the programmes are internationally well-known, such as group assembly at Volvo and Saab-Scania (Agurén, Hansson, and Karlsson, 1976; Forslin and Söderlund, 1977). There are today several hundred other examples of efforts to create more challenging tasks and somewhat greater individual freedom at work, in order to decrease boredom and mental pressure (SAF, 1974). This development has been supported by the Swedish Employers' Confederation, which set up a special department for assisting and stimulating local developments and to publicize results considered to be of more general interest. As a social scientist I regret that it has been part of employer policy not to identify these efforts as scientific research or to call in social scientists to assist in field experiments, or evaluations. Possibly as a result of this policy, documentation has not met acceptable scientific standards and there are difficulties for outsiders who wish to make more independent evaluations of what has been achieved. Nevertheless, available evidence indicates that this employer-initiated development has been of great interest from a more general, human point of view and it represents, no doubt, a most important answer to some of the problems I have mentioned and which we have all experienced to some extent in our own countries.

At the same time, however, it is quite clear that this management approach to problems in working life is conceptualized in too narrow a frame of reference. This is significant not only for the Scandinavian development but for most 'quality of work life' changes that have taken place in Western societies. With a few exceptions most experiments have very little to do with industrial democracy in a sense which involves worker influence on larger economic and technological decisions. By and large these experiments—important as they may be—represent only new ways to increased productivity through increased motivation to work. This means that the approach is not answering all the relevant problems—such as worker claims for a broader base in decision-making—and it also means that its potential is not fully utilized. Basically, the same criticism could be launched at the local developments initiated at the end of the 1960s and the beginning of the 1970s by joint employer–worker bodies, involving also the central organizations on the labour market.

One of the basic problems, I think, is that none of these efforts has been built on a consistent theory from which a functional relationship between the influence of workers at different levels in the company could be developed. For example, it has been shown that autonomous groups and more skilled tasks lead workers to develop aspirations towards increased participation in overall planning and control since they have come to a better understanding of how such functions affect the immediate job (Gardell, 1977a). As a rule such an expansion of worker influence has not been accepted by management, which has led to frustration and feelings of powerlessness. In Sweden repeated experience of this kind finally led the central trade unions to ask for a new legal regulation of power-sharing in the economic system. Similar discussions are going on in several European countries. I think, however, it may be justifiable to use the Swedish example as an illustration of an alternative approach based on legislation and collective agreements in a joint effort to change the conditions of work.

SWEDEN AS AN EXAMPLE OF LEGAL/TRADE UNION BASED STRATEGIES FOR WORK REFORM

On the basis of a new legal framework, alternative strategies for work reform are materializing in Sweden today, which try to cover a much wider range of issues related to the organization of the production system, and to the position of man in this system. In this broader programme restructuring of work still plays an important role—not mainly for productivity reasons but for reasons related to the larger aim of developing a democratic working life, including greater concern for worker health and well-being and for non-material rewards from work. At the same time proponents of these programmes feel that such concern is not incompatible with long-range economic goals. During the present economic crisis the feeling that increased worker participation and better utilization of human resources also represents an economic asset seems to have deepened.

I think you could say that we are at present witnessing a large-scale break-through in the Swedish economy with respect to worker participation and influence in matters related to company affairs in general, but especially per-haps with respect to work environment and work organization. The basis for this breakthrough is the new legal framework regulating our industrial re-lations system and working conditions: the Act of Co-determination put in effect on 1 January 1977 and the Act of Work Environment put in effect on 1 July 1978.

The Act of Co-determination gives the trade unions the right to influence de-cisions at all levels in the company and all questions related to work and work environment are open for collective bargaining. Nationwide agreements on co-determination are expected in areas such as personnel policy, work organiz-ation, use of computers, top management. The Work Environment Act specifies that working methods, equipment, and material should be adapted to man both from a physiological and a psychological point of view. Work should also be organized in a way which furthers skill, self-determination, and vocational responsibility.

In this reform strategy, the concept of work environment has been seen as central, in several different respects.

First, through the new legislation worker resources may be organized to cope with work environment issues in a way which substantially adds to what might be accomplished through public control and expertise alone. The basis for action lies at the workplaces where the problems are to be found. In principle, local union representatives of two kinds will be found at each work site, one dealing with health and safety problems and one dealing with other conditions related to worker participation. Time and other costs for their work will be carried by the production. These local representatives have a legal right to all information they think is necessary to promote worker interests. They will have the right to call on outside experts to assist them in technical matters, evaluate new equipment, etc. Under the law they will probably also be able to ask for assistance from research groups if the central union agrees. The legal right to shut down hazardous operations given to the safety stewards under the present Act of Work Environment will be extended also to solitary work.

Second, I would like to stress that human constraints related to job design and job content have been treated as part of the concept of work environment and this has led towards an enlarged meaning of that concept (Forsman *et al.*, 1972). For practical purposes it has been felt that the behavioural sciences have made it sufficiently clear that job fragmentation and mechanization may result in mental strain and related psychosomatic malaise to warrant an enlarged health concept and a wider meaning of damage from work (Korn-hauser, 1965; Bolinder and Ohlström, 1971; Gardell, 1971, 1976a, 1976b, 1979; Frankenhaeuser and Gardell, 1976; Johansson, Aronsson, and Lindström, 1978; Levi, in press; Karasek, 1979; Wahlund and Nerell, 1977). The enlarged health-concept has made it possible to secure trade union interest in psychosocial aspects of work organization and technology and to ensure that concepts like Quality of Working Life and Humanization of Work are not used only to further productivity goals.

The third point I would like to make in this context concerns the impact that job content may have on the activity level of the individual worker. Impoverished and constrained work is related not only to impaired health but also to a generally low level of activity. This passive attitude and loss of initiative makes the worker less inclined to deal with even the most obvious health risks caused by chemical and physical factors in their own work environment (Gardell, 1977b; Karlsen et al., 1974; Karasek, 1980). You have here another example of the paradox found in much social science research: the people who most need changed conditions are the ones who are least active in bringing change about. The conclusion to be drawn from these studies is that it is important, but not enough, to organize bureaucratically worker resources through local safety committees and shop stewards. To make this organization effective you must also create an active interest in work-related issues among the ordinary workers. It seems as if increased skill demands and increased autonomy in relation to one's own job are the key factors in bringing about increased involvement in work and thus key factors in a more widespread use of worker resources and in coming to grips with bad and dangerous working conditions in general (Gardell and Gustavsen, 1980).

ENLARGED JOB CONTENT AS PART OF INDUSTRIAL DEMOCRACY

In addition to their implications for health and well-being, and for safety work, job content and organization of work have been made part of trade union programmes for industrial democracy. I would like to stress that—in contrast to the management-centred reform programmes—it has been important in the emerging legal/trade union based approach to industrial democracy not to make any theoretical difference between worker influence on different levels in the company. The trade unions' attitude all along has been that they want influence on all levels of the company. Influence for the individual worker on the shop floor level in relation to his own work, and collective forms for worker influence on company affairs, are seen as mutually supporting (LO, 1976; TCO, 1976). This view is also substantiated by research into these relationships as well as by field experiments, even if good data and evaluations are rare (Eldon, 1977; Andersson, 1976; Gardell and Svensson, 1981).

An early illustration of this growing trade union interest in work organization at the shop floor level may be found in a four-year-old joint policy statement on work organization made by the Metal Workers' Union and Swedish Union of Foremen and Supervisors.

In this document the parties compare the methods of the era of handicraft with present-day production methods, pointing out that fragmentation and mechanization of work have meant that dignity of work and intrinsic satisfaction from work have been lost. To restore some of these values the parties feel that it is necessary—within the framework of advanced technology and complex production systems—to enlarge the area of creativity and self-determination in work for each individual worker. I quote:

> To accomplish this, work organization should be based on groups of workers including the supervisor. These groups should be given a greater responsibility for planning, organization, and control over the work of the group. Functions now to be found in specialized staff-groups should be brought back to the producing work-teams.
>
> The motives for a change in this direction rest on demands for a richer job content and demands for improved quality of life. However, we are convinced that the effectiveness of our production system also will increase if this view of work organization is put into practice. (Metall-SALF, 1974)

This statement makes it clear that problems related to mass-production technology are at the focus of the debate. In this context health implications are not stressed, but job satisfaction and the dignity of work are. This position coincides well with the results of much social science research over the years, and shows that monotony, strain, and impoverished work are important problems, valid for large groups of workers. Not only industrial workers but also, to an increasing extent, office and service workers suffer from strain and impoverished work. Mental fatigue and passivity brought about by coercive and fragmented jobs also seem to spill over into less participation in cultural, social, and political life. These tendencies seem to increase with more use of advanced technology even if it is often claimed otherwise (Dahlström et al., 1966; Meissner, 1971; Braverman, 1974; Gardell 1978). The determination to abolish monotony and fragmented work has also quite recently been expressed in the outline for national agreements on work organization put forward by the blue- and white-collar unions jointly (LO/PTK, 1977). In this outline the work group is seen as the basic entity in the work organization to which decision-making power should be extended. In order to avoid hierarchy, technical experts and supervisors should work within the decision-making framework of the production groups. A work organization with such production groups as the primary building blocks is assumed to have the potential to counteract the problems of job fragmentation and mechanization on several grounds:

—within a group context the individual can expand his or her possibilities for attaining some amount of freedom and competence in work;

—the possibilities for learning, variation, and all-round use of human resources will be improved;

—the individual and the group will be able to achieve wider control over the work system and the work methods;

—human contact and solidarity between people will be more likely (LO, 1978; Gardell and Gustavsen, 1980).

To be able to reach such a development workers obviously also need to influence larger decisions and planning processes in the company. This is thought to be achieved through worker representation on boards, in management groups, and so on, and through bargaining procedures under the Act of Co-determination. This explicit connection between worker influence on the shop floor and worker influence through representatives is most important. It represents an understanding of the need for a multi-level strategy for bringing about a more democratic working life and for a consistent theory of worker influence at different levels in the production system. In my view this multi-level strategy constitutes the core difference between the traditional management approach to job reform programmes and the legal/trade union based approach which is emerging in Scandinavia today.

Of course, there will be many difficulties in realizing the goals, and this certainly is an area where much research and experimentation is needed and, in fact, being prepared. Tendencies within the groups to exert excessive pressure or exclude weaker members of the labour force must be observed. There is also a risk that in practice trade unions will fall back on central power and bargaining traditions at the expense of building up knowledge related to technology and job design. Nevertheless, the Act of Co-determination may be seen as an answer to the workers' need to influence not only the distribution of the results of production in the population, but also the methods of production including technology, job design, and the working environment. You could say that the political emphasis has shifted from the worker as a consumer to the worker as a producer.

THE ROLE OF RESEARCH IN WORK REFORM

Finally, some comments on the role of research in present and future developments. The role of research in relation to changes in working life should not be overstated. On the other hand, I think it is quite clear that both legislation, trade union policies, and management-initiated changes have been influenced by research findings on ill-health, stress, and discontent related to present production methods. I have tried throughout this paper to indicate something of this relationship between research and social action. The role of research is quite clear in relation to the legal regulation of physical and chemical risk factors in the work environment. To my mind it is also obvious that the emphasis on work organization and job content has been nourished both by descriptive research and action-oriented field experiments with autonomous groups and enlarged jobs. What has happened in Scandinavia is in effect that traditional descriptive research and research aiming at local problem-solving have entered into a new and fruitful relationship. The essential outcome of this relationship is that subjective experience among individuals and groups has been made a legitimate base for intervention through legislation or national agreements as well as for local measures. This is interesting since it implies an additional role of science to the traditional one of giving so called 'objective scientific' criteria for threshold-limit value regulation and the like—an approach that obviously is quite impossible for regulation of production methods and the organization of work in accordance with human needs and limitations. This merging of scientific outlooks has focused on concepts like worker control and worker well-being, both as effects of technology and job content and as resources for changes in working life in general. These concepts constitute the core of the psychosocial aspect of the working environment which is now included in the legal framework in Scandinavia as well as in action programmes officially accepted by the central worker organizations. I think this approach is very powerful and will make it possible for research to play an even more important role both with respect to health aspects and to democratic aspects of future production systems, in industry and elsewhere.

In this context it is important to underline the significance of values in social science research (Myrdal, 1971). Traditionally, psychological knowledge used in working life has been applied to problems which basically have to do with economic goals and the effectiveness of organizations. A classical example, of course, is the use of personality research for purposes of selection and training, e.g. in connection with career planning. In this case, the extra-scientific values on which psychological research is based are very clearly part of a competitive, growth-oriented, economic system. Psychological knowledge is regarded as an effective instrument for enhancing productivity and the survival of the organization. Even if somewhat disguised, however, the same basic conditions for the use of psychological research and knowledge also apply to other branches of psychology such as group dynamics and human relations, learning theory and motivation, perceptual and motor skills, etc. Also many of the experiments with job enrichment, autonomous groups, etc., are based on the same basic values. The basic approach has been to provide an answer to problems posed by management in its search for more adequate means of motivation and control. The ultimate goal is the competitiveness and effectiveness of the organization—not the well-being of people in our societies.

This approach to problems of working life has little to do with workers' protection as a basic goal. To be able to place behavioural science research within an enlarged concept of health and safety, I think it is necessary to anchor research not in economic but in social and humanistic values, where health, well-being, and the use of creative resources are fundamental goals in their own right, but also part of a larger value system of equity and solidarity, which today is weak but badly needed in world affairs. Our claim to play a role in relation to practical, political processes should rest on these values and on knowledge which research based on these values can provide. I deliberately play economic and administrative goals against human and social goals in an effort to make clear the basic differences of approach to the practical use of psychological knowledge which are inherent in these two models. In practice, of course, the problem is not as simple as that, but I think the distinction is necessary, in order for us to see clearly the potentials of behavioural science as a relatively independent force, and behavioural scientists as relatively independent actors in relation to policy-making. Also, definitions of strategic areas of research will be different for these different models, as will be our understanding of what practical measures should be taken to avoid conditions creating ill-health and passivity and what conditions should be stimulated to enhance well-being and individual control.

As a consequence of recognizing the fact that extra-scientific values always play a part in scientific work, not least in the definition and formulation of problems, there seems to be a growing understanding of the dialectics between theory and practice. Today, many social scientists believe that the distinction between 'basic' and 'applied' research is not a very fruitful one in our sciences, and that research dealing with problems of great extra-scientific value might in fact add incentive to high-quality research from an intra-scientific point of view. High academic standards are especially important in research of great practical implication if it is to be able to stand the test of practical evaluation.

But it is important to underline that this view of the role of science in society also leads the scientific community to demand that they be able to work under autonomous conditions—not in isolation or in ignorance of society, but under organizational conditions which support and give shelter to independent thinking and make it possible to pursue those criteria of truth which are the essence of all scientific work.

REFERENCES

Andersson, A. (1976). Företagsdemokrati vid Tobaksfabriken i Arvika (Industrial democracy at the tobacco plant at Arvika. An evaluation), mimeograph, Stockholm.
Agurén, S., Hansson, R., and Karlsson, K. G. (1976). Volvo Kalmarverken. Erfarenheter av nya arbetsformer (The Volvo Kalmar plant. The impact of new design on work organization), The Rationalization Council, Swedish Employers' Confederation and Swedish Confederation of Trade Unions, Stockholm.
Berglind, H. (1976). Strukturförändringar, arbetsmiljö och utslagning (Structural change, work environment and redundancy), Rapporter i psykosociala frågor (Reports on Psychosocial Issues), Swedish Government Official Reports (SOU), 1976, 3, 27–41.
Bolinder, E., Englund, A., and Magnusson, E. (1976). Kemiska hälsorisker i arbetsmiljön (Chemical Risk-factors in the Working Environment), Prisma, Stockholm.

Bolinder, E., Ohlström, B. (1971). *Stress på svenska arbetsplatser (Stress in Working Life.)*, Prisma, Stockholm.

Braverman, H. (1974). *Labor and Monopoly Capital*, Monthly Review Press, New York.

Dahlström, E., Gardell, B., Rundblad, B., Wingårdh, B., and Hallin, J. (1966). *Teknisk förändring och arbetsanpassning (Technological Change and Work Satisfaction)*, Prisma, Stockholm.

Eldon, M. (1977). Political efficacy at work: More autonomous forms of workplace organization link to a more participatory politics, paper prepared for the Seminar on Social Change and Organization Development at the Inter-University Center for Graduate Studies, Dubruvnik, Yugoslavia.

Forslin, J., and Söderlund, J. (1977). Automation and work organization – a case study from the automotive industry, mimeograph, Swedish Council for Personnel Administration, Stockholm.

Forsman, S., Bolinder, E., Gardell, B., Gerhardsson, G., and Meidner, R. (1972). The human work environment. Swedish experiences, trends, and future problems. A contribution to the UN Conference on the Human Environment, Royal Ministry for Foreign Affairs, Stockholm.

Frankenhaeuser, M., and Gardell, B. (1976). Underload and overload in working life: Outline of a multidisciplinary approach, *Journal of Human Stress*, **2**, 35–46.

Gardell, B. (1971). *Produktionsteknik och arbetsglädje. En socialpsykologisk studie av industriellt arbete (Technology, Alienation, and Mental Health)*, Swedish Council for Personnel Administration, Stockholm. English summary in *Acta Sociologica*, **19**, 83–93.

Gardell, B. (1976a). Psykosociala problem sammanhängande med industriella produktionsprocesser (Psycho-social aspects of industrial work), *Rapporter i psykosociala frågor (Reports on Psychosocial Issues)*, Swedish Government Official Reports (SOU), 1976, **3**, 67–86.

Gardell, B. (1976b). *Arbetsinnehåll och livskvalitet (Job Content and Quality of Life)*, Prisma, Stockholm.

Gardell, B. (1977a). Autonomy and participation at work, *Human Relations*, **30**, 515–533.

Gardell, B. (1977b). Psychological and social problems of industrial work in affluent societies, *International Journal of Psychology*, **12**, 125–134.

Gardell, B. (1978). Produktionsteknik och arbetsvillkor (Technology and conditions of work), in *Attityder till tekniken (Attitudes to Technology)*, ed. P. Sörbom, the Bank of Sweden Tercentenary Foundation and the Swedish Academy of Technological Science, Stockholm, 149–158.

Gardell, B. (1979). Tjänstemännens arbetsmiljöer: Psykosocial arbetsmiljö och hälsa. Preliminär rapport (Psychosocial work-load and health among white-collar workers), Research Unit for the Social Psychology of Working Life, Report No. 24, Department of Psychology, University of Stockholm.

Gardell, B., and Gustavsen, B. (1980). Work environment research and social change. Current developments in Scandinavia, *Journal of Occupational Behaviour*, **1**, 3–17.

Gardell, B., and Svensson, L. (1981). Co-determination and Autonomy. A Trade Union Strategy for Democracy at the Work Place. Swedish Centre for Working Life, Stockholm. (In press.)

Johansson, G., Aronsson, G., and Lindström, B.O. (1978). Social psychological and neuroendocrine stress reactions in highly mechanised work, *Ergonomics*, **21**, 583–599.

Karasek, R. A. (1979). Job demands, job decision latitude, and mental strain: Implications for job redesign, *Administrative Science Quarterly*, **24**, 285–308.

Karasek, R. A. (1980). Job socialization and job strain: The implications of two related psychosocial mechanisms for job design, in this volume.

Karlsen, J. I., Naess, R., Ryste, Ø., Seierstad, S., and Sørensen, B. A. (1974). *Arbeidsmiljø og Vernearbeid (Work Environment and Workers' Protection)*, Tanum Forlag, Oslo.

Kornhauser, A. (1965). *Mental Health of the Industrial Worker*, Wiley, New York.
Levi, L. (ed.) (in press). *Society, Stress and Disease, Vol. IV: Working Life*, Oxford University Press, London.
LO (1976). *Solidariskt medbestämmande (On Co-determination)*, Swedish Confederation of Trade Unions (LO), Stockholm.
LO (1978). *Grupporganisation (Group organization.)*, No. 1: Medbestämmande i arbetslivet Co-determination in working life, Swedish Confederation of Trade Unions (LO), Stockholm.
LO/PTK (1977). Förslag till medbestämmandeavtal, (Outline of central agreement on co-determination), Swedish Confederation of Trade Unions (LO), Stockholm.
Magnusson, M., and Nilsson, C. (1979). *Att arbeta på obekväm arbetstid. Vad säger forskningen om konsekvenser för människan och behov av för bättringar beträffande arbetstidens förläggning?* (Work at inconvenient working hours. What does research say about consequences for man and needs for improvement as regards the scheduling of working hours?), Prisma, Stockholm.
Meissner, M. (1971). The long arm of the job: A study of work and leisure, *Industrial Relations*, **10**, 239–260.
Metall/SALF (1974). Uttalande om arbetsorganisation (Statement on work organization), mimeograph, Swedish Metal Workers' Union (Metall) and Swedish Union of Foremen and Supervisors (SALF), Stockholm.
Myrdal, G. (1971). *Objectivity in Social Research*, Duckworth, London.
SAF (1974). *Nya arbetsformer (New Methods of Work)*, Swedish Employers' Confederation (SAF), Stockholm.
TCO (1976). *Villkor i arbetet. En skrift om personalpolitik (Conditions of Work. A Report on Personnel Policy)*, Swedish Confederation of Salaried Employees (TCO), Stockholm.
Wahlund, I., and Nerell, G. (1977). *Work Environment of White Collar Workers. Work, Health, Well-being*, Swedish Confederation of Salaried Employees (TCO), Stockholm.

Part 1

Psychosocial Effects of Advanced Technology

Working Life
Edited by B. Gardell and G. Johansson
© 1981 John Wiley & Sons Ltd

Work and Health.
Some Psychosocial Effects of Advanced Technology*

ROBERT L. KAHN

INTRODUCTION

Successive changes in technology—that is, tools and the rules for using them—have brought about many other changes, some hotly disputed and others beyond dispute. For example, increases in material consumption can be granted without argument as an outcome of technological advancement.

The costs of those increases, however, are arguable. Bertrand Russell (1930) once summed up the case by asserting that 'mankind decided to submit to monotony and tedium in order to diminish the risks of starvation'. Certainly industrialization has increased the number of people engaged in small-muscle, short-cycle, machine-paced work—along with exposure to such hazards as noise, chemical poisons, and radioactivity. But industrial work has also reduced the demand for large-muscle physical effort, the imposition of work pace by slave-drivers or gang-bosses, and the exposure of workers to the natural hazards of wind and weather. Moreover, it has also reduced the proportion of time spent at work—hours per day, days per year, and years per lifetime.

Beyond these arguments of good and ill is the brute fact that technological increases in production have been bought with fossil fuels. Boretsky (1975) notes that the consumption of BTUs per employed civilian in the United States, which he calls the single most comprehensive indicator of overall technological advancement, was about 62 per cent higher in 1972 than it had been in 1950, and that Gross National Product per person employed in the private economy (measured in constant prices) went up by 74 per cent during the same period. The reason for this close correlation ($r = 0.93$), he goes on to point out, is that the essence of most technological innovations, thus far in human history, has been the substitution 'in all kinds of equipment and mechanical implements, of BTUs for human and animal energy' (p. 71).

---

*This paper is adapted in part from Chapter 17, Work and Health, in the Social Psychology of Organisations (2nd Edition), by Daniel Katz and Robert L. Kahn. New York: John Wiley & sons, 1978.

How long this kind of exchange can continue, whether or not it should, on what energy sources it can draw, and with what risks, are among the crucial questions that confront the human race. Those questions are more likely to be dealt with wisely, I believe, if the outcomes of human organizations are appraised more broadly than has usually been the case, and are defined to include not only the goods and services that are created but the well-being of the people who create them.

This idea is not new, but it has been persistently neglected. The great societal dialectic has been acknowledged in the abstract—human beings create social institutions and are in turn created by them—but ignored at the level of individuals and organizations. Even the open-system model of organizations, which has the potentiality for including outcomes at the individual and societal levels, has for the most part failed to realize that potential for reasons of inappropriate simplification. The brief litany of input–transformation–output has been recited; examples have been given in terms of raw materials, manufacture, and sales, and the rest has been ignored. As some modest documentation of this general point, consider the subject of work and health. Three major handbooks on work and organization have been published in the United States, two of them since 1976. None contains either a chapter on or an indexed reference to health or illness.* Texts and books of readings, old and new, confirm this pattern. The well-being and illness of individuals are not ordinarily regarded as organizational outcomes, even in part.

The central proposition of this paper, on the other hand, is that the demands and opportunities, the stresses and supports of organizational work roles affect the health of the individuals who enact those roles. We consider their health, physical and mental, to be a complex outcome determined in part by properties of the organizations in which they work and the positions they occupy in those organizations. Such effects are thus part of the organizational output.

They are usually among the 'unintended' effects of organizations, however, or at least they stand low on the list of organizational priorities. Partly for that reason, such effects are seldom measured, seldom counted, and almost never included in the major accounting procedures of organizations. Moreover, the effects of organizations upon their members are less easily observed than the main organizational throughput; organizational effects on individuals merge with other effects, environmental and genetic, present and past.

There are some exceptions to these observations, most of them having to do with accidents and physical illnesses conspicuously associated with particular occupations. Folk wisdom and experience had identified certain occupational diseases long before systematic data became available, and the documentation of such occupational hazards has now become extensive in some countries.

Moreover, in recent years research findings have begun to accumulate on

---

*The Dunnette (1976) handbook does contain a chapter by Joseph McGrath on stress and performance.

more subtle occupational effects—physical and mental, immediate and delayed, positive as well as negative. The University of Stockholm and the Karolinska Institute are leaders in such research, and it is on the increase in the United States. In the remainder of this paper, we propose a model in terms of which the findings of that research can be reviewed, attempt such a review, and in the light of those research findings return to the question of technological change.

APPROACHES TO STUDYING WORK AND HEALTH

We can think of the individual in terms analogous to those of the organization. The individual is also an ongoing system, with criteria of well-being and requirements for continuing life quite separate from those of the organization. Some such individual requirements are beyond argument—air, water, food, and sleep in appropriate quantities. Criteria of social and psychological well-being are less well established. There is some convergence, nevertheless, around the Freudian definition of well-being as the ability to work, love, and play, around the idea of freedom from distressing symptoms (gastric discomfort, inability to sleep, etc.), around veridicality of perception, and around positive affect towards self and towards life. These criteria of individual well-being, objective and subjective, are quite separate from the criteria of organizational effectiveness.

The enactment of an organizational role by an individual can thus be thought of as an intersection and partial overlap of two separate systems, the person–system and the organization–system. The overlap consists of certain cycles of behaviour (the enactment of the organizational role) that are shared in time and space—indeed, are identical—for the person and the organization. The behaviours themselves are part of the ongoing life of the individual and of the organization; they define in part both systems.

We are accustomed to studying the extent to which these shared or overlapping cycles of behaviour contribute to efficiency, productivity, growth, and other criteria of organizational effectiveness. Has the individual performed his or her work role with energy, skill, regularity, and judgement sufficient for the continuing success of the organization? It is equally appropriate to ask the complementary questions: Does the enactment of the organizational role enhance or reduce the well-being of the individual? Does it enlarge or diminish the person's valued skills and abilities? Does it increase or restrict the person's opportunity and capacity to fulfil other valued life roles?

Several kinds of comparisons have been used to investigate the answers to such questions in work situations. The most common (and least satisfactory) is a comparison of different sets of individuals engaged in differing tasks, with an attempt to explain observed differences in health in terms of the differing jobs. Such analyses present obvious and difficult problems of self-selection. Do bureaucrats acquire bureaucratic personalities because of their work, or are people of such characteristics attracted to and selected for bureaucratic positions?

Such problems of interpretation are eased when comparisons can be made of the same individuals in two or more different work situations. What happens, for example, when people are promoted, or move to jobs of different technology or organizational characteristics? A special instance of such longitudinal comparisons involves changes into and out of work roles. Are there, for example, predictable consequences to the movement from non-work to work roles (student or housewife to employed worker)? And from work to non-work, either voluntary or involuntary?

Finally, investigators have studied the effects of jobs by looking at substantial numbers of people engaged in the same job (occupation) and attempting to discover uniformities, although this gives in itself only a weak basis for inference.

These, of course, are methodological observations; they do not in themselves say anything about the theories, hypotheses, or models in service of which such comparisons might be made. A number of such models have been proposed for the study of stress (Scott and Howard, 1970), but almost none of them emphasizes the work role (Selye, 1956; Janis, 1958; Lazarus, 1966). An exception is the model proposed by French and Kahn (1962) and elaborated by them and their colleagues in the course of subsequent research (Kahn, 1974; French, 1974; Cobb, 1974). Its purpose is to provide a framework for research on the effects of the work role on health, and it serves that purpose for a continuing series of

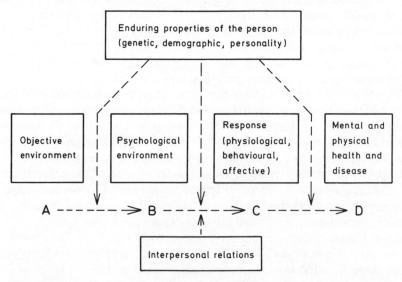

Figure 1 Theoretical framework for research on the effects of work role on health. *Source:* French and Kahn, 1962

investigations at the Institute for Social Research of the University of Michigan (see Figure 1).

The ISR model is extremely broad when presented in these terms; it is in fact a set of conceptual categories rather than the representation of a theory. It becomes both more restrictive and more informative as concepts are introduced into the several categories (boxes) and hypotheses are proposed (arrows). Thus, hypotheses of the A → B category have to do with the effects of the objective work environment on the psychological work environment (the work environment as the individual experiences it). For example, people whose jobs require them to engage in transactions across the organizational boundary (a fact in their objective work environment) more often report that they are subjected to incompatible demands on the job (a fact in their psychological environment).

Hypotheses of the B → C category relate facts in the psychological environment to the immediate responses that are invoked in the person. For example, the perception that one is subject to persistent conflicting demands on the job is associated with feelings of tension. The C → D category deals with the effect of such responses on criteria of health and illness. The relationship of sustained job tension to coronary heart disease (perhaps more arguable with respect to the empirical evidence) illustrates the C → D category.

Finally, the three categories of hypotheses just described must be qualified by an additional class, represented by the vertical arrows in Figure 1. This class of hypotheses states that relationships between objective and psychological environment, between psychological environment and response, and between response and health or illness are modified by enduring properties of the individual and by interpersonal relations. For example, the extent to which a person experiences tension on being exposed to role conflict depends very much upon the personality characteristic of flexibility–rigidity; people who are flexible rather than rigid respond with greater tension to the experience of role conflict. On the other hand, supportive relations with others seem to buffer or modify some of the relationships between the stressful demands of the work role and the consequences for the individual. For example, French (1974) found in a study of a government agency that quantitative work load was related to diastolic blood pressure ($r = 0.33$), but not among those employees who had supportive relationships with their supervisors. In similar fashion, other properties of the person and his or her interpersonal relationships act as conditioning or modifying variables in the causal sequence that leads from the work role to health or illness.

Given this framework, we can define an adequate explanatory sequence; it would consist of a chain of hypotheses beginning with some characteristic of the objective work environment, ending with some criterion of health, specifying the intervening variables in the psychological environment and in the immediate responses of the individual, and stating the ways in which this causal linkage is modified by the differing characteristics of individuals and their interpersonal relations. Such a causal chain might be called a theme, and a set of such themes, logically related, would constitute a theory of work and health.

No one could claim that such a matured theory yet exists, much less that its components have been subjected to empirical test. The framework serves to remind us, however, of one form that such a theory might take. It reminds us also of the cumulative meaning of such empirical fragments as are at present available to us regarding the social–psychological aspects of work and health.

OCCUPATION, INDUSTRY, AND CLASS OF WORKER

One aggregation of findings that link work and health consists of the differential incidence of certain diseases and disabilities among workers in different industries, different occupations, or different 'classes' (that is, private industry, government, and self-employment). Such findings often fail to specify the causal factors within these labour force categories and they omit the intervening explanatory structure required by our model. They are nevertheless a useful point at which to begin an empirical summary of things known about work and health.

The US Bureau of the Census recognizes eight major industrial categories: agriculture, mining, construction, manufacturing, transportation and public utilities, wholesale and retail trade, finance and real estate, and service. Gross differences in these categories in reported disability are not large, but the reasons for disability show a plausible pattern. Farm workers have the highest proportion of musculo-skeletal disability, for example, and white-collar workers the highest proportion of cardiovascular disability (Haber, 1971). The pattern for accidents reflects the hazards of blue-collar jobs and the industries—manufacturing and construction—in which they are concentrated.

Disabilities categorized as nervous or mental are about 8 per cent of the total, but they are most likely to be classified as severe, especially among blue-collar workers. Almost three out of four blue-collar workers with such problems were rated severely disabled (unable to work regularly); the proportion of severe disability among all workers disabled for any reason is only one in four. The magnitude of such differences between industries, for all injuries and illnesses combined, is shown in Figure 2.

A great deal of information has been accumulated for the purpose of specifying in more detail the categories of physical illness associated with different occupations and industries, and identifying the physical substances and modes of exposure that account for such associations. The collection, interpretation, and use of such information is central to a number of professions other than sociology and psychology. It is known, for example, that fatality rates attributable to certain kinds of chemical exposure are extremely high.

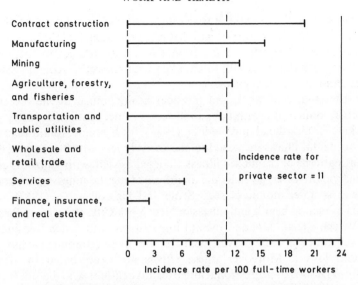

Figure 2 Injury and illness incidence rates by industry division, United States. *Source:* Bureau of Labor Statistics, US Department of Labor (unpublished data), 1973

Asbestos workers have about five times the normal expected rate of fatal lung cancer in the United States, and the ratio of actual to expected deaths increases with years of exposure (Selikoff and Hammond, 1975). Twelve per cent of all working coal miners and 21 per cent of non-working miners showed x-ray findings of pneumoconiosis (Leinhart *et al.*, 1969). Abnormal births—infants with congenital abnormalities—appear to be about twice as frequent among women workers exposed to anaesthetic gases in operating rooms as among similar workers not so exposed (American Society of Anesthesiologists, 1974). Meatwrappears using polyvinyl chloride wrapping materials and price labels have distinctive respiratory and related symptoms (69 per cent) and characteristic week-end and vacation remissions (77 per cent; Bardand, 1973).

Since the passage of the Occupational Safety and Health Act in 1970, there has been a rapid establishment of standards in the United States for the use of these and other materials. At least twenty-five such standards were set in the period 1972–1975, for stressors ranging from the commonplace to the exotic— from heat and noise to beryllium and toluene diisocyanate. The task of developing such standards meanwhile continues to grow. The development of new technologies implies the possibility of new hazards and the need for discovering and limiting them.

Neither the research workers who discover such occupational hazards nor the people who promulgate ways of protecting workers against them believe that the problems are thereby solved. Indeed, it could be argued that the problems move from the domain of toxicology and traditional occupational medicine to the domain of organizational theory, persuasion, and the introduction of change. Nevertheless, steps have been taken with respect to these physical hazards of work that have still to be taken with respect to social psychological stresses and their consequences.

Like the studies of work and physical health, much of the research that links work to mental health does so in terms of occupation, industry, or class of worker. Hollingshead and Redlich (1958), for example, found that the incidence of mental illness increased in successively less advantaged social classes and that patterns of diagnosed illness changed as well, with schizophrenia conspicuously more often given as the diagnosis of mental illness among people in the lower socio-economic classes. Srole and his colleagues (1962), studying patterns of mental health and illness in New York City, show a similar association between social class and mental impairment, with a ten-fold increase in 'sick–well ratios' as one moves from the top socio-economic category to the sixth and lowest. Moreover, these effects are exacerbated by downward mobility. The sons of professional and executive fathers who did not themselves enter such occupations show twenty times the symptoms (sick–well ratio) of sons who followed their fathers into these advantaged occupations.

NATIONWIDE STUDIES OF WORK

Quinn and his colleagues (1974, 1977) have done research that provides more recent data along similar lines, and has the advantage of being based on succssive nationwide samples. It also has the characteristic limitation of such representative data sets; it is based wholly on self-report. Beginning with issues of safety and health, the data include nineteen aspects of working conditions that have been the subject of government action, legislation, and labour negotiation in the United States.

Only about one worker in ten reported no problem in any of the nineteen areas of specific inquiry, and the overall average number of problems mentioned was three. As expected, more problems were mentioned by wage-and-salaried workers than by those self-employed, more by blue-collar than by white-collar workers, and more by operatives (machine workers) than by those in any other occupations. This general finding of disadvantage of blue-collar, industrial, and service jobs summarizes a pattern of almost unbroken specific disadvantages. Moreover, the pattern is exacerbated in regard to such economic matters as wages and employment security. Unsteady employment is essentially a problem of certain occupations and industries. It is reported by only 1–3 per cent of white-collar workers in government, finance, insurance, and real estate; but it is reported by 40 per cent of construction workers, 20 per cent of miners, and more than 20 per cent of unskilled labourers regardless of industry.

The model we have proposed (Figure 1) leads us to look for patterns of response—affective, behavioural, and physiological—that reflect the differences in occupational and industrial categories that we have now reviewed. With respect to affect, feelings of satisfaction or dissatisfaction about work, those expectations are fulfilled. Overall job satisfaction, as measured by Quinn and Shepard (1974), varies among occupational groups from − 42 to + 24, with machine operatives and labourers at the bottom of that range and professionals and managers at the top. The pattern is particularly sharp with respect to the content of the job (challenge), and is not at all apparent for some other facets, especially satisfaction with one's co-workers.

These ecological patterns of correlations tell us a good deal about the nature of work, and encourage interpretations and hypotheses of greater specificity. The development and testing of such hypotheses, however, requires three additional kinds of research: (1) laboratory experiments, in which causal relationships between specific work-relevant stimuli and predicted responses can be tested; (2) non-experimental field studies, in which the broad categories of occupation and industry can be disaggregated in ways that identify their significant components for representative populations of workers; and (3) field experiments, in which major hypotheses about the improvement of work can be tested on a scale that is significant for social policy as well as social science. To some extent, all three of these lines of research have been developed during the past decade, and we will summarize the results of that work very briefly in the following sections of this paper.

LABORATORY EXPERIMENTS WITH WORK-RELEVANT VARIABLES

The most general result of this laboratory work has been to demonstrate relationships between a very considerable number of stressful conditions and an equally impressive number of responses indicative of strain, both for animals and human subjects. The experiments, as McGrath (1976) has pointed out, deal with three broad stimulus categories: intrinsic aspects of task content, social–psychological conditions under which the experimental task is carried out, and physical conditions under which past performance is required.

The performance of physical experimental tasks produces physiological signs of strain (elevated heart rate, increased secretion of adrenaline and noradrenaline, elevated systolic blood pressure, etc.) only if the physical demand is heavy or if it is perceived as heavy (Frankenhaeuser, 1971). Mental tasks (e.g. mental arithmetic) have also been shown to evoke physiological strain, especially when the tasks are performed under distracting conditions. These have included recorded workshop noise (Frankenhaeuser, 1971), flickering light (Raab, 1966), and other irritating factors presumably of the kind encountered at work (Frankenhaeuser and Patkai, 1964). All these experiments involved characteristically brief periods of task performance, but Levi (1972) conducted one experiment in which subjects (army officers and corporals) engaged in a simulated electronic firing of rifles against moving targets for a period of 72 hours. There was a marked decrement in performance and a marked increase in physiological indicators of strain (adrenaline and protein-bound iodine), together with considerable subjective distress.

Physiological signs of strain have been evoked experimentally by embarrassing interrogation (Hamburg, 1962), by the anticipation of uncomfortable or annoying situations (Berman and Goodall, 1960), and by the anticipation of tasks characterized by uncertainty of success or penalty (Frankenhaeuser, 1971). Other experiments have shown similar effects from the experience of task failure, interpersonal disagreements during task performance, low status, and other social disadvantages.

Most experiments involving physical conditions of task performance as stressors have been done with animals, for reasons of ethics, and the extrapolation to human beings in general and the work role in particular remains uncertain. Many of the findings, nevertheless, remind us of the stresses of work. Moreover, the damaging effect of stresses increases very sharply when they are imposed in combination rather than singly. Heat, altitude, and random vibration as separate conditions caused death in rats at rates varying between 0 and 7.5 per cent; the same stress factors in pairs caused death in 65 per cent of the animals subjected to them (Dean, 1966).

Another line of animal experimentation that seems important for understanding the work role has involved the imposition of punishment for failure to perform to standard. Some of these experiments (Corson, 1971) suggest that unavoidable tasks, insoluble problems, and inescapable punishment cause greatest strain (heart rate, respiration rate, and temperature in dogs). Other laboratory studies, including the small but much publicized 'executive monkey experiments', seem to show that strain is maximized when punishment can be avoided but only by successful performance of a strenuous task and when the experimental subject has 'responsibility' for averting the punishment both from self and from a visible other. The 'executive monkeys', whose pressing of a bar could prevent electric shock to themselves and their partners, died of gastro-intestinal lesions in periods varying from 9 to 48 days. None of their 'non-executive' partners, equally shocked but without any means of prevention, died and none showed any gastro-intestinal pathology.

The stressfulness of extreme sensory deprivation has been demonstrated beyond question. Hebb's (1958) subjects, who were required to remain in small isolation rooms but were not otherwise restrained, rated the situation 'unbearable' after three or four days. Frankenhaeuser (1971) reported increases of adrenaline and noradrenaline under more moderate conditions of under-stimulation—the requirement to press a button in response to an irregular signal under conditions of isolation from others. The signs of strain increased when the task was made more complex—the matching of responses by buttons and pedals to multiple signals. This combination of specialized overload and general under-stimulation (lack of opportunity for interaction with others, limitation of activities to a small but demanding repertoire) is suggestive of many work roles, white-collar and blue-collar, in advanced technologies.

A few experiments have been done that attempt the simulation of complete work roles under realistic conditions. Levi (1972) had groups of subjects sort ball-bearings according to small differences in size. There were time pressures to complete the job, critical observations about performance, variations in light, and a background of recorded workshop noise. About two hours of such work produced subjective ratings of unpleasantness and physiological changes of increased heart rate and blood pressure, increased secretion of adrenaline and noradrenaline, and increased concentrations of triglycerides and free fatty acids in the blood plasma. The experimenter comments that 'it is tempting to speculate about the effects of the socio-economic or other real-life stressors, which may be repeated over months and surely may represent a threat to the individual far exceeding that implied in our laboratory situation' (Levi, 1972, 91–105).

STRESS AND STRAIN: FIELD STUDIES

Real-life settings do not partition stress so neatly into task, social–psychological, and physical categories. Studies of stress in such settings tend to involve contrasts between groups with very different life experiences, responses of groups to extreme situations of many kinds, and responses to crisis events. The populations contrasted in these studies are many—blacks and whites, soldiers and civilians, prisoners and publics, communities in disaster and communities spared. Haas and Drabek (1970) cite more than 300 studies of extreme situations and point to some convergence in the results—decrements in performance, undesirable changes in personality, and physiological signs of strain.

The convergence is welcome in a sense, but it lumps together a baffling variety of stresses. One interpretation of that agglomeration is that any event that requires a response of coping or adaptation is likely to evoke some indication of strain. Holmes and Rahe (1967) have taken exactly this view, and treat all such events as stressors, regardless of whether they are sought or unsought, and experienced as positive or negative. Thus their 42-item Schedule of Recent Experiences (SRE) includes the death of one's spouse, the purchase of a new car, marriage, losing one's job, etc. Only the element of situational change and therefore change-demand seems common throughout the list. This approach is in some respects consistent with Selye's, which also regards stressors in terms of an underlying continuum ranging from under-stimulation to over-stimulation. The task of the researcher involves assigning the proper weight or magnitude to all of the relevant stressors. In principle, a combined stress score then could be constructed for any work situation and any technology.

Other investigators, concerned more specifically with the stresses and strains of work, have used detailed comparisons within occupational categories as a means of testing specific hypotheses. Russek (1962) confirmed a predicted ordering of hypertension and coronary heart disease within three professions—medicine, dentistry, and law. For medicine, the ordering increased from dermatologists to pathologists, and then to anaesthesiologists and general practitioners; for dentistry the incidence of these diseases was successively higher among the following groups: periodontists, orthodontists, oral surgeons, and general practitioners. For law the ordering was patent law, other specialties, trial law, and general legal practice. These comparisons are compelling, but they leave us in some doubt as to the source of stress. Both for scientific and pragmatic reasons we want to know *why* general practitioners show more strain than pathologists. Is it the irregularity of demand on time, the quantitative pressure of work, the direct responsibility for the well-being of others, or what?

Differentiation of stress

One way of developing answers to such questions is through the successive differentiation of the stress variable. This approach is characteristic of the Michigan group, and some of the work of Gardell and Frankenhaeuser and their colleagues at Stockholm has proceeded along similar lines. We can illustrate the process with the concept of role conflict, one of the work stresses first investigated in terms of the ISR model (Figure 1). Role conflict was measured initially in terms of the expectations of the individual members of fifty-three role sets in industry (Kahn *et al.*, 1964). Conflicts or discrepancies between the wishes of the role set and the behaviour of the focal person were shown to have negative effects (correlations) on that person's feelings about the job and the people associated with it. Subsequent research (Sales, 1969) demonstrated that often the effective stress was overload, the perception that one is being asked to do more than time permits, although the required activities themselves are neither intrinsically incompatible nor beyond one's abilities. People often experienced such overload as a conflict between quality and quantity, given the constraints of time. Coping could consist of doing less than was expected, doing less well than was expected, or taking more time than was expected; the constraints of quantity, quality, and time could not be met simultaneously. Such overload in the work role has been shown to produce signs of physiological as well as psychological strain.

Caplan (1971) measured overload objectively (visitors, telephone calls, work interruptions) and subjectively, and found both objective and subjective overload to be related to heart rate and serum cholesterol among employees of a government agency. There is some evidence that overload should itself be differentiated, and that quantitative overload (having too much work to do) has different effects from qualitative overload (having work that is too difficult to do).

Cobb (1973) has undertaken research on a special form of work load, responsibility, and, still more specifically, responsibility for persons as compared with things. He notes that both such responsibilities are associated with cigarette consumption, and that responsibility for the future of others is associated with diastolic blood pressure and cholesterol level. Among the government employees who took part in this research, however, these findings hold only for those who showed 'Type A' personality characteristics—an impatient, work-seeking, hard-driving life-style first described by Friedman and Rosenman (1959).

Cobb further distinguishes between responsibility for things and responsibility for persons, and was particularly interested in stresses generated by the latter. These he investigated by means of a quasi-experimental comparison of two large sets—4325 air traffic controllers and 8435 second-class airmen. Hypertension is four times more common among the air traffic controllers, and diabetes and peptic ulcer more than twice as common. Moreover, all three diseases show earlier dates (ages) of onset, and two of them (hypertension and peptic ulcer) show a 'traffic effect'—that is, they are more common among traffic controllers assigned to the busier airports.

Overload and under-utilization

All the stresses in the preceding differentiated succession represent too much of something—conflict, work-load, responsibility, and the like. The same series of research projects, however, generated a parallel series of findings, which we cannot here describe in detail, that illustrate the stressfulness of having too little. Even the early research on role conflict and overload indicated that all people did not find the same magnitudes of conflict stressful, nor the same work-loads optimal. And the ISR series of nationwide studies of work (Quinn and Shepard, 1974) identified *challenge* as the factor rated most important in jobs but cited most often as an area of deficiency.

The combination of overload and under-utilization seems unhappily characteristic of many jobs in technologies usually considered advanced. Workers may be responsible for extremely expensive machinery and equipment; their safety and that of others may require continuous vigilance, and yet the job may use few of their skills and abilities. The demands are heavy but narrow.

Gardell (1976) and Johansson et al. (1978) report an intensive study in sawmills and lumber-trimming plants that illustrates well the stress pattern of overload and under-utilization. Moreover, it includes independent measures in the main categories specified in the ISR model—the objective work situation, its perceptions by the workers, their responses to the situation, and its effects on their health. The basic data consist of comparisons across three categories of jobs, a 'risk' group and two control or comparison groups. The risk group consisted of jobs with extremely short operating cycles (usually less than ten seconds), total dependence on machines (saws, edgers, trimmers, etc.) for determining the work pace, sustained positional and postural constraint, and a need for unremitting attentiveness. The first comparison group included jobs in the same factories but not subject to the same control by machines; these jobs were also less skilled than those in the risk group. The second comparison group consisted of maintenance workers, whose jobs are high in skill and autonomy. Other factors are comparable across jobs—age, sex, seniority, and (with exceptions) hours of work and methods of pay. The results show a sharp and consistent pattern of perceived stress, negative affect, and symptoms of strain in the risk group compared with the other two groups. Consistent with that pattern is the higher rate of absence, both general and stress-attributed. Workers in this group also showed lower patterns of off-the-job participation in organizations, and even their participation in union activity was quite low.

Physiological stress reactions were also measured for men in these groups, by means of the amount of adrenaline and noradrenaline in the urine. The risk group had a secretion rate during the work day that was about 150 per cent of its rate at rest, while the average secretion rate of the control group at work was little higher than its rate at rest. The pattern of difference during the work day is even more impressive and is congruent with the subjective reports of the two groups.

The control group begins the day with a secretion rate only a little above resting levels, peaks early, and 'winds down' gradually to an end-of-day reading slightly below rest level. By contrast, workers in the risk group show considerable anticipatory stress at the beginning of the work day and, after a mid-morning reduction to rest level, become increasingly stressed, so that their peak reading (more than twice their own base level) occurs at the very end of the work day. This pattern of catecholamine secretion fits their statements of reluctance and anxiety about going to work and their avoidance of social activities after work. As one of them said, 'It takes at least a few hours to get all that work rhythm and noise out of your system before you even feel up to ... [being] with the family.'

These findings are consistent with those of current work at Michigan (Caplan et al., 1975) involving a sample of approximately 2000 men in twenty-three selected occupations. Especially in the blue-collar occupations workers reported less task complexity than they preferred, less use of their skills and abilities than they wanted, but often in combination with overload and unwanted overtime. These job characteristics in turn predicted to boredom and dissatisfaction with the job itself, to more general negative affect such as depression and anxiety, and to somatic symptoms.

FIELD EXPERIMENTS AND SOCIAL POLICY

We suggested earlier that different kinds of research play distinctive parts in revealing and improving the human experience of work. Field experiments have a unique place in this pattern, as yet more potential than actual. They can test the correlations of non-experimental field studies and replicate the findings of the laboratory under real-life conditions. When field experiments are conducted on a sufficiently large scale, as in the negative income tax experiments in the United States, they can also serve as 'trial runs' for proposed social and organizational policies. They are in short the essential element in what Donald Campbell (1971) has called 'the experimenting society'.

The record of social science in initiating field experiments in organizational change is all too modest. At least in the United States, sociologists have tended to avoid such activities entirely. Psychologists have more often engaged in organizational change, but usually in the role of consultants to management. Coincidentally or consequentially, field experiments conducted in these circumstances have emphasized the induction of individual or small-group change within an existing structure of authority, allocation of rewards, and division of labour. The literature of organizational experiments thus includes few direct attempts to change *organizational* variables, in spite of the fact that non-experimental studies and, in their way, laboratory experiments point to organizational variables as the most potent means for changing organizational outcomes.

Few as they are, these structurally-oriented experiments have accounted for more than their share of successes in organizational change. Thirty-four such 'case studies in the humanization of work' are cited in the United States in 1973 (*Work in America*, 1973), and major experiments along similar lines are now under way in a number of countries. These and their predecessors can be thought of in terms of four substantive categories, each indicating the sector of organizational structure taken as the primary target: (1) participation and authority, (2) rewards and incentives, (3) division of labour and task definition, and (4) goodness of fit between the social and technical aspects of organization.

The clerical experiment of Morse and Reimer (1956) is an early example of studies in which the authority structure is the primary target of change. In two divisions of a large commercial organization the distribution of control and regulation was moved upward, and in two others it was moved downward. These two experimental treatments, known respectively as the 'hierarchically controlled' and the 'autonomy' programmes, extended over several years and involved several hundreds of workers. Increased production was attained in both sets of experimental divisions, but attitudes moved in opposite directions, becoming more negative under increased hierarchical control and more positive under increased autonomy.

A later experiment conducted by the same research group was built around the acquisition of an authoritarian, conventionally managed company by its major competitor, an organization committed to the participative principles of management described by Likert (1961, 1967) as System 4. Each company manufactured articles of clothing and at the time of the acquisition each employed about 1000 workers. Marrow, Bowers, and Seashore (1967) report comprehensive quantitative data on attitudes and performance for both companies, for the years immediately preceding and immediately following the experiment (1962 and 1964). During this two-year experimental period the data for the acquired company show significant change towards the System 4 pattern in every one of six substantive attitudinal areas, along with substantial economic gains. Return on invested capital changed during the two-year period from − 15 per cent to + 17, and hourly earnings increased by 26 per cent. Five years after the termination of the experiment these tendencies were shown to have continued; the changes were durable.

In this experiment the increases in rewards were significant, but they were secondary; the reward structure was not the primary target of experimental change. Indeed, it is difficult to find examples of field experiments that make the reward structure their primary target, in spite of the fact that non-experimental studies have demonstrated the importance of extrinsic rewards as sources of motivation and satisfaction. The single set of exceptions to this statement is provided by research on the Scanlon Plan, a comprehensive programme based on monetary rewards for increased organizational productivity and on employee representation in decisions affecting productivity.

Over a 40-year period some 180 companies have installed plans that closely approximate the Scanlon specifications, and there have been several reviews of the change process and the effects on attitudes and performance (Lesieur and Puckett, 1969; Frost, Wakely, and Ruh, 1974). The first formal step in establishing the Scanlon Plan in a company is agreement between management and union as to what the base performance shall be for the organization as a whole and how company earnings above that base shall be allocated. The Scanlon Plan is an action programme, but some research has been done to evaluate its effects. Typical results show wages 25 per cent above union contract levels and positive effects in other organizational sectors.

A third category of field experiments takes the division of labour itself as the primary target of change. Such changes can be initiated very modestly—as the enlargement of a few jobs, for example—or on a very ambitious scale. Experiments in job design (also called job enlargement, job enrichment, and work structuring) have become numerous in recent years, and several summaries of their results have been made (Ford, 1969; Maher, 1971; Alderfer, 1976). Their success in improving the quality of the work experience while maintaining or increasing productivity is well established, but their limitations are equally apparent. Job enrichment seems not to diffuse beyond the experimental 'pockets' in which it is begun, but rather tends to reduce or revert to the pre-experimental condition. Furthermore, job enrichment, if it is to be organization-wide, implies changes in authority and rewards, and in technology. If the roles that make up an organization are to change significantly, the 'tools and rules' cannot remain constant.

This interdependence of the social and technical aspects of organizations is the key assumption in the fourth and last category of organizational experiments—those based on the socio-technical approach to organizational change (Rice, 1958; Emery and Trist, 1959). That approach takes as its primary target a complex emergent variable: goodness of fit between the social and technical aspects of organization, and by extension between those aspects of organization and the needs of individuals to perform meaningful tasks, to exercise control over their own task activities, and to have satisfactory relationships with people performing related tasks.

In principle, congruence between the social and technical aspects of an organization could be improved by changing either; in practice the early studies concentrated on the social aspects of organization, especially at the level of the primary work group. Rice's (1958) work in the calico mills of India, while ahead of its time in many respects, accepted the new looms as they stood. The problem of improving socio-technical fit then became one of discovering or inventing a work group structure that used the new technology but met more of the psychological needs of workers.

TECHNOLOGY CONSTRAINING AND CONSTRAINED

More recent experiments, especially in Norway and Sweden, have attempted to improve socio-technical fit by changing the technology as well as the social structure through which it is operated. The Norwegian experience has been described by Thorsrud and his colleagues (Thorsrud, Sørensen, and Gustavsen, 1976). It is unusual in breadth of sponsorship (Trade Union Council, Employers' Association, and national government) and in the number and range of structural variables directly altered. These have typically included enlargement of individual work roles, allocation of increased authority and autonomy to work groups, changes in the reward structure to provide a base wage and a bonus for group or departmental accomplishment, and some adjustment of technological arrangements to fit the new social structure. Results have been favourable with respect to worker responses and productivity, but mixed with respect to the responses of managerial and technical staff. Diffusion has been encouraging but by no means general or uninterrupted.

It is in Sweden, however, that the modification of technology to improve socio-technical goodness of fit is most apparent. The Saab-Scania engine plant at Sodertalje and the Volvo plant at Kalmar have become famous precisely for that reason. Both plants are engaged in manufacturing processes (engine assembly and car assembly) for which the assembly line and the extreme fractionation of tasks have been considered economically essential, and both are operating without conventional assembly lines. Nor are they isolated examples; other 'new factories' and experiments in older factories show similar innovations, with sustained productivity and improvements in the quality of the work experience.

It has been argued that the Swedish experiments have been possible only because of a combination of contextual factors—labour–management harmony, trade union strength, advanced technology, democratic political practice, and growing public interest. Such arguments can be answered only by the continuing history of work experiments and work reform in Sweden, and by experimental developments in other countries and contexts.

As social experiments in organizations have increased in range and depth, the constraining effects of technology have become more apparent. At the societal level, social and technical factors intersect and it is not useful to argue that one always precedes the other. At the organizational level, however, there is a sense in which the technical factors precede the social. Factory buildings are planned and constructed, machine tools are designed and manufactured long before the workers in a particular plant assume their roles. To the extent that those roles are to be unconventional by present standards, the temporal chain of decisions affected grows long. Conventional technologies are ready for the organization to acquire, but they imply conventional jobs. If the job specifications are unconventional, the new jobs may require technologies yet to be developed. When Volvo made the decision to assemble cars without assembly lines, they had to assume the responsibility for discovering or inventing an alternative; their social goals had become technological constraints.

In the early years of industrialization, such constraints were few. Increments in material product were wanted too greatly to permit them to be risked for the sake of avoiding monotony or reducing hazards at work. Moreover, decisions about such trade-offs were made for the most part by people who did not perform the risky and monotonous tasks. Technology became the leading or driving subsystem in industrial society. But the material gains of technology have created the conditions for its constraint or, more properly, the conditions for choice: increasing material affluence, less work, or the transformation of work itself.

The first choice in industrial history was for increased product. The second, which by no means replaced the first, was for less work—fewer hours per day, days per year, and years per lifetime. In the century from 1850 to 1950, the work week in the United States was reduced from about 70 to about 40 hours and retirement from work at the age of 65 became both possible and, in many organizations, mandatory. In recent years, however, the work week has remained stable and the idea of mandatory retirement has been challenged. Further increases in consumer products and further reductions in work may be even less attractive. The third option under conditions of affluence—improving the social and technical content of work so that it is more rewarding in itself—has only begun to be explored. The experiments that we have examined are part of the exploration.

The choices between product and leisure, increasing the quantity of organizational output or the quality or organizational life, are not likely to be easy. They are complex expressions of values and they must be made under complex circumstances. Material affluence is a fact of life for only a small part of the world's population, and its attainment and maintenance consumes resources for which no satisfactory replacements are known. The thesis of this paper has been that choices about work and human organization are likely to be wiser as research illuminates the relationship between work and well-being, individual and social.

REFERENCES

Alderfer, C. P. (1976). Change processes in organizations, in *Handbook of Work, Organization, and Society*, ed. R. Dubin, Rand McNally, Chicago.

American Society of Anesthesiologists (1974). Occupational disease among operating room personnel: national study, *Anesthesiology*, **41** (4), 3–42.

Bardand, E. J. (1973). Results of current investigations of disability among meatwrappers in the Portland metropolitan area, University of Oregon Health Sciences Center.

Berman, L., and Goodall, McC. (1960). Adrenaline, noradrenaline, and 3-methoxy-4-hydroxy-mandelic acid (MOMA) excretion following centrifugation and anticipation of centrifugation, *Federal Proceedings: Federation of American Societies for Experimental Biology*, **19**, 154, cited by W. Raab in *Society, Stress, and Disease, Vol. I, The Psychosocial Environment and Psychosomatic Diseases*, ed. L. Levi (1971), Oxford University Press, London.

Boretsky, Michael (1975). Trends in U.S. technology: A political economist's view, *American Scientist*, **63**, 70–82.

Campbell, D. (1971). Methods for the experimenting society, paper presented to the American Psychological Assocaition.

Caplan, R. D. (1971). Organizational stress and individual strain: A socio-psychological study of risk factors in coronary heart disease among administrators, engineers, and scientists, doctoral dissertation, University of Michigan, *Dissertation Abstracts International*, 1972, **32**, 6706b–6707b (University Microfilms, 72–14822).

Caplan, R. D., Cobb, S., French, J.R.P., Jr, Harrison, R. D., and Pinneau, S. R., Jr (1975). *Job Demands and Worker Health: Main Effects and Occupational Differences*, US Government Printing Office, Washington, DC.

Cobb, S. (1973). Workload and coronary heart disease, *Proceedings, Social Statistics Section*, American Statistical Association, December.

Cobb, S. (1974). Role responsibility: The differentiation of a concept, in *Occupational Stress*, ed. A. McLean. Thomas, Springfield, Ill.

Corson, S. A. (1971). Pavlovian and operant conditioning techniques in the study of psycho-social and biological relationships, in *Society, Stress and Disease, Vol. I, The Psycho-social Environment and Psychosomatic Diseases*, ed. L. Levi, Oxford University Press, London, 7–21.

Dean, R. (1966). Human stress in space, *Science*, **2**, 70.

Dunnette, M. D. (ed.) (1976). *Handbook of Industrial and Organizational Psychology*, Rand McNally, Chicago.

Emery, F., and Trist, E. L. (1959). Socio-technical systems, paper presented at the 6th Annual International Meetings of the Institute of Management Sciences, Paris.

Ford, R. N. (1969). *Motivation Through the Work Itself*, American Management Association, New York.

Frankenhaeuser, M. (1971). Experimental approaches to the study of human behavior as related to neuro-endocrine functions, in *Society, Stress, and Disease, Vol. I, The Psycho-social Environment and Psychosomatic Diseases*, ed. L. Levi, Oxford University Press, London 23–35.

Frankenhaeuser, M., and Pàtkai, P. (1964). Inter-individual differences in catecholamine excretion during stress, *Scandinavian Journal of Psychology*, **6**, 117–123.

French, J.R.P., Jr (1974. Personal-role fit, in *Occupational Stress*, ed. A. McLean, Thomas, Springfield, Ill.

French, J. R. P., Jr., and Kahn, R. L. (1962). 'A programmatic approach to studying the industrial environment and mental health, *Journal of Social Issues*, **18** (3), 1–47.

Friedman, M., and Rosenman, R. H. (1959). Association of specific overt patterns with blood and cardiovascular findings, *Journal of the American Medical Association*, **169**, 1286–1296.

Frost, C. F., Wakely, J. H., and Ruh, R. A. (1974). *The Scanlon Plan for Organizational Development: Identity, Participation and Equity*, Michigan State University Press, Lansing, Mich.

Gardell, B. (1976). *Arbetsinnehåll och livskvalitet (Job Content and Quality of Life)*, Prisma, Stockholm.

Haas, J. E., and Drabek, T. E. (1970). Community disaster and system stress: A sociological perspective, in *Social and Psychological Factors in Stress*, ed. J. E. McGrath, Holt, Rinehart, Winston, New York, 264–286.

Haber, L. D. (1971). Disabling effects of chronic disease and impairment, *Journal of Chronic Diseases*, **24**, 482.

Hamburg, D. A. (1962). Plasma and urinary corticoid levels in naturally occurring psychological stresses, in ultrastructure and metabolism of the nervous system, *Association for Research of Nervous Disease Processes*, **25**, 406.

Hebb, D. O. (1958). *A Textbook of Psychology*, Saunders, Philadelphia.

Hollingshead, A. A., and Redlich, F. C. (1958). *Social Class and Mental Illness*, Wiley, New York.

Holmes, T. H., and Rahe, R. H. (1967). The social readjustment scale, *Journal of Psychosomatic Research*, **2**, 213–218.

Janis, I. (1958). *Psychological Stress*, Wiley, New York.

Johansson, G., Aronsson, G., and Lindström, B. O. (1978). Social psychological and neuroendocrine reactions in highly mechanized work, *Ergonomics*, **21**, 583–589.

Kahn, R. L. (1974). Conflict, ambiguity, and overload: Three elements in job stress, in *Occupational Stress*, ed. A. McLean, Thomas, Springfield, Ill., 47–61.

Kahn, R. L., Wolfe, D. M., Quinn, R. P., Snoek, J. D., and Rosenthal, R. A. (1964). *Organizational Stress: Studies in Role Conflict and Ambiguity*, Wiley, New York.

Lazarus, R. S. (1966). *Psychological Stress and Coping Process*, McGraw-Hill, New York.

Leinhart, W. S., Doyle, H. N., Enterline, P. E., Henschel, A., and Kendrick, M. A. (1969).

Pneumoconiosis in Appalachian Bituminous Coalminers, US Department of Health, Education and Welfare, Cincinnati.

Lesieur, F. G., and Puckett, E. S. (1969). The Scanlon Plan has proved itself, *Harvard Business Review*, **47**, 109–118.

Levi, L. (1972). *Stress and Distress in Response to Psycho-social Stimuli*, Pergamon, Oxford.

Likert, R. (1961). *New Patterns of Management*, McGraw-Hill, New York.

Likert, R. (1967). *The Human Organization*, McGraw-Hill, New York.

McGrath, J. E. (1976). Stress and behavior in organizations, in *Handbook of Industrial and Organizational Psychology*, ed. M. D. Dunnette, Rand McNally, Chicago.

Maher, J. R. (ed.) (1971). *New Perspectives in Job Enrichment*, Van Nostrand Reinhold, New York.

Marrow, A. J., Bowers, D. G., and Seashore, S. E. (1967). *Management by Participation*, Harper & Row, New York.

Morse, N., and Reimer, E. (1956). The experimental change of a major organizational variable, *Journal of Abnormal and Social Psychology*, **52**, 120–129.

Quinn, R. P., and Shepard, L. (1974). *The 1972–1973 Quality of Employment Survey*, Survey Research Center, University of Michigan, Ann Arbor, Mich.

Quinn, R. P., Walsh, J. T., and Hahn, D. L. (1977). *The 1972–1973 Quality of Employment Survey: Continuing Chronicles of an Unfinished Enterprise*, Survey Research Center, University of Michigan, Ann Arbor, Mich.

Raab, W. (1966). Emotional and sensory stress factors in myocardial pathology, *American Heart Journal*, **72**, 538.

Rice, A. K. (1958). *Productivity and Social Organization: The Ahmedabad Experiment*, Tavistock, London.

Russek, H. I. (1962). Emotional stress and coronary heart disease in American physicians, dentists, and lawyers, *American Journal of Medical Science*, **243**, part 6, 716–725.

Russell, Bertrand (1930). *The Conquest of Happiness*, Liveright, New York, 152.

Sales, S. M. (1969). Differences among individuals in effective, behavioral, biochemical, and physiological responses to variations in workload, doctoral dissertation, University of Michigan, *Dissertation Abstracts International*, **30**, 2407–B (University Microfilms, 69–18098).

Scott, R., and Howard, A. (1970). Models of stress, in *Social Stress*, ed. S. Levine and N. A. Scotch, Aldine, Chicago, 259–278.

Selikoff, I. J., and Hammond, E. C. (1975). Multiple risk factors in etiology of environmental cancer: Implications for prevention and control, unpublished data cited in *Health and Work in America*, available from the Superintendent of Documents, US Government Printing Office, Washington, DC, November.

Selye, H. (1956). *The Stress of Life*, McGraw-Hill, New York.

Srole, L., Langer, T. S., Michael, S. T., Opler, M. K., and Rennie, T. A. C. (1962). *Mental Health in the Metropolis: The Midtown Manhattan Study, Vol. I*, McGraw-Hill, New York.

Thorsrud, E., Sørensen, B. S., and Gustavsen, B. (1976). Sociotechnical approach to industrial democracy in Norway, in *Handbook of Work, Organization, and Society*, ed. R. Dubin, Rand McNally, Chicago.

Work in America (1973). A report of a special task force to the Secretary of Health, Education, and Welfare, Massachusetts Institute of Technology Press, Cambridge, Mass.

Working Life
Edited by B. Gardell and G. Johansson
© 1981 John Wiley & Sons Ltd

Chronic Effects from the Physical Nature of Work

Donald E. Broadbent

INTRODUCTION

This paper supports the view that physical conditions of work may have lasting effects on mental health, one way or the other; and that there is tentative evidence to show some of the relationships involved. In particular, pacing of work, rather than short cycle time, is suspect. Although many others have helped with my research, I should say at once that it has been conducted in close collaboration with Dr Dennis Gath, Clinical Reader in Psychiatry in Oxford. He therefore shares none of the blame for errors, but most of the credit for good points in the following discussion.

CAUSES AND EFFECTS IN THE STUDY OF WORK

(a) Causes

Any real job has aspects which are social, aspects which are physical, and aspects which are socio-technical. An obvious example of the first factor is the existence of autonomous work groups on the one hand, or of hierarchical chains of command on the other. Physical factors might include the design of controls or instruments for easy operation, or the level of noise in the environment. Socio-technical factors appear when the layout of the work imposes a certain social relationship. For example, when workers require their work to be moved by cranes operated by other people, the first group becomes dependent on the second group, and 'in their power', unless some special precaution is taken. Each of these conditions of work can be altered separately from the others, and when practical improvements are made in factories it is quite common for the entire situation to be changed. A familiar example is the new Volvo plant at Kalmar, where changes in physical layout and group structure have taken place simultaneously, with probable changes in socio-technical relationships. It is useful, however, to try to consider each factor by itself, because changes in all of them are certainly expensive and disruptive,

39

and may in some cases be impossible. Therefore we need to know the effects of each change on its own, so that effort can be directed at those changes most likely to show good effect. From this point of view, the physical conditions are sometimes taken as fixed, and determined by technology. This is not a fair picture; engineering design allows different options, and at least within limits we can change a productive process so as to produce better conditions of work. This paper in fact concentrates on such physical conditions, without in any way denying the simultaneous importance of the other factors.

If we now look at possible effects on human beings, rather than the causes which produce them, we have again a choice of variables. We can look at the efficiency of the worker, at physiological changes in him, at his satisfaction in his work, or at lasting changes which appear after work.

(b) Effects on efficiency

The first of these is the one which has been most closely related to the physical details of the work and we can now say a great deal about factors which decrease working efficiency. An example which will be relevant later is the question of pacing; the extent to which a man must work in time with a machine, rather than speeding up and slowing down as he thinks fit. In laboratory experiments many years ago, exactly the same task was given under two conditions (Broadbent, 1953). A mechanically paced task showed a drop in performance when the man had been working for some time; whereas a self-paced version of the task went on showing the same average performance for long periods. The reason was that any momentary variation in performance averaged out in the self-paced condition; whereas with mechanical pacing, it caused a failure which could not later be compensated for. Similar results were shown in industry (Conrad and Hille, 1955), and a good deal of attention was paid to methods of combining the engineering advantages of assembly line work with the human ones of self-paced work. This could be done, for example, by placing barriers across an assembly line so that a bank of work developed between each position, freeing the worker from the need to spend exactly the same time on every item.

A particularly striking instance was the development of machines for sorting letters, in which each letter is shown to a human being so that he can read its address, and press keys to determine its destination. The obvious engineering solution is to present the letters at equal and mechanically spaced intervals of time; one of the possible machines, however, was arranged to work self-paced, presenting a fresh letter only when the keys had been pressed for the previous one. It may appear contrary to common sense, but the rate of work with such a machine is much higher than that possible with mechanical pacing; the reason is that the time taken to read a letter varies very considerably, being much longer for rare destinations such as Builth or Poughkeepsie than it is for familiar destinations such as London or New York. Consequently, unless errors are to be frequent, the mechanically paced system must go at a speed slow enough to include the slowest reactions, while the self-paced system can go at the average speed, which is very much faster (Conrad, 1960). The difference is of major economic importance. Thus changes in the physical details of work can make large changes in human efficiency.

(c) Effects on physiology

Efficiency alone, however, is not an adequate goal for human beings, and we must think of possible costs to the worker. Physiological changes are of importance; examples are the changes in excretion of catecholamines. The excretion of noradrenaline, for example, has been found to be greater in sawmill workers on machine-paced work than it is amongst those on self-paced work (Frankenhaeuser and Gardell, 1976). Similarly the length of the work cycle appears to have some effect, though not perhaps the same kind; adrenaline excretion was higher in people with the shortest cycle time. This line of attack is clearly hopeful, but our immediate question is whether the change in physiological state reveals itself in chronic changes in behaviour.

(d) Effects on satisfaction

A third effect of work conditions shows itself in the satisfaction felt by the worker; there is a large literature in this area, but most of it is concerned perhaps with general aspects of the job rather than detailed physical ones. There are well-established methods of measuring the degree of satisfaction with various aspects of the workers' situation, such as pay, promotion prospects, supervision, or the work itself; a classic example is the Job Description Index (Smith, Kendall, and Hulin, 1969). There are more recent modifications and developments of such methods, for example, for a British rather than American workforce (Cross, 1973). It is usually found that general satisfaction is related more closely to the nature of the work itself than it is to peripheral factors such as the quality of supervision (Cross, 1973; Hulin and Smith, 1967). Yet the effect of physical conditions of work upon satisfaction has been much less closely studied than their effects upon efficiency; only one aspect has been examined in much detail, and this is perhaps socio-technical rather than truly physical.

The aspect in question is the degree to which the job allows personal achievement of success; the Job Diagnostic Survey of Hackman and Oldham (1975) provides one way of assessing this. The idea is that a job will be unmotivating if the worker cannot find out how successful his performance is; or if he does not possess responsibility for the work; or if the work is lacking in variety, identity, or value to others. In trying to measure the quality of a particular job, the factors of variety, identity, and significance add together, so that a lack of variety and even a lack of social importance may to some extent be compensated for if the worker takes part in the whole job from beginning to end. Similarly, a monotonous task which is only part of the total achievement of the work group may be acceptable if it is of great social significance. Although, therefore, these three factors can compensate for each other, their total is *multiplied* by the degree of personal responsibility, and by the presence of feedback information in the final assessment of the job. That is, no matter how varied the task, and no matter how much the worker is responsible for its success, the task will be seriously unattractive if he never finds out whether he has in fact succeeded.

Such an analysis is likely to appeal to many who read this paper, because their own work would measure highly on such a scale. However, we must beware of another important factor, that of individual differences. Some people find it more important than others that their job should allow the opportunity for achievement and success, and the nature of the job itself may be more important for them than it is for people who treat the work as a necessary evil in order to secure pay, social contact, and other forms of satisfaction. This point was fully recognized by Hackman and Lawler (1971), and is well verified in other results (Blood and Hulin, 1967; Hulin and Blood, 1968; Brief and Aldag, 1975). We have preliminary indications that car workers performing repetitive jobs tend to describe themselves as persons who prefer a fixed routine, more than do other workers in the same plant, and on similar rates of pay, who do jobs which do not repeat themselves. (Even so, the former seem less satisfied with their jobs than the latter!) To predict perfectly the level of satisfaction with a job, we shall need to know the social and other factors which determine what an individual expects and prefers; and we also need more analysis of the exact details of jobs.

(e) Chronic effects and health

The topic of satisfaction begins to touch upon that of health. There is a low but significant correlation between measures of dissatisfaction with work, and the number of times medical facilities are used (Caplan *et al.*, 1975), and much higher correlations between dissatisfaction and reported emotional feelings of anxiety or depression. In predicting how anxious or depressed a person will say he is, it appears once again that the nature of the job alone is less important than the discrepancy between the job and the preference of the particular person. Caplan and his colleagues (1975) sent questionnaires to people in a wide variety of jobs, from professors to drivers of forklift trucks, and found that although feelings of depression were related to the complexity of the job, the relationship was not significant; whereas such feelings were significantly related to the difference between the actual and the desired complexity of job. People get depressed with a job that is too hard, as well as one that is too easy.

Such subjective feelings seem likely to lead to poor health, although of course one must be cautious in drawing the inference. The admission rates to mental hospitals in the state of Tennessee do show quite severe differences between different occupations (Colligan et al., in press), operatives (such as assemblers, weavers, or press workers) showing an abnormally high rate. In addition to factors in the job itself, however, hospital admissions must of course be contaminated by social factors. Jobs connected with medicine, for example, are also very highly represented, and one might suspect that people working closely with doctors are more likely to be taken into hospital when they show signs of disturbance.

There are also questions of the social status and esteem attached to particular jobs; Kornhauser (1965) has provided evidence that car assembly workers may show low self-esteem and other related feelings, which are certainly undesirable for mental health. Yet, it is difficult to know how much such feelings may reflect the view of a job held by the surrounding society.

Furthermore, very large scale surveys of this kind can scarcely examine the detailed characteristics of the job. It is insufficient to describe a man as, for example, an assembly line worker. Different people whose jobs are described by the same name may actually do extremely different things during the day (Walker and Guest, 1952). In car assembly, for example, one man may have a very short cycle time, repeating the same operation several times on each car; while another has a long cycle time, working only on every second or third car. Some may work close to each other and be able to talk, others be widely separated. Some may be strictly paced while others are in fact able to work at their own speed; one welder, for example, may fabricate a number of parts, which he places ready for another to fix to cars as they pass. The one on the track itself must get each job done before the car moves out of range of his equipment, while the other can build up a bank of components and then wait. If factors of this kind bear any relationship to health, they will weaken any comparisons made between broad occupational groups.

PHYSICAL FACTORS AND EFFECTS ON HEALTH: SOME PRELIMINARY OBSERVATIONS

In order to explore the effects on health of physical variables, it seems reasonable to examine first the factor of pacing in repetitive work. As already noted, it has been much studied from the point of view of efficiency; and the work of Caplan et al. (1975) included a comparison between a sample of paced assembly workers with one of unpaced workers. The latter assembled components on trucks rather than on a line, and moved the trucks to the next station when they had finished. Although the two groups were not significantly different in general job satisfaction, they did differ in boredom and in feelings of anxiety, the paced workers reporting more of such feelings. There was also a borderline difference in feelings of depression; for that score, however, the level of statistical significance is a little doubtful ($p = 0.052$). It should also be noted that the main purpose of the study was comparison of a large variety of jobs rather than a specific comparison of these groups, and the paced workers were both younger and less well paid than the unpaced ones.

Nevertheless, this suggests that pacing is indeed a suitable physical factor for examination.

(a) Medical records

If we wish to go beyond subjective feeling, one point of departure is to take disability which is sufficiently serious to cause medical intervention. In one large British car plant, separate records are kept of diagnosis for all workers attending the works hospital. Such a visit is required whenever the worker has been absent for six weeks or more to ensure that he is fit to restart work; there are also some cases where the person seeks assistance without having been absent, but these are a minority, and the following results have been checked to ensure that they do not affect the conclusions. In each case, the doctor records a diagnosis. Figures were supplied by the medical officer in charge for the numbers of patients receiving some psychiatric diagnosis throughout a two-year period ending in 1974. From the job title it was possible to decide whether a patient was a track worker, or of some other type. The caution given above should be remembered; the jobs of the same title are often different in detail, but it was hoped that such factors might cancel out sufficiently for a preliminary examination.

As might perhaps be expected, the number of patients appearing is only a small proportion of the workforce, less than 1 per cent, and the size of the workforce also varies considerably from time to time. This means that it is not possible to draw conclusions about the overall risk of sickness of this kind for track workers and for others. However, amongst the ninety-seven patients, several interesting differences appeared between the cases coming from the track and those of non-track manual workers. Again it should be emphasized that these are merely suggestive; when a doctor sees the patient, his judgement about the detailed diagnosis or other information to be included in his notes may well be coloured by his knowledge of the man's job. There are also selective factors: for example, only 24 per cent of the patients from the track had some previous history of psychiatric illness whereas 39 per cent of these from other work had such a history. It seems likely that people with a record of nervous disturbance would never obtain jobs on the assembly line. If we keep these qualifications in mind, however, two results appeared which suggest that further work would be useful. It should be noted that these differences appeared among cases seen by each of the doctors employed in the hospital, and are similar for every doctor.

First, it often appears that the records contain some reference to a provoking episode, precipitating a disturbance, such as the loss of a wife, or some legal difficulty. Forty per cent of non-track patients have some such episode, but 37 per cent of those whose job is on the track. This difference appears in five different age groups, none showing a reversed result, which borders on statistical significance. On the face of it, the track workers tend to become sick without other apparent reason.

Again, one can consider the category of the diagnosis; broadly speaking, psychiatric cases in a working population are described as anxiety, depression, or a third category which receives various names such as chronic fatigue or debility. The proportion of cases described as 'anxious' was 32 per cent of the patients from the track, but only 25 per cent of the other cases. The excess is entirely amongst the cases described as having no provoking cause. Thus patients from the track work are more likely to be anxious than those from other work.

These results are, for reasons given above, of little value as evidence; they merely justified the researches to be described.

(b) Psychiatric symptom levels amongst laundry workers

If one is to improve on the clinical judgement of a doctor concerned with his patient rather than with research, a set of standardized questions is needed. There are a number of questionnaires which have been shown to distinguish neurotic patients from the general public, but most of them make no distinction between different kinds of neurosis. One inventory, the Middlesex Hospital Questionnaire (MHQ), does provide questions which are associated with distinguishable kinds of neurosis, and in view of the suggestive findings already noted this was used as the basis for our own interviews (Crown and Crisp, 1966). Some of the questions were dropped as unsuitable for industrial use (for example, questions about sexual behaviour). In addition, it was thought wise for questions to be asked by a human interviewer rather than by the distribution of questionnaires, and this has proved justified. Quite apart from the orientation of most factory workers towards speech rather than writing, problems of ambiguity or misunderstanding appear in face to face interview which would have escaped notice in a questionnaire. The original MHQ has been validated against psychiatric diagnosis, and used in a number of other investigations (Crown, 1974). We have confirmed the validity of the questions with our modified set, and with a human interviewer. That is, we have checked that the total number of symptoms found is much greater in a population of neurotics under treatment than it is in the general population. In our revised form, we have separate measurements for Anxiety, Depression, Obsessional personality, Temporary obsessional symptoms, and the presence of Somatic symptoms.

As another measure of disturbance, with less direct validity, we have devised a series of questions concerning everyday failures of attention, concentration, memory, and so on, known for brevity as the Cognitive Failures Questionnaire.

With regard to the job, we have compiled a number of questions concerning the exact details of the work done, such as the amount of physical effort, the extent of any interruptions or breaks, the degree of precision of movement needed, the presence of noise or temperature disturbances, cycle time, and, in particular, the degree of pacing.

As a first step, a complete interview was conducted with each of eighteen women workers in a hospital laundry. Their jobs varied considerably, although most were doing repetitive work with a cycle time of between one minute and half an hour. The tasks included the loading of drying machines with wet articles, the feeding of bed linen into ironing machines, the placing of clothing in the steaming, pressing, and folding machines, the sorting of linen from a conveyor belt piles of the same kind of articles, and so on.

Before any data on psychiatric symptoms had been examined, the list of job questions was considered, and a decision was taken by the investigator about the answer to each question which would indicate the higher degree of stress. For example, being in a position where no talking was possible was regarded as more stressful than being able to speak to others. The total number of stress points was added for each person, and varied from five to sixteen.

The women with the greatest number of stress points in their job also tended to have the largest number of psychiatric symptoms; the tau correlation between the two measurements was 0.58, which is highly significant statistically even on such a small number of people. Similarly, the women with the greater stress also showed the larger number of cognitive failures, the tau correlation being 0.43 which is still highly significant, $p < 0.01$.

Once again, it is important not to take such results at face value. We have in this case no check on the statements made by the workers themselves about their jobs, and possibly those with neurotic tendencies describe their work in a more gloomy fashion than other might do. More probably, those who are showing a number of symptoms of strain, conceivably for reasons outside the job, might be unpopular amongst their colleagues, and end up with the least the attractive jobs. There remains the possibility, however, that the job itself is producing a state in the person which increases the number of symptoms.

Our continuing interest is in the effect of pacing; two stress points were allotted if the job was one where each action had to be performed within a certain time, and one point if each action could vary but the average of a series of actions had to be faster than a certain limit. This measure of pacing gave a tau correlation of 0.30 with the Anxiety scale of the MHQ, which is of borderline significance statistically ($p = 0.05$ only by a one-tailed test). It is interesting to note that there is no relationship at all to depression, or to the total number of symptoms of all kinds ($\tau < 0.03$ in each case). This is, in other words, the same kind of relationship as that found in the medical records: pacing goes with anxiety but not with other forms of neurosis. In view of the small scale of the study, however, it is still only a suggestion for further work.

PHYSICAL FACTORS AND HEALTH: PACING IN CAR PRODUCTION

A second car plant provided interviews with ninety men engaged in car production. A few others were also interviewed, but the results were kept separate because the men were used as replacements for other workers and thus did many different jobs, or because they were shop stewards, representing the men in negotiations with management, and might therefore spend quite long periods in discussion or negotiation rather than in the same type of work as their colleagues. In general, however, these extra interviews gave similar results to the others, and they were kept separate merely for reasons of caution.

(a) General features of the work

All the 90 men carried out some form of repetitive work. Fifty-three had cycle times of less than one minute, and 80 had cycle times of less than five minutes. The shortest cycle times were predominantly from press workers, of whom 48 were seen; the remaining 42 were engaged in assembly, 23 being paced and 19 unpaced. The unpaced assemblers operated with a bank of work, so that they could slow down provided they had already completed a fair number of items; the paced workers were partly on a true mechanical track, and partly on a compromise arrangement, whereby each unit of work was moved on manually, but with no bank of work. There was therefore some pressure not to hold up the previous person or push the one following. It should be noted, however, that this degree of pacing is less than that found in some other situations.

Of these 90 men, 89 said that their minds sometimes wandered at work; when asked why this was, 79 indicated that the job needed no thought. If asked what aspects of their job made them 'fed up', each man replied in his own words, but it was possible to code the responses into those referring to the work itself, those referring to some problem with management, and those referring to some other social problems, such as relationships with fellow workers. At least 63 per cent, in each of the groups interviewed, mentioned the job itself, about 10 per cent mentioned each of the other categories, the remainder giving complaints about the general environment, about the public view of the car worker, or something of that sort. Thus the main source of dissatisfaction is boredom or repetition, rather than some social factor. There were even some unfavourable comments on recent attempts to improve the social climate by increased participation and democracy, these attempts being seen by certain individuals as irrelevant to the pressing problems of the work. It should, of course, be noted that our questions were directed at grumbles rather than compliments; we do not know how many men were happy with the trend to participation, because they were not asked about it. Only 10 per cent would keep the same job if they had a totally free choice but kept the same talents; usually, they would choose to do some job without the repetitive character.

The average age of the paced assembly workers was 41, and of the unpaced ones 40; the press workers were slightly younger, averaging 34. Only 3 of the men had never been married, and 82 were still married; the average number of children was 2. If asked what they looked for in a job, between 39 and 47 per cent of each group mentioned money. Of the 82 wives, 63 were working at least part-time. This is probably an indication of financial pressure since in some cases the wife worked in the evenings while the husband looked after the children. It should be emphasized that the concern with money is scarcely a matter of grasping pursuit of excessive luxury. Considering the husband's net wage alone, the income for each person in a family of four would be only about £3.00 per week above the basic welfare income available in Britain for those with no other source of support; it would be less than half the grant given to a university student.

It is clear that the work itself was regarded as inherently unsatisfying, but justified by the need to support a family. This supports the analysis conducted some years ago in a different British car plant by Goldthorpe et al. (1969).

Other compensations or balances could be seen for the monotony of the work. Thus, a number of the men commented that their work was necessary if cars were to be built at all, and this emphasis on social value is supported by other answers to the question about their requirements from a job. Between 45 and 65 per cent of each group mentioned satisfaction, achievement, or some such phrase as well as, or instead of, money; that is, more mentioned satisfaction than mentioned money. Again, many commented that they found their main purposes in life outside work altogether. Out of the 90, 71 went out for recreation at least once a week, and no fewer than 78 described themselves as spending a fair amount or a lot of time on activities, interests, and hobbies at home. The range of spare-time activities was considerable, from church work to the repair and maintenance of the cars of friends. Within the job itself, a number of the men reported using methods of occupying their minds while doing parts of the work which needed no thought. This, of course, meant that a physical action must be infrequent; suitable activities are crossword puzzles, and the playing of games such as chess. Each of these allowed a movement to be made in a moment of rest, while allowing thought about the next problem during return to the monotonous job.

(b) Comparison of paced and unpaced assembly

As noted previously, press workers differed from assemblers in average age, and also in a few other features of their work. In particular, they moved from one task to another on different days, whereas those engaged on assembly kept the same job for long periods. The most useful comparison, therefore, is between the paced and unpaced assemblers. These groups did not differ in general environment, rate of pay, marital status, or any other factor we could discover; it is particularly important to note that this company has a policy of paying all production workers the same rate, regardless of job. As might be expected, the paced workers reported significantly less freedom in leaving their work place, but this, of course, is inherent in the nature of the job.

One unexpected difference was that non-smokers were significantly more common amongst the paced group, of whom 65 per cent fell in this class. Only 26 per cent of the unpaced workers were of this type. Such a difference appears reasonable on reflection, since hardened smokers might well try and move away from a job which allowed no opportunity for informal breaks. It is, of course, worrying with regard to other health comparisons, particularly since data from the press workers showed that non-smokers tended to have a higher score on the scale of obsessional personality. This makes it extremely reasonable that the paced workers had higher scores for obsessional personality than the unpaced workers, the exact figures being 4.13 and 3.16, which are significantly different. However, smoking does not appear to be the explanation for the other differences to be mentioned.

There were no differences between the paced and unpaced workers in terms of job satisfaction, somatic symptoms, or symptoms of depression. When, however, we consider symptoms of obsessional state (as distinct from underlying obsessional personality) we find that the paced workers give significantly more than the unpaced ones, the average score being 3.22 rather than 1.73. Similarly, and perhaps most important, the number of symptoms of anxiety is significantly higher for the paced workers, the average score being 3.13 as opposed to 1.58. Thus we have again a difference in anxiety rather than in the general level of symptoms.

This result is of the same kind as the suggestive indications already noted amongst the medical records and in the preliminary study of laundry workers. Anxiety is associated with pacing, but depression is not. The degree of bias in the interview, and the level of statistical significance, are more satisfactory than in those cases. However, the result must still be taken with considerable caution, because in a single plant it is possible that some unsuspected factor has caused anxious people to gravitate towards the assembly line work, or to be more willing to be interviewed while on that work. Preliminary studies in another plant have shown the same result yet again, and I am now reasonably confident that the result is a general one.

One further point should be made, concerning the length of cycle. Both paced and unpaced assemblers had a similar range of cycle times, the maximum being less than half an hour, and the minimum less than a minute. In neither group, however, was there any sign of increase of symptoms as the cycle time was shorter, rather the reverse. Although, therefore, we have results which are at least consistent with an effect of pacing upon mental ill-health, we have no sign that a very short cycle is worse than a longer one, when the task is still repetitive. This is particularly interesting, since there is much social pressure to increase cycle times. However, it is by no means certain that such an increase is desirable. If we remember the methods of compensation used by many of the workers, such as solving puzzles or games while working, it is clear that these depend upon mechanical or automatic execution of the simplest and least demanding parts of the task. Increasing the cycle is perhaps of doubtful value, when it will in any case be repeated hundreds of times each month. Perhaps any benefits of the longer cycle are in these circumstances offset by the greater difficulty of performing a longer task automatically; it thus allows less conversation or thought while working. Whatever the reasons, we have found in this plant no evidence to support pressure for longer cycle times. It will be recalled that the physiological results of Frankenhaueser and Gardell also make a distinction between effects of the two features of work, and it should not be assumed that they are equally damaging, or at least not in the same way.

CONCLUSIONS

It is perhaps over-ambitious to speak of conclusions, since one can point only to suggestions, and to a possible method of advance. However, the emphasis of this paper was stated initially as being the effects on mental health, from physical conditions of work. It is perhaps fair to claim that we have some evidence that such effects may exist. I personally have little doubt that similar effects will appear from social or from socio-technical aspects of the job, although it may be much harder to identify the precise features of of an organization or a social structure which may tend to produce neurotic symptoms. However, the physical nature of the work itself, rather than its social context, is a matter which looms large in the eyes of the worker, and we ought to give it a fair share of importance. We need not accept the pessimistic view that engineering and technology prescribe the role which a human being plays in the productive process, and that he must adapt to it. In many cases, quite small changes of organization can convert a paced into an unpaced task. Other factors also, such as the opportunity for conversation, need to be analysed, so that we can in future arrange work to avoid conditions which produce chronic effects.

ACKNOWLEDGEMENTS

This research was supported by the Medical Research Council under commission from the Department of Employment and the Employment Medical Advisory Service. The Medical Research Council are also the employers of Donald E. Broadbent. Thanks are due to the interviewers, Margaret H. P. Broadbent, Adrienne Garrod, and Carol Hill; and also the management, workers, and medical officers of the plant studied.

REFERENCES

Blood, M. R., and Hulin, C. L. (1967). Alienation, environmental characteristics, and worker responses, *J. Appl. Psychol.*, **51**, 284–290.

Brief, A. P., and Aldag, R. J. (1975). Employee reactions to job characteristics: A constructive replication, *J. Appl. Psychol.*, **60**, 182–186.

Broadbent, D. E. (1953). Noise, paced performance, and vigilance tasks, *Brit. J. Psychol.*, **44**, 295–303.

Caplan, R. D., Cobb, S., French, J. R. P., Van Harrison, R., and Pinneau, S. R. (1975). *Job Demands and Worker Health*, NIOSH Research Report, USHEW, US Government Printing Office, Washington; DC.

Colligan, M. J., Smith, M. J., and Hurrell, J. J. (in press). Occupational incidence rates of mental health disorders, *J. Human Stress*.

Conrad, R. (1960). Letter sorting machines—paced, 'lagged' or unpaced? *Ergonomics*, **3**, 149–157.

Conrad, R., and Hille, B. (1955). Comparison of paced and unpaced performance at a packing task, *Occup. Psychol.*, **29**, 15–28.

Cross, D. (1973). The Worker Opinion Survey: A measure of shop-floor satisfaction, *Occup. Psychol.*, **47**, 193–208.

Crown, S. (1974). The Middlesex Hospital Questionnaire (MHQ) in clinical research, *Mod. Probl. Pharmacopsychiat.*, **7**, 11–124.

Crown, S., and Crisp, A. H. (1966). A short clinical self-rating scale for psycho-neurotic patients, *Brit. J. Psychiat.*, **112**, 917–923.

Frankenhaeuser, M., and Gardell, B. (1976). Underload and overload in working life, outline of a multidisciplinary approach, *J. Human Stress*, **2**, 35–46.

Goldthorpe, J. H., Lockwood, D., Beckhofer, F., and Platt, J. (1969). *The Affluent Worker in the Class Structure*, Cambridge University Press, Cambridge, England.

Hackman, J. R., and Lawler, E. E. (1971). Employee reactions to job characteristics, *J. Appl. Psychol. Monog.*, **5**, 259–286.

Hackman, J. R., and Oldham, G. R. (1975). Development of the Job Diagnostic Survey, *J. Appl. Psychol.*, **60**, 159–170.

Hulin, C. L., and Blood, M. R. (1968). Job enlargement, individual differences, and worker responses, *Psychol. Bull.*, **69**, 41–55.

Hulin, C. L., and Smith, P. A. (1967). An empirical investigation of two implications of the two factor theory of job satisfaction, *J. Appl. Psychol.*, **51**, 396–402.

Kornhauser, A. (1965). *Mental Health of the Industrial Worker*, Wiley, New York.

Smith, P. C., Kendall, L. M., and Hulin, C. L. (1969). *The Measurement of Satisfaction in Work Retirement*, Rand McNally, Chicago.

Walker, C. R., and Guest, R. P. (1952). *The Man on the Assembly Line*, Harvard University Press, Cambridge, Mass.

Working Life
Edited by B. Gardell and G. Johansson
© 1981 John Wiley & Sons Ltd

Metallurgy in a Social Context

SVEN EKETORP

The metallurgy of iron and copper has a long tradition in Sweden. The term 'Swedish steel' is still, rightly or wrongly, synonymous with quality and precision. Mines and ironworks were to a great extent centres of early industrial development in Sweden. It is thus natural to take the steel industry as typical example of Swedish industry.

Tradition has assets but also drawbacks. Radical technical developments are rare in the metallurgical industry and the metallurgical processes used throughout the world are still based on the 500-year-old blast furnace and the Bessemer invention made 120 years ago. Investment costs are high in this type of technology, and this restricts the possibilities for rapid change. Some 95 per cent of our research activities therefore deal with piecemeal corrections of failures in existing processes. Little effort is spent on rigorous research in order to find really new methods of operation.

If we want to make radical changes in metallurgy and the steel industry and create something new—which is absolutely necessary if we in this small country are going to survive in competition with Japan and other countries— we must develop a metallurgical industry in which we can make use of all the knowledge and potential we have now. We must produce new thinking not only in technology and economics but also in the social sphere. The developments so far have been based on technological inventions and strict business economy. Our main driving force has been expansion. Other growth mechanisms certainly, should be possible to apply.

I find it rather hopeful that so far, we have used only to a minor degree the knowledge we already possess in many different fields. We have a scattered knowledge of the fundamentals of metallurgical science and technology, of the solutions to internal and external environmental problems, of how to plan transport and buildings, of effective organization systems, of economy of scale and of special products, of the importance of education, etc. We even have a deep knowledge, as is shown by this symposium, of which conditions are needed if we are to arrive at conditions providing satisfaction, responsibility, and creativity for the people involved. What we have not known is how to let all this knowledge shape and steer the industry. We have given up too early and have been satisfied with suboptimizing instead of attempting total optimization. Why is it that a modern steel plant looks very much the same in Sweden, Japan, and the USSR? Why have the very different social and economic systems not influenced the technological processes, buildings, and products? Certainly this must be due to the fact that in technological developments social factors are not allowed to play any role at all.

At this symposium many facts about man's position and aims in working life will be presented. My hope is that this knowledge will be used to form future technical and economic systems. Such a future would certainly be different from that which results from an extrapolation of our present conditions.

A new approach must be based on an integration of a variety of factors of different nature from pure technical science to the adaptation to psychological rules. Such an immense task of integration and cooperation between different disciplines, however, will be impossible to carry out if there is no central idea on which to base discussions and suggestions. This central idea, around which most people can unite, is that man himself should be in the centre. Do we not all agree that everything is pointless if the needs of man are not satisfied?

Figure 1 illustrates that hitherto technological developments and activities have started with capital and the wish or need to earn a reasonable interest on this money. It is easy to draw the second figure and put man in the centre. It is, however, extremely difficult to make this model a reality and to define how the needs of man can be satisfied by a correct choice of technical, economic, and social systems.

When building industrial projects today we start with a definition of the economic goal and decisions about the product to be made and the technical process to be used. At a very much later date we discuss the organization system to be used, and at the very last stage we let the people who are going to work in the plant enter discussions about some minor details. It is my firm belief

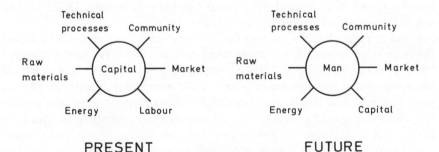

PRESENT   FUTURE

Figure 1 Structure and planning of industry (steel works)

that if we are going to create anything like our idea of an industry suitable for human beings to work in we must let *all* factors, and especially the human viewpoint, play a part right from the beginning. Furthermore, if we decide that the human factors should act as absolute criteria, taking precedence over all other criteria, we will find that the problem is very much less complicated than if we have freedom to combine technical and economic factors at will. It might be said that this is putting social issues before profitability. I think, however, that this is necessary. You might believe that metallurgy today makes use of our latest scientific and technical discoveries. This is by no means the fact. As I said before, our metallurgical processes are very old and do not nearly fulfil requirements, i.e. a cheap, uniform metal using a minimum amount of energy and with no environmental problems. In fact our present techniques make it almost impossible to produce an acceptable environmental solution at a reasonable cost.

Fortunately we have clear indications, based on fundamental principles, of in which directions we should move in order to reach the optimal technology. The same is true for energy minimization, for environmental solutions, for personal fulfilment in working life, for buildings and transport, for marketing, etc. We certainly do not lack basic knowledge. But we hesitate to use it and to integrate it.

Let me list a few examples of what could be done if we were to apply some of our basic facts. In my opinion these proposals, which are designed to arrive at a plant run economically with modern techniques, will also give us very much improved human conditions of work.

—The blast furnace process necessitates the agglomeration of ores and coal to sinter and coke. Kinetics (the science of reaction and transport speed) states that the largest possible surface should be utilized. The obvious conclusion is the use of powders directly contacted in the iron- and steel-making processes. Reaction time can be lowered from 5 hours to a fraction of a second.

—Today's casting (solidification) technique is based on uncontrolled cooling. Again, by using desintegration of the metal stream into small droplets the cooling speed can be increased from 10 to 10 000 °C/sec and a uniform product be obtained in a controlled process.

—Today's rolling technique involves breaking down the coarse crystalline metal structure. By using the above solidification method a large part of the expensive metal-working processes can be removed.

—The steel plant of today has a very complex system for the transportation of materials. A very much simpler flow of materials could be realized. If several process steps can be removed and material flow simplified, for instance by using oxygen instead of air.

—Energy consumption could best be improved from the present figure of

Table 1

Positive answers, 38%	Partition %
Varying job tasks	31
Working independently	18
Learn something new all the time	11
Responsible work	8
Nice fellow-workers	5
Good foremen	3
Well paid	2
Negative answers, 58%	
Monotonous work	52
Bad physical environment	22
Shift work	5
Poorly paid	2
Problems with foremen	2
No possibility for improvement	1

30 per cent efficiency to perhaps 60 per cent by excluding many steps in the processing and by avoiding repeated cooling and heating.

—The environment can hardly be improved beyond the point achieved at great expense in modern mills. However, costs can be reduced by the adoption of a technology specially designed to minimize environmental problems.

—We know enough of the necessary criteria for job motivation. In a recent inquiry (The Working Environment of the Steel Industry, 1975) among Swedish steel plant workers they were asked if they found their job interesting and stimulating. Some 38 per cent answered yes and 58 per cent no. The result, shown in Table 1, is very illuminating. Here we have indications of the different measures that should be used in order to increase the positive and decrease the negative answers.

—Productivity is today measured in units like tons of steel per man and year (Japan 500, Sweden 200 for ordinary steel). This seems to be an altogether oversimplified viewpoint. The quality and type of the product naturally comes into play but, still more important, the quality of the working hour should also be measured. There is a difference between people who use only their left thumb or their right arm and those who are lucky enough to engage their whole personality. Only in the latter case are we using our human resources.

—The steel plant buildings are today extremely monotonous and architects have seldom had anything to do with them. The potential of the building as part of the process functions and as a stimulating environment for the people who work there has so far been completely neglected.

—The steel plant of today is often directed to regions 'for environmentally dangerous industries'. The use of such a term is in itself a disgrace. By using the best possible modern techniques—or directing money to the development of such techniques—it should be quite possible to integrate the steel plant in the community.

These examples should show that we have great possibilities for changing our present processing systems, and at *the same time* improving man's working life in order to reach a state where he can experience an interesting, creative job full of meaning and responsibility. The task is now to integrate all our knowledge while never losing sight of the human criteria. Such an integration might mean compromises but also inspiration from different groups (Eketorp, 1978.)

A few examples of such influences are discussed below.

(1) It is well known that capacity for work is low and the stress level high at certain periods during the night. It would therefore be highly desirable to eliminate the night shift.

This is technically possible—but not with our present technology. The blast furnace cannot be stopped for regular intervals. A new technology must be found where the reactors can be started and stopped frequently without detrimental effects on the processing performance. Such a processing system is possible to find, and I think we are close to the realization of it. The capital cost of such equipment, furthermore, must be as low as possible as it will be working only part of the day.

(2) Experts in psychology—and in the application of common sense—advocate that the industrial unit should not exceed 100–200 people in order that every one should be able to identify himself with the plant and its products and policy. Furthermore, it might be stated that the work group should be no larger than 10–15 people and that no one should be allowed to work in isolation. Such restrictions will immediately influence not only the size of the plant but will perhaps also result in plants consisting of parallel units. The arrangement of the processing units must be such that a social relationship can exist between them. It is obvious that such rules must be introduced at the very first moment of planning the plant.

(3) Steel scrap is today mainly melted in electric arc furnaces. The noise level there often exceeds 110 dB(A). It is almost impossible to reduce the noise and dust from such furnaces to acceptable levels even if costly arrangements are introduced. There exist, however, other electric units, induction furnaces, where the noise and dust problem is almost completely eliminated due to the nature of the electric system itself. A steel plant based on such a technique offers the opportunity for very much improved working conditions.

(4) The product of the present steel plant—and adjoining mechanical shop— is decided upon by market and sales experts. In the near future it is quite likely that the people in the plant will take part in and be responsible for the choice of product to be produced. This will be so not only because of their wish to steer production towards the most interesting and useful markets but also because

they want to influence the production method by which the product is produced. Work environment is a function of the product.

(5) The 'steel plant of tomorrow' will surely be more computer controlled than that of today as we will install processes that are amenable to computerization. This technical and economic improvement must not, however, be allowed to result in systems where people are caught in monotonous and meaningless observation jobs. The computer terminal placed in an 'activity room' might well be an inspiring information centre. This would necessitate the correct arrangement of technical equipment and close cooperation between engineers and psychology experts.

Such systems also require adequate and continuing education. However, job education today is mainly carried out in times of unemployment.

(6) It is quite likely that in future salaries will be paid for total working time including travelling time. This might be a good way to decentralize industry. Today total time away from home tends to increase in spite of decreasing working hours at the plant. Such restrictions introduce a new way of looking at industrial activity and force the community to integrate its functions with those of the industry. The plant could use offices, centres, and even homes for certain activities, and the community could place such things as swimming pools and nursery schools inside the plant. (Why should not the small children spend some of their day at the metallurgical laboratory studying fascinating chemical reactions, or rolling plasticine as modelling material? And there would for the possibility of contact with their mothers and fathers at their work place.)

Clearly such close cooperation between plant and community requires readily available information on planning for an increase or decrease of production, new products to be marketed, raw materials to be used, the volume of transport to and from the plant, etc.

In the fashion described above we are working on a recently started large-scale project called 'Future Steel Works' administrated by the Swedish Board for Technical Development. Twenty different research groups are working together: five of them deal mainly with technical development and equipment, three with environmental questions (physical and psychosocial), three with buildings and the surrounding community, three with organization systems, three with products and production economy, and three with markets and marketing (Eketorp, 1976).

This ambitious undertaking could perhaps be called a study in 'social metallurgy'. Astonishingly enough, this seems to be the first time that so many disciplines have been brought together in order to formulate and create the conditions under which a really modern technology should operate. To me such cooperation seems both natural and necessary.

REFERENCES

Eketorp, S. (1976). A proposal for a future steel plant and a research program, *J. Iron & Steel Inst. of Japan*, **16**, 1–10.

Eketorp, S. (1978). Decisive factors for the planning of future steel plants, *Proceedings of the 3rd International Iron & Steel Congress, Chicago, USA*, 16–20 April.

The Working Environment of the Steel Industry (1975), Swedish Government Official Reports (SOU), 83, Stockholm.

Working Life
Edited by B. Gardell and G. Johansson
© 1981 John Wiley & Sons Ltd

Discussant's Comments

CARINA NILSSON

It is my pleasure as a representative of LO, the Swedish Trade Union Confederation, to receive this opportunity to present some observations on the psychosocial effects of advanced technology on working life. I would like to start by briefly summarizing the recent progress made in this field in Sweden, chiefly with regard to the new Work Environment Act and the Act of Co-determination, and I would then like to go on to comment on some of the papers that have been written for this symposium.

The new Working Environment Act covers psychosocial health risks at work in various ways. For one thing, it attaches great importance to the employees themselves being able to influence their own work and the design and layout of their workplace. Hours of work are also considered an important part of the working environment.

The new Act also makes changes in prior inspection. Prior inspection of machinery and other equipment is already possible under present legislation, but the new Act goes further. Compulsory notification and licences may be required in order to start certain types of activities, and the inspection of machine design and the approval of work processes can be obligatory. Under the Act the National Board of Occupational Safety and Health has the authority to forbid the use of a machine, tool, or chemical product or to ban the implementation of a work process.

The Act further stipulates that the safety representative has the right to stop solitary employment. Solitary employment is often a product of modern technology and is an organizational problem which is one of the primary targets of the new Act.

Commenting on the proposal for the new Work Environment Act, LO expressed the opinion that it ought to contain more precise rules governing the psychosocial working environment. For example, it was felt that the Act should have stated that the employee himself should be the one to adjust his rate of working and that the job should not be of a monotonous nature. However, it was preferred to have the general rules now decided upon in the body of the Act and instead to append regulations defining those rules in the Act.

We believe that the significance which will be given to the regulations drawn up by the National Board of Occupational Safety and Health must result in the employees' side gaining considerable say in determining the areas that such regulations will cover.

This is also a (trade union) demand with regard to the Act of Co-determination which stipulates the degree of influence that trade unions are permitted over the workplace, and also covers matters associated with work organization. A large number of the psychosocial problems in working life are related to work organization. As for co-determination in working life, LO is still hoping that an agreement will soon be concluded which will enable us to increase our influence over the way work is organized.

Another important event is the investigation of the Industrial Health Service, its resources and content, that is at present being conducted. This investigation will report on the advisability of starting a psychosocial section within the Industrial Health Service, an area sparsely covered today.

LO's working environment committee has formulated its opinions on what should be covered in the local work on the psychosocial working environment in conjunction with the current investigation. The Work Environment Act does not clearly define psychosocial problems in working life, and the papers presented here today will also given an idea of the scope of the psychosocial sector.

LO is of the opinion that the psychosocial working environment mainly relates to matters covering:

—work organization,
—the disposition and content of work,
—work tempo,
—monotony in work,
—the need for attention and concentration,
—forms of wage,
—working hours,
—introduction to and training in work.

We are also of the opinion that the problems of the physical environment also have important psychosocial consequences, for example noise which can cause both stress and isolation in work. We believe that the extensive problem of industrial accidents is closely linked to shortcomings in the organization of the work and the way in which production engineering has developed.

I think that there is some justification for saying that we have acquired quite a lot of scientific knowledge about the psychosocial problems in working life today, but it now remains to find practical solutions to these problems. Measures should include practical experiments, legislation regulations, agreements, work by occupational safety and health authorities, the Industrial Health Service and not least by local trade unions. The indecision that is sometimes evident in the trade union's position on psychosocial problems is to a great extent, I believe, due to the fact that it is only now that we have obtained a practical apparatus, mainly through the new Work Environment and Co-determination Acts, to tackle at source these types of working environment problems.

The improved opportunities now given to the trade union to work on psychosocial matters has stressed the need to review from a trade union perspective the available research data on the psychosocial working environment.

The trade unions place a high priority on the ability to influence technical development in working life in a more human and democratic way. Both physical and psychosocial working environment problems are related to the development of production engineering. We believe that trade union participation in technical research and development work, together with an increase in the preventive measures taken by occupational safety and health authorities aimed at the designers of production engineering equipment, are among the factors which will improve the working environment and work organization. The problem must be solved at its roots. And therefore we must also increase and improve the methods by which we can predict the negative effects that technology can have on man in his working life.

I would now like to address more directly some of the matters arising from the interesting papers which have been presented at this symposium.

First, the quotation from Bertrand Russell used by Dr Kahn: 'mankind decided to submit to monotony and tedium in order to diminish the risks of starvation'. This is true for a lot of people. However, it is curious that the few people who have a job which is interesting and allows freedom of thought and action are often those who are the least likely to starve!

Many people in the industrial countries of the West have reached a certain economic standard. One of the great differences remaining between the social classes is the heavy work and the work with many hazards performed by the workers. It is for this reason that it is important for us to be reminded of the conditions under which the workers earn their living, as described by Dr Kahn in his paper. Having had the condition of workers' health described for us, I think it is important to ask: Why does not our society pay more attention to the effects that the organization of work has on health? Are these effects regarded as 'troublesome', and is there any doubt that such working conditions can be basically changed so that they meet essential human needs instead of, as is often the case today, causing ill-health and accidents?

As Dr Eketorp says in his paper, technological development so far has been based on strict business economy and technical inventions, but social facts are hardly allowed to play any role at all. We must now change this and in future design technological systems in which social and human criteria play an important part from the beginning. Therefore, Eketorp's ideas of a new steel plant are very important and I hope we will have the same kind of projects for other branches of industry.

Both Dr Kahn and Dr Broadbent report some scientific complications when studying the effects of work organization on individuals. Self-selection has been mentioned as a problem in this context. I do not think that self-selection is such a big problem in those jobs where the effects that are most detrimental to health are encountered, e.g. assembly line jobs in industry. It is still the case that a large number of people do not have much freedom in choosing a job which suits their own qualifications and abilities. The problem is rather that the weakest are often pushed out of the labour market, and so many studies mainly deal with the 'elite', thereby resulting in less negative data on the effects of the job.

Dr Broadbent's paper includes research results which indicate that the way in which the job is run rather than the length of the work cycles has effects detrimental to mental health. It is possible that job control is the gravest problem, but even so I wonder if surveys have not shown that both the work cycles and the way the job is run have effects that are sufficiently deterimental to health to cause measures to be taken to rectify conditions of work organization such as these.

Dr Kahn describes the modern industrial job in one short sentence which I think sums up the problem: 'The demands are heavy but narrow'. I believe that there is a risk that it will be possible to use this description in the future, also, if our technical development continues in its present vein. Process technology and computerized jobs often seem to make heavy demands on attention while at the same time the content of the work appears to be very constrained.

Some of the research results on the effects of process technology and computerization lead one to believe that there is a danger that the psychosocial effects associated with assembly line jobs will be inherent in the production technology which is at present being developed.

Do we possess sufficient scientific evidence to draw that conclusion or don't we? It is important that our research establishment can not only verify that problems exist once a special technology has been introduced, but that they have the ability to predict problems as well. Is research managing to do that today? It is with this question that I would like to end my contribution to the discussion.

Working Life
Edited by B. Gardell and G. Johansson
© 1981 John Wiley & Sons Ltd

Discussant's Comments

JAN EDGREN

Work forms, production technology, and the physical work environment of Swedish industries are changing at a rapid pace. Great changes have come about in many companies, specially during the 1970s.

Much of the attention has been focused on the physical work environment. Many companies have made a big effort to eliminate health risks and to improve the work environment. They strive to abolish monotony and rigid, machine-paced work. The creation of more meaningful and varied work roles and of team work towards a common goal are what they try to bring about. New forms of organization attempt to decentralize decision-making and to widen the individual's influence over his own work.

Factories and places of work that have separated themselves from the old ideas of work organization have come into existence: Motor car factories without an assembly line, large function-divided workshops which are now reorganized into smaller, product-oriented workshops, the complete mechanization of machine-paced work with short task cycles, dust-free foundries painted in light colours, and paper-processing machinery that seems noiseless compared with older models (see Agurén and Edgren, 1980; Agurén et al., 1976; Arbete, Teknik, Miljö, 1977; Job Reform in Sweden, 1975).

These are some developments in which Swedish industries are very far advanced. What lies behind these developments?

An important driving force in many companies has been to create attractive working conditions around production work. This is done in order to be able to recruit new personnel and also to get them to stay. The companies must meet the increasing demands that people today place on their work.

Another driving factor has been the trade unions' striving for the betterment of working conditions and the work environment for their members. Cooperation between management and the unions in the companies has contributed to the fast development.

A third and often crucial factor has been that the demand on increased productivity work and continuing economic development in many cases harmonized with a development of working forms and organization.

Progress in production technology has provided new opportunities to design production systems that at the same time meet demands for more efficient operations and better jobs for individuals.

NEW CRITERIA FOR PRODUCTION DESIGN

These driving forces and lines of development have brought about the emergence of new criteria of what is a 'good production system'. Among others, the following three criteria are characteristic for the new production system of the 1970s (see also Agurén and Edgren, 1980).

Meaningful work roles in a good environment

Not the least of which has behavioural research contributed to that we, during the last ten years, changed the view on which demands people place on good work, and how a motivated work role is put together. Job enlargement, team work, integration of quality responsibility and other indirect activities in production work roles have become established elements in the doctrine of job design of the 1970s. Our knowledge is as yet far from sufficient and more research is needed. An important point is that people are different and have completely different ideas about satisfying work.

Reliable production systems

An important factor of production efficiency is that production functions safely and smoothly in spite of disturbances and variations in the conditions of production. An objection to the assembly line is that it makes for a production system that is very rigid and sensitive to disturbance. In the cases where production has been changed successfully from assembly line to, for instance, production in parallel groups or stations, the most important advantage to effectiveness has usually been a disturbance-tolerant and more adaptive production apparatus. At the same time new job design has eliminated a rigid chain of production with much specialization and fragmentation, and created more flexible working roles where each individual or production group can function relatively independently of the others and be responsible for a larger related task (such as the preassembly of television apparatus or motor car engines).

Disengagement of man from machine

An important criterion of the job design doctrine of the 1970s is to strive to disengage man from rigid, machine-paced work processes. The most common way is to mechanize our automate short-cycled and repetitive man-machine operations. In this way tasks which consist solely of looking after machines can be reduced or abolished. Now their is the opportunity to create flexible work roles consisting of servicing, supervising, resetting, and loading machines, repairing, and toolwork. From the point of view of effectiveness this disengagement normally means a certain saving in personnel. But even more important is that the disengagement really leads to an increased use of machinery, i.e.

machinery will run for more hours a day. The successful disengagement of men from machine-spacing is thus characterized by more satisfactory work roles as well as by better use of invested capital.

Let us now, with three examples of new production technology, show how the creation of most satisfying work roles in effective production systems are achieved.

LINE-OUT AT SAAB-SCANIA IN TROLLHÄTTAN

Since the end of the 1960s the car-body workshops at Saab-Scania in Trollhättan had experienced serious problems of absenteeism, personnel turnover, and recruitment. The situation was worst at the production line for the welding and grinding of car bodies. It was often difficult to man all the stations, and so there were considerable production losses. The line consisted of a straight track where the car-bodies were transported past a number of welding and grinding stations. The task cycle time at every station was approximately three minutes. An additional problem was unsatisfactory quality which caused high costs for revision, adjustment, and control.

After a careful investigation and much preparation carried out with the participation of the workers, the old line was torn out during the summer vacation of 1975. One month later a completely new production system was built. This system consists of about twenty parallel stations where partly assembled car bodies are finished. At every station two people work together. They take 45–60 minutes to perform all welding and grinding work depending on which car-body model is involved.

The new arrangement means that work is done at a fixed work station. Welding and grinding thus take place on a stationary car body which has been placed on a work table that can be raised and lowered. Thus the work positions have been essentially improved.

An important requirement was to find a new, flexible transportation system for the car bodies. From a common buffer track the car bodies are transported automatically, at the operator's order, to their proper 'destinations'—some of the parallel stations.

The work organization is built on work teams where the parallel work stations have been grouped in threes. Every work team thus consists of six ordinary members. In addition, a seventh person is included on the work team. He is the contact person of the team and takes care of different indirect work tasks which are integrated in the work team's realm of responsibility. Examples of the foreman's indirect tasks are maintenance of tools, cleaning, requisitioning of material, and quality control. The operators take turns at acting as contact person.

In this new arrangement of parallel stations which turn out complete bodies the responsibility for the production quality has been placed directly with the operators. The transportation system has been formed with a return conveyor so that the defective car bodies can be sent back from the final control station and be checked and adjusted by the responsible operators. A merging in this way of responsibility, quantity and quality for both would not have been possible on a conventional assembly line.

The result of radically changing the production system is in many ways a most satisfactory job: longer work cycles, completely unpaced work, team work with common responsibility for indirect tasks, and the operators' own responsibility for finished car bodies. The personnel problems have also decreased sharply and absenteeism, which earlier was the highest of any department in the company, is now lower than average.

The rearrangement has also resulted in a better production economy. The most important factor here is the resistance to disturbances provided by the parallel system. A stoppage in one station affects only that station and does not bring the work on the whole track to a stop as with an assembly line. Production losses have therefore been small and, further, have proved easy to make up. Another important factor is that it has been possible to cut the control and the adjustment costs. Furthermore, the production volume can now be smoothly adapted without it being necessary to change the balance of the system. Even the model change of the Saab 900 did not demand any large rearrangements.

AUTOMATED PRESSING OF CAR BODIES AT VOLVO

The Volvo Olofström work is Volvo's car body factory. Here they press and assemble different components of sheet metal for car bodies. The manufacturing is done in large series and is, as by other motor car companies, performed in a number of press lines. Until just recently it has been taken for granted that the work tasks at a press line must be very monotonous and short-cycled.

A conventional press line consists of five or six heavy press machines which stand in a line. The car body components are shaped by being pressed by one machine after another. The work is often divided up into as many different operations as there are presses in a press line. The last press in the line gives the component its final shape.

Ten years ago the work was set up so that a pair of operators put a sheet in the press machine every six or ten seconds and pressed on the press release. On the other side of the machine another pair of operators took out the pressed sheet and placed it so that the next pair of operators could take it and feed it to the next press. The work was thus very binding, monotonous, and short-cycled. The changing of tools and the changing and adjustment of the machines were done by other specially trained operators.

Little by little it has been possible to mechanize different working elements. Today there are a number of completely automated press lines. At the beginning of each of the new press lines there is a sheet magazine with approximately 400 sheets of metal. The transportation to the first press is automatic. When one magazine is empty an operator replaces it with a new one. This work takes only a few minutes each time. The removal of the sheet out of one press and into the next is done with the help of a dip-feeder, i.e. a loading and unloading device. This dip-feeder completely replaces the manual handling work. This means that the physically heavy and machine-paced work at the press lines has been eliminated. On the other hand, new working tasks have been created through a carefully planned change in the organization.

The automation has created possibilities for group organization. The tasks of a press group consist of control, supervision, and adjustment of the processes. Inspection and packing are manual as before. All tasks are rotated among the operators. But the major change in the organization of the work is that the operators now make tool changes and adjust the process themselves. The operators have been trained to perform these specialized tasks, which used to be performed only by specialists. A work-tool change takes 4–8 hours and usually occurs two or three times a week. The groups which work in this way are very independent.

The automation has brought about considerable savings in personnel and a better production economy. These have naturally been qualifications for investment in new techniques. But more attractive working roles have also been created. It is no longer a problem to recruit and keep press workers at the press line. In addition, the broader and more qualified tasks have made the press line workers more interested in occupational training. In this way the company has obtained a new source for recruitment of tool makers and for maintenance workers.

CONTROL ROOM FOR GROUPS AT HOLMEN'S NEW PAPER PULP FACTORY

Bråviken is Holmen's new paper and pulp plant for newsprint. It is located outside the city of Norrköping. The pulp mill is highly automated and equipped with an advanced computer system. The production process is completely steered from an integrated control room. Here two to four operators are responsible for all the work. It is naturally more efficient to integrate the supervision of as many process activities as possible to one larger control room. This also makes for a better environment for the operators. The operators do not need to work in the noise and heat of the factory, as is the case in many less advanced plants. The integrated control room environment promotes greater operator interaction. Each operator is less bound to his work position and has greater freedom to exercise secondary functions or take a break.

The control room's work consists of many different tasks. One main task is to monitor the flow of the production process. For this a number of visual display units (VDUs) have been installed. The VDUs show different diagrams representing the processes. The diagrams give a good overview of the processes and provide a legible basis for intervention by the operators.

Another task for the operators is to examine the pulp's quality. Special laboratory equipment which is installed in the control room is used for this purpose.

A third task for the operators is to go round the factory at regular intervals in order to check the state of the process. This task often places large demands on the operators' professional knowledge.

Part of an operator's responsibility is to make independent decisions should the conditions for production change. As example, the finished pulp is pumped up into a storage tower from which it is, via a pipeline, distributed to the company's paper factory in the city of Norrköping. Should the volume in the storage tower reach a certain level, one of the operators contacts the paper factory to find out their current need of pulp. The operator now makes a decision about how the pulp process shall be governed and even decides if the process needs to be stopped. In such highly technical production systems as modern pulp manufacturing, the boundary between the factory (blue-collar) and office (white-collar) workers disappears. There is a participation in both the practical production process and in the administrative decision-making process by most of the employees.

DEMANDS FOR MORE EFFICIENT OPERATIONS AND BETTER JOBS

We have with these examples from different types of production briefly pointed out how new thinking in production technology gives new opportunities for the creation of better jobs. Less constraining work, team work, enlarged work roles, responsibility for a larger related task, and responsibility for results in both quality and quantity are aspects of job design which come to mind in the three examples. We have not said that new, advanced technology alone makes for better jobs. *New ideas* are also required if advantage is to be taken of the technical possibilities for good job design.

Behavioural scientists are quick to emphasize that new technology brings with it the risk of negative effects on industrial work (see Gardell's paper). It is clearly true that such risks exist, and it is important that the companies' attention is drawn to the problems which different types of production techniques can cause. There exists however, a risk of prejudiced, negative criticism against new technology as such. It is by new production technology and by new industrial engineering ideas that we can create new possibilities for more satisfying work. Renewal of technology within the companies also promotes the improvement of working life.

There is a tendency within Swedish work life research to ignore the economic restrictions under which industry must work. We have throughout this comment tried to stress that every new step in development must concentrate on attaining more satisfying work and at the same time higher effectiveness. It is not a solution to strive after increased job satisfaction and a better working environment through decreased productivity. Neither the individual company nor the industry as a whole can afford such an economic equation. This applies directly to the severe competitive situation in which Swedish industry finds itself today.

In principle Professor Kahn's thesis holds true that successive periods of 'industrial history' have given us the choice between three alternatives (see Kahn's paper):

—increased production and material welfare;
—decreased amount of work, fewer working hours;
—and now: 'under conditions of affluence—improving the social and technical content of work so that it is more rewarding in itself. . .'.

However, in reality it is not a question of alternatives, it is three demands which are simultaneously made on commercial and industrial life. The task during the 1970s has been to meet the demands for better jobs as well as increased standards and shortened work time. There are no signs that the demands will decrease in the coming years. The only realistic way is, therefore, to find solutions which combine more satisfying jobs and increased efficiency. For this purpose new production technology is necessary.

REFERENCES

Aguré, S., and Edgren, J. (1980). New Factories. Job Design through Factory Planning in Sweden, Swedish Employer's Confederation, Stockholm.

Agurén, S., Hansson, R., and Karlsson, K. G. (1976). *The Volvo Kalmar Plant. The Impact of New Design on Work Organization*. The Rationalization Council, Swedish Employers' Confederation and Swedish Confederation of Trade Unions, Stockholm.

Arbete, Teknik, Miljö—bilder från svensk industri (1977). (Work, Technology, Environment—Pictures from Swedish Industry), Swedish Employers' Confederation, Stockholm.

Job Reform in Sweden (1975). (Conclusions from 500 shop floor projects) Swedish Employers' Confederation, Stockholm.

Part 2

The Time Aspect of Production Systems: The Work–Leisure Relation

Working Life
Edited by B. Gardell and G. Johansson
© 1981 John Wiley & Sons Ltd

Job Socialization and Job Strain: The Implications of Two Related Psychosocial Mechanisms for Job Design

ROBERT ALLEN KARASEK

INTRODUCTION

While there is almost universal agreement that some relationship exists between the work environment and workers' mental health and psychological functioning (Gardell, 1976), there is disagreement about the magnitude and the specific nature of the associations. Such disagreements have left practitioners who would like to make use of such findings for job redesign with few firm foundations. Debate on these basic points seems to have absorbed much of the research effort that might otherwise have been devoted to the important task of testing for a variety of different mechanisms to be included under the broad umbrella of psychosocial effects of the work environment.

The result has been that much of the research deals with global outcome measures such as 'job satisfaction' or 'motivation', and devotes little attention to submechanisms which might predict quite independent, even counteracting psychosocial outcomes—based on a variety of different job characteristics. The goal of this paper will be to take the limited further step of proposing and testing two mechanisms of socio-psychological functioning which have related but basically independent effects. The two mechanisms predict job-related psychological strain (mental and physical illness) and job-learned behaviour patterns carried over from work to life outside the job (job socialization). These two mechanisms are both based on the interaction of job decision latitude and job demands, two job characteristics which are rarely investigated for their joint impacts.

THE JOB STRAIN—JOB SOCIALIZATION MODEL

A truly comprehensive discussion of the literature linking job conditions and psychological functioning in the areas of mental strain and job socialization is beyond the scope of the paper (see Karasek, 1978c; Karasek, 1979; Gardell,

75

1976; Hackman and Lawler, 1971; Staines, 1977). Summarizing my perspectives on the mental strain literature, I feel that many contradictory findings in this area can be traced to incomplete models derived from two mutually exclusive research traditions. One tradition focuses on job decision latitude (decision authority or skill level and variety) and another treats 'stressor' on the job. Most of the vast literature on job satisfaction and mental strain focuses on job decision latitude alone (for example, Kornhauser, 1965; and the skill variety and autonomy scales of Turner and Lawrence, 1965, and Hackman and Lawler, 1971). The second research area, the 'life stress' tradition of epidemiological studies of mental health, focuses on the mental and physical illness induced by environmental stressors, and more recently job stressors (Theorell, 1976; Sundbom, 1971). Unfortunately, job decision latitude research rarely includes systematic discussion of job demands; and the job demand literature rarely includes systematic discussion of job decision latitude (Karasek, 1978c). An exception must be made for several organizational case studies, which have referred, if indirectly, to the important interactive effects of job demands and job decision latitude. For example, Whyte's restaurant workers (1948) experienced the severest strain symptoms when they faced heavy customer demands, which they were not able to control; and Gouldner (1954) notes that personal and organizational tensions increase when close supervision is applied to miners under heavy work-loads (also Crozier, 1964, and Drabek and Hass, 1969). But these case studies and their consistent findings appear to have had little effect in encouraging comprehensive models for survey research.

It is my contention that a correct analysis must distinguish between two important elements of job content at the individual task level: the demands of a job and the discretion the worker is permitted to decide how to meet these demands. These two aspects of the job situation represent, respectively, the instigators of action (job demands or stressors which place the individual in a motivated or energized state of 'stress') and the constraints on the alternative resulting action which makes use of that energy. The individual's job decision latitude is the constraint which modulates the release or transformation of 'stress' (potential energy) into the energy of action.

Both job demands and job decision latitude must be analyzed to avoid misinterpretation and/or inconsistencies. A typical paradox which arises from omitting one of them is alluded to by Quinn and his colleagues (1971, 411): they found that both executives and assembly line workers could have stressful jobs, but they could not explain differences in their job satisfaction. It is probable that the obvious differences in the omitted variable of decision latitude for executives and workers account for the differences observed in their strain symptoms and satisfaction.

Failure to distinguish between job stressors and job decision latitude is also reflected in the tendency to describe all structurally determined job characteristics as 'job demands', regardless of their drastically different effects on psychological functioning (Hulin and Blood, 1968, 268). Failure to distinguish between work-load stressors and job decision latitude (skill level and decision authority) and their different effects could account for such an inconsistent finding that 'time pressure demands' are associated with strain symptoms, while 'intellectual demands' are not (Ritti, 1971). Kahn (1981) finds a similar difference in effects for 'qualitative vs. quantitative job demands'. Another version of this interpretive ambiguity occurs for a few conventional measures of job content, such as 'responsibility', which mix aspects of both job demands and job decision latitude (Turner and Lawrence, 1965, 53).

A related problem is that the empirical association between job conditions and mental strain or dissatisfaction disappears in some well-known research findings, leading some authors (Hulin and Blood, 1968) to conclude that cultural values or individual differences overwhelm the effects of job condition on the individual. Two types of analytical errors could account for the lack of relationships. First, studies which fail to distinguish between demands and discretion and add the measures together would find relationships with strain symptoms cancelled out if, as we propose, the opportunity to use skill and make decisions *reduces* the undesirable effects of job demands. Second, failure to account for the possible non-linear, non-additive associations with mental strain that could occur from the interaction of two independent variables would produce different relationships for different subgroups, or insignificant relationships when findings are examined for linear trends (Turner and Lawrence, 1965; Hulin and Blood, 1968; Caplan *et al.*, 1975; Andrews and Withey, 1976). A conclusive analysis thus requires examining broad representative data which include all types of working situations.

Another type of difficulty occurs with current definitions of 'overload' (or 'underload') as a source of strain (McGrath, 1970; Harrison, 1978). Overload is usually defined as occurring when the environmental situation poses demands which exceed the individual's capabilities for meeting them. While this formulation correctly identifies the mediating role played by personal capabilities, it introduces the individual level of analysis prematurely. Attention should first be directed to other types of environmental variables which can moderate job stressors, such as decision latitude, and then to the moderating effects of individual capabilities or perceptions. Mixing both the environmental and the individual characteristics into a single measure, such as 'overload', not only shifts attention away from environmental moderators but makes it difficult to derive unambiguous implications for either work environment or personnel policy.

Figure 1 summarizes in a simple manner our model of the types of jobs that might result from different combinations of job demands and job discretion. Two interactions are actually represented by the labelled diagonals: one representing *disproportional* levels of job demands and job discretion (A), and the second representing the situation where they are *matched* (B). It is

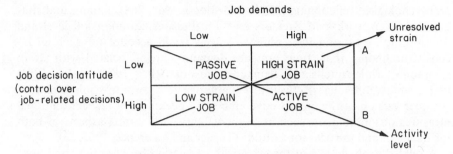

Figure 1 Job strain model

the first situation, when demands are relatively greater than discretion, that we predict mental strain will develop. In the second situation the match of demands and permitted decision latitude is likely to result in the optimal learning (or 'unlearning') situations.

Moving to the upper right along diagonal A, strain increases as job demands increase (Friedman, Rosenman, and Carroll, 1958; Quinn *et al.*, 1971) relative to decreasing job discretion (Frankenhaeuser and Rissler, 1970; Glass and Singer, 1972; Langer and Rodin 1976; Beehr, 1976). If the individual is faced with a difficult situation and yet no satisfactory actions can be taken (Zeigarnik, 1927) or if other desires of the individual must be forgone because of low decision latitude (Henry and Cassel, 1969, 179), the unreleased energy may manifest itself internally, as mental strain symptoms.

The second interaction, where demands and decision latitude are matched (diagonal B) is just as likely to occur in reality. We hypothesize that incremental additions to competency (i.e. learning) occur most often when the challenges in the situation are matched by the individual's control over alternatives or skill in dealing with the challenge (an 'active job' in our terminology— see also Csikszentmihalyi, 1975). In these circumstances opportunities for constructive reinforcement are optimal: the situation will not be unchallengingly simple (thus unimportant) nor so demanding that even appropriate corrective action cannot be invoked (that latter situation will simply result in frustration and the 'strain' discussed above). An important implication of this mechanism is that 'negative learning' can also occur. Individuals may lose their ability to make judgements, solve problems, and tackle challenges if there is long-term adaptation to low decision latitude and low job demand situations (a 'passive job' in our terminology—see Suomi and Harlow, 1972). Related 'learned helplessness' findings (Maier and Seligman, 1976; Weiss, 1968) show that restriction of control in acutely stressful situations leads to reduced problem-solving ability in animal subjects. Berkowitz and Green (1965; Green and Berkowitz, 1964) in their 'disuse theory' also find evidence for the atrophication of unused skills in human subjects over the lifespan.

Our formulation is consistent with a broadly interpreted form of social learning theory and the related 'expectancy theory' model of motivation: the desirability of the challenge may be viewed as a 'stressor' (albeit desirable), and the expectation of attaining the goal may be seen as being dependent on the individual's control over the situation (decision latitude). Thus challenging, high decision latitude situations are 'motivating' or conducive to new learning according to both theories. In social learning theory the effectiveness of the feedback sequence (whereby a succession of reinforcements lead to learning) depends on the degree to which the subject feels he can 'control' the flow of reinforcements through the effectiveness of his actions (Rotter, 1966).

The utility of this model is based on the separation of job demands and job decision latitude. Ideally these two aspects of the job should be highly correlated: 'authority is commensurate with responsibility'. In fact, there is considerable empirical evidence that the correlation is quite low ($r = 0.17$ in US, $r = 0.05$ to 0.26 in Swedish studies, Karasek, 1978b), which implies that there are substantial groups of workers with discrepant demands and discretion.

MEASURING THE DIMENSIONS

Data for testing the stress-management model comes from recent national surveys in the United States and Sweden. The Swedish surveys (Levnadsnivåundersökningen, Johansson 1971) are a two-panel random sample of the full adult population (approximately 1 : 1000), ages 15 to 75, with a response rate of 92 per cent for 1968 and a response rate of 85 per cent for 1968–1974. The US survey, the University of Michigan Quality of Employment Survey for 1972, is based on a national stratified sample of housing units, with a response rate of 76 per cent. The Swedish data contain both expert evaluations and self-reports for some job content characteristics and are also a longitudinal data set: the same workers are interviewed in 1968 and in 1974. The US data are not longitudinal but are richer in detailed job descriptions. Both data sets represent attempts to sample randomly the full national working population in the two countries. This analysis is based upon male workers only; other research has indicated that the relationship between work and mental status for women is often complicated by the additional demand of housework (Karasek, 1976). Only employed workers (82 per cent of male workforce) are included in the analysis of the first Swedish data set.

Theoretical and methodological issues relevant to the construction of the job demand; job discretion; and mental strain, job satisfaction, leisure and political participation indicators from each data set are discussed in detail elsewhere (Karasek, 1978a, 1979; the specific questions included in each measure are listed in the appendix to the latter). Briefly, the job decision latitude indicator measures the working individual's control over use of skills on the job and his authority to make decisions about the organization of his work.

These job characteristics are similar to those discussed by Kohn and Schooler (1973; intellectual job complexity) and Gardell (1971; discretion and qualification level) and to the two central components of the Hackman and Lawler (1971) and Turner and Lawrence (1965) derived job content measures: autonomy (in task organization decisions) and variety (in skill use). Time pacing and repetitive activity are closely related to these measures. Another aspect of decision latitude is the worker's ability to exert control over uncertainties at work (Gardell *et al.*, in preparation). Some of these uncertainties originate in the inherent unpredictability of the operating environment, while others reflect the impact of the organizational decision structure. A measure of physical freedom of action is a major correlate of several psychosomatic illnesses (heart disease symptoms and back ache; Gardell *et al.*, in preparation).

Because intellectual discretion and decision autonomy indicators are so highly correlated in the US data ($r = 0.48$), they are treated as a single scale in the following analyses. The Swedish measure of decision latitude is more specifically related to decisions about the use of skills. Experts' ratings of the training required of a particular job are also available in the Swedish survey and correlate highly with the self-report measure above ($r = 0.65$) which corroborates other findings (Kohn and Schooler, 1973; Gardell, 1971; and Hackman and Lawler, 1971, for five of six measures).

The goal in constructing the scale of job demands is to measure the psychological stressors involved in accomplishing the work-load, stressors related to unexpected tasks, and stressors of job-relate personal conflict. All of these measures have been shown to be significantly related to a range of strain indicators in a large study of Swedish white-collar workers (Gardell *et al.*, in preparation).

Questions about job demands clearly measure the work-load pressure of the job in the US data. The Swedish dimension measures hectic and psychologically demanding work. Neither measure reflects the physical demands of a job which could affect the health of the individual through mechanisms quite different from those proposed here. It should also be noted that both the US and the Swedish data contain adequate evidence that the job demand indicators do reflect 'objective' psychological demands of the work situation; however, a component of personal assessment of stressfulness probably also enters into them (Lazarus, 1966).

The two dependent variables indicating mental strain, exhaustion, and depression are constructed from responses available in both US and Swedish data bases. In each case the depression measures include reports of nervousness, anxiety, and sleeping problems; and the exhaustion indicator is based on reports of severe exhaustion and inability to relax during the evening and trouble getting started in the morning. The job satisfaction measure in the US data is the average of two multiple component indicators measuring willingness to change jobs and job-related depression.

The twenty-eight 'leisure activity' measures used from the Swedish data emphasize active community-level participation in discrete, easily identifiable recreational and political pastimes (significant areas that are omitted in the data are generally leisure 'relaxations': watching television unspecified rest and relaxation, and family socializing activities). Eight leisure and political activity patterns are generated (Karasek, 1976) using Varimax rotation: Intellectual Cosmopolitan Leisure, Active Physical Leisure, Evening Social Leisure, Religious Participation, 'Suburbanite' Leisure, Mass Cultural Leisure, Elite Political Participation, and Mass Political Activity. Two composite variables are constructed representing respectively the sum of both the political activity indicators and all of the leisure activities except Mass Cultural Leisure. Variety in Leisure is the overall number of different activity pattern in which the individual participates.

THE FINDINGS

Figure 2 displays the findings of the test of the 'stress-management' model with both US and Swedish data. The dependent variable is a (0.1) variable representing the presence of a severe problem, such as 'very often depressed'. The percentage of workers with severe exhaustion or depression is displayed as the vertical axis of a three-dimensional diagram. Job demands and job discretion are the other two axes. The three-dimensional diagram allows the separate additive and interactive effects to be immediately assessed. The cell size is determined by cutting the job demand and job decision latitude indicators roughly at their third points (see discussion in Karasek, 1979).

Inspecting Figure 2 we find that the symptom variations conform to the predictions of the model for both countries. When we examine the full national working population it is primarily workers with jobs simultaneously low in job discretion and high in job demands who report exhaustion after work, trouble awakening in the morning, depression, nervousness, anxiety, and insomnia or sleep disturbance. (It must be noted that the meaning of a severe symptom report differs somewhat in Swedish and in English. Therefore, absolute level differences probably cannot be compared in our tables. Of course, relative difference between groups with different job characteristics can be meaningfully compared.) Second, the relationship between job content and mental strain is similar for both Swedish and US workers, using self-report data. In general both increased job demands and decreased job decision latitude contribute to high symptom level. It is noteworthy that at every level of job demands workers with greater control over their job situation experience less mental strain.

Judgements about job characteristics by both workers and experts are possible only with the Swedish data base. It is noteworthy that the findings based on the objective ratings of the job decision latitude (Karasek, 1979) are ap-

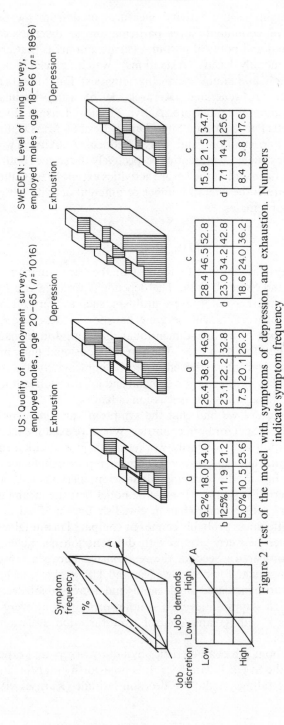

Figure 2 Test of the model with symptoms of depression and exhaustion. Numbers indicate symptom frequency

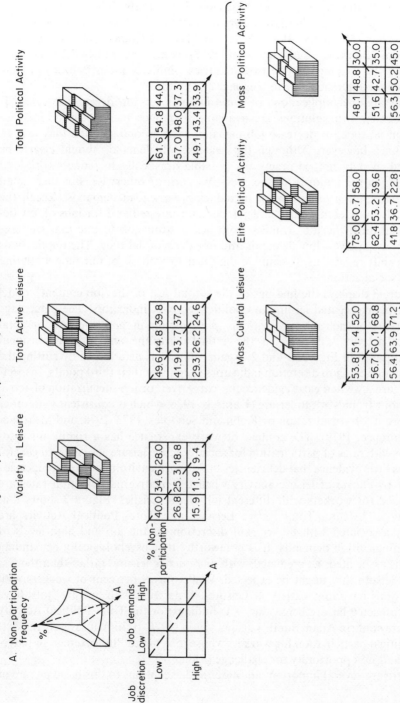

Figure 3 Test of the model with political and leisure participation. Numbers indicate non-participation frequency

proximately the same as those based on the workers' self-reports (see also Gardell, 1971). The alternative hypothesis that the findings represent only social values (Hulin and Blood, 1968), i.e. biased self-reports of workers about their jobs (Björkman and Lundqvist, 1978), is also contradicted by the similarity of the findings for the two countries (similarly industrialized) in spite of potential differences due to language and culture.

What are the implications of these findings for job design strategies? It appears that two solutions are available to reduce mental strain: increase decision latitude, or decrease job demands. The second solution may lead to difficulties, however. Although the heaviest job demands should clearly be avoided, it may not be practically possible drastically to reduce work-load demands in the majority of societies—Western or otherwise. But there is an even more important problem in reducing work-load demands. Recall the four-celled model in Figure 1: if job demands are reduced for jobs of low decision latitude, the job switches from heavy strain job to one that we have defined as passive—low demands and low decision latitude. The implications of this shift require us to examine the other hypothesis of our model relating to job socialization.

Figure 3 displays the findings of the second test of the 'job content' model using the aggregated leisure and political activity indicators. The percentage of workers of each job type with *non-participation* in 'active leisure' or 'total political activity' is displayed as the vertical axis of the same three-dimensional diagram used in Figures 1 and 2. Again, cell size is determined by cutting the job demand and job discretion indicators roughly at their third points. Inspecting Figure 3 we find clear evidence for 'carry over' or job socialization of active behaviour from work to leisure (Karasek, 1976, which is consistent with other findings of job socialization by Kohn and Schooler, 1973, 1978, and Mortimer and Lorence, 1979). The content of work experience has a significant association with rates of participation for socially active leisure activities. In general there is little evidence that deficiencies in the work environment are compensated for by choice of leisure activity when the relative participation rates are examined for workers with different job characteristics. Figure 3 shows that Variety in Leisure, Total Active Leisure, and Total Political Activity are clearly associated with higher skill discretion on the job and high levels of psychological job demands. It is noteworthy that psychologically demanding work is associated, as predicted, with *more active* leisure, rather than the less active leisure that might be expected. While only 9 per cent of workers with active jobs have low Variety in Leisure, 40 per cent with 'passive' jobs have such restricted leisure behaviour. The findings for the Total Political Activity measure confirm Adam Smith's dismal vision (1976, p. 304) of severely restricted political participation for workers whose jobs permit little exercise of judgement and no opportunity for challenge (Elden, 1977).

There are several important additions and exceptions to this basic picture of 'active jobs–active leisure'. Participation in adventure magazine reading and window shopping (Mass Cultural Leisure) is *lower* for workers with more active jobs in Figure 3; and, indeed, those activities do appear to reflect relatively little use of judgement by the participant. Another very important exception occurs in the case of Total Political Activity. This composite indicator actually masks two quite different, independent effects for Elite and Mass Political Participation. The strongest relationship between any of the activity indicators and our model occurs for Elite Political Activity (75 per cent nonparticipation for 'passive jobs' versus 23 per cent for 'active jobs'). For Mass Political Activity, however, the relationship is markedly different, if equally strong (using cross-sectional data). Workers with 'heavy' jobs (i.e. 'oppressed workers' with high demands and low decision latitude) are the active participation for Mass Political Activity. The mechanisms for coping with 'unresolved strain' seem more important than those relating to 'job socialization' in this case. This finding suggests that Mass Political Activity is, in every way, a protest reaction. Workers with the most demanding and restrictive jobs are most active in labour and political organizations, which in Sweden have a record of success in the improvement of working class conditions (Scase, 1972). We cannot say, therefore, that the 'socialization' process, which can account for the majority of our other activity patterns, applies universally.

It is possible that more 'global' measures of psychosocial job effects, such as 'job dissatisfaction', would show effects of both job strain and job socialization. In Figure 4 we return to the job dissatisfaction measures. We originally discarded them because they could mask overlapping or counteracting tendencies, which we claimed should be analysed by more focused investigations. Now we search for evidence of just such aggregated effects. It is evident from these diagrams that the overall relationships are quite complex and that the joint *interaction* of demands and decision latitude appears to determine job dissatisfaction. Clearly a model which considers only linear relationships of either demands or decision latitude alone could come up with unclear or contradictory findings, particularly if the studies are performed in small, specialized subpopulations (for a critique of such studies see Karasek, 1979). In spite of the complexity, the results are basically consistent with our joint job strain–job socialization model. The job dissatisfaction indicator displays a very strong increase (6:1 top virsus bottom decile) for workers with low discretion and high demands, in the same manner as the mental strain indicators of Figure 2 (also observable is a secondary upturn in dissatisfaction at very low strain, which we did not predict). The other obvious feature of the dissatisfaction distributions is the secondary peak for 'passive' jobs. This phenomenon is consistent with the second mechanism of the model (p. 78): activity-level change. Although the mental strain symptoms showed no marked relationship to 'passive' work, the full model proposed a separate mechanism to govern the development of active and passive behaviour patterns on the job.

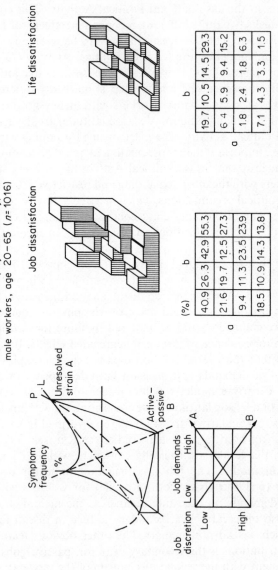

Figure 4 Test of the model with reports of job and life dissatisfaction. Numbers indicate symptom frequency

It is our contention that passive job content is also associated with job dissatisfaction. Very likely an 'active' job, which may lead to stimulating life outside the job and which is associated with only moderate levels of mental strain, represents the most 'satisfying' job situation.

The implication of both the mental strain findings and job socialization findings taken together is probably our most significant conclusion. It seems clear that there are multiple and distinct problems that can arise from poor job design: on the one hand mental strain and increased risk of physical illness (Karasek *et al.*, 1978), and on the other passivity in political participation and community-oriented leisure. Thus there would be a danger in focusing on only one outcome—for example, mental strain problems—and attempting to alleviate strain by restricting job demands. Job induced 'passivity' may be the result of low demands and low discretion. It must be noted, however, that although multiple problems are revealed, progress along one dimension of job content would alleviate the problems of both 'passivity' and 'strain': increased control by workers over skills and actions on the job. Changes in this single dimension of work experience might indeed allow a politically unified treatment of at least these two major social-psychological impacts of work.

ALTERNATIVE EXPLANATIONS

There is the strong likelihood that other factors such as personality and socioeconomic status also have significant effects on mental strain symptoms and leisure and political activity patterns. Any claim that the findings above represent the 'causal' effects of the job situations would have to be supported by a simultaneous analysis of the effects of these alternatives, a difficult task. While a full discussion of empirical tests for alternative explanations is beyond the scope of this article (see Kohn and Schooler, 1973; Karasek, 1976, 1978c, 1979), we can give a brief summary. Evidence from both cross-sectional and longitudinal studies shows that neither social status nor several important individual background characteristics (those who could effect job selection processes, the mechanism by which 'personality' could account for our findings) appear to account for the major portion of the associations displayed in Figures 2 and 3. This is especially true in the case of the mental strain symptoms. In the case of leisure and political activity, socio-economic status measures as well as job content can account for the findings in high status groups, but for less variance for the majority of the population. Of course, personality and socioeconomic status also make independent contributions to explanations of strain and activity patterns, but the fact that these major alternative hypotheses do not account for the bulk of the associations observed above makes the suggestive case for causal effects of job content stronger.

One example of the effects of secondary controls on our hypothesis may be seen when education is held constant (Karasek, 1976). We examine the relationship between job content and the leisure and mental strain variables for members of the Swedish male workforce with only the statutory minimum 7 years of education (about 50 per cent of the Swedish workforce in 1968). Although the associations are not quite as strong and regular as in the full population, the basic pattern remains for both leisure and mental strain. Mental strain symptoms are hardly affected at all by holding education constant. Examination of the leisure and political activity findings reveals, for example, that intellectual, cosmopolitan elite leisure, which is certainly related to social class, still varies dramatically by active–passive job content: there is still over double the non-participation for 'passive' as opposed to 'active' jobs for workers of the same educational backgrounds. At least for workers with little education in Sweden, it appears that the job is a primary classroom for transmitting patterns of leisure and political behaviour (Pateman, 1970).

More exacting tests of the job socialization hypotheses could be proposed. One is to ascertain whether the effects are cumulative with job experience, and another is to determine what effects can be observed in longitudinal studies where the effects of individual background can be held constant. If workers' behaviour patterns are 'carried over' continuously, then the strength of association between the job content and the leisure indicators should increase with increasing job experience in the cross-sectional population (making the assumption that job content has been constant (see Lipset, 1956) or, more correctly, that any changes which have taken place in the job type have no systematic effect on the work–leisure associations). Differences in participation by job content for workers with little job experience must indeed reflects the impact of childhood background or personality, but they are barely statistically significant (Karasek, 1976). However, workers with over 30 years of working experience show substantial differences in leisure participation: there is over double the frequency of non-participation for 'passive' as opposed to 'active' job holders—four times that in the least experienced cohort (Karasek, 1976). These cross-sectional findings are corroborated by longitudinal analyses using panels from 1968 and 1974. Swedish workers whose jobs had become more 'passive' during this period became more passive in their leisure and political participation, and workers with more 'active' jobs became more active (these findings were significant in eight out of nine subpopulations controlled for education and family background: Karasek, 1978a). These relationships are congruent with an explanation that children begin their lives with relatively equal tendencies toward: active and passive life-styles, are 'tracked' (Rosenbaum, 1976) into different life-style tracks during adolescence, and then are further 'socialized' as adults in the work environment—society's most heavily obligated sphere of life.

DISCUSSION

In general we find significant evidence for both the 'unresolved strain' and 'job socialization' components of our model. The evidence is based on nationally representative data from two industrialized countries and covers a wide range of mental strain symptoms and leisure and political participation measures. Some of the data reflect both expert evaluations and worker self-reports of job conditions. The longitudinal data available in Sweden also support the inferences drawn from the cross-sectional findings. Furthermore, the joint involvement of both mental strain and job socialization effects in the prediction of job satisfaction highlights the importance of considering these two mechanisms simultaneously.

While the consistency of these supportive findings is noteworthy, there are limitations to both the data and the simple format used for testing the hypothesis which suggest the need for further research. The undeniably important effects of social relations at the work group or organizational level should be studied. The data on psychological work-load demands should be related to more objective criteria than are available in the present data bases. More detailed investigations should be undertaken into the 'processes' of strain and learning, with data that can test for intermediate steps in the process over time. Furthermore, more comprehensive multivariate analysis with the leisure and political activity indicators is necessary to delimit the multicolinear effects of social status at high status levels and the mediating effects of strong kinship and family ties.

Given these limitations, what are the implications of our findings? The mental strain findings have an obvious implication: it may be possible to reduce the mental strain side effects of modern work organization by increasing decision latitude in the organization, particularly for low status workers. Since this effect may operate independently of work-load effects on mental strain, there is a significant possibility that beneficial changes may be accomplished without affecting organizational output (although further research would be necessary on the work-load/organizational output association). If these inferences are correct, they imply that alternative organizational structures with wider participation in decision-making would be optimal from the perspective of both the individual worker and the organization as a whole.

This implication is in direct contradiction to very early 'job design' strategies, such as those proposed by Frederick Taylor (1947). Thus it is not surprising that Taylor's strategies met with severe opposition from workers and have recently been regarded as a major source of feelings of job dissatisfaction and job 'meaninglessness'. Taylor advocated increasing output pressure on the worker while simultaneously drastically reducing his decision latitude. In the 'bargain' the worker was to get a higher wage, but the magnitude of the unanticipated negative consequences in terms of workers' mental strain and motivation were rarely discussed (or apparently even ascertained).

Most working individuals in advanced economies such as the United States and Sweden find that the 'requirement' of using intellectual skill on the job represents an opportunity to exercise judgement, which enhances the individual's feelings of efficacy and ability to cope with the environment. Figure 2 demonstrates that the opportunity for a worker to use his skills and to make decisions about his work activity is associated with reduced symptoms at every level of job demands in the US and Swedish data. We do not find, therefore, support for the belief that individuals 'overburdened' with decisions face the most strain (Janis and Mann, 1977) among the full distribution of jobs in an industrialized economy. Literature lamenting the stressful burden of executive decision-making misses the mark. It is the constraints on decision-making rather than decision-making itself which are the major problem; and this problem affects not only executives, but workers in low status jobs with little decision freedom. Indeed, if we search the US data for the most common occupation codes with high levels of job demands and lowest levels of job discretion, we find that they are assembly workers, garment stitchers, freight and material handlers, nurses' aides and orderlies, and telephone operators. It is the working individual with few opportunities to make job decisions in the face of output pressure who bears the job strain burden (Kerckhoff and Back 1968.

The implications of the 'job socialization' process are less immediately apparent, perhaps because even the possibility of job socialization is rarely discussed in social science research. Adult learning processes in general have received little attention, and most 'learning' of the broad behaviour patterns displayed in adult life is presumed to be imparted during childhood by family and educational institutions. The potential importance of a significant 'job socialization' effect, then, must be judged by the iconoclastic perspectives it provides about the functions performed by some major social institutions in Western societies.

A job socialization finding carries significant implications about the distribution of rewards from work activity. If work patterns 'carry over' into leisure, workers with low status and low paying jobs could be doubly miserable when these non-economic outcomes of work are also tabulated (a 'compensatory' leisure, by contrast, might eliminate the distributional inequalities of the economic reward structure). A more conventional economic implication relates to demoralization and low productivity on the job, which are of such great concern for management scientists and macroeconomists. Workers made 'passive' by restricted decision opportunities and lack of challenging work can hardly be expected to assume initiative and contribute creatively to the organization on the rare occasions when job restrictions are temporarily lifted. Furthermore, the economic equilibrium in Western societies is heavily dependent on 'consumer demand'. Our leisure activity indicators represent important areas of social consumption which are sources of demand for the society's labour force, both in direct service and in related leisure-good production. If people's desire to indulge in leisure services (and goods) is formed on the job, then the economic equilibrium of advanced 'service-oriented' societies might be substantially affected by unexplored consumer dynamics, which are dependent on the content, not the income, of the work experience. It may not be consistent with the employment constraints of advanced industrial societies to promote industrial policies which lead to 'passive' leisure and diminish the 'services' demanded of other potential workers.

More disturbing is the finding that political participation declines as jobs become 'passive'. Sweden and the US are both societies with increasingly centralized private industry, disappearing small business opportunities, and traditions of job design that emphasize 'work simplification' (now changing in Sweden). If these changes are accompanied by fewer jobs offering substantial decision latitude and challenge, then they could result in a gradual withdrawal from political participation by many and an increasingly dominant role in social decision-making by the few who retain 'active' work opportunities in their jobs. The political findings extend to the area of labour union activity as well. Of particular importance for organized labour is the possibility that trading decision-making authority over work processes for a bigger pay cheque (Aronowitz, 1973) may ultimately lead to a rank-and-file passivity that threatens the viability of the union as an independent political force. While further research would be necessary to determine what political affiliations were associated with 'passive' jobs, they may well be associated with labour union apathy and represent the conservative tendency to let the *status quo* remain and not 'rock the boat' (it should be recalled that active labour union participation was associated with the distinctly different, high strain jobs).

The institutional responsibility for social and political policy must be reformulated if substantial job socialization effects exist. Theories of political participation in democratic societies emphasize the need for educational institutions which instil democratic values and habits in adult life. Yet, if job socialization occurs, patterns of behaviour learned at work should certainly affect the patterns of political activity outside the job (a consequence that was forecast by no less an advocate of modern economic institutions than Adam Smith (1976, 304). This job-centred educational process may only be successful to the extent that the work environment de-emphasizes 'passive' work that is emotionally undemanding and intellectually restrictive and encourages 'active' tasks involving psychological challenge and use of judgemental capacity. Thus, the tests that are now posed for the educational system of modern democratic society should also be posed for its work environments: can they serve as the educational basis for meaningful participation in the social decision-making process, and can they serve as a training ground for self-growth and competence either on the job or outside? The alternative is that the job will continue to serve as the hidden socialization setting, contributing to an increasing number of 'unexplainable' outcomes from other social policies and increasing the disparity in non-economic rewards between those who control the production process and those who are controlled by it.

REFERENCES

Andrews, F. M., and Withey, S. B. (1976). *Social Indicators of Wellbeing: The Development and Measurement of Perceptual Indicators*, Plenum, New York.

Aronowitz, S. (1973). Trade unionism and workers' control, in Hunnius G., Garson, G., and Case, J. (eds), *Workers' Control, A Reader on Labor and Social Change*, Random House, New York.

Beehr, T. (1976). Perceived situational moderators of the relationship between subjective role ambiguity and role strain, *Journal of Applied Psychology*, **61** (1) (February), 35–40.

Berkowitz, B., and Green, R. (1965). Changes in intellect with age: V, Differential changes as functions of time interval and original score, *Journal of Genetic Psychology*, **107**, 179–192.

Björkman, T., and Lundqvist, K. (1978). Försämrade arbetsmiljöer eller ökad medvetenhet, en krtik av spegeltesen, Nordic Conference of Research on Working Life Conditions, Arresøhøj, Denmark, 18–23 June.

Caplan, R. D., Cobb, S., French, J. R. P., Van Harrison, R., and Pineau, S. R. Jr (1975). *Job Demands and Worker Health: Main Effects and Occupational Differences*, US Department of Health, Education and Welfare, Washington, DC (USGPO Stock No. 1733–00083).

Crozier, M. (1964). *The Bureaucratic Phenomenon*, Chicago University Press.

Csikszentmihalyi, M. (1975). *Beyond Boredom and Anxiety*, Jossey-Bass, San Francisco.

Drabek, T. E., and Hass, J. E. (1969). Laboratory simulation of organizational stress, *American Sociological Review*, **39**, 222–236.

Elden, M. (1977). Political efficacy at work: More autonomous forms of workplace organization link to a more participatory politics, Seminar on Social Change and Organizational Development, Interuniversity Center, Dubrovnik.

Frankenhaeuser, M., and Rissler, A. (1970). Effects of punishment on catecholamine release and efficiency of performance, *Psychopharmacologia*, **17**, 378–390.

Friedman, M., Rosenman, R. H., and Carroll, V. (1958). Changes in serum cholesterol and blood clotting time in men subjected to cyclic variation of occupational stress, *Circulation*, **17**, 852–861.

Gardell, B. (1971). *Produktionsteknik och arbetsglädje*, Personaladministrativa Rådet, Stockholm.

Gardell, B. (1976). Reactions at work and their influence on nonwork activities, *Human relations*, **29**, 885–904.

Gardell, B., Karasek, R., Rissler, A., and Lindell, J. (in preparation). *Control and Social Support in the Workplace; Its Psychosocial Effects; A report on Working Conditions, Wellbeing and Social Participation for the Swedish Confederation of Salaried Employees*, Stockholm University, Stockholm.

Glass, D., and Singer, J. (1972). *Urban Stress: Experiments on Noise and Social Stressors*, Academic Press, New York.

Gouldner, A. W. (1954). *Patterns of Industrial Bureaucracy*, Free Press, New York.

Green, R., and Berkowitz, B. (1964). Changes in intellect with age: II, Factoral analysis of Wechsler-Bellvue scores, *Journal of Genetic Psychology*, **104**, 3–18.

Hackman, J. R., and Lawler, E. (1971). Employee reactions to job characteristics, *Journal of Applied Psychology Monographs*, **55**, 259–286.

Harrison, R. Van (1978). Person–environment fit and job stress, in Cooper, C. L., and Payne, R. (eds), *Stress at Work*, Wiley, New York, 175–209.

Henry, J., and Cassel, J. (1969). Psychological factors in essential hypertension, recent epidemiological and animal experimental evidence, *American Journal of Epidemiology*, **90** (3), 171–200.

Herzberg, F., Mausner, B., and Snyderman, B. (1959). *The Motivation to Work*, Wiley, New York.

Hulin, C. L., and Blood, M. R. (1968). Job enlargement, individual differences, and worker responses, *Psychological Bulletin*, **69**, 41–55.

Janis, I., and Mann, L. (1977). *Decision Making: A Psychological Analysis of Conflict, Choice and Commitment*, Free Press, New York.

Johansson, S. (1971). *Om Levnadsnivåundersökningen*, Låginkomstutredningen, Allmänna Förlaget, Stockholm.

Kahn, R. (1981). Work and health. Some psycho-social effects of advanced technology, in this volume.

Karasek, R. (1976). The impact of the work environment on life outside the job, doctoral dissertation, MIT, distributed by Institute for Social Research, Stockholm University.

Karasek, R. (1978a). Job socialization, a longitudinal study of work, political and leisure activity in Sweden, paper presented at IX World Congress of Sociology (RC30), 15 August (working paper, Swedish Institute for Social Research, Stockholm University).

Karasek, R. (1978b). Managing job stress through redesign of work processes, paper prepared for American Public Health Association Meeting, Los Angeles.

Karasek, R. (1978c). A stress-management model of job-strain, working paper, Swedish Institute for Social Research, Stockholm University.

Karasek, R. (1979). Job demands, job decision latitude and mental strain, implications for job redesign, *Administrative Science Quarterly*, **24**, 285–308.

Karasek, R., Baker, D., Marxer, F., and Theorell, T. (1978). Job demands, job decision latitude, and coronary heart disease—a cross-sectional and prospective study of Swedish men, memeo, Department of Industrial Engineering and Operations Research, Columbia University.

Kerckhoff, A., and Back, K. (1968). *The June Bug*, Appleton-Century-Croft, New York.

Kohn, M., and Schooler, C. (1973). Occupational experience and psychological functioning, an assessment of reciprocal effects, *American Sociological Review*, **38**, (February), 97–118.

Kohn, M., and Schooler, C. (1978). The reciprocal effects of substantive complexity of work and intellectual flexibility: A longitudinal assessment, *American Journal of Sociology*, **84**, 24–52.

Kornhauser, A. (1965). *The Mental Health of the Industrial Worker*, Wiley, New York.

Langer, E., and Rodin, J. (1976). The effects of choice and enhanced personal responsibility for the aged: A field experiment in an institutional setting, *Journal of Personality and Social Psychology*, **34**, 2, 191–198.

Lazarus, R. (1966). *Psychological Stress and the Coping Press*, McGraw-Hill, New York.

Lipset, S., Trow, M., and Coleman, J. (1956). *Union Democracy: The Internal Politics of the International Typographic Union*, Free Press, New York.

McGrath, J. E. (1970). A conceptual formulation for research for stress, in McGrath, J. E. (ed.), *Social and Psychological Factors in Stress*, Holt, Rinehart, Winston, New York.

Maier, S., and Seligman, M. (1976). Learned helplessness—theory and evidence, *Journal of Experimental Psychology—General*, **105** (1) (March).

Mortimer, J., and Lorence, J. (1979). Work experience and occupational value socialization: A longitudinal study, *American Journal of Sociology*, **84**, 1361–1385.

Pateman, C. (1970). *Participation and Democratic Theory*, Harvard University Press, Cambridge, Mass.

Quinn, R. P., Seashore, S. E., Kahn, R., Magione, T., Campbell, D., Staines, G., and McCullough, M. (1971). *Survey of Working Conditions, Final Report on Univeriate and Bivariate Tables*, Washington, U.S. Department of Labor, Employment Standards Administration, Washington, DC, August.

Ritti, R. (1971). Job enrichment and skill utilization in engineering organizations, in Maher, J. (ed.), *New Perspective in Job Enrichment*, Van Nostrand, New York, 131–156.

Rosenbaum, J. (1976). *Making Inequality, The Hidden Curriculum of High School*, Wiley, New York.

Rotter, J. (1966). Generalized expectancies for internal vs. external control of reinforcement, *Psychological Monographs, General and Applied*, **80**, (1).

Scase, R. (1972). Industrial man, a reassessment with English and Swedish Data, *British Journal of Sociology*.

Smith, A. (1976). *The Wealth of Nations* (1776), University of Chicago Press.

Staines, G. (1977). Work and non-work: Part I—A review of the literature, in Quinn, R. (ed.), *Employee Responses to Work Environments*, Survey Research Center, University of Michigan, Ann Arbor.

Sundbom, L. (1971). *De förvärvsarbetandes arbetsplatsförhållanden*, Låginkomstutredningen, Allmänna Förlaget, Stockholm.

Suomi, S., and Harlow, H. (1972). Depressive behavior in young monkeys subjected to vertical chamber confinement, *Journal of Comparative and Physiological Psychology*, **80**, 11–18.

Taylor, F. (1947). *Scientific Management*, Harper Bros., New York.

Theorell, T. (1976). Selected illnesses and somatic factors in relation to two psychological stress indices: A prospective study on middle aged construction building workers, *Journal of Psychosomatic Research*, **20**, 7–20.

Turner, A., and Lawrence P. (1965). *Industrial Jobs and the Worker*, Harvard University Press, Boston, Mass.

Weiss, J. M. (1968). The effects of coping response on stress, *Journal of Comparative and Physiological Psychology*, **65**, 251–260.

Whyte, W. F. (1948). *Human Relations in the Restaurant Industry*, McGraw-Hill, New York.

Zeigarnik, B. (1927). Das Behalten erledigter Handlungen, *Psychologische Forschung*.

Working Life
Edited by B. Gardell and G. Johansson
© 1981 John Wiley & Sons Ltd

Time Aspects of Production and Reproduction

RITA LILJESTRÖM

INTRODUCTION

I intend here to explore time both as a qualitative social dimension and as a limited quantity at our disposal. In order to make my problem clear, indeed in order to grasp my questions firmly in the first place, I shall deal with contrast. For this purpose I shall emphasize that which separates social life and economy, as well as private life and paid work.

First of all I shall contrast what could be called archaic, feudal, or preindustrial societies with industrial capitalism. In the former the economy is integrated with the whole of social life; in our societies it is an institutional sphere set apart from the others.

How is the consciousness of men and women affected by structural differences in the factors determining technological production and factors in the private life sphere? The second section of this article seeks to cast light on that question. What is striking here is how the institutional features I contrast coincide with modal notions of female and male. The allocation of roles between the sexes has traditionally encompassed a division into two systems of time budgeting.

What is happening now that sex equality as an avowed goal of public policy is bringing women and men into a common time system? The concluding section discusses the findings of a study on families with children in which mothers have been helped to land 'male' industrial jobs. Both my empirical examples and my general discourse focus on factory workers, and so as to sharpen the definition of the problems even more I shall deal with that phase of the life cycle in which wage earners are also parents. However, I think the problems formulated here should also have a more general validity.

SYMBOLIC AND PRODUCTIVE INVESTMENTS IN TIME

Men and women still relate to time in rather different ways. This is traceable to various causes. One aspect may be seen in their different attitudes to sexuality. Let me begin with what a young man says in the course of an interview

95

on sexual matters. His remarks, stated rather frankly and off the cuff, may be paraphrased as follows:

> 'When I finally get her to agree to go to bed with me, I start to think only of my own gratification. Because up to that point everything has been about her. All our time together has orbited around her. I have courted her, tried to hit upon things that she likes, interested myself in what she thinks and does. I've sacrificed lots of time that I could have put to other uses in listening to her when she talks about herself. So when I've reached my goal, I feel that I now have the right to think of myself, that it is now my turn to get something in exchange.'

He had to postpone his own gratification, while his courting and showering her with attention gratified her. The example illustrates the distinction between instrumental and expressive orientation. But it tells us something more, too. It gives us an example of *symbolic investment meant to hide an asymmetry in the partners' interests*. Bourdieu (1977) distinguishes between symbolic and economic investments, between the good-faith economy and the crass self-interest economy. The archaic economy encompassed not only land, tools, and implements, but also kinsfolk and servants, networks of alliances, relationships to manage, a legacy of undertakings and debts of honour, a found of rights and obligations that had taken shape through the generations. Here was a socially safeguarded reserve that could be tapped as needed and mobilized whenever extraordinary circumstances arose. Economic interests were interwoven with friendship, family feeling, honour, and loyalties.

The strategy of accumulating a fund of honour and esteem also postulates the personal ability to recruit supporters/clients who will uphold the honour and the esteem to which one lays claim. It takes a great deal of work to acquire honour of the kind that runs up credit. To set up and maintain binding social relationships costs substantial material and symbolic investments: donations to ceremonies, alms to the poor, visible hospitality. The question is also one of *investing time*, because the value of symbolic work cannot be determined unless allowance is made for the time that has gone into it. To squander time upon others has been one of the most expensive gifts that any person can bestow. Besides, social relationships require constant unkeep, attention, and frequent confirmation.

From this it follows, Bourdieu argues, that symbolic capital can only be accumulated at the expense of economic capital. One converts material capital into symbolic capital and then back again into economic capital. The symbolic work creates a fiction alleging that economic relationships are really based on voluntary reciprocity. Its purpose is to give an appearance of altruism, to deny the existence of cost/benefit analysis. It conceals dominance and submission. Festivities, gifts, ceremonies, making visits, and paying personal attendance all enter into the work whose purport is to hide the function of the social exchange—which is no less vital to the existence of the group than the reproduction of the economic bases of its existence. The labour required to conceal the function of the exchange is as important an element as the labour needed to carry out the function.

The Kabyle peasants whom Bourdieu studied did not see their toils as 'labour', nor did they see nature as a source of raw materials. Because of their symbolic relationship with nature, work, and social relations, the peasants do not interpret the economy as such, i.e. as a system of interest calculations, competition, and exploitation. Any objective picture of the economic activities and true representations of production and exchange are socially suppressed.

With the advent of capitalism, things like friendship, family feeling, honour, and loyalty were kept apart from business dealings. Business is business. According to Bourdieu, when the economy openly avows self-interest, the result is to reveal those costs which the good-faith economy has had to bear for its refusal to calculate profitability. The monetary economy casts light on the institutional mechanisms of the archaic economies (exchange of gifts and incurring debt) whose purpose was to cover up and limit economic interests. Once the economy has been disengaged from the system of social obligations, all the time that used to be spent on strengthening relations and on concealing the interests behind them is liberated. The social reproduction of the existing order and the preservation of dominance of interest gradually pass over to objective institutions, such as a self-regulating market, an educational system which distributes competencies, and legally objective rights. They all function in a spirit of impersonal universalism.

If we return to the young man in the interview cited above, we can regard his courting of the girl as a symbolic investment, which is also intended to hide from both partners what he is after. As is well known, it is considered unseemly to start off a relationship by confessing openly to sexual motives. His courtship builds up a fiction of altruism and disinterestedness. But in his closing words he asserts the convertibility between his symbolic investment and his right to unilateral sexual gratification. If the young man wants to continue associating with the girl, he must be prepared to shower attention on her and to keep confirming the nature of their relationship.

So where does the point of the foregoing story lie? Bourdieu is well aware that his method of accounting for symbolic exchange imputes to the archaic societies a differentiated product taken from an alien ethos or mental model of the world. In his analysis he emphasizes how different types of societies reproduce relations of dominance from generation to generation. This gives his exposé of the preservation strategies a cynical tinge. The whole of social life becomes subordinated to the 'struggle for power over production'. Bourdieu obviously feels at home in a materialistic tradition which proceeds from production.

Table 1 Summary of difference between two worlds

	Institutional framework: symbolic interaction	Systems of purposive-rational (instrumental and strategic) action
Action-orienting Level of definition	Social norms Intersubjectively shared ordinary language	Technical rules Context-free language
Type of definition	Reciprocal expectations about behaviour	Conditional predictions; conditional imperatives
Mechanisms of acquisition	Role internalization	Learning of skills and qualifications
Function of action type	Maintenance of institutions (conformity to norms on the basis of reciprocal enforcement)	Problem-solving (goal attainment, defined in means–ends relations)
Sanctions against violation of rules	Punishment on the basis of conventional sanctions: failure against authority	Inefficacy: failure in reality
'Rationalization'	Emancipation, individuation; extention of communication free of domination	Growth of productive forces; extension of power of technical control

Source: Habermas (1970).

What interests me are *the different time dispositions* which prevail in societies that integrate symbolic and economic relations, as contrasted with societies that segregate the two yet still have some degree of overlapping and intermixing between them.

Habermas (1970, 1971) describes the advent of two cultures out of segregation between, on the one hand, life worlds which are maintained in social inter-action and, on the other hand, the world of work where rational conduct is controlled by technical rules based on empirical knowledge. The goal of work is to satisfy needs for 'utilities', i.e. for economic rewards. By contrast, interaction seeks to arrive at an understanding of the environment or to make oneself understood. Habermas summarizes the difference between the two worlds in outline form as shown in Table 1. The 'two cultures' characterize different subsystems in the society where either behavioural mode dominates. Family life and leisure harbour 'the subjective facts of social life', whereas production or working life is controlled by objective rationality in relation to established goals.

The archaic societies with their world pictures of myths, shared norms, and 'suppression' are pushed back by the diffusion of goal-oriented subsystems. Work pushes interaction aside. In a first phase a dualism arises between the two words, but Habermas warns that the spilling over and insti-tutionalizing of economic and techno-scientific rationality is already beginning to obscure the dualism between work and interaction in people's minds.

SOLD TIME

The segregation of work and the maintenance of symbolic interaction in different life spheres alter our whole conception of time. Berger (1977, p. 73) distinguishes different levels in a new time dependence which displaces the time perspective from the past and present into the future:

—the daily round is subjugated to the clock. Bodily rhythms are adapted to clock time;
—life is built up into a career, as a sequence of coveted steps in a plan for upward social mobility;
—at societal level planning increases, as well as five-year plans, seven-year plans, demand for forecasts, and scenarios of alternative futures.

Man seeks hegemony over time. With the aid of the clock and the calendar, time is to be mastered, booked in, and filled with foreseeable events. Time gains hegemony over man. Hours of work are fixed, and they exercise control over remaining time. In its turn the demand to have time yield a maximum pay-off impoverishes work.

Braverman (1974) analyses *work as sold time*. He observes that what the worker sells and the employer buys is *not an agreed-on quantity of work, but dominion over the work for a contracted period of time.* The employer, therefore, has every incentive to increase the pay-off from the working period or time on which agreement has been reached. Scientific management specifies methods to maximize the output per hour worked by cutting up production into small motion elements ('therbligs'), which are priced according to their degree of difficulty.

The labour force is segmented between those whose time is expensive and the rest whose time fetches a low price. Intellectual work is removed from the shop floor and centrally placed in a planning department. Time is meticulously checked down to the last second.

So the worker becomes a cog in a machine, as interchangeable and manipulable as the cogs he handles in a process where everything can be taken apart and put together again. Like the cog, he forms part of a sequence: call it 'step four', if you like, in a process consisting of twelve steps. Since means and ends are kept apart, it is not necessary for the worker to grasp how the components, he himself and the cog, form part of the final product. It will suffice to incorporate precise hand motions in a technical process at a high level of abstraction (Berger *et al.*, 1973).

Since the individual's knowledge of his work is at once specific and abstract, this knowledge ends up in a separate compartment of the conscious mind. Both the learning and the type of thinking which permeate work become divorced from other knowledge and types of thinking within other life areas. The all-important thing is to keep work and private life separate from each

other. Berger and his colleagues (1973) analyse this segregation at the consciousness level.

According to Berger, different action systems give rise to different fantasies.
A technological work process directs the individual to solve a certain kind of
problem: plod away at this, fix that, mend this. It shapes a type of attitude
which pushes aside other types of dispositions. Workmates appear at one
and the same time in their concrete individuality and as anonymous cogs in
abstract processes. In the same way a process of self-anonymity unfolds.
A person begins to regard himself in a partial and segmented way. The self
comes to consist of components.

> Put differently, the componentiality of the cognitive style pertaining to
> technological production extends to identity. Again, a specific kind of
> double consciousness develops. In this case the dichotomy is between
> concrete identity and anonymous identity. The individual now becomes
> capable of experiencing *himself* in a double way as a unique individual
> rich in concrete qualities *and* as an anonymous functionary. (Berger *et al.*,
> 1973, pp. 33–4)

The conditions of work also presuppose a special type of emotionality. Subtle-
ties of feeling are suppressed while a certain amount of joking is allowed,
as long as it stays within the bounds of the work ethic. As a result the individual
experiences a cleavage in his emotional budgeting, which compels him to learn
the art of emotional management.

Berger points to how technological production brings with it a quest to
maximize, to increase productivity. This idea of maximization, bigger and
better, more and more and cheaper, stronger and faster, rubs off on the worker's imagination and spreads along that route to other parts of his social
life.

Berger continues:

> One of the important characteristics of technological production is that
> from the point of view of the individual 'many things are going on at the
> same time'. This is true both of the production process itself and of the
> multifold social processes that are connected with it. We individual
> must keep in touch with all of these. His relations, both with material
> objects and other people become very complex. To keep up with this
> complexity necessitates a particular tension of consciousness characterized
> by a quick alertness to ever-changing constellations of phenomena. This
> feature...we would term multi-relationality. (1973, pp. 36–7)

Whereas man in archaic societies lived in a more uniform social world,
his twentieth-century descendant migrates between different subworlds such

as working life and private life. A number of scholars have called attention to the compensatory relationship between work and family/private life. According to Berger: 'This private world will provide him with an order of integrative and sustaining meaning. In other words, the individual attempts to construct and maintain a "home-world" which will serve as the meaningful center of his life in society.' (1973, p. 66) There can be no doubt that this 'solution' has worked for many people. But according to Berger it has a number of built-in weaknesses, all of them directly related to the location of the private sphere in society and to the structural characteristics that are the consequence of this location.

THE PRIVATE SPHERE

The private sphere has emerged as a residual, as something that got left over in the seam between the modern society's large institutions. As such it is 'under-institutionalized'. It forms a world of unparalleled individual liberty and vulnerability. That is because the basic task of institutions is to protect the individual from having to face too many choices by assigning him to tried and tested and ready-made roles, roles which set limits to freedom of action.

The private sphere's detachment from social interaction with the environment took place step by step: it went by way of the local community to the neighbourhood, and from there into the dwelling unit. Jobless persons gravitated towards factories. This drew them to urban settleinents, where they set up house in areas that were built up for a specialized function, that of shelter itself. The interpersonal relations that stil characterize neighbourhoods are restricted to the after-hours time segment or to non-members of the labour force, i.e. women and children.

The flats were small and primitively equipped. The residents used common wells, laundries, woodsheds, and privies. A courtyard became the domicile for everything for which there was no room in the flat but which belonged to the household. The shelter and leisure functions were integrated in the neighbourhood.

With the concentration of capitalistic enterprise, people continue to migrate and form even denser residential clusters. Cities grow to form metropolitan areas. Their central precincts are vacated to make room for government agencies and business offices. The residential areas are built instead on the outskirts of cities in so-called suburbs. The segregation of workers from their dwellings becomes even more pronounced than before. Separating distances now lengthen both in time and space. The technical standard of the flats has been raised. It is no longer necessary nowadays to have different kinds of dependence-inducing jobs in the neighbourhood. All that is needed is to be found inside the four walls of home.

A third phase could be observed during the 1970s: the road that led back to the individually owned garden patch, an emigration from estates of multi-family houses to single-family tracts. In these areas the family is protected from the surrounding world, released from dependence on it, and given access to a richer, closed-in environment. Recreational activities may be located in the dwelling (Fryklind and Johansson, 1978).

(But not quite: the monolithic design of the residential environment assumes the presence of supplementary milieus, not least to cater for leisure activities.)

Married women (and children) thereby lost their base in a multifunctional social world of adult cooperation, or rather cooperation across all ages, which itself integrated productive and symbolic functions. They are reduced to the special life world of the home habitat, where the most important duties they perform are symbolic services.

The women have to set up a countervailing force against the impoverished conditions in the world of work; they have be responsible for socialization, uphold the unity of the whole and the sense of purpose, answer for primary interaction which supports identities by developing sympathetic understanding, and give the individual an opportunity to make himself understood. That is to say, they have to cultivate qualities of the kind that are usually designated as the family's emotional function.

Their time is not controlled, since the work they do is unpaid. They are assumed to act disinterestedly and without selfish motives. In all this they are economically dependent on their husbands. But the basic asymmetry between the two life worlds reappears as asymmetry between the spouses; it has put the woman in a state of economic and social dependence on the man (Young and Willmott, 1973). The 'feudal' relation between the spouses in a rational tech-noeconomic society must be concealed by means of symbolic investments: rituals of courtship, romantic jargon, sex play of dissimulation, repeated affirmations that he loves her gifts and family ceremonies revolving around birthdays, a common leisure—all in order to maintain the good-faith household in a larger economy of self-interest.

At the same time efforts to integrate different subworlds pose never-ending difficulties, with the risk that different time dispositions and motivation systems will be mixed together.

The concomitant of a low degree of institutionalization, seclusion in the dwelling unit, attenuated social ties, and diffusion of 'self-interest' has been to create a fertile soil for egocentricity. No one can rely on anybody, no one dares to become dependent on some other person. The migration between subworlds imparts distance to each of them, makes for a sort of alienating perspective switch. Lasch describes this phenomenon in an article, 'The narcis-sist society' (1976). He argues that the people of our day and age are in the process of losing their sense of historical continuity, the feeling of being a link between the generations, of carrying traits of what used to be and traits

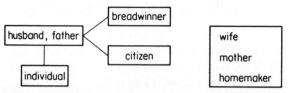

Figure 1 Family in which husband is job-holder and
wife is mother and homemaker
Source: Liljeström et al. (1978).

of what is going to come. In days gone by most people did not live with the thought that 'this is the only life I've got'. Today, 'self-realization' is the key word. Words like 'love' and 'meaning' no longer allude to a way of relating to others, but refer instead to satisfaction of the individual's own immediate needs.

These sombre strains contrast a diffuse wrenching-loose and absence of institutional programming in the private sphere with the goal-oriented organization of production.

To a very great extent the modern society's solution, which was to create a screened-off private sphere as a counterweight to production's rigorous dictates, meant that men and women each accounted for a subworld of their own.

The first modern human beings were men, modern in the sense that they had to segment themselves to meet the demands which segregated, specialized subworlds imposed on them. They had to learn how to keep apart the job-holder and the private person, the citizen and the individual. The functions of the married woman were still tied to the family. Her roles as wife, mother, and homemaker were interwoven. Symbolic functions and unpaid work were integrated with one another (see Figure 1). But the family with equal parents and two breadwinners, which is the model that public policy in Sweden is now striving to achieve, envisions that women and men shall partake of the same life areas. This represents a transition from specialized to shared roles, as shown by the normative model in Figure 2.

What is happening today, when the politically endorsed aspirations of equality are starting to bridge the gap between production and private life?

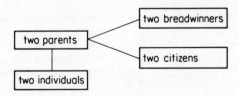

Figure 2 Family in which husband and wife
share roles
Source: Liljeström et al. (1978).

TWO SYSTEMS OF TIME BUDGETING

In societies with economic growth and expanding productive energies, the symbolic investments become subordinate to the economic investment. A policy that goes in for equality between the sexes points up tensions between different ways of orienting oneself to time. In Table 2 I compare two ideal typical ways of investing in time: the one is called 'good fatith' (unpaid work and symbolic acts), the other is called 'self-interest calculus' (paid work/ leisure).

Differences in interaction between women and men have been observed (Parsons and Bales, 1955) in terms of socio-emotional and instrumental leadership. Parsons has captured the distinction between two cultures in his pattern variables (1952). The distinction between instrumental and expressive orientation contrasts immediate satisfaction with postponed telic satisfaction. The latter has been portrayed as a higher stage, more difficult and more demanding of discipline. This bias has stirred up a vague revolt in me. As I see it, the time dimension between instrumental future action and expressive satisfaction in the present is unclear and misleading.

Would it not be truer to say that the distinction overlays an orientation towards *visible results*, which disregard the expressive actions' character of symbolic investments in secular norm-building, maintenance of motivation,

Table 2 Investment in time

Good faith	Self-interest calculus
1. Time that is spent on creating and upholding social relations, on safeguarding reserves for extra-ordinary needs	Time that is taken into use for objective economic interests, exchange relations with an admitted self-interest
2. Unpaid time, there are no quantitative yardsticks to measure the value of work and of symbolic social acts	Paid time, wages fix the value of the exchange
(According to Bourdieu, time must be spent on concealing existing asymmetry in value determination)	
3. Integrated time, time to switch between and keep together several parallel activities	Segregated time, uninterrupted time concentrated on a single task
4. Diffuse programming of time, unpaid work, symbolic interaction and relaxation as a continuous process	Strict programming of time, finished time units, clear-cut transitions between work and leisure
5. Less visible results. Welfare work, e.g. seeks to promote the personal growth and independence of others (Waerness, 1978). Rests on qualitative social norm-setting.	More visible results, quest for quantitative maximization
6. Expressive orientation towards satisfaction in the present	Instrumental orientation towards future goals

and social sanctions and attempt to integrate conflicting interests? In that sense the expressive action upholds long-term symbolic strategies (social reproduction).

Women's tasks have been to uphold social relations, to work for family cohesion, to socialize those who are growing up, to mobilize kinsfolk and friends on extraordinary occasions, and to care for the aged and sick. The material base for these activities rests on man's biological life cycle of long, helpless childhood, old age's diminishing energies, and risks of illness and injury. All this (biological reproduction) makes him socially dependent and necessitates symbolic acts for good social relations.

The social life's time budget cannot reasonably be reduced either to 'concealment of objective interests' or to 'immediate satisfaction'. The clock, the calendar, and the forecast restrict the 'new time conception' to a mechanical read-out function and lock the future in a strait-jacket. The question is whether the ingredients of the instrumental time perspective are not actually permissible self-interest, increased control, and simpler unidimensional calculuses. On the other hand, the socially and biologically reproductive orientation upholds open, long-term strategies of social reaffirmation and normative integration.

If we cast a last glance at the young couple in our introductory example: Is it so certain that the young man satisfied the girl's immediate needs with his courtship? Perhaps most of her satisfaction lay in a hope for a future marriage. . . .

The next section will ask questions about how spouses in families with children seek to synchronize their time.

THE FAMILY AND WORKING LIFE

The illustrations are taken from a study of working-class families which concerned a labour-market pilot scheme of experiments with women in 'male' industrial jobs (Liljeström et al.,—1978). Our research design was based on comparing the normative model for equality (see Figure 2, p. 103) with the real-life conditions of these families. The question of time kept cropping up in many guises.

(a) Synchronization during the 24-hour day

When both spouses go out to work they must be able to synchronize work and care of the children over the 24 hours of a single day. We made two striking observations. One is that many families have had time to try out a number of solutions during different phases of the family life cycle. This means that the wife alternates between home and gainful employment.

The other striking observation is the inventiveness and flexibility shown by the spouses when they set out to combine their respective working hours; either one spouse may take over at home when the other one goes to work, or the wife will arrange her working hours so as to fit in with her husband's. For one thing is perfectly clear: by far the most common practice is for the spouses to try to manage the day care of children by themselves. Which combinations are possible?

If the wife does cleaning work in the late evenings, night duty in a hospital, or delivers newspapers to homes in the early morning hours, her hours of work will not overlap those of her husband. Such an arrangement makes it easy for him to take over the home chores.

Another possibility is for the wife to take on a job that can be performed at home while she keeps an eye on the children, e.g. day care of other people's children, or making dresses at home under contract to an clothing manufacturer. The advantage of this solution is that it does not prevent the enjoyment of shared leisures and it exempts the men from taking over responsibilities for the children after the workday ends. Working at home provides financial rewards but less in the way of contacts and variety.

> 'It's better to work at the factory. As it was, I had more than enough cleaning up to do after littering up the house. Sometimes I missed having workmates. Things got pretty lonely. I felt as though I didn't have anybody.'

Some women look for breathing spaces or safety valves in odd jobs, seasonal work, or other temporary leaps into the labour market. An inevitable time limit is set on this sort of work from the outset. All solutions have a makeshift character. The father, a grandmother, a neighbour's wife, or a woman friend will have undertaken to look after the children on a provisional basis. One makes do for a while with arrangements that would not endure in the long run.

> 'Oh gosh, don't remind me of it. I'm awfully grateful for the extra work, otherwise I'd never have managed it. Not for the sake of the money for my own sake. I'm going to start working in August. I'll be glad to escape from the youngsters; I'm going to fob them off on my poor mother instead.'

The woman's employment outside the home becomes adapted to the man's in-plant (and sometimes out-of-plant) circumstances. Either that, or the family will accept some sort of makeshift arrangement for a while.

A more equitable distribution of the breadwinning and child-raising functions is enjoyed by those families where the parents work different shifts. A typical week for Isa and Lars is shown in Figure 3. When Lars comes home

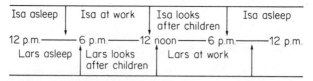

Figure 3 Typical week for couple working different shifts
Source: Liljeström et al. (1978).

from work, Isa and the children are asleep. He finds it hard to fall asleep immediately. It takes time to unwind after eight hours on an assembly line. The children wake Lars up in the morning. People on evening shift seldom get enough sleep. By the time he gets up, Isa has gone off to work. When Isa comes back, Lars has already left. Isa goes to bed before Lars comes home. This married couple see each other on Saturdays and Sundays.

In these families, each parent works an eight-hour factory shift and devotes an additional six to eight hours looking after children and doing the household chores. Saturdays are earmarked for laundry, the weekly clean-up, and shopping. Both the men and the women feel hard pressed by this rigidly scheduled existence. Even so, the arrangement confers substantial economic benefits. Both parents receive a shift work bonus and avoid having to pay for child supervision.

Present combinations of working hours among the spouses in families with children:

—split shift, spouses relieve one another;
—one on day-work—one on shift;
—same hours for both, shift or day-work;
—one on full-time—one on part-time (although part-time may entail regular working hours, it seems to relate just as often to evening cleaning work, early morning newspaper deliveries, and night duty in hospitals);
—housewife doing odd jobs or work in the home, e.g. day care of children, subcontracted sewing;
—'housewife'—or husband at home due to illness or unemployment;
—'solo parents' due to divorce or separation, or because husband's job ties him to another locality.

The working-hours combinations result in three basic solutions to the division of labour between the spouses:

Relief systems

We usually find the most equally responsible parents in families where the parents relieve one another.

Do-it-together systems

Full-time work done at the same times usually leads to shared parental responsibility, but as a rule the mother does the most.

Specialized systems

Here the woman provides most parental solicitude. This unilateral solution becomes most pronounced in 'solo parent' families.

Current trends in the Swedish labour market seem to be providing married couples with greater opportunities to synchronize their worktimes.

(b) Inconvenient working hours

In 1974–75 the Swedish Central Bureau of Statistics worked out the extent of inconvenient or 'unsocial' working hours. Society's 'normal rhythm' of motion and rest and nature's diurnal rhythm run side by side. Hours of work which do not fall within the span beginning with 7 a.m. and ending with 6 p.m. are considered unsocial. It turned out that 31 per cent of the wage earners put in inconvenient hours every workday and that up to 49 per cent have inconvenient working hours sometimes during the work week.

The scheduling of time entails a series of consequences for health, family life, and social life otherwise. As will have emerged from the foregoing account, many parents solve their childminding problems by relieving one another. Here the scheduling of worktimes around the clock increases the combination possibilities. However, the social consequences of inconvenient and irregular working hours are often dubious. One need only look at the hospitals, where the hours of work cannot possibly be contained inside some 'normal rhythm'. Solving Mårtensson (1977) has called attention to the efforts that parents' worktimes have on the life rhythms of children:

> Children of different ages to a varying extent need the security that a life governed by routines will provide. Routines in the large structure of daily experience probably provide the confidence to dare to try new and unknown things which alter the details of that structure. Repetition and predictability are probably also the basis for the child's development of a concept of time.
>
> To what an extent the preschool child has a long-term stable daily routine is primarily a matter of the parents' working hours. A distinction can be made between 'regular' and 'irregular' children. A 'regular' child arrives at the child-care at the same time every day, and thus he always enters at the same phase of the group's daily programme. He recognizes the events and is able to predict what will happen next. This should be important to a small child who cannot tell the time by the clock but who longs for

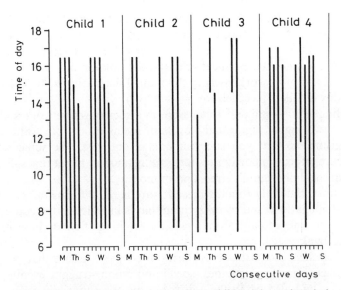

Figure 4 Attendance times for four children in a hospital nursery during a 14-day period. Child 1 may be called a regular full-timer (mother is student nurse), while child 2 is a regular part-timer (mother is student nurse working part-time). Child 3 is an irregular part-timer (mother is senior nurse working part-time) and child 4 is an irregular full-timer (mother is seniossenior nurse working full-time)

Source: Mårtensson (1977).

particular events at least as intensely as an adult. Thus the sequence of routines divides the day in the same way as the hours and minutes used by the adults.

An 'irregular' child does not get the same support from routines. Departure from home takes place at varying phases of the home routine. On different days he joins the child-care group at varying phases of its programme. It must be difficult for such a child to tell what will happen next, when his parents will return, and so on.

We do not know how common these situations are. Figure 4 shows two weeks of attendance for four children in a nursery open only to children whose parents work in the local hospital. It follows that the hours of stay reflect the hospital's work schedules.

(c) Block leisure and piece leisure

Another vital question for the future has to do with the shape that a possible cut in working hours might take. In 1972 an overwhelming majority or persons in a poll said they would prefer shorter worktime to take the form of a longer, unbroken block of time ('block leisure') around weekends or—alternatively— longer vacations, a lower retirement age, or sabbatical leave. Later investigations on a smaller scale indicate that public opinion has shifted somewhat in favour of a shorter workday (Fryklind and Johansson, 1978). The free time per workday is called 'piece leisure'.

According to Fryklind and Johansson, in a society where work and family/ leisure are two highly segregated worlds, it seems rational to want long, unbroken leisure 'so that you can really relax and rest, "be someone else"'. Block leisure affords opportunities for leading another life at times, for getting away from the daily round's stress and monotony.

By contrast, the daily round's piece leisure is tightly constrained by necessary social obligations and by everything that is included in the concept 'gross worktime' : journeys to and from work, the fetching of children, visits to post offices and banks, etc.

The researchers stress that it is during their piece leisure that people take part in society-changing activities, social and union struggle, evening studies, and the like, and also see to the redistribution of responsibilities for children and homemaking. It is the piece leisure that changes the daily round. Block leisure is by its nature a drawing-back, a way to disengage oneself from society, to devote oneself to private solutions.

A six-hour workday has been described in Sweden as a reform for women, while men strongly favour a four-day week. The whole issue has been shelved for the time being.

On the subject of worktime in our study, we asked the families: 'Which of the alternatives, a six-hour workday or a four-day week, would you prefer for yourself?' It turned out that the majority of women chose a six-hour workday. Time shortages are particularly hard on most of the mothers who work full-time. The majority of men favour a four-day week. They would like an unbroken stretch of free time to pursue their leisure interests.

'I probably want a four-day week. I don't know what I would do with two hours extra per day.'

Some men put a finer shade of meaning on their answers:

'A four-day week for me and a six-hour day for my wife.'

That the majority of women and the majority of men prefer different alternatives illustrates the traditionally dissimilar meanings that work and leisure have for women and men. Block time suits the person whose leisure activities are characterized by physically discrete locales, such as the garage, the garden, the housebuilding plot, the football field, an angling expedition, or a hike. Shortening the workday would make for too much disjoined activity.

(d) Part-time employment

At present a spontaneous adjustment is being made to the day's fixed number of hours, as well as to the conflict between responsibility for children and the demands of the job, in that more and more women are going in for part-time employment. Nine out of ten part-time workers are women (part-time = less than 35 hours a week). Whereas as recently as only a few years ago the majority of those who took part-time jobs were older women, it is the women between 25 and 34 years of age who now comprise a quarter of part-time employees. Among the men it is chiefly the very young and the older ones who work part-time (National Labour Market Board, 1978).

The rationale for part-time work stems from various factors, notably problems with child care, poor communications, and the greater availability of such employment. In our study of working-class families, the part-timer housewives assumed sole responsibility for all the household chores. Indeed, they sought part-time work precisely because they could not count on any help in the home. Whereas the men divide their time between paid work and leisure, their wives obtain less of each for themselves because their time budgets must also provide for unpaid work and symbolic work.

Our study tried to grasp the quality of interaction between fathers and children. Responsibility for children has to do on the one hand with practical care and on the other with emotions as a form of work. Children demand emotional presence. That sort of presence is mentally strenuous. It calls for concentration, attention, and empathy. Emotional work means being ready to offer comfort, to look, to admire and to deter, to guide and to divert. It means being ready to be aroused from deep sleep if the child is woken by a bad dream or has kicked its bed clothes off. It means being ready to answer questions while watching a television programme, to capture the gist of a message hurled through defiance and screams, and at the same time to prevent the child from disturbing other people, from causing damage or hurting itself.

Symbolic work with children takes time. Even the parent–child relationship requires constant upkeep, attention, and frequent affirmation.

In the investigated group of families, our conversations with the parents gave us the impression that about one-third of the fathers undertook intimate emotional work with their children. Here are some quotations from fathers who surrendered the emotional work to their wives:

'I don't wake up at night if one of the kids wakes. And if they ask questions while the TV's on, I just shout "Shut up!" Then the wife takes over.'

'Yes, she's probably shown more patience in explaining things that are obvious to anyone else. And mostly they manage themselves. They've got their pals.'

(e) Synchronization over different life areas and over life itself

In the foregoing I have given examples of how attempts by married couples to synchronize their worktimes and parental responsibilities impose restrictions on family life and the joint use of leisure. Although the increase in inconvenient working hours also enables the spouses to enlarge the combination possibilities, it does entail risks that more time programming for the children will be dictated by the irregular working hours of their parents.

Leisure habits and stated worktime preferences reflect the different systems of time budgeting practised by men and women, with presumably far-reaching consequences for participation in community life.

Spontaneous adaptation to part-time working on the part of women seems to take place at the expense of preserved sex roles. Any discussion of worktime is bound to involve questions of how *individuals coordinate their time resources in various respects:*

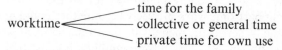

(a) Coordination of worktimes with other societal times for business hours: consulting hours for doctors, classroom hours in school, visiting hours, meeting and course times, etc.

(b) Coordination of times across different activity areas of the kind illustrated by the activity spectrum above.

(c) Coordination of time uses between different members of the household, usually married couples, who either relieve one another or would like to spend time together.

(d) Coordination of the burdens imposed on the family and at work during different phases of the life cycle, i.e. coordination of the family life cycle and the 'career cycle' for both spouses.

In all this, synchronization time is not only a limited quantity at our disposal but also a qualitative dimension in maintaining social and biological reproduction. Whereas the productive aspects of time are well institutionalized and conceptualized, reproductive time is both more loosely institutionalized and neglected in the formation of concepts around time use. Men's time consumption in terms of paid worktime and leisure does not do justice to the 'female time continuum' with its segments of paid work, unpaid work, and symbolic acts (e.g. emotional work with children). There is great risk today that a productive time conception will become more widely diffused at the expense of reproductive time. The examples given above show some of the social apprehensions bound up with synchronization of time.

To deal more appropriately with the period of time engineering which lies ahead, Berger (1977, p. 74) would like to have a critical analysis of where the boundary line should be drawn for the present-day time conception: 'The question is how and in what areas of social life it may be possible to do without clocks and calendars.... The political component of such a critique must, above all, deal with the human cost of every long-range project or plan that bases itself on an allegedly certain future.'

REFERENCES

Berger, P. L. (1977). *Facing up to Modernity*, Basic Books, New York.
Berger, P. L., Berger, B., and Kellner, H. (1973). *The Homeless Mind*, Random House, New York.
Bourdieu, P. (1977). *Outline of a Theory of Practice*, Cambridge Studies in Social Anthropology, London.
Braverman, H. (1974). *Labour and Monopoly Capital*, Monthly Review Press, New York.
Fryklind, P. U., and Johansson, S. O. (1978). Fritiden i framtiden (Leisure in the future), working paper, University of Karlstad, Sweden.
Habermas, J. (1970). *Toward a Rational Society*, Beacon Press, Boston.
Habermas, J. (1971) *Sturkturwandel der öffentlichkeit*, Luchterhand.
Lasch. C. (1976). The narcissist society, *New York Review*, 30 September.
Liljeström, R., Liljeström Svensson, G., and Fürst Mellström, G. (1978). *Roles in Transition*, Liber, Stockholm.
Mårtensson, S. (1977). Childhood interaction and temporal organization. Mimeo, Department of Geography, University of Lund, Sweden.
Parsons, T. (1952). *The Social System*, Tavistock, Routledge & Kegan Paul, London.
Parsons, T., and Bales, R. F. (1955). *Family, Socialization and Interaction Process*, Free Press, Glencoe, Ill.
Waerness, K. (1978). Omsorgsarbeid og ressursforvaltning, Mimeo, University of Bergen, Norway.
Young, M., and Willmott, P. (1973). The Symmetrical Family, Routledge & Kegan Paul, London.

Working Life
Edited by B. Gardell and G. Johansson
© 1981 John Wiley & Sons Ltd

The Work–Leisure Relationship under Changing Economic Conditions and Societal Values

STANLEY PARKER

INTRODUCTION

In this paper I propose to look at several aspects of the relationship between work and leisure, both in the lives of individuals and in the structure of the societies in which they live.

My paper is divided into three parts. In the first I examine the forms that work and leisure have taken in earlier and simpler societies, in order to place our contemporary experience of and attitudes towards the work–leisure relationship in cultural and historical perspective. In the second part I consider various group patterns of work and leisure, the debate between those who maintain that work and leisure are becoming more alike and those who maintain that the spheres are tending to polarize, the theoretical types of work–leisure relationship, and the mutual influence of the two spheres. In the final part of my paper I am concerned with the future of work and leisure, with the potentialities for human and social development which each sphere holds, with alternative social policies to deal with relevant problems, and with the possibility of moving from linear to more flexible life-styles.

Much of what I have to say in this paper is based upon findings and ideas which are dealt with more fully in my books (Parker, 1972, 1976, 1977). However, some of the material—particularly on flexible life-styles—is presented here for the first time.

WORK AND LEISURE IN SIMPLER SOCIETIES

Historical meanings of work

Work, wrote Marshall McLuhan (1964), does not exist in a non-literate world: it begins with the division of labour and the specialization of functions and tasks in sedentary, agricultural communities. Obviously this is a narrow view of work. A more defensible statement is that work (in its widest sense, including labour) is a basic condition of the existence and continuation of human life. This does not, of course, apply to all forms of work. Only some are necessary to the production and reproduction of the means of life, others may be required in the development and preservation of particular types of social institution, while yet others result in the production and distribution of relatively inessential goods and services. The development of civilization corresponds in one sense to the diversity of employments in which men engage and to the expansion of the area of goods and services which are regarded as necessities. At different stages of social development, societies have various ways of defining the scope of human work in terms of the goods or services required. But there is a deeper meaning of work as itself a value that is at least partly independent of its product.

It is only for the last few decades that we have any reasonably objective documentation of the meaning of work for the mass of people. We have little or no evidence of how 'the common man' conceived of work in earlier times. The clues that we have to the various historical meanings of work must be gained from philosophical and religious writers and refer to the ideal of work held by an elite. For the rest, the 'problem' of the meaning of work did not exist. For most of history men have *been* what they *did:* a man's work provided him with an identity that was recognized both by others and by himself.

To the ancient Greeks, in whose society mechanical labour was done by slaves, work was a curse and nothing else. Physical work of every sort was regarded as drudgery. Work was seen as brutalizing the mind, making man unfit for thinking of truth or practising virtue; it was a necessary material evil which the visionary elite should avoid.

Like the Greeks, the Hebrews thought of work as a painful necessity, but added the belief that it was a product of original sin. Primitive Christianity followed the Jewish tradition but added a positive function: work is necessary above all in order to share what is produced with one's needy brothers. But no intrinsic value was recognized in labour—it was still only a means to a worthy end. Early Catholicism did something to dignify labour, but mainly of the religious and intellectual kind.

Protestantism was the force that established work in the modern mind as 'the base and key of life' (Tilgher, 1931). In Luther's teachings work was still natural to fallen man, but all who could work should do so. With the idea that the best way to serve God was to do most perfectly the work of one's profession, Luther swept away the distinction between religious piety and worldly activity: profession became 'calling' and work was valued as a religious path to salvation.

Calvin developed these ideas further: all men, even the rich, must work because it is the will of God. But they must not lust after the fruits of their labour. From this paradox—the command to ceaseless effort, to ceaseless renunciation of the fruits of effort—the motive power and ideological justification of modern business derives. This is the foundation of the nineteenth-century cult of work for the sake of work, and the abhorrence of idleness and pleasure.

But there was a reaction to these ideas about the religious motivation of work. Since the Renaissance some men had held the view that creative work could be a joy in itself. The early Utopians looked forward to a society in which people would be joyful because each would have work suitable to his character and need do it for only a few hours a day. The nineteenth-century socialists held similar views. When production is carried on solely for use and not for profit, when men are no longer compelled to work at unpleasant or boring jobs to earn a living, they will have more zeal for work. It will be better organized and require less time for a greater output. Workers will have leisure time for a freer and more truly human life.

The foregoing is a brief historical sketch of some meanings attached to work. Many of our contemporary ideas are still influenced by these older conceptions.

Historical development of leisure

Thorstein Veblen (1925) went back to the barbarian stage of social development to find the origins of his 'theory of the leisure class': 'During the predatory culture labour comes to be associated in men's habits of thought with weakness and subjection to a master. It is therefore a mark of inferiority, and therefore comes to be accounted unworthy of man in his best estate. By virtue of this tradition labour is felt to be debasing, and this tradition has, never died out'. To gain esteem it is not sufficient merely to possess wealth or power—it must be put in evidence. This is partly achieved by conspicuous abstention from labour. The leisurely life of a ruling class is thus a means of their gaining the respect of others.

During most of the seven or eight millennia of civilization the majority of people have had to work so hard to sustain themselves and their families that their lives have been almost devoid of leisure and spontaneous activities. The life of the peasants is a continuous round of labour. In the countries affected by the Hebrew tradition there is the Sabbath, but that is not so much a day of leisure as a day of ceremonial inactivity, a day of restraint. It was only at the centres where wealth accumulated or where a strong element of nomadism remained that holy days lost their severity and became holidays.

In preindustrial societies the majority of people had leisure only in the sense of rest from oil and of participation in ceremonies. This was not conscious leisure, or the result of an exercise of choice, but part of the regular pattern of living. The same applies to many non-industrial societies today. In his study of the Equadorean Indians, Beate Salz (1955) notes that all their time is used, if not in work, then in other 'structured activities'. Such festive occasions as

weddings, christenings, birthdays, and fiestas are common, and seem to have
an obligatory character as well as serving as leisure activities.

Work and leisure in non-industrial societies

Under preliterate conditions the line between labour and leisure is not sharply
drawn. In so far as there is no separate 'leisured class', the separation of productive activities into work and labour is also less obvious than in more civilized
societies. Primitive people tend to approach a great many of their daily activities as if they were play. The orientation of life is towards long periods of work
interspersed with occasional periods of intense expenditure of energy. In these
societies there are no clearly defined periods of leisure as such, but economic
activities, like hunting or market-going, have their recreational aspects, as
do singing and telling stories at work. Though there are things done for enjoyment and recreation, the idea of time being set aside for this purpose is unfamiliar.

Work in cooperation is a frequent aspect of primitive economic life. The
stimulus given by work in company with others singing and telling jokes
lightens drudgery and gives it a flavour of recreation. H. Ashton (1967) describes the cooperative work-parties (*matsema*) among the agricultural Basuto:
'These are gay, sociable affairs comprising about 10–50 participants of both
sexes.... These matsema are useful though not very efficient. They assemble
in the morning about 9 o'clock and work, with frequent breaks for light re-
freshment, until about 3 or 4 o'clock in the afternoon, to the accompaniment
of ceaseless chatter and singing.' If labour is seen merely as a factor in production then this kind of behaviour is 'inefficient'. But the point is that it is
useful to the people involved and is a preferred pattern.

However, some preindustrial societies do make a distinction between work
and leisure, in a way that is quite close to the contemporary, although not to
the traditional, Western pattern. Thus the lives of the Baluchi of Western
Pakistan are divided into a sphere of duty or obligation necessary for life
in civil society and an area which they call the sphere of one's own will (Wax,
1958). They seem to regard the latter as being a sphere of freedom and dis-
traction from the workaday world. But whereas the Western tradition is to
see the workaday world as the foundation of existence, the Baluchi invert
the emphasis. For them—as indeed for growing numbers of people in Western
society today—the world of their own will is the cherished area, the one in
which they spend their energy, imagination, and ingenuity.

One of the biggest differences in the meaning of leisure is that between
urban and rural communities. Leisure in agricultural societies is structured
by the rhythm of necessary daily tasks and of the seasons, and is embedded
in life rather than a separate part of it. The point is illustrated by the reaction
of Texan homesteaders to the possibility of inheriting a large fortune. Some

thought they would take time off to go hunting and fishing but no one considered complete leisure a possible way of life (Vogt, 1955).

What are the general conclusions to be drawn from studies of work and leisure in types of society other than our own? First, work seems usually to have been identified with the constraint of labour, though the forms that this constraint has taken—as an obstacle to 'higher things', as a purgative, or as social duty—are today absent or muted themes when compared with the economic constraint to earn a living. Secondly, sandwiched between the earlier religious views of work and the nineteenth-century Protestant cult of work for the sake of work, there was the Renaissance view of work as creative, intrinsically satisfying activity. Thirdly, the absence of a sharp demarcation between work and leisure in most preliterate and rural societies has two aspects: the more leisurely character of work, and the greater importance of non-work obligations as compared with the more individual type of leisure experienced in modern industrial societies.

WORK AND LEISURE IN CONTEMPORARY SOCIETY

Group patterns

Data are available on the relation between work and leisure characteristic of a wide variety of occupational groups. To consider first the manual group: the decreased physical strain of work has brought about a change in the function of leisure for some. Thus it has been observed that the jobs of steel workers have now become relatively so lacking in strain that the worker leaves the plant with a good deal of energy left which carries him readily through his leisure hours. However, in occupations like mining and fishing leisure tends to have a more traditional role. Jeremy Tunstall's (1962) study of distant-water fishermen showed the leisure during the three months in the year they are ashore fulfils the functions of status seeking of explosive compensation for arduous working conditions.

Something of this violent reaction to work can be seen in the leisure activities of some non-manual workers. Georges Friedmann (1960) quotes a study of the leisure habits of employees at the Postal Cheque Centre in Paris, whose jobs are completely routine: on leaving the office, these clerks are either much more active or, in contrast, withdraws into themselves, in a sort of apathy. But a different pattern of work and leisure is shown by those non-manual employees whose work demands more involvement and responsibility. Among professional engineers studied by Joel Gerstl and S. Hutton (1966), 23 per cent said they had hobbies connected with the field of engineering, and as many as 73 per cent claimed work-connected reading as one of their hobby interests.

Heckscher and DeGrazia (1959) concluded from their survey that the way of life of American business executives permits no clear-cut distinction between work and leisure. To counteract the encroachment of work on leisure time, the executive's work is penetrated by qualities which we would ordinarily associate with leisure. On the other hand, David Riesman (1952) remarks that the professional or business person is apt to leave his work with a good many tensions created by his reactions to interpersonal situations, and so he may have to satisfy his leisure 'needs' before he can rise from the level of recreation to the level of creation. He may move from a job where he is constantly faced with others and their work expectations to leisure pursuits, again in the company of others, where workmanlike performance is also expected of him.

The penetration of the businessman's work into the rest of his life is a function of the demands of the work itself rather than of the culture. This is illustrated by the close similarity of the Japanese businessman's life to that of the American. Ezra Vogel (1963) reports that in Japan business is combined with community activities, recreation, and personal activities. It is difficult to distinguish working time from leisure time. Vogel also notes that, like successful businessmen, doctors rarely make a sharp separation between work and leisure, partly because to some extent working hours are determined by the arrival of patients. It is the salaried man who makes the sharpest distinction between working time and free time. In contrast to the businessman who mixes business and leisure, and to the doctor whose leisure is determined by the absence of patients, the salaried man generally has set hours so that he can plan certain hours of the day and certain days of the week for himself and his family.

The type of leisure activity chosen may reflect the type of work and work situation. Even differences in *style* of a given type of leisure activity may be related to work experience. Thus K. Etzkorn (1964) note that 'public campground' camping, which is routinzed, is practised more by individuals with routinized jobs, while 'wilderness' camping is preferred by individuals in more creative occupations. Fred Blum (1953) goes more deeply into the relation between work and leisure experienced by the typical packing-house worker. This type of worker has a tendency to carry work attitudes on into the weekend in spite of a strong psychological fatigue and desire to get away from work and everything it stands for. Since it is almost impossible to work eight hours intensively and switch over suddenly to a new, creative way of life, workers are pushed into some kind of activity which keeps them occupied without reminding them of their work. Fishing is one of the favourite pastimes of these workers. It has elements which are just the opposite of the work process— relaxation, being outdoors, 'getting away from it all'—yet it also has elements akin to the work process. While not requiring any initiative, it allows the psychological mechanisms of busy-ness to go on. It makes it possible to carry over work attitudes into leisure time without making leisure experience similar to work experience.

Fusion versus polarity

The type of relationship between work and leisure spheres is to be seen at both the societal and individual levels. There are arguments for and against the proposition that work and leisure are becoming similar to each other. At the societal level the evidence for both 'fusion' and 'polarity' consists of changes that have allegedly taken place in the content of work, the way it is organized and the setting in which it is done. At the individual level fusion is experienced as spillover of work into leisure and vice versa and polarity as opposition, or at least differentiation, of these spheres.

Harold Wilensky (1964) cites as evidence of work–leisure fusion the long coffee break among white-collar girls, the lunch 'hour' among top business and professional people, card games among night shift employees; and off work, the do-it-yourself movement, spare-time jobs, 'customers' golf' for sales executives, and commuter-train conferences for account executives. Also, many devices are being invented for creating spaces of free time within the working day and at intervals throughout the career. In America the subbatical year is no longer restricted to academic employees. One firm has for some time been granting twelve months' paid vacation after ten years of service, and other employees have the chance of a quarter sabbatical—three months off after five years' service. Another type of work–leisure fusion, the integration of sex into work, is noted by Herbert Marcuse (1964): 'Without ceasing to be an instrument of labor, the body is allowed to exhibit its sexual features in the everyday work world and in work relations.'

No doubt with evidence such as the above in mind, Gregory Stone (1958) has asserted that 'more and more we work at our play and play at our work... our play is disguised by work and vice versa. Consequently, we begin to evaluate our leisure time in terms of the potential it has for work—for us to "do it ourselves", and we evaluate our work in terms of the potential it has for play'.

There are other observers, however, who take a different view about what has been happening to work and leisure. Dismissing evidence of fusion such as that cited above as marginal to the main structure of modern industry, they seek to show that work has become more concentrated and demanding. It may be less arduous physically than it used to be, but its present standards of efficiency are said to require one to key oneself to a higher pitch of nervous and mental effort. The theme of alienation from work is relevant here, since it implies that work as a sphere of human experience is estranged from other spheres such as that of leisure. Under conditions of present society, it is said, the 'break in consciousness' between work and socialized play, begun during the Industrial Revolution, has been completed. Certainly it is arguable that the institution of employment has brought about a fairly sharp distinction between working life and private life, between sold time and unsold time. The 'evasion

of work', according to Daniel Bell (1954), is the characteristic fact about
work in the life of a contemporary American:

> Work is irksome, and if it cannot be evaded it can be reduced. In the old
> days the shadings between work and leisure were hard to distinguish. In
> modern life the ideal is to minimise the unpleasant aspects of work as
> much as possible by pleasant distractions (wall colours, music, rest
> periods) and to hasten away as quickly as possible, uncontaminated
> by work and unimpaired by its arduousness....

The ideal may be to split the unsatisfying life of work from the more rewarding
life of non-work, but we must reserve judgement on the extent to which the
ideal is actually being achieved.

We may conclude that the evidence for fusion or polarity of work and
leisure at the societal level is conflicting. Perhaps the whole argument has been
confused by the reference to different levels—that of society in general and that
of occupations and work situations in particular—each of which requires
its own methods of analysis and conclusions.

Types of work–leisure relationship

I dealt above with 'fusion' and 'polarity' of work and leisure in respect of social
developments in these two spheres. But what of work and leisure as parts of
our own lives? We may speak of fusion if we refuse to divide our lives in this
way, and of polarity if we insist on such a division. The corresponding functions
of leisure have been labelled by Harold Wilensky (1960) as 'spillover' and
'compensatory'. Work may be said to spill over into leisure to the extent that
leisure is the continuation of work experiences and attitudes; leisure is compensatory if it is intended to make up for dissatisfactions felt in work.

My own research has involved carrying the analysis of these two types of
relationship further, and led to the addition of a third. I distinguish extension,
opposition, and neutrality. With the *extension* pattern the similarity of at least
some work and leisure activities and the lack of demarcation between what is
seen as work and leisure are the key characteristics. This pattern is typically
shown by social workers, successful businessmen (perhaps they *are* successful
because they have little or no time for leisure), doctors, teachers, and similar
people. The key aspects of the *opposition* pattern are the international dissi-
milarity of work and leisure and the strong demarcation between the two.
People with tough physical jobs like miners and oil-rig workers may either
hate their work so much that any reminder of it in their off-duty time is unpleasant, or they may have a love–hate attitude to it. A third pattern of *neutrality* is only partly defined by a 'usually different' content of work and leisure
and an 'average' demarcation of spheres. It is *not* intermediate between the other

two patterns because it denotes detachment from work rather than either positive or negative attachment. It often goes along with jobs which Peter Berger (1964) has called 'gray'—neither fulfilling nor oppressive. People in such jobs tend to be as passive and uninvolved in their leisure as they are in their work.

My own and other research suggests that each of these three patterns of work–leisure relationship is associated with a number of other work and non-work variables. People with a high degree of autonomy in their work are likely to have the extension pattern, and those with low autonomy the neutrality pattern (the effect of autonomy on the opposition pattern is not clear). Extension is usually accompanied by a feeling of being 'stretched' by the work, neutrality by being 'bored' with it, and opposition by being 'damaged' by it. The likelihood of having some work colleagues among one's close friends seems to be high among those with the extension pattern and low among the neutrality group. Level of education usually goes from high to low among the groups with the extension, neutrality, and opposition patterns.

These and other conclusions about the three patterns are tentative and remain to be verified or modified by further research. As critics have pointed out, the three-fold typology leaves many questions open. People do not always find either the kind of work or leisure they want, so their needs and wishes cannot necessarily be assessed from their behaviour in a given situation. Also the existence of patterns between people's work and leisure is no guarantee that there is any causal relationship between experiences in the two areas of life.

Kenneth Roberts (1974) has suggested that it is important to distinguish ideas from behaviour, because relationships discovered between work and leisure on the ideational plane will not necessarily be reflected in behaviour. Leisure could be more potent than work in giving meaning to an individual's life, yet it could be his job that influenced his leisure behaviour more than vice versa. Roberts notes that the division between individual and societal levels of analysis cuts across the distinction between behavioural and ideational planes. Leisure has, he claims, advanced most in the individual-behavioural and ideational-societal spheres, reflecting respectively more time freed from work and the marketing of leisure values by the relevant industries. In the individual-ideational and behavioural-societal spheres, however, work values and socially structured behaviour still indicate a rhythm of life dictated by the demands of work.

Two fairly recent theoretical articles have aimed at clarifying and simplifying the various concepts and theories which have grown up. Kando and Summers (1971) draw attention to the need to integrate the study of *forms* of work and leisure and their underlying significance or *meaning*. Similar forms of work or non-work may have different meanings for various individuals participating in them, and different forms may have similar underlying meanings. The authors' model attempts to conceive the complex set of relationships within which work influences non-work. Two paths are suggested: (1) work leads to the development of certain psychological, social, and behavioural skills and life-styles which may spill over into leisure, and (2) work, when it leads to a certain subjective experience of deprivation, may result in efforts to compensate for this in non-work activity.

John Kelly (1972) is also concerned with the problem of meaning, but he thinks that asking why participants engage in an activity is a dubious procedure, since all of us 'construct' reasons to fit situational expectations and self-images. He prefers reports by self and others of behaviour and activity. He believes that work–leisure relation and discretion are the two most important dimensions. Leisure may be either independent of work or dependent on the meaning given it by work. It may also be either freely chosen or determined by work constraints or the pervasive norms of the society. This analysis gives four cells: (1) chosen and independent: 'pure' leisure, as in the Greek ideal; (2) chosen but related to work: 'spillover' leisure; (3) determined by the structural or social factors of work but independent of the work relation: 'complementary' leisure; and (4) determined by and related to work: 'preparation' or 'recuperation' leisure.

The above sketches are intended to give an idea of the range of theories which have been put forward in recent years to explain the relationship between work and leisure. Most researchers agree that there is a long way to go, both in terms of empirical inquiry and of theory construction, before we can feel confident that we understand this complex process. The subject is of wide interest and concerns not only the way we attempt to influence and control social behaviour and institutions but also the way in which we handle work and leisure problems and make choices in our own lives.

The influence of work on leisure

Experience in, and attitudes to, work influence leisure in a number of ways. The scheduling of the work will determine how much and when time is available for leisure, and the content of the work may affect the amount and type of energies left over for leisure. Some jobs will permit 'leisure at work' more than others, and some occupations are more frequently associated with certain kinds of leisure activities than others. Cultural differences enable the same kind of work to affect leisure variously from country to country.

Child and Macmillan (1973) have taken a comparative look at the leisure lives of managers in Britain, the United States, and other countries. Results from several surveys suggest that many American managers are completely job-oriented, intellectually narrow, and uninterested in the humanities or liberal arts. The typical American executive enjoys his work and his way of life permits no clear-cut distinction between work and leisure. The picture emerging from surveys of British managers, however, is quite different. Work-related activities do not take up a major part of their leisure time. They generally spend most of their leisure time at home, and few devote any appreciable part of it to activities that in any way directly further their work and career.

Several studies throw light on aspects of the work and leisure lives of manual workers. Richard Brown and his colleagues (1973) show that, while home-based and family-based activities predominate in the leisure of shipbuilding workers, some of their leisure activities take place in work time. Very often the social meeting places at work are more fixed and permanent than the places in the yard where the work is actually done, and shipyard workers talk about their 'leisure-at-work'. James Mott (1973) traces the historical association between miners and weavers and pigeon racing and breeding. Drawing on research carried out by French sociologists in a mining area, he suggests that the complex business of pigeon racing provides individual and social compensations, and the opportunity to exercise many kinds of skill lacking in mine work.

Several American studies have sought to establish a relationship between type of occupation and choice of leisure activity. Leonard Reissman (1954) found that people in higher class positions were more active and diverse in their social and leisure participation than those in lower classes. Saxon Graham (1959) concluded that the proportion of professional workers participating in strenuous exercise was nearly twice that of unskilled workers. The general conclusion of studies by Alfred Clarke (1956) and Rabel Burdge (1969) is that people in higher 'prestige' classes participate in a greater variety of leisure activities than do people in lower classes, although a few pursuits such as bowling and gardening are more favoured by the lower classes. But one wonders whether the faily gross categories of 'prestige level 1', etc., conceal more specific differences between occupations which may be linked with characteristic forms of leisure behaviour.

In an article entitled 'The long arm of the job', Martin Meissner (1971) poses the question: does work affect leisure? He is particularly interested in three dimensions of both work and leisure: the amount of choice or discretion that is possible or demanded, the extent to which the activity is purpose-directed or carried out for its own sake (instrumental or expressive), and the amount of social interaction involved. He concludes that when choice of action is suppressed by the constraints of the work process, the worker's capacity for meeting the demands of spare-time activities which require discretion is reduced: he engages less in those activities which necessitate planning, coordination, and purposeful action, but more in sociable and expressive activities. Lack of opportunity to talk on the job is associated with much reduced rates of participation in associations, that is, in activity commonly believed to help integrate individuals into the community.

Apart from specific research findings, general observation leads us to the conclusion that people often use leisure for work purposes, like the American managers quoted above. The popular game of bingo shows another facet of the influence of work on leisure. It has several features which are similar to the work experience of many of those who take part in it: it involves concentration and regulated patterns of physical movement, it is supervised by someone else, and it allows breaks for refreshments. Indeed, many sporting and artistic activities have more in common with physically and mentally demanding work than with the idle and carefree attitude that is often thought to be the essence of leisure.

The influence of leisure on work

Joffre Dumazedier (1967) has assembled a number of findings from his studies in France to support his contention that the effects of leisure on work are now more marked than vice versa. Many young people are looking for the leisure possibilities in any job that is available to them. Executives and their wives are refusing to accept a job in a locality where the opportunities for after-work life are limited. Company organization itself is often based upon methods of emulation, cooperation, and competition borrowed from sports, and numerous methods of job improvement and training have been inspired by techniques well known to sports instructors. While Dumazedier appears to favour most of these developments, he also draws attention to the negative side of the picture: enjoyment of recreational activities often results in denial of any commitment to either company or union. It should also be noted that his general approach to work and leisure is based on an assessment of trends in France: the situation in other countries, with a different balance between industrial and agricultural activities, may lead to different conclusions.

The influence of leisure on work is also seen in the fact that a substantial and growing proportion of the population is employed in one or other of the leisure industries. These include industries providing entertainment, sports and gambling facilities, holiday amenities, materials for hobbies, a considerable part of transport, book production, the care of gardens and pets, and so on. Employees in these occupations often face the paradox that other people's leisure is their own work. Compared with most other occupations, people in the leisure industries tend to allow considerable scope for 'role style' or personalized performance; authority and sanctions when rules are broken are likely to be asserted only when the public are not present; and there are special strains and tensions resulting from playing a role—waitress or comedian, for example—which must closely match the expectations of the paying customers.

THE FUTURE OF WORK AND LEISURE

The potentialities of work and leisure

To adapt a marxist phrase, it scarcely seems an exaggeration to say that there are two classes in modern industrial society: the privileged with respect to a unified and fulfilling work–leisure life, and the underprivileged. As Henry Durant (1938) remarked, for some men and women the problem of leisure does not arise:

> They all obtain satisfaction from their work. All of them have some sphere of independent action, or they are presented with problems and difficulties with which they must grapple and solve; none of them are automata.... Because of this, and because, finding satisfaction in their work, they do not desire to flee from it as soon as the immediate job is completed, the impact of their profession or work is clearly discernible in all their activities. There is for them no sharp break. They read books which relevance to their job; similarly they attend lectures and follow courses of study; they move predominantly amongst people who have the same interests.... In short the method of earning their livelihood determines for them their mode of living. And it does this in such a way that they obtain satisfaction. Hence they need not search for compensations in other directions; they do not require soporifics from the world of amusement ... they will tend to bring to such aspects of their lives the same attitude and qualities of mind as are required and developed by their work.

My research confirms that there is a group of people who tend to have such a work–leisure pattern, and that there are two other groups who do not. I have labelled these three groups extension, opposition, and neutrality, although I hesitate to claim that the first is in every way preferable to the other two.

Some men in the past have led, and some today do lead, 'unitary lives in which the excellence obtainable during leisure characterizes the work in which they engage' (Weiss, 1960), while others—the underprivileged–have excellence in neither sphere. The question arises: to what extent is this distribution of excellence the inevitable product of personality differences rooted in human nature, or the potentially changeable product of a particular type of society which distributes the 'means to excellence' unevenly?

The quality of the work and leisure lives of the mass of people in any society becomes a problem when the confrontation of the two spheres reveals shortcomings in either or both, or when a minority appears to have achieved conditions and satisfactions which give the majority a sense of relative deprivation. The view that there are two kinds of person with respect to seeking fulfilment in either work or leisure makes the problem a narrow one: how to adjust kinds of person to kinds of potentially fulfilling situations within something like the present societal division of labour and leisure. But if we reject the view that there are two such kinds of person, the problem becomes much wider: what kind of social structure is necessary to give *all* people opportunities for fulfilment in work *and* leisure, and how can various individual needs be reconciled with the 'needs' of society itself? Such a new social structure would involve a radically new division and integration of work and leisure.

A large number of people today have work and leisure lives which are neither satisfying nor creative. What should be done? A number of detailed answers are possible, but they may be grouped into two broad types. The guiding principles of these answers are respectively *differentiation* and *integration*.

Those who advocate the differentiation of work and leisure as the answer to at least some of the problems in either sphere do so on the assumption, explicit or implicit, that the segmentation of spheres is a characteristic and desirable feature of modern industrial society. It is the task of society, the argument runs, not to impose a pattern of social relationships on the individual but to offer him a set of alternatives. A society in which failure to 'adjust' in one sphere means failure to 'adjust' in all spheres is said to be less desirable than a society in which failure is compartmented and therefore restricted.

Most people would agree that it is better to have a choice of opportunities to adjust and find fulfilment in different ways than to be compelled to adjust to the dictates of a totalitarian society. But we must beware of imagining that the lives of individuals and the institutions of modern democratic societies are more autonomous than they actually are. It may sound a superficially attractive solution to say, 'If our work doesn't offer us a chance to think and be creative we must compensate for this in leisure.' But there must be considerable doubt about the quality of 'success' obtainable in one isolated sphere.

Those who propose an integration of work and leisure disagree with the advocates of differentiation not only in their proposed solution to the problem but also in their perception of the present state of affairs. The first group see a *relationship* between present work and leisure, though not yet an organic one, whereas the second group see work and leisure as separate compartments of life and society.

The case in favour of an integration of work and leisure arises from a critique of what various forms of differentiation have failed to achieve. This is perhaps unavoidable at the present stage of social development. We have no set of social institutions and corresponding cultural patterns which represent an integration of work and leisure—we have, at most, the behaviour and attitudes of a comparatively few individuals sharing certain patterns of living which indicate what that integration could be. Even this kind of guide may be misleading, because change at the societal level is not, for example, a matter of seeking to extend the life patterns of social workers to embrace all kinds of workers.

The wider realization of human potentialities is clearly a long-term goal, although this does not mean that we cannot take short-term steps in that direction. To reconcile work with leisure, to show how the one can enhance the other, may take some time, because we have long thought of work as the opposite of leisure. Making efforts here and there to improve working conditions or to enhance the joys of leisure are valuable activities, but they may do no more than help us to hold our own against the sweeping tide of technological and bureaucratic society. A sociological imagination that reminds us of the real range of social behaviour is necessary so that we can collectively decide the range of work and leisure experiences which should be open to individual choice.

Alternative social policies

As a starting-point we may consider the three 'solutions to the problem of stultifying labour' outlined by Wilensky (1960):

(1) develop patterns of creative, challenging leisure to compensate for an inevitable spread in dehumanized labour; (2) offer vastly better compensation to those condemned to alienating work situations (the trade union solution of more money for less working-time...); (3) redesign the workplace and the technology to invest work with more meaning, and hence enhance the quality of leisure.

These three proposed solutions may be related respectively to the three patterns of work–leisure relationship: neutrality, opposition, and extension respectively. Although the first solution includes 'compensation' and so implies some kind of relationship between work and leisure, it suggests that 'dehumanized' labour can be tolerated if it is kept separate from a creative, challenging leisure. But there must be grave doubts about whether this kind of split life can be achieved.

The second solution is a more straightforward acceptance that leisure is the opposite of work. With the first solution the compensation offered is entirely in non-work terms: in turn for acceptance of 'dehumanized' labour, a more attractive leisure package is offered. In the second case the compensation is both within and outside the work sphere. The difference between the two solutions may be expressed as society making two compensatory propositions to those whose work it recognizes to be intrinsically unpleasant or unsatisfying: (1) 'We know it's boring, but put up with it and we shall make it up to you in leisure', or (2) 'We know it's damaging, but you need only do it for a short time and we shall pay you well for it.'

In contrast to the other two, the third of Wilensky's solutions is concerned with the patterning of society as a whole. Although it embodies specific proposals for dealing with work or leisure problems, it does so within a framework of thought that recognizes the interdependence of spheres. This type of policy may be called *holist*, to distinguish it from the *segmentalist* approach implicit in the other two solutions.

Most holist policies for dealing with work and leisure have a basis in work, although the relevant concepts apply both to work and leisure. One such concept is the 'productive orientation' put forward by Erich Fromm (1956).

This refers to the active and creative relatedness of man to his fellow man, to himself, and to nature, and is expressed in the realms of thought, feeling, and action. The productive orientation is set against both the exploitative and hoarding orientation (the exploitation of man by man and the pleasure in possession and property, dominant in the nineteenth century) and the receptive and marketing orientation (the passive 'drinking in' of commodities and the experience of oneself as a thing to be employed successfully on the market, dominant today). In contrast, the productive orientation sums up a situation in which people *participate* in what they do, whether it is called work or leisure.

It is possible to start from the angle of leisure as well as that of work. Instead of using concepts such as the 'productive orientation', which stem mainly from work, we can inquire what is the optimum role of leisure in life and society and then seek to integrate this with other spheres, notably work. Leisure as the opposite of work—that is, leisure as detachment, passivity, and general absence of effort—is not reconcilable with work; but leisure as interest, pleasurable activity, and a general sense of creative self-expression can be seen as continuous with aspects of work. Our aim can thus include the growth of leisure time in which to do the work we wish. Thus the integration of work and leisure means more than just introducing a few bits of leisure-like activity into certain parts of the working day or task—it means a whole new pattern of daily activities.

Flexible life-styles

Most of us have life-styles which are predictable and standardized, with fairly rigid periods of education, followed by full-time career work with limited leisure, followed at the end of life by a not always satisfying period of retirement. A different plan for the future has been put forward by Best and Stern (1977). The plan may be summed up as: substitute for the present linear progression of education, work, and leisure a cyclical pattern in which all three elements can alternate at various stages in the life cycle. The authors give figures showing that, during the twentieth century, work has become increasingly bunched into the middle period of the life cycle, while non-work time has increased substantially in the earlier and later years of life. Although the compression of work into the middle period of the life cycle is the culmination of a long historical trend which has had basically healthy features (for example, child labour laws and the possibility of retirement with a pension), there is evidence that the trend has now gone too far. The present situation is especially frustrating for youth and the elderly, who both want more work, independence, and responsibility. There is also evidence that a significantly large minority of prime-age workers want more leisure without having to sacrifice too much by way of economic security and job status to get it.

One possible answer to many present dissatisfactions would be to enable people to develop more cyclical life patterns and hence more flexible life-styles.

This new approach would enable and encourage mid-career people to leave their jobs temporarily and engage in leisure, education, or community service activities. If enough workers were to choose such an option, a labour shortage or job vacancy situation would be created which could be filled by unemployed or underemployed persons. In terms of leisure, more people would be able to do the active things they want to do before they become too old to enjoy them, and they could return to some suitable kind of useful occupation instead of vegetating in retirement.

The idea of cyclical life patterns and flexible life-styles is ambitious and far-reaching in its consequences for people and institutions. But, as Best and Stern point out, a unidimensions focus upon education, work, or leisure without careful integration with the other two is neither likely to engage public interest nor solve pressing social problems. The achievement of flexible life-styles could bring us a new kind of leisure and a new kind of work, and a range of activities that would partake of the nature of both work and leisure.

REFERENCES

Ashton, H. (1967). *The Basuto*, Oxford University Press, London, 131.

Bell, D. (1954). *Work and its Discontents*, Beacon Press, Boston.

Berger, P. (1964). *The Human Shape of Work*, Macmillan, New York.

Best, F., and Stern, B. (1977). Lifetime distribution of education, work and leisure, Washington (unpublished).

Blum, F. (1953). *Toward a Democratic Work Process*, Harper, New York, 109.

Brown, R., Grannen, P., Cousim, J. and Samphier, M. (1973). Leisure in work, in *Leisure and Society in Britain*, eds. M. Smith, S. Parker and C. Smith, Allen Lane, London.

Burdge, R. (1969). Levels of occupational prestige and leisure activity, *Journal of Leisure Research*, Summer.

Child, J., and Macmillan, B. (1973). Managers and their leisure, in *Leisure and Society in Britain*, eds. M. Smith, S. Parker and C. Smith, Allen Lane, London.

Clarke, A. C. (1956). The use of leisure and its relation to levels of occupational prestige, *American Sociological Review*, **21**, 301–307.

DeGrazia, S. (1962). *Of Time, Work and Leisure*, Twentieth Century Fund, New York.

Dumazedier, J. (1960). Current problems of the sociology of leisure, *International Social Science Journal*, **12**, 522–531.

Dumazedier, J. (1967). *Journal of Society of Leisure*, Collier—Macmillan, London.

Etzkorn, K. (1964). Leisure and camping, *Sociology and Social Research*, October.

Friedmann, G. (1960). Leisure and technological civilization, *International Social Science Journal*, **12**, 509–521.

Fromm, E. (1956). *The Sane Society*, Routledge, London, 32, 361.

Gerstl, J., and Hutton, S. (1966). *Engineers*, Tavistock, London, 138–139.

Durant, H. (1938). *The Problem of Leisure*, Routledge, London.

Graham, S. (1959). Social correlates of adult leisure-time behaviour, in *Community Structure and Analysis*, ed. M.B. Sussman, Crowell, New York, 347.

Heckscher, A. (1963). *The Public Happiness*, Hutchinson, London, 161.

Heckscher, A. and DeGrazia, S. (1959). Executive leisure, *Harvard Business Review*, July.

Kando, T., and Summers, W. (1971). The impact of work on leisure, *Pacific Sociological Review*, July.

Kelly, J. (1972). Work and leisure: A simplified paradigm, *Journal of Leisure Research*, **4**, 50–62.

McLuhan, M. (1964). *Understanding Media*, Routledge, London, 149.

Marcuse, H. (1964). *One-Dimensional Man*, Routledge, London, 74.

Meissner, M. (1971). The long arm of the job, *Industrial Relations*, **10**, 239–260.

Mott, J. (1973). Miners, weavers and pigeon racing, in *Leisure and Society in Britain*, ed. M. Smith, S. Parker and C. Smith Allen Lane, London.

Parker, S. (1972). *The Future of Work and Leisure*, Paladin, London.

Parker, S. (1976). *The Sociology of Leisure*, Allen Unwin, London.

Parker, S. (1977). Work involvement and its alternatives, in *The Sociology of Industry*, 3rd edn, Allen Unwin, London.

Riesman, D. (1952). Some observations on changes in leisure attitudes, *Antioch Review*, December.

Reissman, L. (1954). 'Class, leisure and social participation', *American Sociological Review*, February.

Roberts, K. (1974). The influence of leisure upon work, in *Concepts of leisure* (ed. J. F. Murphy), Prentice-Hall, New Jersey.

Salz, B. (1955). The human element in industrialization, *Economic Development and Cultural Change*, October.

Stone, G. (1958). American sports: Play and dis-play, in *Mass Leisure*, eds. E. Larrabee and R. Meyersohn, Free Press, Glencoe, 285.

Tilgher, A. (1931). *Work: What it has Meant to Man through the Ages*, Harrap, London.

Tunstall, J. (1952). *The Fishermen*, MacGibbon & Kee, London, 137.

Veblen, T. (1925). *The Theory of the Leisure Class*, Allen & Unwin, London, 36.

Vogel, E. (1963). *Japan's New Middle Class*, University of California Press, Berkeley, 21.

Vogt, E. (1955). *Modern Homesteaders*, Harvard University Press, Cambridge, Mass., 114.

Wax, R. (1958). Free time in other cultures, in *Free Time: Challenge to Later Maturity*, ed. W. Donahue, W. Hunter, D. Coons and H. Maurice, University of Michigan Press, Ann Arbor.

Weiss, R. (1960). A philosophical definition of leisure, in *Leisure in America: Blessing or Curse?* American Academy of Political and Social Science Monograph, No. 4, 29.

Wilensky, H. (1960). Work, careers, and social integration, *International Social Science Journal*, **12**, 543–560.

Wilensky, H. (1964). Mass society and mass culture: Interdependence or independence?, *American Sociological Review*, **29**, 173–197.

Working Life
Edited by B. Gardell and G. Johansson
© 1981 John Wiley & Sons Ltd

Discussant's Comments

CARL THAM

The three introductory talks illuminated in a very stimulating way the complex and partly contradictory attitudes to work and leisure that coexist in our culture.

One characteristic feature in society is the very strong emphasis on the importance of work for the whole life of the individual. That evaluation is supported by a very long moral tradition and its impact is obviously confirmed by a great deal of empirical research. Dr Karasek concluded that we in general find 'clear evidence for "carry over" or job socialization of active behaviour from work to leisure'. This insight is now comparatively well established in our view of working life. Dr Parker talked about a holistic perspective: we dream about working life without sharp demarcation lines between work and leisure, work as a cultural act and leisure as personality-molding work.

An important reflection of this evaluation is the view that the individual is entitled to work; this formula has replaced the old formula of 'full employment'. This is not merely a change of words; it also reflects a change of policy. Labour market policy nowadays is far more ambitious than it used to be when it comes to dealing with various obstacles to labour market participation and to the adaptation of working conditions to the capabilities and requirements of the individual.

The massive entry of women into the Swedish labour market can also be seen as a reflex of the strong emphasis on work values. The fundamental presumption here is that equality between men and women can be attained if both sexes can undertake productive work on an equal footing.

This high value placed on work generates strong demands for a transformation of working life, a change in production patterns that can give the individual a greater share of responsibility, satisfaction, and a sense of sharing. But changing the conditions of work is a cumbersome process and it will take time.

In this context I should like to emphasize the significance of a flexible and preferably expansive labour market that gives the individual good opportunities to change jobs: voluntary mobility can be a very efficient way of attaining a greater measure of satisfaction in working life. Alfred Hirschmann (1970), in a book that has now become a minor classic, talks about 'voice' and 'exit' as two options of individual protest. In working life, both options should be available.

It need hardly be added that we are very far from the ambitious goals of the transformation of working life and the satisfaction of the individual—and hence also from the balanced relationship between leisure and work that both Karasek and Parker discuss. It might even be true that the significant gap between the officially stated and ceaselessly repeated political ambitions in this field and the everyday experience of most people have given birth to frustration and to a certain disenchantment instead of a sense of evolving emancipation.

The present situation is full of contradictions. We have more people than ever before in the labour force in spite of the present recession. Yet at the same time both opinion polls and actual social behaviour, as reflected in statistics and empirical studies, seem to confirm that people are increasingly oriented towards life-styles and activities outside the sphere of work. Expressions of this are the demands for shorter hours, and longer holidays, and the sharp increase in part-time work.

But maybe this is just an apparent contradiction. Higher employment gives households more economic resources and hence a better chance to succumb to the temptations of leisure. Expensive life-styles are established in youth. At the same time our productive and social life are badly adapted to the new situation in which an average family works a total of 70 hours outside the home instead of the 48 hours of some twenty years ago. As Rita Liljeström said, the demands of productive life tend to infringe upon those of reproductive life: the need for practical care and emotional presence in the family. Hence, there are mounting claims for more leisure time, flexible hours, and more part-time work. In fact, it is mainly the women who make such claims because our dominant social patterns still give them a particular responsibility for the home—the condition that Rita Liljeström characterized as a combination of paid work, unpaid work, and symbolic acts, e.g. emotional work with children. That is how far we have got—and it is obviously not very far.

Paradoxically enough, then, we can note that when the right to work is beginning to pass from promise to reality, there is a simultaneous drive away from work. And it is not only a yearning for more family life. There are other claims as well. In our hyper-organized society, with great democratic ambitions, the individual is perpetually bombarded with demands for participation in community life. Everybody should attend the trade union meeting, the parent–teacher meeting, the political party meeting, join various community action groups, etc. The reaction against a society in which all collective needs are handed over to professional functionnaires has led to new demands for participation requiring a great deal of time. And this is also visible in the sphere of production where straightforward productive activities are pushed back a little in favour of consultations and other community-oriented activities.

This also leads to a change in values. It is no longer always commendatory to say of a person that he lives for his work. Even if work is seen as a route to self-realization, it must not infringe upon other sides of the personality, or the individual's tasks as a good and active citizen.

It can hardly be avoided that these new claims collide with the claims of productive life, and even if we may find a suitable balance, the economic consequences will have to be reckoned with. In this brilliant study of the social limits to growth, Fred Hirsch (1976) argues that the patent efficacy of the capitalist mode of production supplies the material basis for a more individualistic life-style which, in turn, restricts the opportunities for future growth. The temptations of leisure culture, in combination with stronger social demands on our working life, will tend to threaten the moral preconditions on which the system is built: such values as restraint, acceptance, and obligation. So far as this is true, we can expect a further limitation of expansion in future. Many people believe that this is a good and sound development—that zero-growth is a desirable condition. But the problem—at least in an era of transition from growth to zero-growth—is that the new claims are not always accompanied by a proper insight into the linkage between benefits and costs. More leisure will have some unavoidable consequences for our private and over public powers of consumption.

In a society with a large and expanding service sector, there is also a conflict between, on one hand, the new demands for a more flexible working life and more part-time employment and, on the other, the welfare of the consumer or clients.

Let me give you one practical example of this conflict. In 1977, about 50 per cent of all employees in the Swedish health sector worked part-time. Not only does this create considerable administrative problems, it also has a direct impact on the quality of medical care. With this amount of fluidity, it becomes very difficult to ensure continuity in the interaction between the patients and the medical personnel which is highly desirable from a medical and a social point of view. These problems may to some extent be specific for the health sector, but there are related difficulties in other parts of the labour market. Wherever the employees demand more flexible hours and more part-time work, there is bound to be some loss of convenience for clients, customers, and others. This is particularly true of a society where the real growth centre is the service sector.

There are also some consequences to consider in a discussion about working life. Modern society is strongly dependent on the contributions of those who are prepared to work awkward hours and odd days. This is particularly true in the expanding sector of public care; if everyone insisted on short and regular hours, the weak and the sickly would be the first to suffer. Dr Parker concluded his paper with a very attractive vision of 'flexible life styles', a cyclical pattern in which the individual can alternate between education, work, and leisure more independently than now. I am all for that. But it seems equally important to create a culture in which people develop a strong responsibility for their work and the people who depend upon them.

Economic stimuli are important, of course, but in a society with high taxes and relatively egalitarian income conditions such stimuli can never replace the necessary moral cohesion. And that brings us back to the point of departure: to create such productive conditions that work becomes meaningful and important to the individual.

I would like to conclude these reflections on a point that none of our three contributors dealt with at length: the situation of the elderly in working life. Here, again, we find a great deal of ambivalence in the established pattern. Up to about 65 years of age work is considered to be a right or even perhaps an obligation. Yet when this magical line is attained you are expected to withdraw from productive life and you are condemned to eternal leisure: the companionship of work is at best replaced with some therapy offered by well-meaning authorities.

Retirement, it turns out, is not only a right but also an obligation: a good citizen is expected to withdraw and has no longer a right to work, however fit he may be. This is plainly absurd, from a medical and a social point of view, and I understand that there is complete agreement among gerontologists and other medical disciplines that too little activity is just as pernicious and unhealthy as too much activity. Leisure without work becomes no leisure at all; for many people it becomes nothing but loneliness and boredom. It is high time that we begin to draw practical conclusions from this insight.

REFERENCES

Hirsch, F. (1976). *Social Limits to Growth*, Harvard University Press, Cambridge, Mass.
Hirschmann, A. (1970). *Voice, Exit, and Loyalty*, Harvard University Press, Cambridge, Mass.

Working Life
Edited by B. Gardell and G. Johansson
© 1981 John Wiley & Sons Ltd

Discussant's Comments

GÖSTA REHN

Let me improvise a few variations on themes which have already been discussed by those who have spoken before me.

There is one aspect of the relation between work and leisure, in connection with consumption and life patterns, that we should always keep in mind, because it has a strong influence on the ways in which people choose between work and leisure, and that is the rat-race mechanism, the old story of 'keeping up with the Joneses'. When the individual considers optimal working hours and the resulting income, he believes that a higher income would keep his standard of living higher than his neighbours'. But when, because of this, everybody works long hours, nobody is happier. But everyone again believes that he would be so if he could increase his income again.

This may explain why we have reduced hours of work and increased leisure so slowly in relation to the rapid increase in the income level over the last 20 or 50 or 100 years. In fact, we have compelled each other by law to reduce hours, to some extent knowing or at least feeling that this was necessary in order to counterbalance the rat-race illusion. We cannot persuade each other to reduce our hours of work and our income, or to slow down our increase in income, if we do not apply a sort of compulsion. People wished to be compelled to reduce working hours. But now we hear more and more argument in favour of the idea that we should relax those old rules whereby we compel each other to work less, and that we should give freedom of choice both in the allocation and the length of hours of work (Rehn, 1977). Perhaps we who are advocating this might ask ourselves whether we are just creating unhappiness. Maybe we are opening the gates for a new 'keep up with the Joneses' competition, a new form of rat-race. We should be thinking about how to counteract the evil effects of our good deeds, if we get the opportunity to pursue a line of free choice.

In a way I can see that actually a situation has been created whereby the risk has been reduced of freedom of choice causing such side-effects, namely through high marginal tax rates. We can dare to make length of working time more a matter of individual choice because the marginal tax rates are high, and people realize how little they would gain from working one more hour. This is something we can think about when we discuss the possible reduction in the marginal tax rate. Perhaps here is another case of the type Goethe talks about in *Faust*—the spirit that always attempts evil and achieves good (or perhaps it was the other way around).

The possibility of upside-down effects of various actions in the social field is something that we should always keep in mind. I do not pretend to come up with definite solutions. I am trying to define vexing problems which arise when I advocate new types of freedom. Let me make a confession, however. My preoccupation with freedom of choice on timetable and length of hours of work is to a great extent caused by my belief that less regular work will come by an irresistible social process, where people take advantage, legitimately or illegitimately, of social insurance systems. If this is not to end in a sort of chaos, we should try to bring some order into the process by giving this freedom a rational and equitable form. It must be channelled in order to encourage both the maintenance of full employment and the increase of leisure, and to hamper the tendency towards speeding up the rat-race.

Now I come to another, similar theme, which Carl Tham has also touched upon, and that is the risk of creating or increasing serfdom by promoting security. Nobody can be against security of employment—the right to keep one's job, and so on. There is no question of reversing the trend in this direction, which is pursued in most industrialized countries. But each time governments introduce such protection they should try to see how its negative side-effects can be controlled, how one can counteract the tendency to create a situation where nobody dares to leave the job he has got.

Sociologists are indicating the competition between 'voice' and 'exit' as methods of achieving self-determination and freedom. But, after all, one aspect of the freedom of choice, one part of the individual's power of *voice* in his workplace, is the freedom with which he can threaten to apply *exit*.

Therefore we must continue to stimulate those arrangements in society which make free mobility in the labour market possible for the individual, thus ensuring him some freedom in relation to all his protection. Otherwise we may find one day that we have created protective cages from which people dare not escape. This in turn would reduce their bargaining power, including their power to uphold other types of freedom and protection in the workplace. The bargaining power of an organization is to a great extent dependent upon individual members' own sense of power and freedom. Therefore, I think that all these things which are beginning—possibilites for flexible retirement, opportunities for paid educational leave, job training, everything that improves opportunities for people to alternate between working and not working—should be enthusiastically developed. All this should contribute to creating a work pattern in which young people at least need not worry about job protection until they settle down in the type of work they would like to pursue for life. But even then there should be ways of applying *exit* without great cost or risk.

All these dilemmas which my fellow speakers and I have raised—or at least many of them—could be solved by formula, separating the flow of income and the flow of income-earning work to a considerably greater extent than is the case now. In earlier writings (e.g. Rehn, 1977) I have suggested the introduction of *general drawing rights* for this purpose: a development of the social insurance system whereby part of those taxes and contributions which we all are paying to cover pensions, education, holidays, and unemployment should be made available to us under more related rules than hitherto. Instead of the money being distributed to us only under bureaucratic scrutiny which determines whether we are eligible to use it for a specified purpose at a given moment, we should be able to claim it at times and for purposes of our own choosing. Everybody's life, after basic schooling, should start with a credit giving him certain opportunities to go to school or university or on training courses, and to finance his subsistence during such periods of non-work either immediately or later in life. If somebody did not use the money for education in his youth, he would be permitted to use it later, e.g. for long holidays, an early pension, or a temporary or partial pension.

Introducing greater freedom of choice and self-determination in the use of taxes and social insurance contributions, which in reality implies switching income from one period of an individual's life to another, may be part of the solution of the individual freedom/protection dilemma (and also the pursuit of real self-interest/submission to the rat-race dilemma) that tends to keep us from using our freedom of choice in a rational way.

Possibly this rethinking of the rules for social insurance could also help to solve another problem of modern society, namely the tendency of high marginal tax rates to tempt people not to declare all their income. Unlike the sounder effects of high marginal tax rates, which I indicated earlier, this tends to frustrate any efforts to reduce hours of work and to increase leisure. It encourages the reintroduction of the rat-race mechanism: everybody tries to earn money on the side in order to keep up with all the Joneses who also have work on the side. Perhaps this dangerous tendency would be counterbalanced to some extent, if it were seen that everybody has a high degree of self-determination over a good deal of the money he contributes to society, while undeclared work does not contribute to the state benefits to which he is entitled, and which are protected against inflation and other risks.

An effort to find solutions to the various dilemmas, or goal conflicts, which we have all been discussing, may be a fruitful endeavour. Some of the elements exist already, but if we begin systematically to look for ways of creating greater opportunities for the individual to determine the time allocation of his work and his non-work, maybe Western societies could go further and faster towards the solution of these dilemmas. That might also help to solve another goal conflict, the differences between the interests of men and women. If we provide possibilities for variation in amounts of work and amounts of leisure for

both men and women all through life, during the next 100 years women perhaps would use their rights and possibilities rather differently from men.
But should we see every difference between the life patterns of men and women
as an evil?

We regard it, rightly, as an evil if anybody, man or woman, is pressed by old
conventions into an outmoded sex role on an obsolete pattern of life or into any
pattern that is not freely chosen. We assume that it would cause unhappiness.
Our concept of freedom implies differences between individuals as to life patterns. But there is a tendency to regard every difference between the average behaviour patterns of men and women as suspect, as a hang-over of male chauvi-
nism or female prejudice or whatever it may be. I doubt that this request for con-
formity is in line with the interests of either sex. If elimination of many of the
constraints on how much working time everybody is compelled or permitted
to put in during given periods could create patterns whereby both men and
women have shorter hours during certain parts of life and longer hours during
other parts, perhaps this freedom of variation would be used more extensively
by women than by men. Should it be regarded as something necessarily wrong?
The main thing is that we could, from youth onwards, make both parties
regard a flexible life pattern as the natural order of things rather than those
rigid patterns which, anyway, are on the way out.

Finally I want to mention one more thing. The observations of Karasek
about the tendency of boring work to make the rest of life boring as well, the
effect of dull work to make leisure dull, too, tends to be used as an argument
against those of us who try to reduce the existing pressures on young people
to stay at school until they have acquired the highest qualifications it is possible for them to achieve. Some people argue that if a young person takes an
easy job which soon becomes dull and boring, he will stay there and he will
become boring himself, even if he were not so from the beginning. But school,
too, can be so boring that people can become both bored and boring. There
are those who, because they are compelled—by social convention if not by
law—to attend school for too many years, become school haters, inoculated
against any sort of return to the use of the intellect.

I think that if we apply the freedom of choice principle here, too, from an
early stage, including the freedom of having some command over the time
allocation of one's life's income, we could introduce a new and flexible life
pattern for all the young people, both the intellectually advanced, imaginative,
vivacious ones and those who are less privileged by nature and childhood
environment. If both types of people could from the beginning be taught to
regard it as normal to go back and forth between school and work, this might
be an introduction to a dynamic pattern for the rest of their lives, including
a habit of intermittent education.

We know that natural gifts and social-cultural conditions tend to cause
segregation between one class of people, who become dull through doing dull

work from the beginning and for long periods and never escaping from it, and another class who 'behave well' by going straight through secondary and higher education to the interesting jobs which the former believe they have no chance of attaining. But we should systematically try out methods which could invite both groups to apply other and more flexible life patterns, more conducive to dynamism and activity all through life. Gradually employers would learn that the fact that somebody had taken an irregular school-and-work path through his youth is not a reason to be suspicious of his working skills and capacities. Do not let us be scared by Karasek's observation that dull work tends to make people dull. Even if there is such a tendency, the connection is not very strong, particularly if we think of short periods of such work. Since we cannot weed out all dull and boring tasks from working life, we should promote life patterns whereby those tasks are shared out between us all as temporary jobs rather than let them be concentrated as lifelong tasks (with perfect employment security to imprison them) upon people selected for those jobs from the beginning of their working lives.

REFERENCES

Rehn, G. (1977). Towards a society of free choice, in *Comparing Public Policies*, ed. J. J. Wiatr and R. Rose, Ossolineum, Wroclaw. (Short version in the *OECD Observer*, February 1973.)

Part 3

Social Effects of a Changing Labour Market

Working Life
Edited by B. Gardell and G. Johansson
© 1981 John Wiley & Sons Ltd

Age and Marginality in the Swedish Labour Market

HANS BERGLIND

INTRODUCTION

The Swedish labour market has rapidly changed during the last decade. Two trends seem especially notable; the sharp increase in female employment, and the decrease in male employment. Both trends are well known and hardly unique to Sweden. In fact, they characterize almost all highly industrialized countries (International Labour Office, 1977). They seem to be connected with changes in the economic structure which facilitate demand for labour in traditionally female occupations, while decreasing demand for labour in traditionally male occupations, mainly within the goods-producing sector. As I have discussed these tendencies elsewhere I shall only briefly touch upon them here (Berglind, 1977, 1978b).

Trends in gainful employment have differentially affected men and women, as well as different age groups. Young people face great difficulties in finding a job in today's labour market, and the middle-aged and the old—at least among men—show declining activity rates. Discussion here will focus on the degree to which the decreasing activity rate according to age is exclusively a male phenomenon; reasons for the prevailing trends; and some of their consequences.

Before data are presented, the terms 'marginality' and 'marginal labour' should be clarified. Of their several meanings, at least two are relevant. In one sense, these terms can refer to people whose movement in and out of the labour market depends on the economic cycle. This comes close to the marxist concept of the 'reserve army' (Marx, 1965).

In another sense the terms can be used to describe the fact that certain categories of people run a high risk of becoming permanently redundant or eliminated from the labour market. One main argument of this paper is that, while the young and women are marginal mainly in the first sense, people above a certain age are eliminated or excluded from the labour market in the second, more definitive sense. I shall also argue that this elimination of the old from the labour force in a welfare state like Sweden is officially sanctioned in order to solve growing problems in the labour market.

145

TRENDS

Changes in rates of employment among men and women in different age groups in Sweden can be discerned from Figure 1. It is clear that the increase

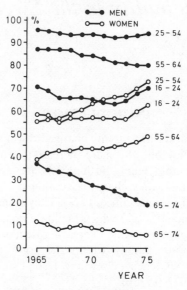

Figure 1 Relative number of employed among men and women in different age groups, 1965–1975 (%). The figures are based on the average for each year according to the labour force surveys. In these surveys a person is classified as employed if, during the survey week, he or she worked at least one hour as a paid employee or in his (her) own business (or at least 15 hours as an unpaid worker in a family enterprise). Persons who are temporarily absent from work due to vacations, illness, etc., are also included in this category. Due to a growing number of non-responses in recent years, the figure for 1975 probably overestimates the employment level to a somewhat higher extent than in preceding years. *Source:* Labour force surveys (raw tables of yearly averages)

in female employment has been highest among women aged 25–54 and a little lower in the age groups 55–64 and 16–24. For women of 65–74 the level of employment has notably decreased. For men also there is a marked variation with age. In the youngest age group (16–24) the employment level was lowest in 1972, a year of recession, but then it rose almost to the same level as in 1965. In the age group 25–54 a slight decrease is noticeable. It is even more marked among the 55–64-year-olds, where the relative number of employed men decreased by approximately 7 per cent in ten years. This decrease was much more marked among non-married than among married men. In the age group 65–74 the employment level for men, as for women, almost halved.

These observations give some support to the idea that the decline of the employment level among the young in the late 1960s and early 1970s was rather temporary, while among the old (men above 54 and those of both sexes above 65) the employment level showed a more steady continuous downward trend. This downward trend, however, cannot be simply interpreted as indicative of elimination or exclusion from the labour market. It may also mean that those who left the labour market did so because they preferred not to work, despite the possibility of gainful employment.

How were these non-working persons occupied? They may have been looking for work, but further analysis shows that this was not the case. The unemployment rate in Sweden was comparatively low with no indication of any upward trend. Rather, the category comprising people outside the labour force has grown in some age groups, especially among men. Labour force surveys reveal some information about why people are out of the labour force. The most important reasons include: household work, student status, institutional confinement, and incapacitation. The 'incapacitated' group is of special interest. It contains the largest numbers and is also the most expansive. Figure 2 illustrates how the proportion of men and women in different age groups has expanded within this category. It is noteworthy that no consistent increase has occurred in the relative number of those 'incapacitated' below the age of 45. Above that age the increase has occurred in *all* categories. Such an increase also occurs among women in spite of the rise in their rate of employment. The reservoir of female labour has been drained through more women taking up gainful employment. At the same time, among those not working, a growing number, both absolutely and relatively, are apparently unable to work, i.e. are excluded from the labour market. In spite of increased female employment, the number of males who are 'incapacitated' is still higher in the corresponding age and civil status categories. For both sexes the figures are remarkably higher for the non-married (including those divorced and widowed) than for the married. These trends seem to confirm the hypothesis that a *growing* number of people have become marginal or unemployable with advancing age.

This development among the non-working population is strengthened by the growing exodus from the labour market among those in higher age groups

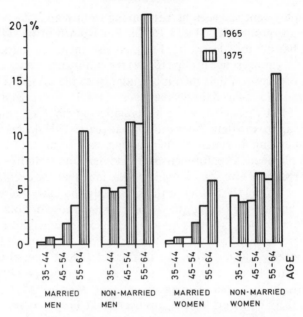

Figure 2 Relative number of 'incapacitated' among men
and women in different age groups, 1965 and 1975.
People are classified as 'incapacitated' who, because of
long-term illness or disability, are ineligible for any kind
of gainful employment; who are looked after (cared for)
by their family or others, and who are not expected to be
able to work again within a period of at least six months.
Those who have withdrawn from work for reasons of
age without medical symptoms other than those related
to higher age should *not* be classified as incapacitated,
according to instructions given to interviewers in the
labour force surveys. It is, of course, impossible to know
to what extent these instructions have been followed

who are currently working. Data from a 3.3 per cent representative sample of
the Swedish working population (defined as those working at least 20 hours
per week) shed some light on this problem. Because this sample was utilized
both in the 1965 and the 1970 census, it facilitated a longitudinal analysis of
the same people on two occasions (Berglind, 1978b). It reveals the extent to
which those working in 1965 were still employed five years later (see Figure 3).
As observed for an earlier period (Meidner, 1954), these data also indicate
that the outflow from the workforce is much higher among women than among
men. This is especially marked among younger women, who tend to leave
their jobs in connection with marriage and childbirth. This higher outflow
for women is compensated for by a higher inflow *to* the labour force which
grows with the age of their children.

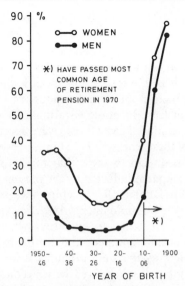

Figure 3 Resignation from work between 1965 and 1970 among men and women in different age groups (%)

It is also evident that outflow values for both men and women decrease until about the age of 40–45, when they again begin to rise. This reinforces our earlier observation of a growing number of 'unemployables' among those aged 45 and above. Results based on the census sample, however, do not reveal whether or not this tendency has changed since 1970; unfortunately more recent data are still not available.

GROWING POSSIBILITIES FOR EARLY RETIREMENT

The official attitude towards older members of the workforce has been ambivalent. In 1970 the law was changed to make early retirement (disability) pensions more easily available to old people undergoing difficulties in securing employment (Berglind, 1978a). This trend was reinforced by further statutory changes in 1972.

On the other hand, in 1974 the Security of Employment Act was launched with the purpose of improving job security, especially for older workers. (The Security of Employment Act; enactment: SFS 1974:12, 367, 378.) The Act contains the fundamental provision that an employer must show reasonable cause for notice. The period of notice (from one to six months) rises with the age of the employee. Longest notice must be given to employees aged 45 or over.

Two other important legal changes were introduced in 1976. First, the age for receiving an old-age pension from the national pension scheme was lowered from 67 to 65 years of age. Secondly, a new type of pension—'partial pension'—was introduced. Available to person between the ages of 60 and 65, it reimburses 65 per cent of the loss in income resulting from a reduction of working hours. The reduction must be five hours or more per week and the remaining work week at least 17 hours (Bratthall, 1976). In September 1978 approximately 40 000 persons, aged 60–64, were receiving this new type of pension. The majority of these worked 17–21 hours per week.

Our preliminary studies seem to show that this reform is especially applicable to employees in companies affected by the present (1977–1978) economic recession (Crona, 1978). Laying off old employees is a difficult procedure because of the Security of Employment Act; thus employers—as well as employees—find it more congenial to have two persons share one full-time positions, with partial pensions compensating for the reduced time.

Thus, at the same time as the state attempts to prevent the expulsion of the elderly from their jobs, it has secured better economic compensation for the growing numbers forced to leave their jobs. The net outcome of these conflicting trends can be studied most easily through changes in the number of people receiving an early retirement pension (Figure 4). The figure shows that growth in the relative number of early pensioners accelerates with age.

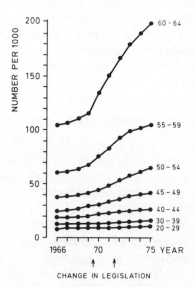

Figure 4 Number of premature retirement pensioners per 1000 inhabitants in different age groups

The increase is only slight in the age brackets below 40, but remarkably high in all categories above 50. This is interesting, because changes in the law in 1970 and 1972 were intended mainly to give support to people of 60 and over who were facing problems in a hardening labour market. Moreover, increase in the number of pensioners had started even *before* the law was changed in 1970. This is quite noticeable among those of 45 and over. It seems as if the problems leading to liberalization of the law had already affected application of the law before its change.

It should be remembered that we are discussing the development of the total number of people receiving early retirement pensions. This number, amounting to approximately 300 000 in the age groups 16–66 at the end of 1975, is the net outcome of both an inflow of new pensioners and the outflow resulting from reasons such as starting to work and losing pensions (a very rare occurrence); passing the upper age limit and thus becoming old-age pensioners; and death. Probably a study of the inflow of new premature pensioners alone would have demonstrated less of an age effect, but it would not have changed the total picture.

What cannot be seen from Figure 4 is that the development has been some- what different for men and women. It was almost parallel for the age groups below 55. From that age the increase became much more dramatic among men.

POSSIBLE EXPLANATIONS

So far our observations seem to confirm the idea that the middle-aged and the elderly—especially the males—are becoming redundant. For women two opposite trends prevail. On the one hand, activity rates are growing among women below the age of 65. On the other hand, the number of 'unemployables' and early retirement pensioners is increasing among women as well as among men. Why is it that the elderly are becoming increasingly dependent on society for public transfers, like early pensions, for their subsistence?

A number of possible factors may explain this development. Some are associated with the individual, such as deteriorating health. Other explana- tions focus on local as well as broader structural changes in society. Still other explanations are based on the interaction between the individual and the so- cial structure. This last assumption will be used as a basis for the discussion which follows.

It should be remembered that our problem is to explain why a certain pheno- menon has *increased* at a rather rapid rate; that is, why increasingly *more* people in the higher age brackets are classified as unemployable. It seems rather unrealistic to argue that this is primarily because of deteriorating health among the elderly. Why should health become worse at such a rapid rate in a welfare society? Another possibility is, of course, that even if the health of the populat- ion has not worsened, standards for judging health may have changed; a person need not be as handicapped as previously to be classified as 'incapacitated' or unemployable. But why should this change have taken place?

When the law regulating the right to an early retirement pension was launched, the main idea was not to adjust medical standards but rather to give greater consideration to those changes in the labour market especially affecting workers of 60 or over (in 1970 the age limit was 63). The number of people pensioned on the basis of labour market conditions, however, has remained rather low during the period of expansion, and does *not* explain the great increase that was experienced, even in age groups below 60. Our interpretation is that while the medical standards probably have become more liberal, this liberalization has taken place because of changes in the labour market. When jobs become more difficult to get, more people become incapacitated in relation to the job openings still available. To be able to compete a person must be stronger, healthier, and more profitable than before. Moreover, not only the elderly face difficulties in today's labour market. Similar difficulties face those who have low education, are single (divorced, widowed, or never married), and who lack practical experience relevant to the jobs that are open to competition.

Some of these negative characteristics are associated with age: for instance, low education, and divorced and widowed status. But what about experience? Young people have little or no work experience, while the elderly as a rule have gained considerable experience during many years of work. Beyond quantity, however, we must inquire into the extent to which the aged have the kind of experience which is demanded in today's labour market. If, for instance, the elderly are over-represented in those occupations that are shrinking, their practical experience might be obsolete, or even an obstacle to obtaining a new job in the competitive labour market. Thus, if this hypothesis is correct, we would expect (1) the elderly to be over-represented in shrinking occupations, and (2) the outflow to be higher correlated with age in shrinking rather than in expanding occupational areas.

To assess developments between 1965 and 1975 we have grouped occupations into three sectors, calculating the change in the number of employed in each. The results are presented in Table 1. The primary and secondary occupational sectors are apparently shrinking while the tertiary (service) sector has expanded. In the earlier period those employed in sectors I and II are older on the average, than those in sector III.

Suppose, for a moment, that a certain number of those in shrinking occupations who are under the general pension age become redundant and seek new jobs. Suppose, furthermore, that a certain proportion of those who are looking for a job never get one. If there is no correlation between age and the possibility of getting a new job we would still expect those who are unable to find a new job to be fairly old, because they come from occupations where the average age is high. But what if the elderly are likely to keep their jobs, or what

Table 1 Men and women age 16–64 according to occupational sector in 1965 and 1975

Occupational sector		Sex	Number (thousands)				Median age	
			1965	1975	Change	%	1965	1975
I	Farming, forestry,	Male	377	179	−198	−52%	47.1	46.7
	fishing, etc.	Female	87	61	− 26	−30%	47.9	47.8
II	Mining, manufactur-	Male	1035	981	− 54	− 5%	40.2	36.0
	ing, etc.	Female	205	194	− 11	− 5%	41.0	38.1
III	Other occupations	Male	824	1113	+289	+35%	38.4	39.3
	(professional,	Female	1024	1440	+416	+41%	37.3	37.8
	technical, admini-							
	strative, clerical,							
	sales and service							
	work)							
I–III	All occupations	Male	2236	2273	+ 37	+ 2%	40.6	38.7
		Female	1316	1695	+379	+29%	38.7	38.2

Source: Labour Forces Surveys (raw tables for 1965 and 1975).

if they have a better chance than younger workers to find new jobs? To answer these questions we studied three age cohorts of working age in 1965 and 1975. The results are shown in Table 2.

It comes out quite clearly that higher age groups are in occupations that shrink most or expand least. This holds for the total number of occupations as for most individual occupations. The highest 'losses', both for men and women,

Table 2 Changes in the relative number of employed (%) 1965–1975, according to age, sex, and occupational category

Occupation	Men, born:			Women, born:		
	1931–1940	1921–1930	1911–1920	1931–1940	1921–1930	1911–1920
Farming, forestry, fishing	−18.3	−17.7	−32.5	+17.0	−10.8	−32.9
Mining, manufacturing work, etc.	− 8.9	−12.0	−30.9	+27.0	−10.6	−48.6
Professional technical work, etc.	+20.7	+ 6.1	− 2.9	+42.5	+51.5	+16.9
Administrative, exe-cutive, managerial work	+27.3	+19.8	− 6.0	+42.1	+33.3	+ 6.7
Clerical work	−26.3	+37.2	+13.6	+40.1	+44.2	−10.2
Sales work	+19.8	− 4.6	− 1.5	− 1.5	+ 7.4	−22.7
Transport and com-munication work	−26.4	−17.1	−32.1	+53.9	+12.0	−27.8
Service work	+83.9	+ 6.1	+15.0	+124.6	+62.2	− 5.5
All occupations	− 0.3	− 5.9	−22.5	+45.4	+29.7	−16.9

are to be found in the primary sector (farming, etc.), in the secondary sector (manufacturing work, etc.) and in 'transport and communication work', a category within the tertiary sector. Total employment in these three categories also decreased between 1965 and 1975. This gives strong support also to our second hypothesis. As long as we cannot follow the same individuals on two occasions, we cannot be sure how the changes between occupations have taken place. It seems highly improbable, however, that the results would have been very different had it been possible to make a follow-up study comparing the same individuals on both occasions. In fact, our above mentioned longitudinal study comparing census data from 1965 and 1975 confirms this trend (Berglind 1978b).

It may be noted that these sectoral movements of labour are quite typical. During early periods of industrialization, workers in manufacturing—especially men—are usually recruited from the primary sector. If the secondary sector stagnates or even begins to shrink while the primary sector continues to decrease its labour force, many old workers are faced with a situation adversely affecting their employment possibilities. At the same time, however, our data indicate that the tertiary sector, with the exception of some occupations, has been growing, and this expansion has favoured female labour and the young—especially those with a good education. This does not preclude the fact that during times of economic recession these groups also face unemployment. But it indicates a kind of marginality which is mostly of a temporary character.

THE PERSPECTIVE OF THE NON-EMPLOYED

In 1975 the non-employed population of Sweden of 20–64 years of age consisted of a little over 1 million persons. Of these 30 per cent were men, and 70 per cent women. Developments during the last decades have led to a levelling between the sexes: non-working men have become more numerous and non-working women fewer. As we have already seen, the number of both men and women who report that they are incapacitated has grown.

How do non-working persons perceive their situation? Do they want a job and do they think that this is possible? In the spring of 1975 the Central Bureau of Statistics performed a survey of the 'economically inactive population' (Undersökning av den icke sysselsatta befolkningen våren 1975, 1977), in which were included some questions about the perceived possibilities and preferences for work among those interviewed. Some of the results are presented in Table 3.

It is interesting to note that both the desire to work and the perceived possibilities of getting a job are fairly constant in the two younger age categories. After 45, both the desire and the perceived possibilities diminish sharply. We noticed earlier that this age limit is critical also for those who have a job. Very few persons who are between 45 and 64 years of age both wish and find it possible to get a job where they live.

Table 3 Propensity to work among economically inactive population (20–64) according to sex and age (%)

Category	Men			Women		
	20–24	25–44	45–64	20–24	25–44	45–64
Want to start working						
Within 6 months	6	17	9	9	12	7
Later	87	76	42	82	69	32
Not interested	7	7	49	9	19	61
Total	100	100	100	100	100	100
Perceived possibility of getting job						
Good	27	28	14	25	27	11
Limited; don't know	29	24	19	43	45	30
None	44	48	67	32	28	59
Total	100	100	100	100	100	100

On the basis of these results, it is impossible to say to what extent this variation of attitudes with age reflects a change of attitudes or is the result of a selection procedure. Those people who wish to work and find it possible to work will probably enter the workforce, while those who are not interested will remain at home and constitute a growing part of the non-active population. At the same time this non-active group receives an inflow of people who have no possibility of continuing to work. It is, however, quite possible that those who stay at home become less interested in finding work and that they—realistically—perceive that their possibilities of taking up gainful employment have diminished.

THE THREAT TO WELFARE POLICY

The fact that increasing numbers are outside the workforce, deprived of the possibility of supporting themselves through work, has led to increasing dependency on societal transfers, and thereby to heightened social costs in the form of premature pensions, unemployment benefits, etc. These transfers are in large measure financed through taxes. Irrespective of the form of financing, they can be easily interpreted as a contribution which the working population surrenders for the support of the non-working population. The situation is sometimes depicted in terms of the bifurcation of the population into those who 'nurture' and those who 'consume'.

In a society characterized by high taxes and stagnation there is thus a risk that growing costs of such transfers can lead to negative attitudes. Such attitudes can be directed against the welfare system, or against those persons for whom transfers are an important source of income. None the less, a row of different factors presumably affects the degree to which such negative attitudes actually prevail. Some are related to the social structure and cultural traditions; some to the place within this structure occupied by those who express such attitudes; and some to the design of the transfer system.

There are studies which indicate that lately the climate of opinion within which welfare policy operates has become harsher. Norwegian opinion studies cited by Kolberg (1978) indicate that the proportion of the population favouring expansion of the economic welfare system decreased from 48 per cent in 1965 to only 20 per cent in 1973. In the USA support for various welfare programmes remained relatively unchanged between 1968 and 1976. On the other hand, negative attitudes towards recipients of social help became more common: the proportion holding such negative attitudes rose from 30 per cent in 1972 to 37 per cent four years later (Miller, 1978).

These same studies also reveal data about which groups react most strongly. According to Norwegian studies (Kolberg, 1978), views on the frequency of abuse vary with education. Of those with only minimum compulsory education, 75 per cent held that cheating among clients was very common, while only 64 per cent of those with high school education and 51 per cent of the university educated subscribed to this view.

On the other hand, American studies display a contrasting picture. Negative attitudes towards people on welfare are more common among persons with at least a high school education, than among the less educated. They are also more common among those with higher incomes, among managers, and among whites compared with coloured (Miller, 1978).

Swedish data illuminating attitudes in this area are scarce. Some data, however, were gathered in connection with an investigation of a sample of voters during the parliamentary elections of 1973 and 1976. Respondents were asked to state their position regarding the following statement: 'Social reforms have gone so far in the country that in the future the state ought to diminish rather than increase benefits and support to its citizens.' The pattern of responses indicated that there was no *overall* shift in attitudes between 1973 and 1976, but there were more bourgeois voters who expressed negative views in 1976. (Petersson, 1977). It is possible that the bourgeois parties received a certain inflow from former socialist voters with negative attitudes towards welfare policy. But whatever the case, it is quite difficult to say if this contributed to the victory of the bourgeois parties in the 1976 election.

On the whole, our knowledge about attitudes towards social policy is very limited. One might guess that such attitudes are quite closely related to the form of transfers. Programmes of general transfers, building on compensatory replacement of income loss, are probably more easily acceptable than programmes requiring income tests or a more comprehensive proof of need. In Sweden, an obvious example of the latter type is social help, continuing to account for only a very small part of total cash subsidies (1.2 per cent or around

850 million Kronor in 1978). This small proportion of total social outlays has probably incurred more resentment than the remaining 99 per cent.

Closely related to attitudes towards welfare recipients is the prevailing work ethic. In most industrial countries—not only capitalist countries—the dominant value system emphasizes the importance of work as a source of livelihood. Men who cannot utilize their labour power are easily viewed with suspicion. The presumed will to work plays a central role in attitudes towards recipients of social help (Berglind and Puide, 1976).

In fact the only way to legitimize transfers to persons of working age has been through a doctor's certification. Without such certification, a redundant worker runs a much greater risk of being considered unwilling to work. Those who are excluded from the labour market often regard themselves as 'incapacitated' or sick, and most recipients of early retirement pensions receive such pensions on medical grounds. This exemplifies the 'medicalization of a social problem' (Illich, 1975), i.e. the lack of suitable jobs for the redundant. Such a development not only tends to hide the real causes behind the trend; it also can force such people into a sick role (Parsons, 1951), making them ardent consumers of the limited resources devoted to medical care and services.

As is known, the rich have always been suspicious of the work ethic of the poor. They rationalize the lay-off of a worker as the result of the worker's lack of will to work, i.e. his own personal 'shortcoming'. This rationalization functions not only as a defence of the prevailing economic system, but also as a defence of the conscience of those who hold such attitudes. In the long run it can lead to fissures in the solidarity which is the foundation stone of a welfare society.

ACKNOWLEDGEMENT

This study is based on a research project financed by the Bank of Sweden Tercentenary Foundation.

REFERENCES

Berglind, H. (1977). Unemployment and redundancy in a 'post-industrial' labor market, in *Work and Technology*, ed. M. R. Haug and J. Dofney, Sage Studies in International Sociology 10, London.

Berglind, H. (1978a). Early retirement pensions in Sweden: Trends and regional variations, *Scandinavian Journal of Social Medicine*, 1.

Berglind, H. (1978b). From industrial to service society, *International Journal of Contemporary Sociology*, **15**, 1 and 2.

Berglind, H., and Puide, A. (1976). Synen på socialhjälpstagarna (Views on recipients of social help), in *Ideal och Verkligheter i svensk socialvård (Ideal and Reality in the Swedish Social Services)* Wahlström & Widstrand, Stockholm.

Bratthall, K. (1976). Flexible retirement and the new Swedish partial-pension scheme, *Industrial Gerontology*, **3**, 3.

Crona, G. (1978). Partial retirement in Sweden—development and experience, paper presented at the 9th World Congress of Sociology, Uppsala.

Illich, I. (1975). Medical Nemesis: The Expropriation of Health, Galder & Boyars, London.

International Labour Office (1977). Labour force estimates and projections 1950–2000, Geneva.

Kolberg, J. E. (1978). Limits to welfare, *Acta Sociologica*, supplement.

Marx, K. (1965). *Das Kapital*, Erster Band, Dietz Verlag GmbH, Berlin.

Meidner, R. (1954). Svensk arbetsmarknad vid full sysselsättning (Swedish labour market at full employment), National Institute of Economic Research, Stockholm.

Miller, A. H. (1978). Will public attitudes defeat welfare reform? *Public Welfare*, Summer.

Parsons, T. (1951). *The Social System*, Free Press, New York.

Petersson, O. (1977). *Valundersökningar (Election Investigations)*, Rapport No. 2. *Väljarna och valet 1976 (Voters and the 1976 Election)*, SCB, Stockholm.

Undersökning av den icke sysselsatta befolkningen våren 1975 (1977). (The economically inactive population survey in spring 1975), *Statistiska meddelanden Am 1977:2.11*.

Working Life
Edited by B. Gardell and G. Johansson
© 1981 John Wiley & Sons Ltd

Some Possible Relations between Stressful Work Events, Other Life Events, and Psychopathology*

BRUCE P. DOHRENWEND and BARBARA SNELL DOHRENWEND

INTRODUCTION

In describing the background to this symposium, the organizers wrote:

> ...it has become evident that conditions in working life must be considered in a social and political framework.... Problems in the external environment are closely connected to the work environment, in which the first signs of health hazards often appear. The need for efficient, profitable forms of production has led to a situation in which profound readjustments are required by large groups of people and in which an increasing number of individuals become redundant.... The development towards increasing equality between the sexes has contributed to a growing number of women in the labour force. This in turn has had a strong impact on the family, on leisure activities, and, in particular, on the children's situation in society.

Our purpose in this paper will be to examine what we have learned from our studies of socio-environmental factors, stress, and psychiatric disorders that may be relevant to the themes of this symposium in general and to this particular session on the effects of a changing labour market. As effects, we will examine rates of functional psychiatric disorders. Under the functional disorders, we shall include schizophrenia, the behavioural manifestations of which come closest to those most people would regard as 'insane'; affective psychosis which is characterized by severe depression; neurosis which is characterized by severe anxiety, and the personality disorders, especially those involving antisocial behaviour and addictions to alcohol or drugs.

*This work was supported in part by Grant MH–10328 and by Research Scientist Award K–5–MH–14663 from the National Institute of Mental Health, US Public Health Service, and by the Foundations' Fund for Research in Psychiatry.

We shall consider, first, whether modern life in industrial societies has produced an increment in such disorders and, second, whether the processes involved centre on the work situation. Needless to say, we shall provide considerably less than complete answers to these questions.

URBANIZATION AND PSYCHIATRIC DISORDERS

In 1900 only two-fifths of the population of the coterminous United States lived in urban settings—that is, in central cities with populations of 50,000 or more and the surrounding areas that are integrated with them economically and socially. This fraction had increased to about half by 1920; to three-fifths by 1950; and to almost two-thirds by 1960. In our most recent census in 1970, almost three-quarters of our population were found to live in urban settings (Dohrenwend and Dohrenwend, 1974a). Nor is the United States alone in this worldwide process. As Carlestam (1971) suggested, 'We should reckon with the possibility that urbanization will continue up to a saturation limit of 80–90 percent of the population in most cases, especially in industrialized countries' (p. 146), with Greater Stockholm itself with 1.3 million residents in 1965 soon likely to rank among the world's 100 largest cities (p. 147). However, as Carlestam noted, 'the influence of urbanized environment on mental stability remains a big unknown' (pp. 145–146).

The dearth of facts about the matter has not, however, inhibited speculation. One particularly vivid example was supplied by Lawrence K. Frank writing in 1936 at a time when the Great Depression had influenced the thinking of many about the nature of society and its impact on its human inhabitants:

> Our so-called social problems...are to be viewed as arising from the frantic efforts of individuals, lacking any sure direction and sanctions or guiding conception of life, to find some way of protecting themselves or of merely existing on any terms they can manage in a society being remade by technology. Having no strong loyalties and no consistent values or realizable ideals to cherish, the individual's conduct is naturally conflicting, confused, neurotic, and antisocial....(Frank, 1936, 339–340)

Popular speculations such as Frank's have far outstripped the number of serious attempts to put them to the test. There are, however, some relevant studies and one of these was conducted by Goldhamer and Marshall (1953) with data on hospital first admissions between 1840 and 1940 in the state of Massachusetts.

Their startling central finding was that rates of functional psychoses of the early and middle years had not varied over the 100-year period. This finding is, however, restricted to treated rates and does not include the full range of functional psychiatric disorders. Moreover, as Goldhamer and Marshall pointed out, it is possible that the conditions of urban life had been sufficiently established in Massachusetts by 1840 so that the investigators would have had to go back another 100 years to test the effects for the most important changes. Unfortunately, such data are not available.

Nevertheless, Goldhamer and Marshall's finding and replications of it elsewhere (Pugh and MacMahon, 1962) are surprising in part because they are based on treated cases. It has long been known (e.g. Jarvis, 1971) that rates of treated psychiatric disorder vary with the availability of treatment facilities, which surely must have increased from 1840 to 1940, and with public attitudes towards their use (cf. Dohrenwend and Dohrenwend, 1969, 5–7). In fact, conclusions about the traumatic psychiatric effects of industrialization have been criticized on just these grounds. It has been argued that because of their reliance on treated rates of disorder, usually treatment in mental hospitals, they tell us nothing about the impact of a changing society on mental health as such (Mott and Roemer, 1948, 140–141).

Fortunately, since the turn of the century, more than sixty investigators or teams of investigators have attempted to estimate the prevalence of untreated as well as treated cases of psychiatric disorder in a variety of communities in North and South America, Europe, Asia, and Africa. However, there are problems in interpreting the results of these studies. Although most of them are alike in reporting brief period prevalence, that is, the number of cases existing regardless of time of onset, during a period spanning a few months to a few years (Dohrenwend and Dohrenwend, 1969; 1974a; 1974b; 1976) we have found in our various analyses of these studies that the rates of disorder reported vary widely. In some communities, rates of 1 per cent and less were reported; in others, rates of 50 per cent and more. Such differences are due more to contrasts in thoroughness of data collection and, especially, to contrasting conceptions of how to define a case of psychiatric disorder than differences in the persons and places studied or the history of the times at which the studies were conducted.

Given the powerful impact of these methodological differences, direct comparisons of overall rates for various types of disorder obtained by different investigators is likely to be misleading. It is possible, however, to compare the relationships they report between various types of disorder and demographic factors such as age, sex, and social class. Moreover, a happy set of circumstances makes it possible for us to obtain a limited number of comparisons within studies at rural and urban sites.

At least seven of the epidemiological investigators reported data from both rural and urban segments of the populations they studied, with two reporting data for two settings, each divided into rural and urban portions (Dohrenwend and Dohrenwend, 1974a). Altogether, therefore, these studies provide nine comparisons of rural and urban rates in which the same methodology is used within the rural–urban pairs. In one comparison, the total rate for all psychiatric disorders combined was higher in the rural setting; there was one tie; and in the remaining seven comparisons the urban rate was higher than the rural rate. However, these differences between rural and urban rates were not large; the median difference for all rates was only 1.1 per cent and the range in individual studies was from an excess of 0.9 per cent in a rural area to an excess of 13.9 per cent in an urban area. The reason for the generally small differences in these rates between rural and urban sites is that while some types of psychiatric disorder were found to be more prevalent in the urban setting, others were found more frequently in the rural setting. Thus

—total rates for all functional psychoses combined were more prevalent in the rural settings (five out of seven studies) and this appeared to be so for affective psychosis (three out of four studies) though not for schizophrenia (higher in the urban area in three out of five studies);
—rates of neurosis were higher in the urban settings (five out of six studies);
—rates of personality disorder were higher in the urban settings (five out of six studies).

Some of these results are consistent with popular speculations about the pathological consequences of stressful urban environments. They are also consistent, however, with plausible alternative interpretations. While cities can be harsh and threatening, they also provide concentrations of industry and commerce, wealth and power, and art and entertainment that make them magnets for rural people. Migrants seeking greater opportunity, challenge, or, perhaps, anonymity are drawn to cities in large numbers. The possibility cannot be overlooked, therefore, that such migrants bring with them the types of psychopathology that show higher rates in urban settings. Unfortunately, no studies exist that have taken pre-migration baseline measures of true prevalence of disorders among potential rural emigrants followed up by post-migration measures of migrants and non-migrants in the urban destination. In the absence of such studies, the issue remains unresolved.

Nevertheless, the findings point to neuroses and to personality disorders as more distinctively urban than rural problems. Therefore, it is highly likely that, whatever their origins, increasing urbanization in modern Western societies will lead to increasing concentration of the load of such disorders in urban centres.

THE IMPACT OF THE INCREASING PROPORTION OF WORKING WOMEN

Since the 1930s, there has been an accelerating trend for women in modern Western societies to enter the workforce, with World War II marking the point at which married women in large number began to take jobs outside the home for the first time. In the United States, for example, only slightly over a fifth of those employed in 1920 were women. By 1930, the figure increased slightly to about 22 per cent. By 1940, it had jumped to about 26 per cent and was near 30 per cent by 1950. Today it is well over 40 per cent and the expectation based on US Labor Department Statistics is that it will continue to increase rapidly in the next few years.

Eli Ginsburg, chairman of the National Commission for Manpower Policy in the United States, has described this rapidly increasing rate of entrance into the job market by women as 'the single most outstanding phenomenon of our century—'. Moreover, it is his opinion that 'its long term implications are absolutely unchartable. It will affect women, men and children, and the cumulative consequences of that will only be revealed in the 21st and 22nd centuries' (New York Times, 1976, 49).

While the facts about the consequences of this change are sparse, there has been no dearth of speculation. Gove and Tudor, in a recent review, found much in the writings of contemporary social scientists to suggest that these changes in women's role have been placing them under increased stress relative to men in modern Western societies. They summarize the argument as follows:

> Women previously had a more meaningful role. Families were large, and during most of their adult life women were responsible for the care of children. Without the conveniences of modern industrial society, housework required more time and skill and was highly valued. Since the family's economic support was frequently provided by a family enterprise, the wife played a role in supporting the family. With the development of industrialization and the small nuclear family, the woman's child-rearing years were shortened, her domestic skills were largely replaced by modern conveniences, and she was no longer part of a family enterprise supporting the family. During this time, both sexes were receiving more education; for the male, education produced occupational advancement and diversity; for the female, education was accompanied by changes in the legal and ideological structure, which held that the same standards should apply to men and women. However, instead of being treated as equals, women remained in their old institutionalized positions. If this analysis is correct, much of the presumed stress on women is a relatively recent phenomenon. (Gove and Tudor, 1973, 816)

It has also been argued, however, that the changes in women's role have been, on balance, positive rather than negative with regard to the stress and strain they entail. As Kolb wrote recently:

> the distribution of contraceptive pharmaceuticals has freed womanhood in a way which has never occurred before, and she has greater latitude for testing and selecting a husband and father, for using sex as a form of

physical intimacy, for competing in the ranks of the employed.... Many
women of the newer generation have an approach to life differing from
their predecessors...conflict over sexual behavior is lessened with dimi-
nution of the associated anxieties, guilts and shame. This, in turn, may
well enhance healthy child bearing and rearing.... (Kolb, 1973, 224–225)

In order to investigate opposing predictions we would, ideally, have data
from epidemiological studies that would enable us to test whether rates of
psychiatric disorders increased or decreased for women over time. Unfortunately, differences in concepts and methods used in pre-World War II
studies by contrast with post-war studies preclude such analyses of absolute
changes over time. However, the majority of studies of true prevalence have
provided some data on relative rates of psychiatric disorders among men and
women. If we assume that the male role did not change as radically as the
female role between the pre-war and post-war eras, we can study the effect of
the presumed female role change by comparing male and female rates of
various disorders in the two eras. Moreover, since Gove and Tudor's conception of the change in women's role is specific to industrialized societies, we can
introduce a rough control for level of industrialization by making separate
comparisons of studies carried out in rural as against urban communities,
within Europe and North America as against the rest of the world. When we
made these comparisons we found that (Dohrenwend and Dohrenwend,
1976)

—there are no consistent sex differences in rates of functional psychoses in
  general (34 studies) or in rates of one of the two major sub-types, schizophrenia (26 studies), in particular; rates of the other, affective psychosis,
  are generally higher among women (18 out of 24 studies);
—rates of neurosis are consistently higher for women regardless of time or
  place (28 out of 32 studies);
—by contrast, rates of personality disorder are consistently higher for men
  regardless of time or place (22 out of 26 studies).

The major issue here is posed by the relatively high female rates of neurosis
and affective psychosis with their possible common denominator of depressive symptomatology (cf. Silverman, 1968; Klerman and Barrett, 1973),
and the relatively high male rates of personality disorder with its possible
common denominator of irresponsible and antisocial behaviour (e.g. Leighton
et al., 1963, especially 266 and 269; Robins, 1966, especially 82–83; Mazer,
1974). The issue is: what is there in the endowments and experiences of men
and women that push them in these different deviant directions? It seems
possible that, where industrialization and modernization produce changes in
sex roles that lead to more rewarding lives for women, we shall see a reduction in
neurotic symptomatology in general and symptoms of depression in parti-

cular among them (Richman, 1977). Where they produce more stress and strain by contrast, we should expect an increase in such symptomatology among women. And, where the roles of women and men become most similar, it would be stunning evidence of the impact of environmental factors on psychiatric condition if their modes of adaptation and maladaptation became more similar than the results of the studies summarized above suggest is possible (Rosenfeld, 1977).

The need for research on these issues is great—on practical as well as theoretical grounds. If we had or could obtain the relevant data on changes in rates of disorder with changes that are occurring in sex roles at different times and in different places, we could be more optimistic than Ginzburg about foretelling and perhaps modifying at least some of the consequences of these changes prior to the time our descendants are confronted with them in the twenty-first and twenty-second centuries!

CONSISTENCY OF SOCIAL CLASS DIFFERENCES

In 1855, a physician and epidemiologist named Edward Jarvis submitted a report to the Governor and Council of the state of Massachusetts on what is probably the most complete and influential attempt to investigate the true prevalence of psychiatric disorder conducted in the nineteenth century (Jarvis, 1971). This investigation took place almost half a century before the Kraepelinian era in psychiatry, and the main nosological distinction that he made was between 'insanity' and 'idiocy'. His most striking finding was that 'the pauper class furnishes, in ratio of its numbers, sixty-four times as many cases of insanity as the independent class' (Jarvis, 1971, 52–53). The basic finding of the highest overall rate of functional psychiatric disorder in the lowest social class has remained remarkably consistent in subsequent epidemiological studies of true prevalence conducted in the United States and elsewhere. Moreover, the inverse relationship with social class holds for important sub-types of disorder. In brief summary, the class findings from the true prevalence studies conducted since the turn of the century are as follows (Dohrenwend and Dohrenwend, 1974b):

—the highest overall rates of functional psychiatric disorder have been found in the lowest social class in 28 out of the 33 studies that report data according to indicators of social class such as occupation, education and income;
—this relationship is strongest in the studies conducted in urban settings or mixed urban and rural settings (19 out of 20 studies);
—the relationship holds for the important sub-types of schizophrenia (5 out of 7 studies) and personality disorder (11 out of 14 studies).

These results have raised and raised again a major substantive issue with very important theoretical and practical implications: are the rates of various types of disorder higher in the lower social classes because of the impact of more stressful environments associated with such class positions; or is it that persons predisposed to or suffering from such disorders are selected into or fail to rise out of lower class groups, which would imply that genetic factors are more important than socio-environmental factors in etiology (cf. Clausen, 1957)? This has come to be known as the social stress–social selection issue and poses the same dilemma of explanation as the one raised with regard to rural–urban differences—namely, is social location a cause or a consequence of preexisting psychiatric disorder? To this day, we do not know the relative importance of social stress in contrast to social selection factors in the rural–urban and social class differences, much less the nature of the interaction of the two processes. While some promising research strategies are being developed to test the issue, it still remains for the present, at least, largely unresolved (cf. Dohrenwend and Dohrenwend, 1969; 1974a; 1974b; Dohrenwend, 1975).

THE ROLE OF STRESSFUL LIFE EVENTS

If socio-environmental factors related to urban location and low social class are important in the etiology of the functional psychiatric disorders, how do they exert their influence on the individual? An appealing hypothesis is that they are associated with exposure to stressful life events. These are occurrences—such as marriage, birth of a first child, loss of a job, divorce, physical illness, and death of a loved one—that alter the usual activities of most people who experience them, thereby requiring adaptation on their part (cf. Dohrenwend and Dohrenwend, 1974c).

A wide variety of correlates of the number and magnitude of life events experienced have been reported in the literature. For example, Holmes and Masuda (1974), in addition to reporting that overall changes in health were related to life events, cited studies showing the following specific correlates: heart disease, fractures, childhood leukemia, pregnancy, beginning of prison term, poor teacher performance, low college grade point average, and football injuries. Among the specific somatic disorders, Hinkle (1974, 38) and Theorell (1974) have focused attention on coronary heart disease, both fatal and non-fatal.

Paykel (1974), Hudgens (1974), and Brown (1974) have added evidence that various types of psychiatric disorder may follow a build-up of life events; specifically acute schizophrenia, depression, suicide attempts, and neurosis. The range of correlates has been expanded to include associations with symptom scales that measure various types of psychological distress rather than outright disorder. Markush and Favero (1974) found that relatively mild symptoms of depression as well as a symptom scale of less specific psychological distress were related to measures of life events. Uhlenhuth and his colleagues

(1974) have reported similar findings. Myers, Lindenthal, and Pepper (1974) have shown with still another measure of psychological distress that symptom scores will fluctuate over time with fluctuations in the nature and number of life events experienced. Such evidence from recent clinical and epidemiological investigations is consistent with Hinkle's conclusion 'that there would probably be no aspect of human growth, development, or disease which would in theory be immune to the influence of the effect of a man's relation to his social and interpersonal environment' (Hinkle, 1974, 10). It would seem that almost any disease or disability may be associated with these events.

SOCIAL CLASS, STRESSFUL WORK EVENTS, AND OTHER STRESSFUL LIFE EVENTS

While direct tests of the role of environmentally induced stress in producing social class differences in rates of psychiatric disorders remain to be conducted (Dohrenwend and Dohrenwend, 1970; Cooper and Marshall, 1976), there is considerable indirect evidence that stress in the form of negative life events is important. For example, a review that we made of the literature (Dohrenwend and Dohrenwend, 1970) suggested that shorter life expectancies in lower class groups imply that more families are likely to be disrupted by premature death of a parent. In addition, the inverse relationship between social class and rate of marital breakdown by divorce or separation indicates that even when both parents survive, the lower-class family is less likely to remain intact. Moreover, some types of physical illness such as cervical cancer are more frequent in the lower class as are accidents and injuries to both adults and children.

Nor do the characteristics of lower-class jobs *per se* appear favourable. For example, there is evidence that paced assembly lines are associated with indications of both mental and physical ill-health as is lack of participation in decision-making about one's job (Cooper and Marshall, 1976). And possibly of central importance, job loss or lay-off is more likely to be the lot of lower-class, hourly wage workers than of the salaried worker from the middle class.

There is considerable reason to give central importance to this last fact. There is, of course, the material deprivation involved in a reduced standard of living. But this is far from the whole story, or, in welfare states, perhaps even the main part of it. As Gross has noted:

At least since the time Freud first described the positive functions of work in the normal healthy personality, many others have pointed to the upsetting effects of lack of work. Christian society has added a grim aspect to the therapeutic view of work by giving the person no choice to do anything else. This attitude appears to be a legacy from Puritanism, with its high evaluation of work and its conception of work as a way of serving God or of proving that one is a member of the elect. (Gross, 1970, 65).

Moreover, there is striking empirical evidence from a study by Brenner (1973) that unemployment may be important in the causation of a variety of serious psychiatric disorders. In this research, Brenner discovered relationships between fluctuations in the economy and mental hospital admissions in New York State over a period of more than 100 years. It is unfortunate, however, that the data were mental hospital admissions rather than true rates of disorder. Thus, as Brenner himself realized, the results may be due to increased intolerance of deviance at times of high unemployment or to use of hospitals as almshouses by unemployed persons rather than to the precipitation of psychiatric symptoms.

The most compelling evidence that stressful life events are important would be provided by verification of the hypothesis that the events or combinations of them will produce psychiatric disorders in previously normal persons. Such tests require a focus not on patients but rather on non-patient groups in the general population. One of the most careful case studies of the health effects of unemployment on such groups was done by Cobb and Kasl (1977). The subjects of their study were 100 male blue-collar workers at two plants that were scheduled to be permanently shut down together with 74 men from two unthreatened plants who were selected as controls. One of the plants facing closure was located in a metropolitan area—a paint-manufacturing plant; the other, involved in manufacturing display fixtures, was located in a rural area. The men facing unemployment were between the ages of 36 and 60, married, and had worked for the company for an average of 17 years. They represented close to 80 per cent of the workers in the plants and were followed from the period of four to seven weeks before the plants were scheduled to close (the period of anticipation) to two years after the plants closed.

Data were collected by public health nurses just before the plants closed, five to seven weeks after the plants had closed, again four to eight months after the plants had closed, again at twelve months, and finally about two years after the plant closing. At each visit, the nurses collected data both on physical and mental health, the latter by means of structured questionnaires that included questions on depressed mood, low self-esteem, anxiety, psychophysiological symptoms, and suspicion. A sub-set of these items were from the Langner (1962) scale and similar screening instruments dating from the Psychosomatic Scale of the Neuropsychiatric Screening Adjunct developed during World War II (Star, 1950). Scales of this kind, although frequently criticized, are widely used as instruments for psychiatric screening (Kasl, Gore, and Cobb, 1975). By design the items in these scales differentiate sharply between samples from the general population and groups of psychiatric patients (e.g. Dohrenwend and

Crandell, 1970) or groups exposed to severe environmental stress such as that experienced by some combat divisions during wartime (Star, 1949).

The median length of unemployment experienced by the men in the closed plants was five weeks. With regard to the psychological outcomes related to this forced unemployment, Cobb and Kasl concluded:

> In the psychological sphere the personal anguish experienced by the men and their families does not seem adequately documented by the statistics of deprivation and change in affective state....Two things probably account for this. First, the measurement techniques for subjective states are imperfect; and second, *the adaptive capacities of man...to reduce the effects are striking. Indeed, in some...[the effects] may have been so transitory as to have been missed.* (Cobb and Kasl, 1977, 180, italics added)

Imperfect as they undoubtedly are, we would nevertheless not expect the measures used in this study to miss altogether any major outbreak of psychiatric disorder that occurred in response to unemployment. The hypothesis about the strong adaptive capacities of these men seems all the more persuasive for this reason. In sum, the findings suggest that relatively brief unemployment, by itself, is not an important etiological factor in persistent psychological distress, much less in severe psychiatric disorder in the general population. If this is so, there is no neat series of bridges from the inverse relationships with social class reported in epidemiological studies, the findings on relations between mental hospital admissions and economic fluctuations in employment rates over long periods of time, and the findings from a careful case study of the psychological impact of unemployment forced by plant shut-down.

We suspect that unemployment contributes strongly to the causation of psychopathology in the general population only when it combines with other stressful events experienced by exposed individuals. The reason is that the growing literature on relations between stressful life events and both physical and psychiatric disorders shows correlations not between single events and such disorders but rather between the number of such events experienced and disorders (e.g. Dohrenwend and Dohrenwend, 1974c; Gunderson and Rahe, 1974). As the investigators in the study of unemployment just described found, 'cases and controls had practically identical mean numbers of events...[therefore] plant closing and job changes did not precipitate other events (e.g., residential moves, wives going to work)...' (Cobb and Kasl, 1977, 111).

HYPOTHESIZED PATHOGENIC TRIAD

If, indeed, stressful life events are pathogenic only when they cumulate, do we have any basis for specifying particular cumulative patterns that are most likely to be pathogenic? Some findings concerning the effects of extreme situations are suggestive.

In an investigation of 2630 soldiers who had broken down during combat in the Normandy campaign during World War II, Swank (1949, 501) estimated that the onset of combat exhaustion occurred even in previously normal soldiers when about 65 per cent of their companions had been killed, wounded, or had otherwise become casualties. The men in this study had been carefully selected for health and ability to cope. As Swank describes them: 'They were of better than average stability and willingness by virtue of the fact that they had passed the various training tests (induction, overseas assignment, battle simulation exercises), had been selected for combat units, and had proved their mettle by remaining in combat varying lengths of time' (p. 476). And while men who were stable prior to combat remained in combat longer without breaking down (pp. 480 and 500), such prior stability did not prevent the eventual onset of combat exhaustion (p. 507).

Nor are the symptoms caused by such situations of extreme stress limited to those most usually characteristic of traumatic war neurosis, combat fatigue, and combat exhaustion. Psychotic symptoms have been observed in the form of what have been called 'three day' psychoses (Kolb, 1973, 438). It is possible, in fact, that such extreme circumstances can play a major role in inducing outright psychotic disorder since, as Paster (1948) found, there is far less evidence of individual predisposing factors in combat soldiers who became psychotic than among soldiers who developed psychotic disorders in less stressful circumstances. It would seem that most of the varied signs and symptoms observed in psychiatric patients in civilian settings have also been observed as reactions to combat (e.g. Kolb, 1973, 436–438). In this sense, war has been indeed 'a laboratory which manufactures psychological dysfunction' (Grinker and Spiegel, 1963, vii).

The extent to which symptomatology and disturbance of functioning produced by such extreme situations in previously normal persons are transient and self-limiting is, however, a matter of controversy (cf. Kinston and Rosser, 1974). Many observers have emphasized the transience of the symptoms (cf. Dohrenwend and Dohrenwend, 1969, 110–130). At the same time, studies in which persons exposed to these extraordinary events have been examined years later have repeatedly found some individuals with more or less severe pathology that apparently began at the time the stressful experience occurred (cf. Kinston and Rosser, 1974, 445–448). Certainly at the extreme of exposure to the brutalities of Nazi concentration camps, there is strong evidence that not only does severe stress-induced psychopathology persist in some survivors (Eitinger, 1964), but also that the survivors are more prone to physical illness and early death (Eitinger, 1973).

Natural and man-made disasters are, fortunately, rare occurrences whose devastating effects are limited to relatively small populations of exposed persons. It is, nevertheless, possible to reason by analogy ways in which more ordinary stressful life events would induce an approximation of the pathogenic conditions involved in extreme situations such as prolonged exposure to heavy combat in wartime or incarceration in concentration camps (cf. Dohrenwend and Dohrenwend, 1978). Consider, for example, that prolonged combat involves unanticipated events that are outside the control of the individual—such as loss of comrades; it involves the individual's physical exhaustion; and it deprives him of the social support of his comrades as the casualty rate rises. Similarly, survivors have reported that life in Nazi concentration camps involved continual exposure to unanticipated events over which the prisoner had no control (Eitinger, 1964; 130) and, for most prisoners, physical exhaustion. Furthermore, the most severe and persistent pathological effects were found in ex-prisoners who were deprived of social support both during imprisonment and after their release by dint of the loss of their families and the destruction of their pre-war homes (Eitinger, 1964, 19–22).

In civil life events such as unexpected loss of loved ones, exhausting physical illness or injury, and, say, migration to a new community with accompanying disruption of usual social supports, if they occur in close proximity to one another, may induce stressful circumstances similar in many important respects to those found in extreme situations. Here, we hypothesize, the cumulation of events would produce psychopathology in most previously normal persons.

If this triad describes the set of life events that is necessary to produce pathology in previously normal individuals, it might help to reconcile some of the seemingly inconsistent results that have been obtained in studies of the effects of work-related stress in industrialized societies. It suggests the hypothesis that workers are most likely to suffer stress-induced changes in health when they can neither anticipate nor control events on their job, such as changes in procedures, when the job is physically arduous, and when they are forced to emigrate from their home town or country in order to obtain work.

Such a complex of work conditions is frequently the lot of rural migrants to urban centres or migrants from countries with relatively little industrial development to highly industrialized countries. These workers typically must take the most menial jobs in factory and service industries that require them to follow others' orders and do physically arduous work, and often must leave family and friends behind at home. They are also most vulnerable to sudden lay-offs and least likely to be able to secure a new job in a depressed economy.

IMPLICATION OF THE TRIAD HYPOTHESIS

Relatively high rates of stress-induced psychological disorders in rural or foreign immigrant workers would be consistent with the observation that, overall, the prevalence of these disorders is greatest in the lowest class. It is pertinent to note here that in his nineteenth-century study of the epidemiology of mental illness in Massachusetts Jarvis (1971) not only reported that the highest rate was to be found in the pauper class but also noted that this class consisted disproportionately of recent Irish immigrants. The triad hypothesis, which focuses attention on immigrant workers, is also consistent with the reported association of increases in mental hospital admissions with economic depression. By dint of their vulnerability to unemployment and lack of social supports, immigrant workers might be institutionalized for mental disorders in disproportionate numbers during an economic depression. Finally, the conditions faced by immigrant workers contrast sharply with those of the native American workers with intact families who were able, Cobb and Kasl found, to endure temporary unemployment without developing mental illness.

Several of the factors studied by researchers more specifically concerned with work-related sources of stress that are hardly limited to lower-class occupations seem to us to be especially likely to promote and/or exacerbate one or more elements in the hypothesized pathogenic triad at any class level in modern, industrial societies. Two of these are objective sources of 'role ambiguity' (Kahn et al., 1964, especially 75–77) and lack of worker control over the job and its performance (Frankenhaeuser, 1971; Gardell, 1971). Other things being constant, these factors would be expected to decrease ability to anticipate the occurrence of stressful events and increase the likelihood that such occurrence was experienced as outside the control of the individual. Similarly, work overload or underload (Frankenhaeuser, 1971), to the extent that it exhausts the worker physically, would tend to exacerbate the impact of other stressful life events he or she experienced. And finally, factors that promote role conflict in industrial organizations (Kahn et al., 1964) would tend to increase the impact of stressful work events and other stressful life events by disrupting work-related networks of social support.

IN CONCLUSION

We have, then, examined what we have learned from our studies of socio-environmental factors, stress, and psychiatric disorders for its relevance to the themes of this symposium in general and to this particular session on the effects of a changing labour market. Of special importance in providing the wider context for our analysis have been findings from epidemiological studies of relations between various types of psychiatric disorders and such important demographic variables as sex, social class, and urban in contrast with rural location.

As we pointed out, these relationships have raised more questions about the role of environmentally induced stress in the functional psychiatric disorders than they have answered. Many of these questions focus on the part played by stressful life events.

In this paper, we have considered some of these questions as they apply to relations between stressful work events, other stressful life events, and psychiatric disorders. In the process, our point of departure was a hypothesized pathogenic triad of certain combinations of events occurring simultaneously or within a relatively brief interval of time. This triad consists of physical illness or injury that exhausts the individual physically, other fateful loss events the occurrence of which is both unanticipated and outside the individual's control, and additional events that disrupt his or her social supports. We have further hypothesized that certain specifically work-related events and conditions such as role ambiguity, lack of control over job, work overload and underload, and role conflict would be highly likely to promote one or more of the elements of this triad.

If we are right about how stressful circumstances related to work may contribute to the development of the pathogenic triad, then it would be important to reduce the impact of such work-related factors on grounds of health as well as other political and humanitarian considerations wherever they are found—whether among immigrant workers at the bottom of the industrial hierarchy or among travelling executives forced by competitive conditions to deal with repeated unpredictable crises during overly long workdays in unfamiliar settings; whether among working men or among working women.

REFERENCES

Brenner, M. H. (1973). *Mental Illness and the Economy*, Harvard University Press, Cambridge, Mass.

Brown, G. W. (1974). Meaning, measurement, and stress of life events, in *Stressful Life Events: Their Nature and Effects*, ed. B. S. Dohrenwend and B. P. Dohrenwend, Wiley, New York.

Carlestam, G. (1971). The individual, the city and stress, in *Society Stress and Disease, Volume 1: The Psychosocial Environment and Psychosomatic Diseases*, ed. L. Levi, Oxford University Press, New York, 134–147.

Clausen, J. A. (1957). The ecology of mental disorders, *Symposium on Preventive and Social Psychiatry* (sponsors, Walter Reed Army Institute of Research, Walter Reed Army Medical Center, and the National Research Council), US Government Printing Office, Washington, DC, 97–108.

Cobb, S., and Kasl, S. V. (1977). *Termination: The Consequences of Job Loss*, US Department of Health, Education, and Welfare (DHEW) (NIOSH), Publication No. 77–224.

Cooper, C. L., and Marshall, J. (1976). Occupational sources of stress: A review of the literature relating to coronary heart disease and mental ill health, *J. of Occupational Psychology*, **49**, 11–28.

Dohrenwend, B. P. (1975). Sociocultural and social-psychological factors in the genesis of mental disorders. *J. of Health and Social Behavior*, **16**, 365–392.

Dohrenwend, B. P., and Crandell (1970). Psychiatric symptoms in community, clinic, and mental hospital groups, *Amer. J. Psychiat.*, **126**, 1611–1621.

Dohrenwend, B. P., and Dohrenwend, B. S. (1969). *Social Status and Psychological Disorder: A Causal Inquiry*, Wiley, New York.

Dohrenwend, B. P., and Dohrenwend, B.S. (1974a). Psychiatric disorders in urban settings, in *American Handbook of Psychiatry, Volume II: Child and Adolescent Psychiatry*, ed.-in-chief, S. Ariati; ed. G. Caplan, Basic Books, New York, 427–447.

Dohrenwend, B. P., and Dohrenwend, B. S. (1974b). Social and cultural influences on psychopathology, *Annual Review of Psychology*, 25, 417–452.

Dohrenwend, B. P., and Dohrenwend, B. S. (1976). Sex differences and psychiatric disorders, *Amer. J. of Sociology*, 81, 1447–1454.

Dohrenwend, B. S., and Dohrenwend, B. P. (1970). Class and race as status related sources of stress, in *Social Stress*, ed. S. Levine and N. Scotch, Aldine, Chicago, 11–140.

Dohrenwend, B. S., and Dohrenwend, B. P. (1974c). *Stressful Life Events: Their Nature and Effects*, Wiley, New York.

Dohrenwend, B. S., and Dohrenwend, B. P. (1978). Some issues in research on stressful life events, *J. of Nervous and Mental Disease*, 166, 7–15.

Eitinger, L. (1964). *Concentration Camp Survivors in Norway and Israel*, Allen & Unwin, London.

Eitinger, L. (1973). A follow-up of the Norwegian concentration camp survivors mortality, *Israel Annals of Psychiatry and Related Disciplined*, 11, 199–209.

Frank, L. K. (1936). Society as the patient, *Amer. J. of Sociology*, 42, 335–344.

Frankenhaeuser, M. (1971). Experimental approaches to the study of human behavior as related to neuroendocrine functions, in *Society, Stress and Disease, Volume 1: The Psychosocial Environment and Psychosomatic Diseases*, ed. L. Levi, Oxford University Press, New York, 22–35.

Gardell, B. (1971). Alienation and mental health in the modern industrial environment, in *Society, Stress and Disease, Volume 1: The Psychosocial Environment and Psychosomatic Diseases*, ed. L. Levi, Oxford University Press, New York, 148–180.

Goldhamer, H., and Marshall, A. W. (1953). *Psychosis and Civilization: Two Studies in the Frequency of Mental Disease*, Free Press, New York.

Gove, W. R., and Tudor, J. F. (1973). Adult sex roles and mental illness, *Amer. J. of Sociology*, 78, 812–835.

Grinker, R. R., and Spiegel, J. P. (1963). *Men Under Stress*, McGraw-Hill, New York.

Gross, E. (1970). Work, organization and stress, in *Social Stress*, ed. S. Levine and N. A. Scotch, Aldine, Chicago, 54–110.

Gunderson, E.K.E., and Rahe, R.H. (1974). *Life Stress and Illness*, Charles C. Thomas, Springfield, Ill.

Hinkle, L. E., Jr (1974). The effect of exposure to culture change, social change, and changes in interpersonal relationships on health, in *Stressful Life Events: Their Nature and Effects*, ed. B. S. Dohrenwend and B. P. Dohrenwend, Wiley, New York.

Holmes, T. H., and Masuda, M. (1974). Life change and illness susceptibility, in *Stressful Life Events: Their Nature and Effects*, ed. B. S. Dohrenwend and B. P. Dohrenwend, Wiley, New York, 45–72.

Hudgens, R. W. (1974). Personal catastrophe and depression: A consideration of the subject with respect to medically ill adolescents, and a requiem for retrospective life-event studies, in *Stressful Life Events: Their Nature and Effects*, B. S. Dohrenwend and B. P. Dohrenwend, Wiley, New York.

Jarvis, E. (ed.) (1971). *Insanity and Idiocy in Massachusetts: Report of the Commission on Lunacy, 1855*, Harvard University Press, Cambridge, Mass.

Kahn, R. L., Wolfe, D. M., Quinn, R. P., Snoek, J. D., and Rosenthal, R. A. (1964). *Organizational Stress: Studies in Role Conflict and Ambiguity*, Wiley, New York.

Kasl, S. V., Gore, S., and Cobb, S. (1975). The experience of losing a job: Reported changes in health, symptoms and illness behavior, *Psychosomatic Medicine*, 37, 106–122.

Kinston, W., and Rosser, R. (1974). Disaster: Effects on mental and physical state, *J. of Psychosomatic Research*, 18, 437–456.

Klerman, G. L., and Barrett, J. E. (1973). The affective disorders: Clinical and epidemiological aspects, in *Lithium: Its Role in Psychiatric Research and Treatment*, ed. S. Gershon and B. Shropsin, Plenum, New York, 201–236.

Kolb, L. C. (1973). The psychiatrist as explorer, *Proceedings of the V World Congress of Psychiatry, Mexico, DF,* Excerpta Medica International Congress Series No. 273, Amsterdam.

Langner, T. S. (1962). A twenty-two item screening score of psychiatric symptoms indicating impairment, *J. of Health and Social Behavior,* **3,** 269–276.

Leighton, D. C., Harding, J. S., Macklin, D. B., Macmillan, A. M., and Leighton, A. H. (1963). *The Character of Danger,* Basic Books, New York.

Markush, R. E., and Favero, R. V. (1974). Epidemiologic assessment of stressful life events, depressed mood, and psychophysiological symptoms—A preliminary report, in *Stressful Life Events: Their Nature and Effects,* ed. B. S. Dohrenwend and B. P. Dohrenwend, Wiley, New York.

Mazer, M. (1974). People in predicament: A study in psychiatric and psychosocial epidemiology, *Social Psychiatry,* **9,** 85–90.

Mott, R. D., and Roemer, M. I. (1948). *Rural Health and Medical Care,* McGraw-Hill, New York.

Myers, J. K., Lindenthal, J. J., and Pepper, M. P. (1974). Social class, life events, and psychiatric symptoms: A longitudinal study, in *Stressful Life Events: Their Nature and Effects,* ed. B. S. Dohrenwend and B. P. Dohrenwend, Wiley, New York.

New York Times (1976). 12 September.

Paster, S. (1948). Psychotic reactions among soldiers of World War II, *J of Nervous and Mental Disease,* **108,** 54–66.

Paykel, E. S. (1974). Life stress and psychiatric disorder: Application of the clinical approach, in *Stressful Life Events: Their Nature and Effects,* ed. B. S. Dohrenwend and B. P. Dohrenwend, Wiley, New York.

Paugh, T. F., and MacMahon, B. (1962). *Epidemiological Findings in U.S. Mental Hospital Data,* Little Brown, Boston, Mass.

Richman, J. (1977). Psychological and psychophysiological distress in employed women and housewives: Class, age and ethnic differences, PhD dissertation, Columbia University.

Robins, L. N. (1966). *Deviant Children Grown Up,* Williams & Wilkins, Baltimore, Md.

Rosenfeld, S. (1977). Sex role polarization and mental health: An exploratory study, PhD dissertation, University of Texas at Austin.

Silverman, C. (1968). *The Epidemiology of Depression,* Johns Hopkins Press, Baltimore, Md.

Star, S. A. (1949). Psychoneurotic symptoms in the army, in *Studies in Social Psychology in World War II. The American Soldier: Combat and Its Aftermath,* ed. S. A. Stoufer, L. Guttman, E. A. Suchman, P. F. Lazarsfeld, S. A. Star, and J. A. Clausen, Princeton University Press, Princeton, NJ, 411–455.

Star, S. A. (1950). The screening of psychoneurotics in the army: Technical development of tests, in *Measurement and Prediction,* ed. S. A. Stoufer, L. Guttman, E. A. Suchman, P. F. Lazarsfeld, S. A. Star, and J. A. Clausen, Princeton University Press, Princeton, NJ, 486–547.

Swank, R. L. (1949). Combat exhaustion, *J. of Nervous and Mental Disease,* **109,** 475–508.

Theorell, T. (1974). Life events before and after the onset of a premature myocardial infarction, in *Stressful Life Events: Their Nature and Effects,* ed. B. S. Dohrenwend and B. P. Dohrenwend, Wiley, New York.

Uhlenhuth, E., Lipman, R. S., Balter, M. B., and Stern, M. (1974). Symptom intensity and life stress in the city, *Archives of General Psychiatry,* **31,** 759–764.

Working Life
Edited by B. Gardell and G. Johansson
© 1981 John Wiley & Sons Ltd

Changing Labour Markets and Labour Market Policy

PETER B. DOERINGER

INTRODUCTION

The problem of changing labour markets can be usefully understood in terms of different theories of economic change. The first is the theory of industrialization, or what is more commonly known as the process of economic development. Economic development involves the transformation of a traditional society into a modern society. Traditional society is based on rural or village forms of social and economic organization, derives its income largely from agrarian production and relies heavily on informal sources of income. The modern economy is organized primarily around urban areas and is dominated by formally structured enterprises which generate *wage* income.

According to this view, all societies start out as essentially agrarian in nature and evolve into modern economies through ever-increasing investments in capital equipment and in education and training. Economies containing both modern and traditional sectors are described as 'dual'. In advanced economies, dualism is supposed to disappear.

The second theory of economic change is less a theory of economic development than a theory of change in economic systems. For this theory, economic development is about the process of creation of an industrial class structure—a class of workers who will be employed in a modern society and a class of capitalists who will invest in it and seek to expand their profits through the control over capital and the workforce. Economic change occurs through a revolution in which work organized according to the rules of play of capitalism is replaced by work organized to suit the objectives of the working class.

This paper is concerned more with the former type of transformation and change in labour markets.

TRANSFORMATION AND STRUCTURAL CHANGE IN ECONOMIC DEVELOPMENT

The change in labour markets associated with industrialization creates both social problems and social benefits. Industrialization inevitably requires a change in working life and accepting change is often painful. The faster the rate of development and the more radical its departure from the ways of the past, the larger the problems created by change.

The dislocations demanded by economic development are several: relocations of population from rural to urban areas, dramatic changes in the scheduling of work and the skills and tasks involved as the structure of production changes, self-employment is replaced by managed employment, work groups grow in size, and the division of labour within the family changes. With these changes come the reactions to change, the most severe being sabotage, strikes, and labour unrest. Less dramatic, but important, are the feeling of personal alienation, changes in the fabric of family life, and the growing inequality of income between those who work in the modern sector and those who remain in traditional forms of employment (Kerr et al., 1960).

The benefits are normally seen in terms of growing income, both for individuals and for society. Those employed in the modern sector clearly experience more affluence; those unemployed, but attached to the modern sector, also experience certain benefits of modern life; even those remaining in rural areas can expect improvements in medical care, nutrition, agricultural methods, and so forth. As the modern sector expands, the theory is that both the direct and indirect benefits will be more widely distributed and that the problems associated with economic transformation will gradually disappear.

This utopian view of change, of course, has its obvious limitations. The benefits of growth do not automatically spread to all corners of society (Hirschman and Rothschild, 1973). Even those working in the modern sector who seemingly have the most to benefit from this process of development at any point in time are often dissatisfied with their conditions. One need only look at the history of rebellion against modernity during the Industrial Revolution—and to more modern periods of labour unrest, worker alienation, concern with worker control and participation in employment decisions, and persistent conflicts over issues of income inequality and inequity—to find signs that economic development need not ultimately remove social ills.

CHANGE IN LABOUR MARKET PROCESSES

What have been the specific changes in labour market processes as a result of industrialization? Traditional economies have relatively simple labour markets. Much work is unpaid and contained within the family unit. Markets for such labour tend to be casual.

Labour markets in the modern sector appear to be very different. In industrialized economies there has been a substantial change in the structure of employment by occupation and by industry (Harbison and Myers, 1964). By occupation there has clearly been a decline in agricultural employment, in self-employment, in unpaid family labour, and in low-skilled and casual labour. Within the modern sector, professional, technical, managerial and middle-skilled, white-collar occupations have been the areas of growth. There have been significant increases in *per capita* income, education and capital investment have risen substantially, and inequality has declined, although less substantially than these other indicators of economic progress. In short, one can look at the data and conclude that the dual economy is being replaced by the modern economy and that increasing economic benefits are being conferred upon the labour force. The inference often drawn from this data is that with the disappearance of the traditional sector, inequality based on anything other than differences in ability, education, and personal preference will be eliminated, work will become more rewarding, and leisure opportunities will increase (Bell, 1973).

There is, however, a more complex view of the change in labour markets which presents a less optimistic picture. Within the framework of the modern economy, there are signs that a new dualism is emerging. While many individuals hold jobs in the *primary sector* that are rewarding and provide meaningful work careers, the coming of the meritocratic age when every individual's employment is based upon his abilities and preferences is not in fact borne out. Certain workforce groups consistently are employed in the *secondary sector* of 'dead end' jobs that do not provide careers (Doeringer and Piore, 1971). As a general rule, youth, females, certain ethnic minorities, and displaced older workers all seem to work in secondary jobs that are unpleasant, often low paid, sometimes unstable and, most important, provide little training or experience or opportunity for economic advancement.

For most male youth this process of entrapment in 'dead end' work is a temporary phenomenon. The average young male worker graduates from unskilled 'dead end' employment to transitional employment, often in a small firm or in an apprenticeship programme providing a supportive work environment with a learning and training process, and then graduates again to adult, career employment. For the other groups, however, modern sector employment is less connected with career advancement than with 'dead end' work analogous to that available in the traditional sector (Osterman, 1978; Wirtz, 1975).

THE ORIGINS OF MODERN DUALISM

Dualism, or more accurately labour market segmentation, presents a view of the labour market different from that of conventional economic analysis. In the ideal labour market of traditional economics everyone who wants to work at prevailing wage rates is employed. There is no surplus or shortage of labour in this system. Everyone's wage rate is determined by a process of supply and demand—the active interplay between employers looking for the best workers and workers looking for the most rewarding jobs. Every worker is in his or her 'rightful place'. 'Rightful place' is defined as every worker receiving what he or she is worth. Highly skilled, highly productive workers get paid more; less skilled, less productive workers get paid less.

According to this view, a worker's skills may be easily carried from place to place and differences in pay reflect differences in ability, motivation, skill, and residential location. Ability is thought to be an inherited trait and motivation arises out of social processes. Skill and location are thought to be determined by rational 'investments' rewarded in the labour market by higher pay. A worker, for example, would add to his skills if he discovered the cost of acquiring new skills was outweighed by the higher earnings that would result (Mincer, 1974).

In this kind of a 'rightful place' theory, if workers were underpaid, or under-educated, they would take steps to correct their economic situation. If workers were overpaid or underproductive, employers would lower their wages or replace them with other workers until a parity between pay and productivity was established. Under this system, 'careers' are determined by worker invest-ments. Workers may invest in more education or learn through on-the-job experience and therefore advance. There may also be 'dead end' workers who make no further investment in their own education, elect not to relocate, prefer leisure to employment, or do not become wiser through experience.

In contrast, the dual or segmented labour market view concedes that certain kinds of labour markets operate according to such 'rightful place' theory. The market for professional athletes, for artists and musicians, for unskilled labour, for entrepreneurs, and for various kinds of professionals may well be governed by these principles. But more often there are other kinds of markets in which the action of individuals and their investment in education or training or relocation may have very little to do with explaining their earnings or their career paths. In such markets the competition for jobs and workers may be far less influential in determining pay and career than the exercise of economic and political power through bargaining or legislative processes (Doeringer and Piore, 1971; Walton and McKersie, 1965).

The structure of the labour market is determined by a number of factors. There is the 'economic' market in which the technology of plant and equipment provides the options within which other structuring influences operate. Part of this market conventionally rewards ability, motivation, and training. It also contains something which economists call 'randomness', but which is known more commonly as 'luck' (Jenks, 1972).

But institutional sources of structure are also key in shaping the primary sector of the modern economy and in distributing employment opportunities between the primary and the secondary or peripheral sector of the dual eco-nomy.

In agrarian societies, labour market institutions—unions, corporations, governmental agencies—rarely exist. The rise of the modern economy, however, is associated with institutionalization of the labour market. It is these insti-tutions that permit workers to shelter themselves against the forces of supply and demand. The ability to erect such shelters is key to the realization by both workers and employers of many of their labour market objectives, both economic and distributional (Freedman, 1976).

Much of the success of either a corporation or a bureaucracy depends on its ability to control its environment. This control in turn relates on the one hand to sources of revenue, either from the sale of products or through legislative processes, and, on the other hand, the purchase of factors—the acquisition of labour, capital, and materials (Galbraith, 1967; Chandler, 1962). Part of controlling the environment involves internalizing, where possible, the supply of labour so that the competitive market need not be relied upon as a source of labour. This encourages an organization of work in which people are hired for entry level jobs and developed within their organization to the maximum extent possible. When the nexus is broken between the internal and external market, managerial decisions can then determine who gets hired, trained, and advanced.

Once the discretion to supplant market forces (and luck) is established, workers, too, will wish to exercise influence over the internal labour market. Here the role of workers' organizations becomes important, either through politics or bargaining, in determining wages, the allocation of work, and working conditions. Beyond the issues of structuring of work and wages, however, both employers and unions have a wider interest in the stability and prosperity of their internal labour markets. The prosperous corporation does not lay off workers and has a greater ability to pay high wages and to provide career opportunities. This encourages both employers and unions not only to look inwards for sources of prosperity, but also to turn outwards to seek protection from the market for their goods and services. This protection may take the form of government subsidies, monopolistic arrangements safeguarding market shares, or international trade protection. This search for economic shelter is pursued both through economic and political power.

The third factor in the development of labour market dualism is connected with what might be broadly described as social processes. For example, the boom in births following the end of World War II has flooded the labour market with young workers, thereby temporarily expanding the supply of labour for traditionally 'dead end' jobs. As this group of workers ages, the effect of the declining birth rate tends to be felt in the labour market. There may be pressures to reorganize the secondary sector to enhance work opportunities. There may also be new pressures from adult workers to reorganize career patterns in favour of a rapid advancement of young adults over older workers. Similar conflicts may arise between the sexes and among different ethnic groups as the demographic composition of the labour force changes. Sometimes these conflicts are resolved through labour market change. At other times, there may be reliance on changes in social welfare programs—welfare, pension plans, unemployment insurance, and the like.

The fourth factor is discrimination. We find, for example, in most countries, a clear pattern of assignment of women or ethnic minorities to 'dead end' employment opportunities. There are attempts to reconcile this consignment with prevailing philosophies of meritocracy. Minorities are said to have poor attitudes; women are said to have patterns of labour market behaviour connected with child-rearing. But there is also ample evidence that discrimination and prejudice are major factors in assigning workers to 'dead end' jobs in the modern sector. In this sense, 'rightful place' for some groups of workers may be socially defined in terms of economic and social status.

The fifth factor pertains to what I would broadly describe as the macroeconomic policies followed by government with respect to economic stability, growth, and unemployment. Part of the development of the primary sector depends upon stability and continuity of employment. Production and, therefore, employment, are often divided into stable and unstable portions. The stable portion is usually reserved for the large corporation, the unstable, uncertain portion is usually transferred to the secondary sector (Piore, 1973). Macro policies which put pressure on an economy to use its resources fully to expand along a stable path are optimal for encouraging the growth of primary employment in the modern sector (Okun, 1973). Fiscal policies, too, can affect market structure as evidenced by the growth of 'black work' lodged largely in the secondary sector.

WHY DOESN'T DUALISM DISAPPEAR?

Nothing in the previous description is necessarily an obstacle to the elimination of secondary employment. Market forces, technological change, market shelters, social forces, and so forth, are as consistent with a growing primary sector as they are with dualism. Yet dualism shows considerable persistence.

This persistence stems from a number of sources. Perhaps the most fundamental cause is that no advanced economy has successfully resolved the conflicting goals of full employment and relative price stability. Time after time governments deliberately induce business fluctuations in order to control inflation. Subsequently they try to return to a path of full employment and rapid growth. This alteration between policy goals introduces instability into the economy, instability which the primary sector seeks to export to the secondary sector or to other economies.

Second is the lure of jobs and of low-cost goods and services. Many countries follow deliberate policies of sustaining or supporting low-paid, labour intensive work because there are political pressures either to hold on to jobs without regard for their quality or because they result in goods and services being provided at a low cost. Immigration policy and other devices for sustaining the supply of low-skilled, low-paid labour in a country are the most common devices used to sustain 'dead end' employment. The secondary sector requires generation after generation of workers willing to work for low pay. Yet experience shows that the second generation of the secondary workforce is far less willing to accept such work and must be continually replaced.

The third feature is the pressure for institutional survival in the face of structural change. While many governments have programmes to ease the dislocations of labour and capital in declining companies and industries, no government has adopted an effective programme for *institutional* survival. Many of the political problems associated with declining industries and declining regions result from institutions seeking to survive. Regardless of how well workers' economic needs are taken care of, they still prefer their 'rightful job'. Moreover, unions do not willingly yield their institutional position. Similar arguments can apply to employers who are reluctant to lose their institutional position in the local economy. Institutional sheltering may work to the detriment of other segments of the workforce or shelters may defend a company or sector of the economy against forces which would bring about a justifiable decline of that sector (Johnston, 1963).

Finally, there is the issue of discrimination. Despite pressure from economic competition and from public policy to end discrimination in employment, discrimination remains a persistent force in modern labour markets.

POLICIES FOR CHANGING LABOUR MARKETS

What are the implications of modern dualism for labour market policy? Society is not a passive passenger in the economic development process. As problems emerge, whether they be strikes, or bad working conditions, or inequality in income or power, the set of institutions associated with modern economy—the corporation, the trade union, the government agency—all search for policies to ease the strain of dislocation. Sometimes these are policies of governments which seek to combat problems facing broad segments of society. Sometimes these are actions of managers seeking to improve morale or productivity or to reduce labour turnover. Sometimes these are actions by trade unions to improve wages and working conditions. Regardless of the source of policy initiative, however, all are responsive to the problems created by change. These policies may either reinforce or ameliorate dualism.

There are three areas of intervention. First is the range of policies invented and fostered in Sweden under the title of active manpower policy. Manpower policy assumes that economic development, particularly when based upon a commitment to strong growth and full employment, produces structural imbalances as a by-product. The solution has been two-fold: to provide a range of training and labour relocation subsidies and substantial income maintenance arrangements to sustain the economic well-being of displaced workers. These policies have been supplemented by temporary employment programmes and by regional development programmes to try to operate on the demand side of the labour market as well (Rehn, 1973).

The second class of policies has involved regulation, sometimes of wages but more often of working standards and working conditions. The third area has involved policies towards collective bargaining and the representation of workers by collective organizations.

Of these three policies, the labour market and income maintenance policy is most clearly based on the view of the competitive market. Indeed, the word 'transparency' is often used to describe the ideal labour market. It is a market without segments, a market without barriers, a market in which everyone is in his competitive 'rightful place' and in which the role of manpower policy is to encourage and advocate transparency whenever and wherever possible. This was the principle thrust of Sweden's active manpower policy for many years.

The second approach, the regulation of the labour market, obviously reflects the view that the benefits of transparency, of everyone being in their 'rightful place', are either unevenly spread throughout the economy or, if evenly spread, do not meet socially acceptable standards. As a result, the errors of the market are corrected through the force of public policy.

The final approach, the industrial relations approach, is directed at the creation of institutions and embodies the notion of countervailing power. In a capitalist system, employers have a tremendous control over the economic destiny of the labour force that needs to be offset by collective action by the workers (Doeringer, 1980).

These approaches have failed to end dualism. The major shortcomings have been their lack of coordination and their failure to recognize the inescapable link between labour market institutions and labour market dualism.

Manpower policy says nothing about institutions. It is a policy basically directed at individuals and at the 'rightful place' theory. It is not responsive to the need for institutional survival. In a country like Sweden, institutional survival may be of less political concern. The employers who are affected by structural change may have little political claim to survival. Also, in a country like Sweden, with virtually all of its workforce unionized and the major proportion in a single union, institutional survival on the labour side is not threatened by worker dislocation. This, however, is a unique situation among industrialized countries. And, even in Sweden, high levels of unemployment may begin to undermine the tolerance for market transparency.

The regulatory approach to labour market policy also neglects institutions. Indeed, it develops rules independent of the configuration of institutions.

The industrial relations approach is the only one which seeks to foster institutional growth and development. However, the rules of industrial relations are in most countries divorced from questions of labour market policy. Industrial relations is about collective bargaining, and wages, and working conditions. Labour market policy is about training and relocation.

The challenge for labour market policy is to find ways of recognizing the strength of institutions in the labour market, recognizing that the forces that create shelters can be used constructively, not only for the purposes of sheltered workers and employers but also for the purposes of society itself. Institutions are neither good nor bad in the labour market, but they are a fact of life. Policy must accept this fact of life and place it much more squarely in the domain of public policy. Not only is such an approach likely to be able to deal with problems of dualism, it is also likely to provide the vehicle for resolving the conflict between inflation and unemployment.

Most of the important labour market decisions: the types of jobs that exist, the career patterns, the pay, the training, the hiring and assignment process, are made by employers' and workers' organizations. Where employers and workers are in agreement they can be a major force in shaping the outcomes of macro policy as well. The key, then, to finding new policy directions is to harness these institutions to the goals of public policy.

In many countries, small experiments are being tried in tripartite collaboration among labour, business, and government to improve economic performance. Whether the issue is incomes policy, regulatory policy, or production bottlenecks, this approach is building a new institutional capability to reconcile social conflict and to devise new solutions to social problems. The changing labour market provides an ideal arena for extending this experimentation in a search for new policies and new procedures for improving economic performance.

REFERENCES

Bell, Daniel (1973). *The Coming of Post-Industrial Society: A Venture In Social Forecasting*, Basic Books, New York.

Chandler, Alfred D. (1962). *Strategy and Structure: Chapters in the History of the Industrial Enterprise*, MIT Press, Cambridge, Mass.

Doeringer, Peter B. (ed.) (1980). *Industrial Relations in International Perspective: Essays in Research and Policy*, Macmillan, London.

Doeringer, Peter B., and Piore, Michael J. (1971). *Internal Labor Markets and Manpower Analysis*, D.C. Heath, Lexington, Mass.

Freedman, Marcia (1976). *Labor Markets: Segments and Shelters*, Allanheld, Osmun, Montclair, NJ.

Galbraith, John K. (1967). *The New Industrial State*, Houghton Mifflin, Boston, Mass.

Harbison, Frederick H., and Myers, Charles A. (1964). *Education, Manpower, and Economic Growth: Strategies of Human Resource Development*, McGraw-Hill, New York.

Hirschman, Albert O., and Rothschild, Michael (1973). Changing tolerance for inequality in development, *Quarterly Journal of Economics*, November 544–566.

Jenks, Christopher (1972). *Inequality*, Basic Books, New York.

Johnston, T. L. (1963). *Economic Expansion and Structural Change: A Trade Union Manifesto*, Allen & Unwin, London.

Kerr, Clark, Dunlop, J. T., Harbison, F., and Myers, C. A. (1960). *Industrialism and Industrial Man*, Harvard University Press, Cambridge, Mass.

Mincer, Jacob (1974). *Schooling, Earnings, and Experience*, Columbia University Press, New York.

Okun, Arthur (1973). Upward mobility in a high-pressure economy, *Brookings Papers on Economic Activity*, 1.

Osterman, Paul (1978). Youth work and unemployment, *Challenge*, May–June, 65–69.
Piore, Michael J. (1973). On the technological foundations of economic dualism, Mimeo, MIT Economics Department Working Paper, 110, May.
Rehn, Gösta (1973). Manpower policy as an instrument of national economic policy, *Manpower Policy, Perceptives and Prospects*, ed. Seymour L. Wolfbein, Temple University, Philadelphia, Pa.
Walton, Richard E., and McKersie, Robert B. (1965). *A Behavioral Theory of Labor Negotiations*, McGraw-Hill, New York.
Wirtz, W. Willard (1975). *The Boundless Resource: A Prospectus for an Education—Work Policy*, New Republic Book Co., Washington, D.C.

Working Life
Edited by B. Gardell and G. Johansson
© 1981 John Wiley & Sons Ltd

Economic and Social Effects of Labour Mobility

BENGT G. RUNDBLAD

INTRODUCTION

During the 1960s poverty was rediscovered in the affluent countries of the industrialized part of the world. In the US, Michael Harrington's book *The Other America. Poverty in the United States* was published in 1962, and in 1964 President Johnson started the war on poverty. Similar developments followed in other countries, and in Sweden the government appointed a special low-income commission in 1965. One of the tasks of this commission was to carry out a nationwide Level of Living Survey, which included not only the level of income of different strata in the Swedish population but also their situation with regard to, for example, health, housing, education, employment, and working conditions.

In the previous chapter, 'Changing labour markets and labour market policy,' Peter B. Doeringer has given an explanation of the existence of poverty, or at least of bad living conditions in the midst of the affluence of the industrialized nations. His explanation is in terms of the dualism or segmentation of the labour market in connection with industrialization. Many individuals get jobs in the *primary sector* that are rewarding and provide meaningful work careers, while others end up in the *secondary sector* of 'dead end' jobs that do not provide careers. He also states that, as a general rule, youth, females, certain ethnic minorities, and displaced older workers seem to work in secondary jobs that are unpleasant, often low paid, and sometimes unstable. For most male youth this entrapment in the secondary sector is a temporary phenomenon, but for the others there is little way out. Hans Berglind, in his chapter '*Age and marginality in the Swedish labour market*', adds to this analysis by describing how the transformation of the labour market makes it increasingly difficult for middle-aged and older workers to hold any jobs at all. This increasing redundancy for older groups in the Swedish labour market holds true for both men and women above the age of 45, but more so for men.

In the following, an attempt will be made to add to the analysis by Doeringer and Berglind by reporting some results from Swedish studies of how the change in labour markets associated with industrialization affects individuals. The studies deal with internal migration and workers affected by the shut-down of their former place of work, i.e. different forms of labour mobility.

GEOGRAPHICAL MOBILITY—ECONOMIC AND SOCIAL EFFECTS

In the middle of the 1960s the Department of Sociology in Gothenburg carried out a study of the adjustment of workers moving to an expanding labour market. (Johansson, Olsson, and Rundblad, 1969). The study was designed as a panel study with interviews, first, one month after the subjects' arrival in Gothenburg, and then seven months after their arrival. Those migrants who had left Gothenburg before the time of the second interview were interviewed wherever they were living in Sweden. The migrants selected for the study were those 820 migrants who, during the months of August–October 1966, were appointed by public or private enterprises with at least 100 employees in Gothenburg. Only Swedish migrants were included in the study, but the problems of foreign workers in the Gothenburg region were taken up in another investigation. After seven months about a quarter of the original population of 820 migrants had left Gothenburg.

Of the Swedish migrants interviewed, two-thirds were below 25 years of age and only about one-tenth were above 39 years of age. There were more men (59 per cent) than women. Another interesting fact is the high education attained by many of the migrants, especially women. This shows how a big city area like the Gothenburg region, with its high concentration of offices, hospitals, and educational institutions, attracts young and highly qualified migrants. Many of them come from areas unable to give them work appropriate to their educational training.

As Doeringer states in his paper, the changes in labour markets associated with industrialization create both social benefits and social problems: benefits in the form of growing income, both for individuals and society, problems in the form of the relocation of population from rural to urban areas, changes in skills, and the scheduling of work and feelings of personal alienation. These effects are also reflected in our results from the Gothenburg study. Two-thirds of the migrants working both before and after the move were earning more in Gothenburg. And those migrants who were unemployed before the move or who entered the labour market in connection with the move got jobs in Gothenburg.

Housing in Gothenburg for the migrants, however, was less modern than the housing they had had before the move. One-tenth even lived in special barracks for migrants at the time of the first interview. The migrants were also less involved in leisure-time activities after the move, and a quarter of the migrants had no steady social contacts with other people in Gothenburg. By the time of the second interview some improvements were apparent for the migrants remaining in Gothenburg with regard to housing and contacts with other people. However, satisfaction with working conditions had lowered between the two interviews for these migrants.

If we compare 'movers', i.e. those migrants who left Gothenburg before the second interview, with 'stayers' we find that the movers were younger and had a lower educational level. This difference in educational level naturally shows up also in the occupational distribution of the two categories of migrants. The movers worked more often in manufacturing jobs in Gothenburg (52 per cent) than the stayers (30 per cent). The movers also more often came from the forestry regions in the north of Sweden and had had a higher unemployment rate before the move. They had worse housing and experienced greater difficulty in establishing contacts with other people in Gothenburg. If we want to sum up the differences between the movers and the stayers, we can say that the movers had fewer resources than the stayers. Their lack of resources shows up, for example, in their greater lack of information about work and housing before moving to Gothenburg.

And when the movers left Gothenburg, most of them (80 per cent) returned to their former places of residence, where the housing was better and where they had family and friends, but where also many of them still had difficulties in finding work. Some of them (12 per cent) were unemployed at the time of the second interview and about a third had been unemployed for some time after leaving Gothenburg. Those who could not find suitable work, therefore, had to start thinking about another move.

It is possible that most of these migrants who returned to their former places of living will, after a period of trial and error, end up in situations that will be satisfying to them both with regard to work, housing, and social contacts outside work. However, some others may end up in the secondary sector with the 'dead end' jobs described by Doeringer. In such jobs we also find some of the stayers, i.e. those migrants who got such jobs in Gothenburg but did not see returning home as a way out.

A follow-up study five years after the migrants' first move to Gothenburg also shows the strong influence of socio-economic status and level of education on the general level of welfare among the migrants (Gustafsson et al., 1975). Those with low socio-economic status and low education at the time of the move to Gothenburg in 1966 had during the following five years, for example, experienced more unemployment, worse housing conditions, and poorer health than those with high socio-economic status and education. In 1971, looking back on the move to Gothenburg, only one-tenth of those with just a basic education thought of the move as 'completely or mostly positive' from their own point of view, as compared with a quarter of those with a high school education or more.

Even though the differences in welfare between migrants with lower and higher socio-economic status diminished somewhat towards the end of the five-year period, it is clear that socio-economic status has a strong influence on the outcome of migration. There are indeed, as Doeringer states in his paper, 'signs that economic development need not ultimately remove social ills'.

SHUT-DOWNS—ECONOMIC AND SOCIAL EFFECTS

Follow-up studies of the shut-down of factories in Sweden show in general that 20–25 per cent of the former employees are unemployed or not in the labour force (retired, sick, etc.) one or even two years after the closing down of their former place of work. Our monthly labour force surveys also show that among the unemployed those who have been laid off because of shut-downs or other forms of reduction of the workforce have especially long periods of unemployment.

These results can partly be explained by the fact that employees who have different forms of physical and social handicaps are especially hurt by shut-downs. In Swedish occupational medicine these employees are sometimes called 'conditionally employable', which means that special considerations have to be taken in the choice and design of work for them (Heijbel, 1976). It has been estimated that in Sweden 10–15 per cent of all employees on the open labour market belong to this category of 'conditionally employable'. This would mean about 400 000–500 000 individuals. Most of these employees, in spite of their handicaps, function well in their jobs. They have a strong work motivation and do not see themselves as sick or handicapped. That they function so well can be explained at least partly by the fact that over time a 'convoy' (Kahn, 1976) of social relations has been built up around them. This 'convoy' consists of fellow workers, supervisors, and occupational health personnel who have developed a readiness to help when the pressures both at work and outside work become too strong.

These 'conditionally employable' people, however, are an especially vulnerable group who can very easily be eliminated from the labour market as a result of lay-offs or job transfers within a workplace. The individual worker can be moved, but it is difficult and takes time to rebuild the relations that made it possible for him or her to function so well in the job. There is, therefore, a great risk that such workers will end up as long-term unemployed after the shut-down of their place of work.

In a follow-up study of the closing down of a small paper pulp mill in Sweden, we tried to detail the consequences of a shut-down (Rundblad, 1976). Many of the older workers laid off as a result of this shut-down had, before their employment in the mill, supported themselves by work in agriculture or forestry. It was rather common that they suffered from physical handicaps caused by this earlier work. Partly because of these handicaps and partly because of the diminishing number of jobs in forestry due to mechanization, they had taken unskilled jobs in the paper pulp mill. And there 'convoys' were built up around these workers. The mill was located in a small community, where everybody knew everybody else, and it was easy to lend a helping hand both at work and outside work. The shut-down of the mill, therefore, hit this group of workers very hard. Many of them became long-term unemployed, a situation which created resignation and passivity among them. These psychological changes made their situation worse and contributed to an extension of their unemployment and a possible final elimination from the labour market as described by Berglind in his paper.

The psychological changes caused by long-term unemployment are also well described in other studies of the consequences of unemployment, e.g. the study of mass unemployment in the Austrian community Marienthal during the 1930s (Jahoda, Lazarsfeld, and Zeisel, 1971). The study of Marienthal shows, for example, how the apathy among the unemployed made them unable to use the few opportunities for employment that still existed.

The concept 'conditionally employable' as used here can also be linked to the discussion of the pathogenic triad in the chapter by Barbara and Bruce Dohrenwend. They describe a process in which certain events occur simultaneously or within a relatively brief interval of time. The triad 'consists of physical illness or injury that exhausts the individual physically, other fateful loss events the occurrence of which is both unanticipated and outside the individual's control, and additional events that disrupt his or her social supports'.

For the 'conditionally employable', the illness or injury can have lasted for a long time, which is different from that in the Dohrenwends' use of the concept 'pathogenic triad'. Otherwise, we have in the shut-down situation for these workers an illness or an injury, and a fateful loss event outside their own control, and also an event that disrupts their social support in the form of the 'convoy' of social relations at their former place of work. The disruption of the social relations at work will also in the long run be likely to affect their social relations outside work, especially if they remain unemployed.

We have here only described the economic and social effects of shut-downs in terms of long-term unemployment and the psychological consequences of this unemployment. It is very likely that there are also consequences in the form of, for example, impaired health. However, even with the results available, it is clear that shut-downs for those in some way socially or physically handicapped, or just old, are among the most stressful events possible in the sphere of work.

REFERENCES

Gustafsson, B. O., Johansson, S. O., Karlsson, S.-E., and Åberg, J.-O. (1975). Flyttning och välfärd—sammanfattning av data (Migration and welfare—summary of data), Mimeo, Department of Sociology, University of Karlstad.

Heijbel, C. A. (1976). Företagshälsovårdens och anpassningsgruppernas roll (The role of occupational medicine and work modification groups, *Socialmedicinsk Tidskrift* (2).

Jahoda, M., Lazarsfeld, P. F., and Zeisel, H. (1971). *Marienthal, the Sociography of an Unemployed Community*, Aldine-Atherton, Chicago.

Johansson, S. O., Olsson, S., and Rundblad, B. (1969). Kvarvarande och avflyttade (Stayers and movers), Mimeo, Department of Sociology, University of Gothenburg, Sweden.

Kahn, R. L. (1976). Mental health, social support, and metropolitan problems. Institute of Social Research, Ann Arbor, Mich. (mimeo).

Rundblad, B. (1976). Arbetslöshet efter företagsnedläggelse—led i en utslagningsprocess? (Unemployment after the shut downs of factories—part of a process of elimination from the labour market?) *Socialmedicinsk Tidskrift*, (2).

Working Life
Edited by B. Gardell and G. Johansson
© 1981 John Wiley & Sons Ltd

Discussant's Comments

OSBORNE BARTLEY

As is well known, we still have serious economic problems in Sweden, for instance the structural ones in our industry.

All economists seem to agree that the basic economic goals are full employment, stable prices, international balance of payments, and a reasonable rate of economic growth. There is also a fairly common understanding that all these goals cannot be achieved at the same time. Several economists argue that full employment cannot be maintained if prices are kept stable. Therefore, the question of which goal is given priority in a country becomes a question of ethics and 'value judgements'. One country can be for full employment at all costs, whereas another may not rank it of primary importance. Most countries seem at present to consider that the pursuit of stable prices is the most important economic goal. That kind of economic policy has resulted in considerable unemployment, low utilization of existing industrial capacity, and a low rate of growth.

It also changes the social situation for the employees. The social effects have been more thoroughly discussed by the previous speakers. I have been asked to comment on the social effects upon the employees from more of an economic point of view and I will try to do so. But, I think it will be in a pseudo-economic way because I am really not an economist.

The major goal of economic policy in Sweden has been, and still is, full employment, which means everybody has right to work. Our labour market policy has been successful in the sense that the unemployment rate is fairly low. But we have not managed to maintain stable prices. In addition, we have got the same problem of low utilization of our production capacity as the countries which have given stable prices higher priority.

As I have already said, the question of which goal is chosen as a major goal is a question of ethics and value judgements. But it is also a question of what kind of an effect a high unemployment rate has on the country's financial situation. If a country wants to guarantee a certain standard of welfare and a reasonably high standard of living for the unemployed, the unemployment benefits are kept at a high level, causing large public expenditure. If, at the same time the tax rates are high, and as a consequence revenues from taxation resulting from a policy of keeping people employed are also high, the net cost for society of giving employment to the previously unemployed is low. Gösta Rehn discussed these problems in a paper in 1976 and showed that if a person was employed instead of unemployed the net income for society was 70 to 90 per cent of the employer's total expenditure. The explanation is that society no longer needs to pay unemployment benefits and, furthermore, it gets a higher income from taxes. The corresponding figure in Sweden in 1976 was approximately 85 per cent, and it becomes over 90 per cent if the effects of, for instance, value added tax are included. Even though the example used by Rehn is somewhat drastic, the fact is that it is society which gets most of the income when a previously unemployed goes back to work. And this is, of course, not only a question of economy, but also a social question in widest sense.

In the light of these facts the Swedish labour market policy seems to me well worked out. Since I believe in the philosophy of the Swedish labour market policy and in the positive social and economic effects of this policy, I have been somewhat surprised at, and doubtful about, the measures taken during recent years aimed at making retirement easier. Berglind, who in his paper pointed out that the elimination of an old labour force has been officially sanctioned, seems to feel as I do. As I have already mentioned, it is now possible to get an early retirement pension from the age of 60 if one has difficulty in securing employment. Moreover, a partial pension from the age of 60 has been introduced. If one considers the beneficial economic effects of giving jobs to the unemployed one comes to the conclusion that the recent legislation relating to the old-age pension is economically unfortunate for the country as a whole. This legislation does not fit in with the overall economic policy of this country, and it seems to me to be either inconsistent or to inply that the government has given up and no longer believes that the country is capable of giving meaningful employment to older people. It seems as if Berglind and I have reached to the same conclusions.

If we consider this problem in the longer term—as Allan Nordin and Carl-Johan Åberg do in their book dealing with the growth, or rather lack of growth, of population and its effects on the economy—we doubt even more that it was right to lower the age of retirement. It is, however, too early to take concrete measures based on forecasts which in their turn, of course, are based on several more or less uncertain assumptions.

But if it turns out that the number of births continues to be low, that the net effect of migration is zero, and that the death rate is constant or diminishing, then we will have a decrease in population, a decrease in the labour force, and an increasing proportion of older, retired people. If we find ourselves in that kind of a situation—or preferably before we reach it—we should face the question of whether we should raise the pension age.

It seems to me impossible to solve our economic or even our social problems if we do not achieve a higher rate of economic growth and use our industrial capacity more efficiently. But it is not easy since, first, we are dependent on the world around us and, second, we have some obstacles in our social and economic system.

My opinion is that one of the major obstacles at present is the decreasing mobility of the labour force. There are several reasons for this.

(1) Since 1974 we have had the Security of Employment Act. This piece of legislation is by no means revolutionary, at least not for white-collar workers. But it legislates the sequence in which employees may be given notice, and thus guarantees higher security for those who have been in the same job longer. I suppose that the employees become progressively less willing to change jobs. There is no doubt that the Act ties an employee more tightly to a certain employer.

(2) The number of women working has rapidly increased and it is becoming more and more common for both the man and the woman in a family have employment. If one of them gets a good job offer somewhere else, the other might have problems in finding suitable employment in the same area. This is naturally an obstacle to higher mobility. The problems which the family may have with child care in the new place may be a further obstacle.

(3) Many feel that the government does not approve of firms closing down. Therefore, people no longer leave their jobs even though they know that their company is facing an economic crisis. I think they feel that they still have their security guaranteed and they choose to stay.

(4) The pension regulations, which I previously discussed, certainly make older people less interested in training for a new job and a move. People prefer to retire early. Mobility certainly diminishes with increasing age.

(5) There seems to be a tendency to increase internal recruitment in various public authorities and perhaps also in private companies. If this is correct the result will be increasing rigidity, decreasing mobility.

(6) The high marginal income tax rates combined with our transfer system have resulted in a system where a better-paid job no longer functions as an economic stimulus for a full-time employee and persuades him to change his job. The net effect of better pay has become smaller and smaller and a change of the tax system is much needed.

Thus, there is a need for increased mobility of the labour force and measures are already under discussion to a certain degree. As regards the Security of Employment Act, I have no reason to criticize. Of course, security should not be diminished, but could a method be found by which scrunity could be guaranteed without tying the employee to a certain employer.

I am aware of the severe structural problems in the Swedish economy and I can see that *ad hoc* measures are sometimes necessary. If they are not taken, drastic changes in the labour market will occur. But at the same time I would prefer a more aggressive economic policy with, for instance, even higher investments in research and development. Such measures ought to increase our productivity and our utilization of industrial capacity. In this connection I would like to point out that we already have a very serious situation in the field of research. And it will certainly become worse.

The benefits to a person when he moves to a new area ought to be considerably higher. Furthermore, there is a need for some sort of social preparedness for newcomers. At the moment they often return in a short time. They are unable to adjust socially.

A necessary structural change, of course, is not achieved merely by means of increased mobility of the labour force. The need for increased interest in research work has already been mentioned. Also existing companies may adjust their production and rationalize in order to consolidate their financial position. If this occurs it is necessary that the employees are able to participate in the decisions. We have legislation in the field of co-determination. It is important that all employees are given the opportunity to take part in decisions which are of importance to individuals. That means increased opportunities to carry out trade union work during working hours. My guess is that such a measure would be a good investment.

Bruce and Barbara Dohrenwend in their paper have discussed what happens when an employee cannot influence his job situation. Lack of control over job may contribute to the development of psychiatric disorders.

As I have pointed out, we have a changing Swedish economy with serious structural problems. Of course, these changes lead to changes also for the labour force both from a social and an economic point of view. It is of the utmost importance that measures are taken such that the problems for the labour force are reduced to an absolute minimum.

Part 4

Quality of Life in Industrial Society

Working Life
Edited by B. Gardell and G. Johansson
© 1981 John Wiley & Sons Ltd

An Attempt at a Discussion about the Quality of Life and Morality in Industrial Society

ERIK ALLARDT

The term 'quality of life' has been frequently used for over a decade in reports on the states of nations, in treatises on public policy, and in social critiques. There is, however, no consensus on what 'quality of life' really stands for and what kind of phenomena it denotes. The vagueness of this term is, so to say, in the nature of things. Quality of life denotes something which is valued, and which is or has been missing. Thereby people with different life-styles will stress different things, societies in different stages of development will emphasize different qualities, and differential need-satisfaction will result in different things being held as crucial to the quality of life. The fact that the concept of quality of life varies in its meaning is part of its usefulness. It is a sensitizing concept useful in critiques of the states of affairs. As a value-related concept it is concerned with good and bad life. The term will be used here in this way. There will be a particular emphasis on social relationships providing individuals with social identities and the moral rules by which they can orientate themselves in the society. As a point of departure some concepts and findings from a comparative study of the state of well-being in the Scandinavian countries will be used.

A BASIC FOUR-FOLD TABLE

The Comparative Scandinavian Welfare Study, conducted by the Research Group for Comparative Sociology at the University of Helsinki, was based on an interview survey in Denmark, Finland, Norway, and Sweden and was carried out in the spring of 1972. In each country a national probability sample of approximately 1000 persons from the population between 15 and 64 years old was interviewed (Kata and Uusitalo, 1973).

In the comparative Scandinavian study welfare was used as the overriding concept, and by welfare was meant the overall state of need-satisfaction in a national population. The aim was to measure and describe welfare or the state of need-satisfaction in Denmark, Finland, Norway, and Sweden.

Welfare as a concept denoting the state of need-satisfaction in a population is usually studied and described by some system of social indicators. The indicators refer to different components or aspects of welfare. However, indicators of welfare are not merely some kind of variables. They are related to the good and bad life, the good and bad society, and as such they reflect values. A basic question in studies of welfare (and in studies of the quality of life for that matter) is from where do we get these values?

In choosing the welfare values there are several problems, but two of these appear as particularly pressing. The first such problem is whether in assessing the level of welfare one should rely on measures of *external, objective conditions*, or on the *personal, subjective evaluations* of the citizens. According to one view, welfare values or dimensions should be established by observations of peoples' goal-directed activities and conditions under which people suffer. According to another view, the welfare values have to be established by studying the subjective perceptions and attitudes of the people. It cannot be overstressed that this issue indeed is a difficult one. Superficially it may appear very democratic to base a survey on peoples' own opinions and attitudes. On the other hand it is well known that there is great variation in the ability to articulate both satisfaction and discomfort, and that underprivileged people usually are less able to articulate their interests than others. To base the choice of welfare values entirely on the subjective views of the people is therefore likely to lead to a fruitless conservatism. On the other hand, a complete disregard of what people themselves say leads in its turn to an inhuman dogmatism. This dilemma would be easier to solve if strong empirical correlations existed between the objective and subjective measures. However, as regards the empirical relationships between objective and subjective indicators, there is no conclusive evidence. In most studies, or rather in most settings studied, the relationship between the objective and the subjective indicators seems to be surprisingly weak. Therefore, it seems fruitful in many studies to use both objective and subjective indicators. This was also the case in the Comparative Scandinavian Welfare Study.

The second major problem is concerned with whether one should focus on the *material or impersonal resources* by which people presumably can master their living conditions, or whether one should emphasize *values which are ends in themselves*. A typical value which can be regarded as an end in itself, a so-called autotelic value, is personal growth or self-realization, whereas income is a typical material resource or a heterotelic value. However, one should be aware of the fact that there are no watertight compartments between resources and autotelic values. Education, for instance, is a resource when looked upon as a means to secure a job in the labour market, but it is an end in itself when regarded as an indication of personal growth. The fulfilment of an autotelic value turns out often to be resource for acquiring other good things in life. Thus, personal growth or self-realization may lead to a greater ability to acquire a reasonable income or to increase the chances for good health. It seemed,

Table 1

	Objective indicators	Subjective indicators
Material and impersonal resources	1. *Level of living:* Objective measures of material or impersonal resources	3. *Dissatisfaction:* Subjective feelings of satisfaction-dissatisfaction as regards the material living conditions
Values which are ends in themselves	2. *Quality of life:* Objective measures as regards peoples' relations to other people, society, and nature	4. *Happiness:* Subjective feelings of happiness and need-satisfaction

therefore, fruitful to include both typical resources and typical autotelic values in the comparative Scandinavian study.

When cross-tabulating the dichotomies implied in the two problems the following four-fold table shown in Table 1 was obtained.

The terminology has been used in a slightly different way in earlier presentations of the conceptual scheme (Allardt, 1975; 1976). However, the terms in themselves are not important but the problems and the phenomena covered are. The distinctions indicated in the table are often blurred. The term 'quality of life' has sometimes been used to cover all four cells in the table, in the same sense as welfare here has been spoken of. More often 'quality of life' has been used to cover subjective evaluations and perceptions in contradistinction to the material level of living. The point here is that both the level of living and the quality of life can be assessed by objective and external approaches in addition to subjective and perception centred ones. It is assumed that all four categories, the objective level of living, the objective quality of life, the feelings of dissatisfaction, and the feelings of happiness are of some importance in pursuing public policy. The important thing is not the terminology but that all four cells in the table somehow are accounted for.

HAVING, LOVING, BEING

Despite the assumption of the multidimensionality of welfare and the intention to cover all four cells in the four-fold table presented above, there was in the comparative Scandinavian study a heavier stress on the objective measures than on the subjective ones.

The objective measures of welfare were assumed to related to the degree of satisfaction of human needs. In order to be able to distinguish between different components of welfare a classification of needs was required. The point of departure was a simple classification of three basic kinds of needs: (1) needs defined by the material or impersonal resources an individual has and can master (*Having*); (2) needs related to love, companionship, and solidarity (*Loving*); and (3) needs denoting self-actualization and the obverse of alienation (*Being*). As can be seen, Having refers directly to the level of living, whereas the value categories of Loving and Being are composite parts of the quality of life.

The questionnaire used allowed for a specification of the following components:

Having, corresponding to the level of living
(1) income
(2) housing conditions
(3) employment
(4) health
(5) education
Loving as part of the quality of life
(6) community attachment
(7) attachment to family and kin
(8) active friendship relations
Being as part of the quality of life
(9) personal prestige
(10) insubstitutability
(11) political resources
(12) interesting things to do (Doing)

Most of the measures consisted of summated scales based on several items. In operationalizing the twelve components the aim was to use measures of actual conditions and overt behaviour although it was not possible to be entirely consistent. The operationalization of the components have been presented elsewhere (Allardt, 1975) and space does not allow for a presentation of them here, but some components deserve a brief mention. Insubstitutability as a welfare value rests on the assumption that the less substitutable a person is in his job, in his family, and among his friends, the more he is a person and the less a thing or number which can easily be replaced. The political resources were measured by studying to what extent a person regularly participates in elections, has tried to influence local decisions, has spoken at meetings, and feels that he can influence decisions in matters concerning his personal fate.

The subjective indicators were constructed by the use of attitudinal scales. The feelings of *dissatisfaction* were tapped by four measures:

(13) perceived antagonisms in the society
(14) perceived discriminatory patterns
(15) perceived unjust privileges
(16) dissatisfaction with one's own income

The category of *happiness* was studied by two scales only:

(17) reported feelings of whether life is happy or unhappy, interesting or dull, easy or hard, socially rich or lonesome
(18) reported satisfaction of social needs

It goes without saying that the subjective indicators used were too few in order to give a comprehensive picture of dissatisfactions and feelings of happiness. Nevertheless the analyses of the relationships between the eighteen components mentioned above point towards some important insights about the multidimensional character of welfare and well-being.

THE MULTIDIMENSIONALITY OF WELFARE

The multidimensional nature of welfare was already assumed in constructing the conceptual scheme presented above. It is nevertheless important and interesting to study this multidimensionality empirically by examining the statistical relationships between the twelve values and the six attitudinal scales presented above.

When the twelve welfare values and the six attitudes were submitted to factor analysis on the basis of their intercorrelations, almost identical factor structures were obtained for the four different countries almost irrespectively of what rotation procedures were used. The factor spaces seemed to be most accurately described by the following set of five factors or dimensions:

(1) a *Resource* factor, defined mainly by the components of Income, Education, and Personal Prestige (the last mentioned component was originally thought of as a measure of personal esteem but it was not possible to isolate it from status or rank);
(2) a *Being* factor, defined mainly by the components of Insubstitutability, Political Resources, and Doing;
(3) a *Loving—Happiness* factor with higher factor loadings on both the components of Loving and the Happiness attitudes. These two categories are to a certain extent correlated which is seen also in other kinds of analyses;
(4) a *Dissatisfaction* factor defined by the attitudinal scales aimed at measuring dissatisfaction. No other variables have loadings in this factor; and
(5) a *Health—Employment* factor, defined, as its name indicates, by the components of Health and Employment. Accordingly, the components related to the level of living split into two factors.

It is obvious that the factor structures correspond very well to the theoretical divisions made at the beginning of the study. The factor analyses also give indications of relationships or absence of relationships more thoroughly described by other techniques.

When studying the relationships between the welfare components by cross-tabulations, correlational analyses, and MCA-analysis it appears that the interrelationships between components and attitudes of different theoretical categories are very weak or non-existent. As the factor analyses indicate, there are positive relationships between two of the categories.

First, there is a positive relationship between the components of Having and Being. The relationship is not very strong but the correlations are nevertheless clearly positive. There is, for instance, a positive correlation between income and political resources (in Denmark 0.30, in Finland 0.25, in Norway 0.17, and in Sweden 0.21). The findings are according to expectations. It seems reasonable to assume that income and political resources are to a certain degree mutually reinforcing. More generally, the results indicate that there is a positive, although not very strong relationship, between the level of living and the absence of alienation.

Second, there is a positive relationship between the components of Loving and the subjective expressions of happiness. There are, for instance, in all countries positive correlations between the existence of active friendship relations and the scale measuring happiness (in Denmark 0.20, in Finland 0.26, in Norway 0.22, and in Sweden 0.16). The relationships are not very strong but it is nevertheless worthwhile to note that subjective, expressed feelings of happiness are related (although weakly) to the existence of positive human relationships but unrelated to all other kinds of indicators or components.

Despite the above mentioned examples of positive correlations between some of the components from different theoretical categories there seems to be ample proof for the multidimensional character of welfare. The idea of multidimensionality is not without implications for the pursuit of public policy. If it can be assumed that all the different theoretical categories (and notably the categories of Having, Loving, Being, Dissatisfaction, and Happiness) are important, then the multidimensionality implies that there are no easy roads to a general welfare. All the different aspects of welfare are worth attention, and they cannot be attained by simply increasing the welfare in one category only.

SOME NEGATIVE FINDINGS

Some of the most remarkable findings consisted of the absence of relationships or zero-correlations. It is, of course, possible that the absence of relationships was due to unreliable variables or the failure to find valid indicators. This has also been indicated in some critical reviews (Johansson, 1977, 57–58). Some of the negative results, however, get clear support from other studies. A certain degree of credibility in the findings is provided by the fact that the results are very similar in all four countries. In any case, many of the negative findings or the absence of relationships have very interesting implications. Three cases of negative findings in particular appear to be important.

(1) It is notable that there are only zero-correlations between the scales measuring dissatisfaction on one hand and the scales measuring happiness on the

other. This result will not be more thoroughly commented upon here. Suffice it to say that it bears a resemblance to the results of Herzberg according to which very different factors in the world of work lead on one hand to dissatisfaction and on the other to satisfaction (Herzberg, Mausner, and Snyderman, 1959; cf. Huizinga, 1970, 73–83). Here we may only conclude that dissatisfaction and happiness do not appear to be poles on one and the same dimension but that they seem to be different phenomena altogether.

(2) The second negative finding of interest is the absence of relationships between the components of Loving, on one hand, and the components of Having and Being on the other. Thus, the social relations of companionship and solidarity do not seem to be related to the material level of living or to the opportunities for self-realization through political activity, leisure activities, or insubstitutability in the world of work. Again caution is called for because the results may particularly depend on unreliable or invalid measures of the relationships of companionship and solidarity. On the other hand, there are enough reasons to be doubtful about assumptions of positive relationship between the material level of living and the possibilities of finding friends, local contacts, and supportive relations in the family or the kinship group. Until there is proof to the contrary, it seems reasonable to assume that companionship and solidarity have about equal chances of emerging and surviving in rich castles and poor huts.

(3) One of the more remarkable findings is that the relationships between the components of the level of living (Having) and the attitudes of dissatisfaction are extremely weak, and for all practical purposes non-existent. This was already indicated by the factor analyses in which the dissatisfaction factor appeared to be highly independent of the objective welfare components. The only slight exception to the general pattern is that there is a weak positive correlation between income and income satisfaction in all the four countries (0.13 in Denmark, 0.14 in Finland, 0.17 in Norway, and 0.12 in Sweden), but that even this relationship is much weaker than one could reasonably expect.

One possible explanation of the unexpectedly weak correlations could, of course, be the lack of reliability and validity of the measures used. However, there are reasonable grounds for considering the dissatisfaction measures good or at least acceptable. There are fairly high correlations between the items on each scale, and the scales are also positively intercorrelated.

Another striking fact is revealed when the dissatisfaction measures are related to common background variables such as social class defined by occupation, education, sex, age, etc. It appears that within each country the overall dissatisfaction level tends to be surprisingly constant across categories defined by social characteristics of this kind. When multivariate analysis (e.g. MCA-analysis) is performed separately for each of the four countries a surprisingly small amount of variance in the dissatisfaction is explained by social background factors. It is hard to avoid the conclusion that the expressions of dissatisfaction are only to a very small degree directly related to the external social conditions.

There is, however, one factor which in all four societies is correlated with dissatisfaction and which in the multivariate analysis appears as a predictor of dissatisfaction. This is *political orientation*. In all four countries the level of dissatisfaction clearly increases when moving from right to left on the political spectrum. It is to be noted that 'political orientation' as a variable is of a different nature from the other background variables. Political orientation is to a large extent an attitudinal variable and reflects more or less a deliberate choice, whereas social class, education, age, sex, etc., reflect external circumstances in which the individual lives. These general tendencies do not disappear when an analysis based on the single items—instead of based on summated scales— is performed. The political right—left dimension is for each single item more strongly correlated with dissatisfaction than income and social class defined by prestige ratings of occupations. Furthermore, the correlations between political orientation and dissatisfaction are as a rule statistically significant, whereas the correlations between income and social class on one hand and dissatisfaction on the other only rarely deviate from zero. Additional insight into the relationship between dissatisfaction and political orientation is provided by the fact that among all objective welfare components (irrespective of whether they belong to the categories of Having, Loving, or Being) only one component, namely Political Resources, seems to have a consistent positive relationship with some of the measures of dissatisfaction. Thus there is a weak but nevertheless positive correlation between Political Resources and Perceived Unjust Privileges (in Denmark 0.18, in Finland 0.17, in Norway 0.16, and in Sweden 0.16). In any case, it appears reasonable to assume that in the four Scandinavian countries variations in dissatisfaction rather than objective, external conditions reflect political consciousness and awareness.

The findings from the comparative Scandinavian study and some other studies simultaneously conducted elsewhere are almost astonishingly similar. In a majority of known studies the general conclusion has likewise been that there is only a low degree of correspondence between the external conditions and subjectively expressed satisfaction–dissatisfaction (see, for example, Campbell, 1972, 441–442; Abrams, 1972, 454–455).

It may be noted, of course, that dissatisfaction measures can be constructed in a number of ways. The dissatisfaction measures can be constructed to match and to correspond to certain external conditions as is the case when one simultaneously measures income and income satisfaction, housing and satisfaction with housing conditions, etc. The indicators can be constructed, on the other hand, as measures of more generalized feelings of dissatisfaction, as doubtlessly has been the case in the comparative Scandinavian study. There is no point in arguing against the possibility of arriving at higher correlations between objective and subjective indicators by making the objective conditions and their corresponding subjective measures match closer and closer. It is doubtful, however, if it would be fruitful to proceed in such a direction except for a particular purpose and in some specific studies. Theoretically, the generalized attitudes of satisfaction–dissatisfaction are the important ones. In the light of the findings it seems definitely worthwhile to separate the objective and the subjective indicators because they both empirically and conceptually represent different phenomena. To try to replace one by the other will only lead to a loss of information.

In view of the fact that the comparative Scandinavian study dealt primarily with generalized dissatisfaction, it is interesting to note the strong resemblance between our results and those reported by Ronald Inglehart (1975) in a large scale comparative study of the US and several West European countries. His study examined dissatisfaction in a very thorough fashion by measures of both generalized and specific dissatisfaction. Nevertheless the overall findings are strikingly similar in Inglehart's studies and our own. The resemblance starts with the general overall findings that the relationship between objective need-satisfaction and subjective dissatisfaction is almost astonishingly loose, but the similarities of the findings can also be observed in their details. Inglehart stresses how the overall satisfaction levels tend to be roughly constant across any set of social categories having stable membership. This is, in fact, also the finding in the comparative Scandinavian study.

DISCONTENTS IN THE WELFARE STATE

Psychologically it is not surprising that there is hardly any relationship between the level of dissatisfaction and the external conditions. A person's level of satisfaction and dissatisfaction is dependent on his or her aspirations, but the aspirations constantly adjust to what has been performed and gained. Overall satisfaction or dissatisfaction is not a substance, but an ever-changing balance.

It seems nevertheless correct to say that today in the so-called welfare societies there exists a kind of discontent which cannot be explained by the conventional theory of the ever-changing aspiration levels. Rather it is a question of a historical situation in which a certain kind of optimism and belief in continued growth has changed into certain forms of pessimism and scepticism as regards both the possibilities and the benefits of growth. It is not a coincidence that some of the more popular societal analyses in the last decades have capitalized on the theme of the limits to growth, either on the limited material resources of growth, as in the reports of the Club of Rome (Meadows et al., 1972), or on the social limits to growth as in Fred Hirsch's (1976) provocative book. In all advanced industrial societies there has been a growth of new forms of protest directed against the speedy development of new technologies such as nuclear power plants, or against new forms of economic concentration, as in the opposition to the EEC and multinational corporations, or against the very foundation of the modern state as in certain terrorist actions.

The rise of the new forms of pessimism, scepticism, and protests against growth has been analysed and described in a number of books and writings. The arguments will not be reported here, but it seems fruitful to dwell upon the negative findings from the Comparative Scandinavian Welfare Study for a little longer. One part of the optimism and the belief in continuous growth in the 1950s and the early 1960s was an assumption that welfare and well-being was all of a piece, and at least that continuous economic growth and a corresponding increase in the material resources of individuals would ensure a sufficient level of welfare in all important respects. The findings from the Comparative Scandinavian Welfare Study as well as from some other studies make the assumption of the unitary nature of welfare highly unlikely. Rather, what is meant by welfare, and what people call for when they speak about welfare, or quality of life for that matter, consists of several independent parts and categories.

It may be kept in mind that the zero-relationships found in the comparative Scandinavian study might be due to the lack of reliability and validity of the indicators, as stated in some critical reviews (Johansson, 1977, 37–58). However, in a sense the reviews of the research report can also be used as an argument in support of the view presented here. Both the inter-Scandinavian *Acta Sociologica* (1977, 301–316) and the Finnish sociological journal *Sosiologia* (1976, 170–175; 1977, 37–38) carried review symposia, each with three reviews of the report. All the reviews were critical but the extreme divergence of critical demands and views was remarkable to say the least. Even without any detailed analysis and comparison of the reviews, it seems fair to say that they not only contained different viewpoints but also contradictory demands. It is hard to avoid the conclusion that there is very little consensus about what ought to be put into a welfare study and about how it should be conducted.

When there are both several independent dimensions of welfare and also divergent views of what is central to welfare it seems natural to ask whether one, instead of constructing batteries of universal indicators, should aim at typologies of persons emphasizing different aspects of welfare or of quality of life. An interesting and provocative attempt in this direction has been made by Zetterberg (1977) who on the basis of Swedish opinion poll data has distinguished between different life-styles in Swedish society. Life-styles are sets of activities that the people who practise a life-style share with some persons but not with others, and that they experience as very engaging and strongly motivating. From this point of view Zetterberg is able to distinguish between those mainly oriented towards work, towards the family, towards consumption, towards party-going and sociability, towards culinary activities and enjoyment, or towards social and political commitments, etc. For those who practise different life-styles different things are engaging and motivating. Clearly also different things and different activities represent the good life.

Zetterberg is theoretically basing his ideas of more or less stable life-styles on some general assumptions from social psychology. The first is the so-called *Identity Postulate* (Zetterberg, 1966, 125–126). It states that 'persons are likely to engage in those actions within their repertoire of actions which maintain their self-evaluation'. Zetterberg states on the basis of empirical studies that persons primarily aim at maintaining their self-evaluation rather than trying to enhance their positive self-evaluation. The postulate clearly assumes that there is a stable core of activities and self-attitudes the preservation of which is extremely important for a person. Thus the Identity Postulate describes the crucial mechanism behind the life-styles. There are, however, other supporting mechanisms. One is formulated by Zetterberg in the theorem of *Social Challenges*: persons try to emit such actions within their repertoire of actions that imply that they have successfully met challenges. Another is described in the *Theorem of Social Motivation*: persons are likely to engage in those actions within their repertoire of actions which maintain the evaluations that their associates give to them.

THE IMPORTANCE OF SOLIDARY RELATIONSHIPS

It seems logical to move from Zetterberg to some other fairly well established and by now almost traditional propositions in social psychology. They are found in Leon Festinger's well-known theory of social comparisons. One of its key concepts is group cohesiveness, and it defines group cohesiveness through the attraction the members feel towards their group. In terms of Festinger's theory we could add a new theorem to those presented by Zetterberg. It could here be labelled the *Theorem of Group Attractiveness* and for our purposes it may read: the more attractive a group, or in other words the higher the group cohesiveness, the more the individuals are able to maintain their self-evaluation.

Festinger's theory has been formalized both mathematically and verbally by specifying hypotheses, corollaries, and deductions, but Festinger's argument can briefly be described as follows: it is assumed that an individual, in order to maintain his self-evaluation, is in great need of opportunities to evaluate his opinions and performances, and that these opportunities are provided by other individuals similar to himself. The more similar the individuals are, the easier it is to perform the comparisons and hence also the evaluations. Furthermore, the easier it is to perform both the comparisons and the evaluations, the more attractive the situation, and the more cohesive the group involved (Festinger, 1954, 117–140). Without extending the argument further it clearly also follows that the more attractive or more cohesive the group the easier it is to maintain one's self-evaluation.

In any case, there are grounds for maintaining that individuals generally are in need of some solidary relationships or groups to which they can feel attracted. This is also the reason for including the category of Loving among the welfare values. Most systems of indicators include components which here have been subsumed in the categories of Having and Being whereas the needs for companionship and solidarity are usually left outside the realm of welfare values.

The Loving values are in some respects very different from the values of Having and Being. The two latter values refer to clearly *individual needs*, whereas Loving always implies *relations of interaction* between individuals. Loving implies that the individual both gives and receives, and love relations are at their best symmetrical relations. Relationships of love, companionship, and solidarity require a common language as the most important tool for mutual understanding, and one may even venture to say that these relationships at least partly exist in the language. In any case, this indicates an important property of the Loving values. To interfere with and systematically plan for value fulfilment in the realm of Loving is ethically very problematic and it would clearly imply an element of brainwashing. While the values related to Having and also to a large extent those related to Being can be made objects of systematic social planning it seems right to expect that relationships in the realm of Loving ought to be given the chance to develop spontaneously.

Even if the Loving values cannot be made objects of direct social planning it is important that they are explicitly recognized as welfare values in order to avoid such planning measures which would destroy the possibilities of solid relationships and in order to provide conditions in which solidary forms might emerge. The emphasis of Loving is important because it also introduces an altruistic element into the work for social welfare. The Having and Being categories, as stated, directly refer to individual needs. Personal growth or self-realization is in some indicator systems thought of as the highest value or as the final end result (Galtung, *et al.* 1975, p. 523), but considered as a value an individual might claim for himself it definitively has an egotistical ring.

It does not seem unfounded to assume that one of the disappointments with the welfare state has been that some of its provisions have promoted egotistical behaviour and neglected moral rules of an altruistic kind. Systems of social indicators provide the citizens with data by which they can evaluate their own positions and conditions in the society. If the citizens are not caught-up in a web of solidary relationships the likely result will be purely egotistical claims without any concessions made in the name of companionship and solidarity.

Many acts of cruelty throughout history have been committed in the name of group cohesiveness and solidarity. It can only be said that small is beautiful when solidary relationships are stressed as welfare values. Groups which provide the best opportunities for social comparisons and the maintenance of self evaluations are mostly small and constitute the direct living environment of the citizens, such as the local community, the kinship group, the immediate work group, or the local branches of various organizations. Typically they are related to the local community, and they exist at least partly for other than purely utilitarian reasons.

THE IMPORTANCE OF IDENTITY AND MORAL RULES

Before summarizing the argument presented here a word of warning is called for. It is important to recognize two social problems which are sometimes presented as political opposites or at least are often advocated by people of different views. The first problem is that there are still many people who, as regards the welfare values, are located below a level under which no individual should be located. In the Third World many live below a level which we are apt to consider inhuman and cruel, but also in the advanced industrial societies there are many who live (at least as regards their social opportunities) below acceptable floor values. This deprived group will continue to be an extremely important target group in all welfare policy as well as in level of living studies and social reporting. The second problem is that disappointment really exists in the results of welfare policies, and that focusing solely on the improvement of material resources will not provide remedies for all societal ills and problems. It is important to recognize both the problems. Discussion of and emphasis on one of these problems should not lead to the neglect of the other.

It has been suggested here that one of the reasons for such disappointment has been the neglect of provisions which facilitate the forming of solid social relationships. Solid social relations have two main functions. Firstly, they provide the individual with an identity since social comparisons and the maintenance of self-evaluation are possible only under conditions of a certain degree of solidarity. Secondly, moral rules, conceptions of right and wrong, and consideration for others are born and formulated in groups and situations of solidarity. It is very much through moral codes that the world becomes predictable for the individual.

The claims for welfare and welfare measures become problematical as soon as they are made into something that most individuals can only claim for themselves. To work for the welfare of others has been the privilege of a few. The latter often fail to see that the problem is not only to help others to attain a decent level of living but also to provide such forms of participation as would provide opportunities for everybody to work for other people. When welfare is made into a purely egotistical goal most people will be deprived of two crucial human necessities: the need to develop a social identity, and the need to internalize morals which help to make the world predictable. Therefore, some of the most important welfare measures today consist in developing forms of social participation which can facilitate the development of solidary relationships.

REFERENCES

Abrams, M. (1972). Social indicators and social equity, *New Society*, **22**, 454–455.
Acta Sociologica (1977). Review Symposium, R. Erikson, J. Partanen, and H. Kristensen:

Erik Allardt's Att ha, att älska, att vara. Om välfärd i Norden, *Acta Sociologica*, **20**, 301–316.

Allardt, E. (1975). *Att ha, att älska, att vara. Om välfärd i Norden (Having, Loving, Being. On Welfare in the Nordic Countries)*, Argos, Kalmar.

Allardt, E. (1976). Dimensions of welfare in a comparative Scandinavian study, *Acta Sociologica*, **19**, 227–239.

Campbell, E. (1972). Aspiration, satisfaction and fulfillment, in *The Human Meaning of Social Change*, ed. A. Campbell and P. E. Converse, Russell Sage Foundation, New York, 441–466.

Festinger, L. (1954). A theory of social comparison processes, *Human Relations*, **7**, 117–140.

Galtung, J., *et al.* (1975). Measuring world development II, *Alternatives*, **1**, 523–555.

Herzberg, F., Mausner, B., and Snyderman, B. (1959). *The Motivation to Work*, Chapman & Hall, London.

Hirsch, F. (1976). *Social Limits to Growth*, Harvard University Press, Cambridge, Mass.

Huizinga, G. (1970). *Maslow's Need-Hierarchy in the Work Situation*, Wolters-Noordhoff, Groningen.

Inglehart, R. (1975). Value priorities, subjective satisfaction and protest potential among Western publics, *paper prepared for the 1975 Annual Meeting of the American Political Science Association*, mimeo, San Francisco.

Johansson, S. (1977). Om 'Att ha, att älska, att vara'. En kritisk granskning av en jämförande undersökning av välfärd i Norden (on 'Having, Loving, Being'. A critical review of a comparative study of welfare in the Nordic countries), *Sociologisk forskning*, **14**, 37–58.

Kata, K., and Uusitalo, H. (1973). On the data, sampling and representativeness of the Scandinavian survey in 1973, Research Group for Comparative Sociology, University of Helsinki, Research Reports, No. 4.

Meadows, D. H., Meadows, D. L., Randers, J., and Behrens, W. W., III (1972). *The Limits to Growth. A Report for the Club of Rome's Project on the Predicament of Mankind*, Eart Island Limited, London.

Sosiologia (1976 and 1977). Reviews by B. Koskiaho, J. Partanen, and N. Christie of E. Allardt's report of the comparative Scandinavian welfare study, *Sosiologia*, **13**, 170–175, and **14**, 36–38.

Zetterberg, H. L. (1966). On motivation, in *Sociological Theories in Progress I*, ed. J. Berger, M. Zelditch, Jr. and B. Anderson, Houghton Mifflin Boston, Mass.

Zetterberg, H. L. (1977). *Arbete, livstil och motivation (Work, Life-style, and Motivation)*, The Swedish Employers' Federation, Stockholm.

Working Life
Edited by B. Gardell and G. Johansson
© 1981 John Wiley & Sons Ltd

Coping with Job Stress—a Psychobiological Approach

MARIANNE FRANKENHAEUSER

This paper considers the quality-of-life concept from the point of view of harmony between fundamental human needs and environmental conditions. It is argued that the knowledge gained by research in human psychobiology can aid in directing technological applications to suit human needs and abilities. Examples are given from a multidisciplinary research programme concerned with the dynamics of stressful person-environment transactions, viewed from psychological and biological perspectives. Emphasis is placed on coping and adaptation by workers exposed to conditions characterized by underload, overload, and lack of control. On the basis of empirical results, it is argued that a moderately varied flow of stimuli and events, opportunities to engage in psychologically meaningful work and to exercise personal control over situational factors, may be considered key components in the quality-of-life concept.

THE DYNAMICS OF HUMAN NEEDS AND MOTIVES

Research on human stress and coping is the meeting place for several disciplines. The psychobiological approach is based on the notion that a highly developed nervous system provides the human being with a wide repertoire of responses among which deliberate choices can be made. Assisted by technology, we have drastically transformed our life conditions, and continue to do so at an accelerating rate. In striking contrast, the structure and size of the human brain have remained essentially the same over some 40 000 years. Thus, we are faced with two seemingly incompatible phenomena: the standstill of genetic evolution and the accelerating pace of social evolution.

This raises questions of human adaptability. How adaptable is the human being? How far can one stretch this old biological construction? What happens if the limits are exceeded? What are the long-term costs?

Questions such as these may be taken to signify a passive acceptance of technological development as a force that obeys its own laws. The possibility of arresting or modifying its influence is considered only when human tolerance is at breaking point or when the costs of adaptation become too high. Viewed in this perspective, stress research serves mainly to provide warning signals of excessive strains. However, research on the processes governing person–environment transactions has a much more constructive role to play: it should aim at providing knowledge that can be used as a basis for directing technological applications to suit fundamental human needs.

The traditional social indicators describe the conditions under which people live, their level of living assessed in terms of material welfare. While these measures have greatly improved the data base for social programmes and preventive actions, they are not the only criteria against which human satisfaction and happiness should be evaluated (cf. Allardt, 1975; Campbell, 1976; Frankenhaeuser, 1977).

There is a growing understanding of the dynamics of human need structure and the fact that people whose basic survival and safety are more or less guaranteed now have the possibility to express other demands and expectations. These involve demands for greater personal control and participation, for awareness of one's role in society, opportunities for meaningful work and other creative activities, for emotional involvement in the main tasks of the day, and for the realization of personal talents and abilities. The generations now growing up are demanding to use their knowledge and capacity in contexts that are experienced as socially meaningful. This combination of knowledge, demands, and expectations constitutes a new driving force in society.

On the political level, the consequences of these changes in human need structure have come to the fore as new and growing groups of people experience demands and expectations that used to be restricted to a privileged minority. There is a deeper understanding of the fact that the production system that has served to generate our material welfare is incapable, in many respects, of meeting the need for meaningful work. Among the workers themselves, among industrial managers, trade unions, and policy makers, there is a growing concern about harmful side-effects, on the psychological and social levels, of increased automation and mechanization.

Moreover, the view that the worker would be able to compensate for a dull and boring job with stimulating and enriching activities in his free time is being replaced by an understanding of the strong links between a job that is circumscribed and repetitive and a leisure that is passive and psychologically unrewarding (e.g. Gardell, 1976b). In other words, those persons whose job is restricted and monotonous are less likely than those who hold interesting jobs to engage in leisure activities requiring planning, participation, and effort. New support for this interpretation of the dynamics of the labour-leisure relationship has recently been provided in an analysis (Karasek, 1976) of follow-up data from the Swedish Level of Living Survey (Johansson, 1970).

Considerations such as these have generated a readiness to pay attention to knowledge gained by research into human stress and coping. And this, in turn, has stimulated efforts among scientists enagaged in basic research to provide data that can be put to practical use. This paper reviews some efforts along these lines.

THE SEARCH FOR 'OPTIMAL ENVIRONMENTS'

Psychobiology and social psychology generally view problems related to stressful person–environment transactions from different perspectives and tackle them by different methods. There is, however, a conceptual link between the two disciplines. Common to both is the emphasis on the human need for a moderately varied flow of stimuli and events as well as the need for social interaction. Another joint focal point concerns the individual's need to exercise personal control over his/her activities.

Our approach to stress in working life (Frankenhaeuser and Gardell, 1976) rests on the assumption that a better understanding of the causes underlying maladjustment related to work can be gained by integrating concepts and methods from psychobiology and social psychology within a common frame. This line of research has much in common with the pioneering work carried out by Caplan, Cobb, French, Kahn, and their associates at the Institute for Social Research, University of Michigan (e.g. Kahn, 1973).

The *social-psychological approach* to underload and overload is based on the assumption that joy and pride in work are fundamental human needs. Critical factors are those which circumscribe people's ability to control their own work and assess their work role in relation to a meaningful whole, as well as factors which limit opportunities for cooperation and fellowship with others (e.g. Gardell, 1976b).

The *psychobiological approach* is based on the concept of arousal. In order to function adequately, the central nervous system requires an inflow of impulses from the external environment. Both lack and excess of stimulation threaten the homeostatic mechanisms by which the organism maintains an adequate degree of arousal. In this context, the concepts of underload and overload refer to the inability of the central regulatory mechanisms to maintain an optimal arousal level at high and low levels of stimulus input. This is the biological principle underlying the inverted-U relationship between psychological functioning and physiological arousal. The optimal level is located at the midpoint of a scale ranging between very low and very high levels of stimulus input. At the optimal level, the central nervous system is moderately aroused, individual resources are mobilized, and full attention is given to the surroundings; the person is emotionally balanced and performs to the best of his/her abilities.

At low levels of stimulus input, the individual tends to be inattentive, easily distracted, and bored. Poor performance is associated with a slowing down of brain processes. Conditions of extreme understimulation, involving both sensory and social deprivation, are accompanied by a state of mental impoverishment and alienation with loss of initiative and capacity for involvement.

At the opposite end of the stimulus continuum, the central nervous system is over-aroused. The ability to select adequate information and to respond selectively to the impinging signals is impaired. Feelings of excitement and tension develop, followed by a gradual fragmentation of thought processes, a loss of ability to integrate the messages into a meaningful whole, impaired judgement, and loss of initiative.

The crucial point is that large groups in society are forced to live and work outside the 'stimulus zone' that provides opportunities for active, goal-directed behaviour. Among these are industrial workers engaged in monotonous, restricted jobs, the elderly, the handicapped, and the poor. Whereas privileged groups in society may have the power to influence their surroundings so as to attain a better person–environment fit, the underprivileged and weak are forced to adapt to conditions shaped by others.

THE COSTS OF ACHIEVEMENT

One of the notions underlying the use of physiological and biochemical techniques in *human stress research* is that the load which a particular environment places on an individual can be determined by measuring the activity of the body's organ systems. One can, for instance, make functional assessments of various organs that are controlled by the brain and reflect its activity and level of wakefulness. With the development of biochemical techniques that permit the determination of exceedingly small amounts of various hormones in blood and in urine, psychoneuroendocrinology has come to play an increasingly important role in stress research. Two neuroendocrine systems are of particular interest: the sympathetic-adrenal medullary system, with the secretion of the catecholamines adrenaline and noradrenaline, and the pituitary-adrenal cortical system, with the secretion of glucocorticoids, e.g. cortisol. These hormones play a key role for several reasons: as sensitive indicators of the stressfulness of person–environment transactions, as regulators of vital bodily functions and, in some circumstances, as mediators of bodily responses leading to pathological states. (For reviews the reader is referred to, for example, Euler, 1967; Frankenhaeuser, 1971, 1975a, 1979, 1980; Levi, 1972; Mason, 1975.)

It should be stressed that these neuroendocrine responses to the psychosocial environment are determined by the individual's cognitive appraisal of the situation and the emotional impact of the stimuli rather than by their objective characteristics. This implies that attitudes and values are potent determinants of stress responses on the physiological level and, hence, associated with the 'diseases of adaptation'.

An important feature of our *research strategy* is the combination of laboratory and field studies, both of which will be illustrated by examples. In the former type of study, specific problems are extracted from natural settings and brought into the laboratory for systematic examination. The latter takes our laboratory-based, experimental techniques into the field and applies them to persons engaged in their daily activities. Both types of study aid in the assessment of 'achievement costs'. They are focused on the risks and benefits involved in meeting situational demands by 'raising the body's thermostat of defense' (Selye, 1974). Will the person who responds in this way have to pay a price for behavioural effectiveness in terms of increased bodily wear and tear?

In the laboratory, questions such as these can be studied by, for example, exposing a person, who is engaged in performing a task, to a sudden increase in task demand. Under these circumstances he may adopt one of two different strategies: either maintaining performance at a constant level by increasing his effort, or keeping his effort constant and letting performance deteriorate. The former strategy exacts a higher subjective cost, as reflected in self-reports of various aspects of psychological involvement. The physiological cost will be higher, too, as reflected in various arousal indices.

In general, the participants in our experiments, under laboratory as well as natural conditions, choose to meet situational demands by investing the effort needed to maintain a high performance level, often showing a remarkable ability to 'pull themselves together'. An example (Figure 1) is provided by experiments in which a cognitive conflict task was performed at two levels of difficulty, one denoted 'single conflict', the other 'double conflict' (Frankenhaeuser and Johansson, 1976). The higher mental load of the latter task was reflected in self-reports of distress as well as in measures of adrenaline excretion and heart rate. In other words, the subjects met the increase in task demand by 'raising the thermostat', and in these circumstances performance remained intact.

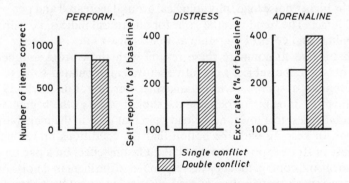

Figure 1 Mean performance in a cognitive task under conditions of 'single' and 'double' conflict, and mean changes (log scale) in subjective distress and adrenaline excretion, expressed as percentages of baseline values. Based on Frankenhaeuser and Johansson, 1976; reproduced by permission of Opinion Publications, Inc.

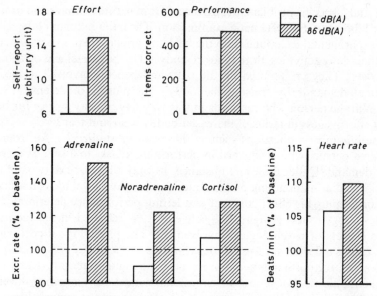

Figure 2 Mean scores for effort and arithmetic performance, and mean changes from baseline in adrenaline, noradrenaline, and cortisol excretion and heart rate in subjects doing arithmetic under exposure to noise of 76 and 86 dB(A). Based on Lundberg and Frankenhaeuser, 1978; reproduced by permission of North-Holland Publishing Company

The picture was similar (Figure 2) when subjects were exposed to one of two intensities of white noise while performing mental arithmetic (Lundberg and Frankenhaeuser, 1978). As predicted, more effort was invested in doing arithmetic at the higher noise load, physiological arousal increased and performance remained intact. The trend was the same for all arousal indices, i.e. adrenaline, noradrenaline, and cortisol excretion as well as heart rate.

It is instructive to compare these results with those from another noise experiment where the subject's cognitive set was manipulated so as to induce a less ambitious response style (Frankenhaeuser and Lundberg, 1977). In essence, this was done by introducing the subject, right at the beginning of an experimental series, to a lower noise load than that used in the main part of the experiment. In keeping with the notion that the conditions prevailing in the initial phase of stress exposure tend to have a lasting effect on a person's mode of adjustment and coping, the subjects responded to the increased noise intensity by letting their performance drop instead of striving to meet the rise in demand. In these circumstances the increase in noise intensity was not accompanied by increased physiological arousal.

Our experimental findings show that, among normal healthy persons, those who secrete relatively more adrenaline tend to perform better in terms

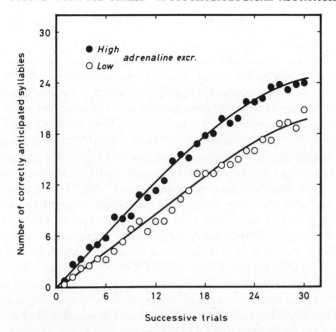

Figure 3 Mean performance on successive trials in a verbal-rote learning task in subjects with high (above median) and low (below median) adrenaline-excretion values. Reprinted with permission of publisher from: Frankenhaeuser, M. & Andersson, K. Note on interactions between cognitive and endocrine functions. *Perceptual and Motor Skills*, 1974, 38, 557–558

of speed, accuracy, and endurance than those who secrete less. This relationship is particularly marked under conditions of low to moderate stimulation (cf. reviews by Frankenhaeuser, 1975b; Lundberg, 1980; O'Hanlon and Beatty, 1976). The example given in Figure 3 (Frankenhaeuser and Andersson, 1974) shows that performance in a learning task was consistently superior in high-adrenaline compared with low-adrenaline subjects (i.e. subjects above and below the median adrenaline-excretion value).

The question that presents itself is whether adrenaline-mediated adjustments to short-term demands will have lasting after-effects, reducing workers' ability to cope with subsequent requirements and threatening their health and well-being. Although there is no direct evidence for a causal relationship between catecholamine secretion and disease, data from several sources suggest that, if secretion is prolonged, damage to various organs and organ systems may occur (e.g. Eliot, Clayton, Pieper, and Todd, 1977; Henry and Stephens, 1977; Raab, 1971). These questions will be considered in the next section.

SLOW 'UNWINDING' AFTER WORK OVERLOAD

The data presented above take us to the question of *after-effects* of acute demands. It seems reasonable to regard the duration of the response evoked by temporary disturbances in daily life as a key determinant of their potential harmfulness. In other words, the speed with which a person 'unwinds' after stressful transactions with the environment will influence the total 'wearing' of his/her biological system. It will also influence the extent to which stress at work is 'carried over' into leisure time (cf. p. 222). Hence, physiological 'unwinding' mechanisms tend to influence the interaction between work and leisure.

It is noteworthy that individuals differ with regard to the temporal pattern of their adrenal-medullary activity during stress. Comparisons between persons classified as rapid and slow 'adrenaline decreasers' support the assumption that a quick return to physiological baseline after energy mobilization induced by short-term exposure to a heavy mental load, implies an 'economic' mode of response. Conversely, a slow return to baseline indicates poor adjustment in the sense that the person 'over-responds' by spending resources that are no longer called for. In agreement with this reasoning, results from a laboratory study (Johansson and Frankenhaeuser, 1973) showed that 'rapid decreasers' tended to be psychologically better balanced and more efficient in achievement situations than 'slow decreasers' (Figure 4).

An equally important finding is that the time for 'unwinding' varies predictably with the individual's state of general well-being. Thus, in a group of industrial workers, the proportion of 'rapid decreasers' was significantly higher

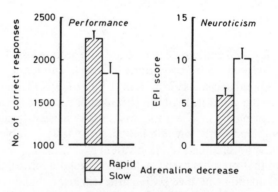

Figure 4 Means and standard errors for sensori-motor performance and neuroticism scores on Eysenck's Personality Inventory (EPI) in rapid and slow 'adrenaline decreasers'. Based on Johansson and Frankenhaeuser, 1973; reproduced by permission of North-Holland Publishing Company

after than before a vacation period, which had improved the workers' physical and psychological condition (Johansson, 1976).

These findings led us to focus on possible after-effects of an extended period of *overtime at work* in a study of female employees in an insurance company (Rissler, 1977; Rissler and Elgerot, 1978). The extra time (an average of 73 hours per employee) was spread over two months but most of it occurred during a four-week period. No new duties were involved, only an increase in the quantity of regular work. The employees were free to choose the schedule for their extra hours and most of them opted for work on Saturdays and Sundays, rather than doing more than eight hours on weekdays. Since these women ordinarily devoted several week-end hours to household duties, they faced a conflict between responsibilities at home and at work.

It was argued that the overtime load would call for intense adaptive efforts, the effects of which would not be restricted to the extra work hours, but would also manifest themselves during and after the ordinary workdays. The results supported this hypothesis in that adrenaline excretion was significantly increased throughout the overtime period, both during the day and in the evening. Figure 5 shows daytime and evening measures of adrenaline excretion on nine occasions, one before, six during, and two after the overtime period. The daytime values were determined in samples obtained at the place of work, the evening values in samples taken at home. As shown in Figure 5, the mean adrenaline level of the group was consistently elevated during the overtime

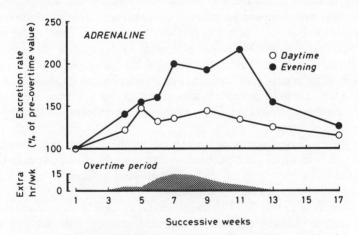

Figure 5 Mean adrenaline excretion in office workers during the day and evening on nine occasions before, during, and after a period of overtime at work. Values obtained during and after the overtime period are expressed as percentages of those obtained before this period. Most of the extra hours were worked at week-ends, and urine samples were obtained on Tuesdays. Based on Rissler and Elgerot, 1978

period, after which it declined and approached the levels typical of ordinary work conditions. The most remarkable finding was the pronounced elevation of adrenaline output in the evenings, which were spent relaxing at home. This was accompanied by markedly elevated heart rate as well as feelings of irritability and fatigue. It is worth noting that there was a time-lag between the work-load peak, which occurred in the middle of the overtime period, and the peak adrenaline excretion, which came at the very end of the period. Hence, the results show that the effects of overload may spread to leisure hours, and that they may accumulate gradually, which delays their full impact.

It should also be noted that there were considerable differences between the women in their response to the overtime work. These differences, which may be partly related to constitutional factors, indicated that slow unwinding tended to be associated with various symptoms of dissatisfaction and psychosomatic disturbances.

CONTROLLABILITY—A KEY TO COPING

In psychobiological research the opportunity to exert control over one's own activities is recognized as a major determinant of the stressfulness of person–environment transactions. It is generally agreed that, in the long run, controllability facilitates adjustment and enhances coping effectiveness, although the effort involved in exerting control may be associated with a temporary increase in arousal (cf. review by Averill, 1973). Conversely, lack of control may have widespread negative consequences, among which is a state of 'learned helplessness' (Seligman, 1975) which, in turn, may lead to depression. According to this theory (Maier and Seligman, 1976), a sense of hopelessness, paired with a reduced motivation to control, is likely to develop when a person experiences that events and outcomes are independent of his/her actions. Research along these lines has obvious relevance for the measures taken to enhance the quality of working life by increasing the influence of the employees in their places of work.

Our psychobiological approach to the issue of control is based on the assumption that a person who is in a position to regulate stimulus input may be able to maintain both physiological and psychological activation at an optimal level over a wide range of stimulus conditions.

Some aspects of controllability lend themselves well to experimental study. Our approach to the problem will be illustrated, starting with some laboratory analogues and proceeding with studies conducted in natural settings.

Conditions characterized by uncertainty, unpredictability, and lack of control usually produce a rise in adrenaline output. In laboratory experiments, the degree of stimulus predictability as well as the availability of adequate coping responses can be systematically varied. An example is provided by a study concerned with the avoidance of aversive stimulation in three differently

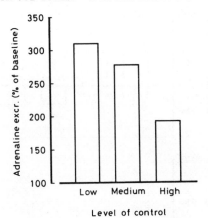

Figure 6 Mean adrenaline excretion in three laboratory situations differing with regard to the level of control. Values are expressed as percentages of baseline level. Based on Frankenhaeuser and Rissler, 1970. Reproduced by permission of Springer-Verlag

designed sessions (Frankenhaeuser and Rissler, 1970). Figure 6 shows that under conditions of low control, i.e. when subjects were exposed to mild but uncontrollable and unpredictable electric shocks, adrenaline excretion was about three times as high as during relaxation. The two other sessions were designed so that the subjects exercised varying degrees of control over the aversive stimulation. As seen in the diagram, adrenaline output decreased successively as the subjects' situation changed from one in which they were helpless into one that they could master.

The pituitary-adrenal cortical system plays a particularly interesting role in relation to the helplessness-mastery dimension. While lack of control is accompanied by a pronounced increase in the secretion of cortisol, secretion may be actively suppressed under conditions characterized *either* by a high level of control and predictability (e.g. Coover, Ursin, and Levine, 1973; Levine, 1978; Weiss, 1972) *or* by strong psychological defences (Friedman, Mason, and Hamburg, 1963).

Recent data from our laboratory (Frankenhaeuser, Lundberg, and Forsman, 1980) illustrate the dissociation between the adrenal-medullary and the adrenal-cortical response to an achievement situation characterized by feelings of complete mastery, safety, and control (Figure 7). This was attained by giving each participant a carefully designed preparatory period in which he was encouraged to try out different stimulus rates on a choice-reaction task in order to arrive at his own 'preferred work pace'. The task proper did not

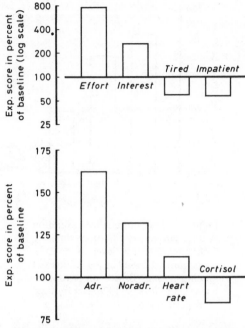

Figure 7 Mean changes from baseline level in
mood variables (upper diagram) and physiological variables (lower diagram) in an achievement situation characterized by high controllability and 'confident task involvement'. Based
on Frankenhaeuser, Lundberg, and Forsman, in
press

start until the subject felt confident about the pace at which to begin a period
of sustained work. Every five minutes he was then given the opportunity to
modify the stimulus rate so as to maintain an optimal work pace. Hence, the
situation was both predictable and controllable to a very high degree. Self-
reports indicated that these experimental arrangements were successful in
creating an atmosphere which was both pleasant and stimulating, providing
excellent possibilities for sustained work. Under these conditions of 'confident
task involvement' cortisol showed a tendency to decrease to a level below the
baseline. At the same time, the increase in adrenaline reflected a sustained involvement in carrying out the task. The interesting point was that, under these
demanding work conditions, the sense of being in control had a pronounced
deactivating effect on one of the organism's main adaptation systems. This,
together with other relevant data (e.g. Sachar, 1970), points to far-reaching
consequences of controllability for patterns of health and well-being.

When interpreting these results, it is worth noting that stress responses to
non-controllable events, as simulated in the laboratory (Lundberg and Franken-

haeuser, 1978), tend to be related to the extent to which persons generally perceive life events as lying beyond or within their sphere of influence as determined
by the internal–external locus of control scale (Rotter, 1966). This underlines
the role of learning in the development of active coping strategies as opposed
to passive psychological defences.

STRESS IN URBAN COMMUTING

Commuting forms part of the day-to-day hassles that add to the stressfulness
of urban life. One of our projects provides an example of how psychobiological
techniques can be used for monitoring human adjustment to pressures of everyday life. Our aim was to identify the stressful aspects of daily commuting
between a suburban home and a central-city job. A period of petrol rationing
during the oil shortage in the winter 1974 provided an opportunity to examine
a group of passengers who made the same journey under different conditions
of crowdedness (Lundberg, 1976). An increase in the number of passengers during the rationing period, although not more that 10 per cent, was reflected in
measures of adrenaline excretion as well as in measures of perceived discomfort
and crowdedness.

Figure 8 shows that adrenaline excretion (left-hand diagram) was significantly
higher during the more crowded conditions of the second trip. In this diagram,
adrenaline measures are expressed as percentages of Sunday values, when the
persons stayed at home.

As to the actual travelling conditions, seats were available for all passengers
on both occasions. The most pronounced difference between the two trips was

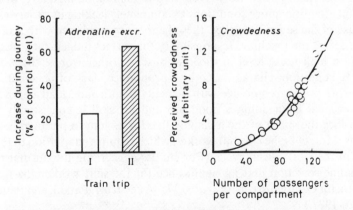

Figure 8 Mean increase (in % of baseline) of adrenaline excretion
during each of two train trips made under different conditions of
crowdedness (left) and ratings of perceived crowdedness (right).
Based on Lundberg, 1976; reproduced by permission of Opinion
Publications, Inc.

that the possibility of selecting a seat and choosing one's own company was much more restricted on the second trip. In agreement with this, we found in another study in the same series that passengers who boarded the train at the first stop secreted less adrenaline than those who boarded midway, when the train was more crowded and seat selection more restricted (Singer, Lundberg, and Frankenhaeuser, 1978). We have interpreted these results as showing that psycho-ecological factors, including controllability, were more important determinants of stress than the length and the duration of the trip.

The right-hand diagram of Figure 8 shows that perceived crowdedness, according to magnitude estimates made at successive points on the journey, increased as the square of the number of passengers. These are the mean ratings of a larger group of passengers, used here to illustrate the ability of 'the man in the street' to quantify his experiences by a simple scaling procedure.

STRESS ON THE ASSEMBLY LINE

Data from a large-scale ergonomics study of sawmills in Sweden—based on experts' ratings, health surveys, and interviews—show that many jobs in the highly mechanized sawmill are characterized by severe physical strain and restriction of social interaction and movement (Ager et al., 1975). The workers report feelings of extreme monotony, repetitiveness, non-participation, and coercion. The work is machine-paced, and the monitoring process demands unfailing attention, since skilled judgements of timber quality have to be made at very short intervals. A striking feature is the short work cycle, in some cases less than 5 seconds. Great effort is required to maintain a high level of performance and attention under conditions as completely lacking in variety as these. In the case of the sawmill worker, these factors are combined with a fast pace of work, set by the machine, responsibility for correct judgements, piecework rush, and a high noise level in the sawhouse. In other words, the worker is exposed to conditions characterized by a pronounced lack of personal control over the work process, combined with elements of both underload and overload. He is prevented from doing a good job and his skill is consistently under-utilized, since the speed of the assembly line forces him to perform below his standards. Moreover, he is a shift worker, which requires adaptation to repeated changes in the work–sleep cycle. (For studies concerning the diurnal rhythm of adrenaline secretion and its significance for the shift worker the reader is referred to, for example, Fröberg et al., 1975; Åkerstedt, Patkai, and Pettersson-Dahlgren, 1977.)

For our study (Frankenhaeuser and Gardell, 1976; Johansson, Aronsson, and Lindström, 1978), we selected a group classified as high-risk workers on the basis of the extremely constricted, machine-paced nature of their assembly line job. This group was compared with a control group of workers from the same mill, whose job was not as constricted physically and mentally.

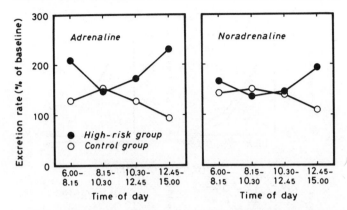

Figure 9 Successive mean values for adrenaline and noradrenaline excretion during an eight-hour work shift in two groups of sawmill workers. Values are expressed as percentages of baselines obtained under non-work conditions. Frankenhaeuser and Gardell, 1976; reproduced by permission of Opinion Publications, Inc.

Figure 9 shows successive measurements of catecholamine excretion, taken during an eight-hour work shift and expressed as percentages of baseline values obtained under work-free conditions at home. The average adrenaline excretion was significantly higher in the high-risk group than in the controls. Furthermore, the time course was strikingly different for both amines, catecholamine release decreasing towards the end of the workday in the control group, but increasing in the high-risk group. The difference between the groups in the last measurement of the day was significant for both amines. Such a build-up of catecholamine arousal during a long workday should be regarded as a warning signal, indicating that the organism is forced to mobilize 'reserve capacity', which in the long run is likely to add to its wear and tear. In other words, the cost of adaptation may be exceedingly high. These assumptions were supported by interview data indicating that an inability to relax after work was a common complaint in the high-risk workers. Moreover, the frequency of psychosomatic symptoms as well as absenteeism was exceptionally high in this group.

The next step was to try to identify those aspects of the work process which induced the psychological and neuroendocrine stress responses. It was hypothesized that the common origin of the high catecholamine level and the high frequency of psychosomatic symptoms in our high-risk group was the monotonous, coercive, machine-paced nature of the job. In agreement with this, correlational analyses showed consistent, statistically significant relations between neuroendocrine response patterns and job characteristics referring to different aspects of monotony and machine control. These relationships were examined further by comparing subgroups of workers differing with regard to specific job characteristics, as determined by expert ratings, e.g. degree of

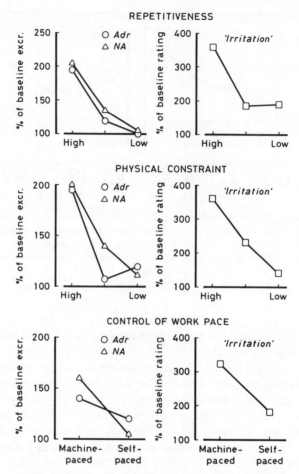

Figure 10 Mean values for adrenaline and noradrenaline
excretion and self-ratings of irritation in a group of
sawmill workers under conditions differing with regard
to repetitiveness, physical constraint, and control of
work pace. Values obtained during work have been
expressed as percentages of baselines obtained under
non-work conditions. Based on Johansson, Aronsson,
and Lindström, 1978; reproduced by permission of
Taylor & Francis Ltd

repetitiveness and physical constraint. Most subgroups were rather small and
the difference between them not statistically significant, but the trends were
consistent and formed a meaningful pattern as illustrated in Figure 10 (for
details see Johansson, Aronsson, and Lindström, 1978). Stress, as reflected
in adrenaline and noradrenaline excretion as well as in self-reports of irritation,

was most severe when the job was highly repetitious, when the worker had to maintain the same posture throughout working hours, and when the work pace was controlled by the machine.

When evaluating these data it should be noted that conditions in the sawmill are representative of a wide range of mass-production industries, e.g. the car industry. It is encouraging to note the successful outcome—in terms of increased job satisfaction without loss of effectiveness—of technological innovations at the Saab-Scania and Volvo plants now operated without conventional assembly lines. This raises the question of the risks and benefits of highly automated production systems, to be considered next.

STRESS IN PROCESS CONTROL

As we have seen, research on job stress consistently points to the same risk factors: short, repetitive work cycles, machine-controlled work pace, restriction of movement and social interaction.

These particular risk factors can be reduced or even eliminated in the completely automated production systems which form a dominant trend in current development. The question is whether work satisfaction will improve and the strain on workers will diminish by a transition to production systems, where the repetitive, manual elements are taken over by machines and the workers are left with mainly supervisory, controlling functions.

One of the advantages of highly automated systems is that many of the tasks are comparatively qualified. The operators supervising a process are allowed at least partial control over their work pace. The work is not regulated in detail, with a pre-set schedule of movements, and the operators are fairly free to move about. All this increases the chances for an active, participatory work role.

Other, less optimistic forecasts suggest, however, that although automation does reduce certain alienatory factors, it introduces new stress components that may be still more detrimental (cf. Bainbridge, 1978; Gardell, 1976a; Johansson, 1978). These are seen most clearly in the control-room of large-scale plants. Monitoring a process calls for acute attention and readiness to act throughout a monotonous period on duty, a requirement that does not match the brain's need to be stimulated in order to maintain optimal alertness. It is well documented (e.g. Broadbent, 1971) that the ability to detect critical signals in a monotonous environment declines rapidly even within the first half hour. The fact that the peocess operator work in shifts means that he has to perform his attention-demanding tasks also when 'out of phase' with his biological rhythm, i.e. when his adrenaline secretion is likely to be low and his ability to concentrate reduced (e.g. Fröberg et al., 1975). To this must be added the strain inherent in the awareness that temporary inattention and even an intrinsically slight error could have extensive economic and other disastrous consequences.

The operator's task is focused on *preventing* a breakdown of the process. To this end he should sound the alarm without a moment's delay and immediately thereafter make a series of rapid decisions and act upon them instantaneously. Empirical evidence indicates that ability to make decisions may suffer a temporary paralysis under conditions such as these. During a brief but possibly critical interval, the operator may be incapable of making use of the information available to him.

Other critical aspects are associated with the high demands on mental skill. The process operator is concerned with symbols, abstract signals on arrays of instruments, and is not in touch with the actual products of his work. Little is known about the psychological implications of such job requirements. Will they meet the workers' demands for comprehending, predicting, and controlling their own activities and linking them to a meaningful whole? These problems are now given high priority in our research programme (e.g. Johansson, 1978).

MAN-ADAPTED TECHNOLOGY—THE SEARCH FOR GUIDELINES

In the preceding sections, examples from stress research have been used to illustrate how technology is being used to create environments which conflict with fundamental human needs. In so far as life conditions are being shaped in violation of basic rules of psychology and biology, it does not make sense to define adaptation as 'harmony between man and his environment'. It seems more adequate to use the concept 'healthy maladjustment' to describe the failure of human beings to adapt to inhuman conditions—a sound revolt against unsound demands on adaptability. There is a risk, however, that the insidious process of 'pseudo-adaptation' may tend to counteract our drive to rebel against potentially dangerous uses of technology. This process, which is associated with the great flexibility of the human nervous system, permits subtle symptoms of maladjustment to accumulate gradually without eliciting corrective responses on the political and cultural levels.

Special attention should be given to risks involved in overstimulation, one of the hallmarks of the technologically advanced society and an inducement to 'live faster' in order to 'keep up'. In the long run, the most serious consequences of overstimulation are likely to lie in the emotional sphere, in the process of habituation. When we are bombarded with too many, too strong, or too frequent stimuli, the response of the nervous system gradually weakens, the stimuli lose their impact, and the reactions are toned down. The physiological stress effects become less intense and feelings of distress and discomfort fade. But so do feelings of involvement, empathy, and consideration for others. By its very nature, emotional erosion is an 'invisible' process and there is a risk that we will not notice the gradual attrition of our capacity for psychological involvement. This capacity has often been mobilized in the past when vital values were at stake, as witness the large groups that became active when it was realized how seriously the environment was threatened by pollution and exploitation. But if man himself is the subject of an analogous impoverishment— if it is human tolerances that are exceeded so that we no longer have an overview and consequently lack initiative—who will there be to sound the alarm and pioneer a new line of development?

Considerations such as these have been neglected in the past when demands on short-term efficiency have furthered the development of production systems which inhibit initiative and suppress creativity. One implication is that workers engaged in jobs where their abilities are constantly under-utilized represent an enormous 'creativity reserve'. Technological innovations should aim at mobilizing this reserve.

There are other unused human resources. In our society where individual effectiveness is at a premium, egotistic values are promoted. Human behaviour patterns characterized by hard-driving competitiveness and an urge to excel thrive in a society that consistently rewards those who think, act, and communicate more rapidly than their peers. If other, altrustic, values were promoted, human resources in the sphere of solidary interpersonal relations would be mobilized. This could guide development along new paths.

ACKNOWLEDGEMENTS

The research reported in this paper has been supported by grants from the Swedish Work Environment Fund (Project No. 76/49), the Swedish Medical Research Council (Project No. 997), and the Swedish Council for Research in the Humanities and Social Sciences.

REFERENCES

Ager, B., Aminoff, S., Baneryd, K., Englund, A., Nerell, G., Nilsson, C., Saarman, E., and Söderqvist, A. (1975). *Arbetsmiljön i sågverk. En tvärvetenskaplig undersökning (Work environment in the sawmill. A multidisciplinary investigation)*, Rapport AM 101/75, Arbetarskyddsstyrelsen (National Board of Occupational Safety and Health), Stockholm.

Åkerstedt, T., Pátkai, P., and Pettersson-Dahlgren, K. (1977). Field studies of shift work: II. Temporal patterns in psychophysiological activation in workers alternating between night and day work, *Ergonomics*, **20**, 621–631.

Allardt, E. (1975). *Att Ha, att Älska, att Vara (Having, Loving, Being)*, Argos, Lund.

Averill, J. R. (1973). Personal control over aversive stimuli and its relationship to stress, *Psychological Bulletin*, **80**, 286–303.

Bainbridge, L. (1978). The process controller, in W. T. Singleton (ed.), *The Study of Real Skill*, MTP Press, London.

Broadbent, D. E. (1971). *Decision and Stress*, Academic Press, London and New York.

Campbell, A. (1976). Subjective measures of well-being, *American Psychologist*, **31**, 117–124.

Coover, G., Ursin, H., and Levine, S. (1973). Corticosterone and avoidance in rats with basolateral amygdala lesions, *Journal of Comparative and Physiological Psychology*, **85**, 111–122.

Eliot, R. S., Clayton, F. C., Pieper, G. M., and Todd, G. L. (1977). Influence of environment stress on pathogenesis of sudden cardiac death, *Federation Proceedings*, **36**, 1719–1724.

Euler, U.S.v. (1967). Adrenal medullary secretion and its neural control, in L. Martini and W. F. Ganong (eds.), *Neuroendocrinology*, Vol. 2, Academic Press, New York, 283–333.

Frankenhaeuser, M. (1971). Behavior and circulating catecholamines, *Brain Research*, **31**, 241–262.

Frankenhaeuser, M. (1975a). Experimental approaches to the study of catecholamines and emotion, in L. Levi (ed.), *Emotions—Their Parameters and Measurement*, Raven Press, New York, 209–234.

Frankenhaeuser, M. (1975b). Sympathetic-adrenomedullary activity, behaviour and the psychosocial environment, in P. H. Venables and M. J. Christie (eds.), *Research in Psychophysiology*, Wiley, London, ch. 4, 71–94.

Frankenhaeuser, M. (1977). Quality of life: Criteria for behavioral adjustment, *International Journal of Psychology*, **12**, 99–110.

Frankenhaeuser, M. (1979). Psychoneuroendocrine approaches to the study of emotion, in H. E. Howe and R. A. Dienstbier (eds), *Nebraska Symposium on Motivation 1978*, University of Nebraska Press, Lincoln.

Frankenhaeuser, M. (1980). Psychoneuroendocrine approaches to the study of stressful person–environment transactions, in H. Selye (ed.),*Selye's Guide to Stress Research*, Van Nostrand Reinhold, New York.

Frankenhaeuser, M., and Andersson, K. (1974). Note on interactions between cognitive and endocrine functions, *Perceptual and Motor Skills*, **38**, 557–558.

Frankenhaeuser, M., and Gardell, B. (1976). Underload and overload in working life: Outline of a multidisciplinary approach, *Journal of Human Stress*, **2**, 35–46.

Frankenhaeuser, M., and Johansson, G. (1976). Task demand as reflected in catecholamine excretion and heart rate, *Journal of Human Stress*, **2**, 15–23.

Frankenhaeuser, M., and Lundberg, U. (1977). The influence of cognitive set on performance and arousal under different noise loads, *Motivation and Emotion*, **1**, 139–149.

Frankenhaeuser, M., Lundberg, U., and Forsman, L. (in press). Psychophysiological reactions in a self-paced reaction-time task, *Biological Psychology*.

Frankenhaeuser, M., and Rissler, A. (1970). Effects of punishment on catecholamine release an efficiency of performance, *Psychopharmacologia*, **17**, 378–390.

Friedman, S. B., Mason, J. W., and Hamburg, D. A. (1963). Urinary 17-hydroxy-corticosteroid levels in parents of children with neoplastic disease, *Psychosomatic Medicine*, **25**, 364–376.

Fröberg, J. E., Karlsson, C.-G., Levi, L., and Lindberg, L. (1975). Circadian rhythms of catecholamine excretion, shooting range performance and self-ratings of fatigue during sleep deprivation, *Biological Psychology*, **2**, 175–188.

Gardell, B. (1976a). *Arbetsinnehåll och Livskvalitet (Work Content and Quality of Life)*, Prisma, Lund.

Gardell, B. (1976b). Technology, alienation and mental health. Summary of a social psychological research programme on technology and the worker, *Acta Sociologica*, **19**, 83–94.

Henry, J. P., and Stephens, P. M. (1977). *Stress, Health, and the Social Environment*, Springer Verlag, New York.

Johansson, G. (1976). Subjective wellbeing and temporal patterns of sympathetic-adrenal medullary activity, *Biological Psychology*, **4**, 157–172.

Johansson, G. (1978). Om psykosociala stressfaktorer i processövervakning. Redovisning och analys av ergonomisk literature (On psychosocial stress factors in process control.

Survey and analysis of ergonomics literature), unpublished manuscript.

Johansson, G., Aronsson, G., and Lindström, B. O. (1978). Social psychological and neuroendocrine stress reactions in highly mechanized work, *Ergonomics*, 21, 583–599.

Johansson, G., and Frankenhaeuser, M. (1973). Temporal factors in sympatho-adreno-medullary activity following acute behavioral activation, *Biological Psychology*, 1, 63–73.

Johansson, S. (1970). *Om Levnadsnivåundersökningen (On the Level of Living Survey)*, Allmänna Förlaget, Stockholm.

Kahn, R. L. (1973). Conflict, ambiguity and overload: Three elements in job stress, *Occupational Mental Health*, 3, 2–9.

Karasek, R. A. (1976). The impact of the work environment on life outside the job, Institute for Social Research, University of Stockholm, Ph.D. thesis, unpublished.

Levi, L. (1972). Stress and distress in response to psychosocial stimuli. Laboratory and real life studies on sympathoadrenomedullary and related reactions, *Acta Medica Scandinavica*, Suppl. 528.

Levine, S. (1978). Cortisol changes following repeated experiences with parachute training, in H. Ursin, E. Baade, and S. Levine (eds), *Psychobiology of Stress*, Academic Press, New York, ch. 5, 51–56.

Lundberg, U. (1976). Urban commuting: Crowdedness and catecholamine excretion, *Journal of Human Stress*, 2, 26–32.

Lundberg, U. (1980). Psychophysiological aspects of performance and adjustment to stress, in H. W. Krohne and L. Laux (eds), *Achievement, Stress and Anxiety*, Hemisphere Publishing Corporation, Washington, DC., ch. 4, 75–91.

Lundberg, U., and Frankenhaeuser, M. (1978). Psychophysiological reactions to noise as modified by personal control over noise intensity, *Biological Psychology*, 6, 51–59.

Maier, S. F., and Seligman, M.E.P. (1976). Learned helplessness: Theory and evidence, *Journal of Experimental Psychology: General*, 105 (1), 3–46.

Mason, J. W. (1975). Emotion as reflected in patterns of endocrine integration, in L. Levi (ed.), *Emotions—Their Parameters and Measurement*, Raven Press, New York, 143–181.

O'Hanlon, J. F., and Beatty, J. (1976). Catecholamine correlates of radar monitoring performance, *Biological Psychology*, 4, 293–304.

Raab, W. (1971). Cardiotoxic biochemical effects of emotional–environmental stressors—Fundamentals of psychocardiology, in L. Levi (ed.), *Society, Stress and Disease*, Vol. 1: *The Psychosocial Environment and Psychosomatic Diseases*, Oxford University Press, London, 331–337.

Rissler, A. (1977). Stress reactions at work and after work during a period of quantitative overload, *Ergonomics*, 20, 13–16.

Rissler, A., and Elgerot, A. (1978). Stressreaktioner vid övertidsarbete (Stress reactions related to overtime at work), Rapporter, nr 23, Department of Psychology, University of Stockholm.

Rotter, J. B. (1966). Generalized expectancies for internal versus external control of reinforcement, *Psychological Monographs*, 80 (1) (Whole No. 609).

Sachar, E. J. (1970). Psychological factors relating to activation and inhibition of the adrenocortical stress response in man: A review, in D.de Wied and J. A. W. M. Weijen (eds), *Progress in Brain Research*, Vol. 32, Elsevier, Amsterdam, 316–324.

Seligman, M. E. P. (1975). *Helplessness. On Depression, Development and Death*, Freeman, San Francisco.

Selye, H. (1974). *Stress without Distress*, Lippincott, Philadelphia and New York.

Singer, J. E., Lundberg, U., and Frankenhaeuser, M. (1978). Stress on the train: A study of urban commuting, in A. Baum, J. E. Singer, and S. Valins (eds), *Advances in Environmental Psychology*, Vol. 1, Erlbaum, Hillsdale, NJ.

Weiss, J. M. (1972). Psychological factors in stress and disease, *Scientific American*, 226, 104–113.

Working Life
Edited by B. Gardell and G. Johanssoon
© 1981 John Wiley & Sons Ltd

Family Life Cycle, Work, and the Quality of Life: Reflections on the Roots of Happiness, Despair, and Indifference in Modern Society*

HAROLD L. WILENSKY

Among the widely accepted myths about the shape of modern society, three are most prominent in popular discussion. First, the nuclear family is in serious trouble, if it is not breaking up. Second, the mass of citizens are increasingly alienated from their work or from ever-more technocratic, bureaucratic, centralized workplaces and are therefore withdrawing from work in spirit if not in hours. Finally, a new 'post-industrial' order is emerging in which intellectuals, scientists, managers, and experts in command of theoretical knowledge dominate the political system, while service occupations (the 'tertiary sector') dominate employment and production, and 'post-materialist' values dominate the culture**. In other words, a vanguard of educated people, occupied in 'health, education, research, and government' (Bell, 1973, 15), is already decisive in every modern political economy, and it is the carrier of the 'cultural revolution'. Older issues are giving way to newer issues, in a major shift in values—a shift from the work ethic to freedom and expressiveness ('do your own thing'), from intellectual calculation to impulse and ecstasy, from hierarchy to equality and participatory democracy, from a competitive rat-race to a quest for community, from economic growth and consumerism to environmentalism and a concern with the quality of life (cf. Davis, 1971; Turner, 1976).

---

*This chapter is part of a forthcoming book on the politics of taxing and spending based on research made possible by the support of the National Science Foundation (Grant SOC77–13265), the German Marshall Fund, the Russell Sage Foundation, the Institute of International Studies, and the Institute of Industrial Relations of the University of California, Berkeley. It is a revision of a paper presented at the International Symposium on Man and Working Life, Stockholm, 12–14 June, 1978. I am grateful to Val Lorwin and Olof Palme for critical comments, and to Susan Reed Hahn, Jeffrey Haydu, and Anne T. Lawrence for research assistance.

**Thus Bell (1973, 1976) and Galbraith (1967); their work draws on themes in Weber, Veblen, Schumpeter, and Burnham. For more empirically grounded arguments regarding such trends, see Inglehart, 1977, and citations therein.

Writers who see this post-industrial era vary in their depiction of both the trends and the generating forces. But they agree that industrialization is the root cause of major changes in the family and in the technical and social organization of work. These changes in turn have produced a population of which a large fraction is educated, secure, affluent, and mobile. These vanguard groups are in a position to demand still more security and freedom. Their restiveness and their consciousness of the possibilities of human liberation are presumably spreading to the masses of people in every rich democracy.

Drawing on my earlier research on work, careers, and leisure styles and my current research on the welfare state and equality, I shall evaluate these myths. I suggest that mass discontent is rooted neither in family break-up nor in the modern organization of work, although some aspects of both make some individuals and groups unhappy. Instead I shall emphasize normal strains of transitions over the family life cycle as they are intensified or lessened by variations in taxes, debt, and real income. If we want to explain life satisfaction and discontent, work alienation or attachment, even some aspects of political alienation, we must look to interlocking cycles of family life, work, consumption, social participation, and morale.

Here is a preview of my explanation of variations in life satisfaction. Life satisfaction or morale is high when people are established in a stable career context and are at a stage in the family life cycle where their resources and rewards balance their aspirations. For most modern populations that balance is least evident in early and late periods when morale sags, especially among young couples with preschool children, solitary survivors, the divorced, separated, or widowed of any age. Obviously, national public policies regarding services and cash targeted towards the young, the aged, and the transition singles vary greatly, so we should find some national variations in life satisfaction among such groups.

My primary aim is to reinterpret data on national and life cycle variations in life satisfaction by applying my notion of 'life cycle squeeze'—a condition where aspirations and rewards are badly out of balance. An incidental aim is to solve the puzzle that appears in many 'happiness' studies: the frequent finding that subjective life satisfaction or sense of well-being is more or less unrelated to objective conditions or the level of living (Allardt, 1977). I shall argue that when we link data on stress and strain to parallel developments in family composition, job patterns, income flows, and debt loads—the most relevant objective conditions—then we discover that how people live and how they feel about life are closely meshed.

By arguing that life satisfaction varies by nation and by stage in the family life cycle I do not deny that some intellectuals, writers, and artists—whatever their country and age—experience an existential despair that cannot be captured in a typical survey interview. But I doubt that their despair reflects the dominant mood of modern society.

Modern populations, like their pre-modern counterparts, are 'apathetic' about the big public issues. Instead, the vast majority are centrally concerned with the daily routines of life with kin and friends. They are rarely preoccupied with the great issues of war and peace, the fiscal crisis of the state, environmental degradation, or the decline of high culture; they are not excited by the prospects of participatory democracy in politics or co-determination at work. So if we are to grasp trends in the quality of life and life satisfaction we should begin with trends in family life. Then we can consider trends in the organization and meaning of work. A final section will bring the two together as a way of locating the sources of popular discontent.

IS THE NUCLEAR FAMILY DISINTEGRATING?

The theme that the modern nuclear family is disintegrating is recurrent (cf. Wilensky and Lebeaux, 1958, 67–83). What is new is a convergence of radical and conservative ideologies about family break-up. Some radical feminists have joined conservatives in the argument that equality between men and women is incompatible with a stable family life. Conservatives bemoan the drift towards equality as a major cause of family break-up. Militant feminists— whether the marxist Group Åtta in Sweden or its radical counterparts in Berkeley—see a new world coming in which true equality will, indeed, subvert conventional marriage and family life; they applaud family break-up as a requirement of the liberation of women from household slavery.

Why do so many intelligent people assert the incompatibility of equality and the stable, companionate family? Although the conservative version of this argument is losing, it is perhaps still the majority viewpoint in most rich democracies. I shall state it in its most forceful form and then evaluate the evidence.

Real equality, this argument assumes, will have three outcomes. First, men will have less incentive to care for families. If women demand that the men continue to work, be committed to careers, *and* share equally in household and child-rearing tasks, most men will prefer their present dominance in work to the newer arrangements. Second, women—freed for competition in careers and political power—will reject child-bearing. They will prefer to pursue the goals typical of men: income, status, satisfying work, power. Third, the increased competition between men and women outside the household will spill over in a struggle for dominance inside the household; such a struggle will destroy affection and sour once intimate relationships.

We lack the baseline data with which to assess these alleged trends and, as usual, we lack systematic cross-national studies of family life. But if growing equality between men and women has these effects, several inferences follow: more people should be avoiding marriage, more couples should be childless, more children should be abandoned or, at least, neglected. Finally,

divorce rates should be rising; and the quality of relationships in marriage—
the steadiness and depth of love and affection—should be diminishing.

A recent summary of evidence for trends in the United States by Mary
Jo Bane (1976) casts doubt on all but two of these inferences:

—*Marriage* enjoys unprecedented popularity. The percentage of single people
over 30 decreased from 1960 to 1974; 90–95 per cent of women marry—
a figure that has climbed in recent decades. Young Americans are merely
postponing marriage, becoming a bit more cautious.

—*Childlessness* rose in the nineteenth century and dropped in the twentieth
century: 8.2 per cent of married women born in 1846–1855 were childless;
the comparable figure is down to 7.3 per cent for women born in 1931–1935.
Of course, we cannot yet know what today's childless young women will
have done about children by the time they are in their forties. But in 1975
less than 5 per cent of wives interviewed in a US Census nationwide cross-
sectional survey expected to remain childless; the expectation of childlessness was uniformly low among various income and educational categories
(Bane, 1976, 9).

—*Child abandonment* has not increased. The percentage of children living with
at least one parent has steadily risen. By 1975, despite rising divorce rates,
only 2.7 per cent of children under 14 lived with neither of their parents.

—*Child neglect* is a more complicated phenomenon. If the question is, 'Are
urban, working mothers less effective in child-rearing than their non-working
sisters?' the answer is almost surely 'No'. The weight of evidence is that,
far from harming children, the mother's work either has no effect or increases
the self-esteem of the child. For the mother herself, it has variable effects on
marital conflict and feelings of adequacy and satisfaction in the maternal role,
depending on the mother's type of work and stage in the family life cycle
(cf. Wilensky, 1968, 243; Nye and Hoffman, 1963; and Veroff and Feld,
1970). If the question is, 'Does divorce harm children?' the answer is, 'Yes,
for a while, but it depends on their age, sex, and the circumstances'. Although
the evidence is strong that during a divorce (and for a couple of years after)
parents and their very young children are in deep trouble, there is little
evidence of enduring effects (cf. Maccoby, 1978, 200–206).

In fact, during the past 40 or 50 years there have been only two major changes
in child care arrangements. Both vary greatly by nation; both are shaped by
public policy. The first is the expansion of child-care facilities for working
mothers. The second, perhaps more dramatic, shift is the increasing use of
television as a 'babysitter'. American children watch television for an average
of 30–33 hours per week, much more time than they spend in school.

Although the effects of heavy slugs of television-viewing are still debatable,
there is good evidence that the broadcast media subvert both reading and
ordinary conversation (Wilensky, 1964, 190; Steiner, 1963). If parents and

children are talking and reading less and watching television more, then perhaps 'child neglect' is a defensible label for the trend. But all this has little to do with equality between men and women or increased labour force participation by women. And the effect of using television as a babysitter versus using day-care centres is not clear. Watching BBC is not the same as watching CBS. Schools and families that expect homework from children will thereby block addiction to television; schools and families that abandon the struggle for children's homework will leave the field open to television. Similarly, a high-quality day-care centre in Sweden is different from an overloaded school classroom for 4-year-olds in France or a poorly staffed, poorly financed day-care centre in the USA. Thus, public policies regarding education, support services and benefits for working mothers, and the programming of television may be strategic for the quality of family life.

In short, the drift towards equality between the sexes has reduced neither the marriage rate nor the willingness to have at least one child (the typical performance is two); nor has it provoked the abandonment or even neglect of children. Then what *has* happened to the nuclear family? What about divorce? And does competition between men and women for dominance in and out of the family threaten intimacy and affection?

There is abundant evidence of recent increases in one kind of family break-up—divorce. In the USA there has been an almost uninterrupted increase in the divorce rate for the entire period known. The rate increased from less than 2 per 1000 married females in 1867 to 17.8 in 1946. (That peak reflects both the typical break-up of hasty, ill-advised wartime marriages and the immediate postwar backlog of delayed divorces.) There was then a decline until the late 1950s (Wilensky and Lebeaux, 1958, 79). By 1973, however, the divorce rate surpassed its postwar peak and continued rising the recent rise is concentrated among women who in 1970 were 45–54 years old. These trends are similar for all Western nations permitting divorce (Ogburn and Nimkoff, 1955, 219); United Nations, 1954, 1960, 1966, 1971, 1975).

It is a popular sport to project death and divorce rates and to conclude that family disorganization will soon get worse. Thus, if recent trends continue, nearly four in ten of the children born in about 1970 will experience a parental death, divorce, or separation sometime during their first 18 years (Bane, 1976, 136). Even recognizing that such projections are shaky, we are still assured of a large minority of transition singles with parental responsibilities, prominent among modern populations dissatisfied with their lives.

To say that divorce rates rise is not to say that the family is breaking up. For remarriage rates have kept pace with divorce rates. Men and women are rejecting their specific partners, not the institutions of partnership.

Now let us turn to the more subtle question of the quality of relationships between the sexes. Although the achievement of equality is slow, it appears to be going on in countries as diverse in culture and politics as Japan, Sweden,

Italy, Austria, and the United States. The main liberating forces are the universal and interrelated accompaniments of industrialization: the reduced economic value of children; rising levels of aspiration for self and children; increased labour force participation by women; and a long-term decline in fertility rates. While the accent on the small nuclear family, the shearing away of members of the extended family may not be a strictly modern development (Scott and Tilly, 1975, 36–64) there is no doubt that the percentage of old people who share bed and board with their adult children *has* declined.* At every age level and marital state, adults prefer an independent household, a trend apparent at least since 1940 (Bane, 1976).

Although contemporary feminist movements are accelerating the shift towards equality in family life, it is apparent that the major liberating forces I have listed preceded such movements. (Recent survey data in the USA confirm the point: the best predictors of the shift towards more equalitarian role definitions from 1964 to 1974, among high- and low-status women alike, were not their exposure to the women's movement but instead their level of education and whether they worked (Mason, Czajka, and Arber, 1976.)

With production removed from the household, extended kin sheared away, and family size reduced, a great deal of emotional intensity has probably been directed towards the few persons left (Wilensky and Lebeaux, 1958, 72). Does intensified competition in the labour market and competition for dominance in the family render this emotional intensity poisonous? What does the effort to combine work, marriage, and parenthood do for the quality of family relationships? The research that could answer these questions has not yet been done. However, an exploratory study conducted by Karen Paige in California among 64 married couples—lower-middle and upper-working class, 30–44 years old—provides some clues. She compared the emotional life of dual-career couples with no children, dual-career couples with children, and traditional families where the wife had not worked for ten years. Their work patterns neatly fit the couples' attitudes towards women's roles, with the traditional family most conventional and conservative, the dual-career

---

*The argument that the three-generation household was not the norm in either nineteenth-century America or Europe misses the relevant time period for comparing pre-modern with urban-industrial society. If we consider household composition for an early modern period we find some contrasts. From the sixteenth to the eighteenth centuries, if there were two- rather than three-generation households, it was because of low longevity rooted in famine, malnutrition, and pestilence. Life was 'nasty, brutish, and short'. Many grandparents and other relatives could not 'live in' because they were dead. Others, the minority who reached old age, typically formed three-generation households. Or if the aged parents survived the adult children, or if the latter moved far away, the aged would often make a contract with a younger friend or couple and their children to share a household under specified conditions of mutual care. While the nuclear family may have been the prevalent form in western Europe, compared with its modern counterpart it much more readily expanded to include other kin. In Natalie Davis's phrase, the early modern family 'breathed' in a way the contemporary family does not; see Davis, 1976, 88.

couples with children moderately liberal, and the childless couples most liberated. In feelings of affection for one another, the childless working couples had a clear edge, the dual-career couples with children scored medium, and the traditional couples were least loving. What these findings suggest is that the more liberated model of the future—the double-earner pattern—will if anything enrich the emotional life of husbands and wives. Of course, we can also assume that the transition to these newer patterns will often be painful; it may involve much bargaining over the division of household labour and child care. We can expect much turmoil and tension among partners who are differentially liberated or come from different political generations. Among partners who are equally committed to careers—a tiny but growing *avant-garde*—we can anticipate sometimes unbearable tension about whose work should determine place of residence.

The announcement of the death of the nuclear family, then, is premature. Divorce rates have risen but marriage and remarriage remain popular. While fertility rates have declined and the aged and singles prefer independent households, having children is not going out of fashion. Abandoning children is even rarer than childlessness; and the fact that more mothers work does not mean more child neglect, although divorce imposes transitional strains on both children and parents. If my analysis identifies any major problems flowing from the transformation of family life—widespread private troubles that might be reduced by public policies—they are the need for (1) financial and emotional cushions for transition singles; (2) services and benefits for working couples with young children; (3) a family policy that strives to ensure diversified excellence in schools and television—the two big time-consumers and socializers in children's lives. In general, income maintenance programmes could be redesigned to take more systematic account of changing family composition, with special attention to the problems of income and time pressures among single parents and dual-career couples with young children.

In most rich countries, there is an increasing pool of people who are temporarily poor in both time and money because of changes in household composition; many of these harried people have an urge to save time and money and gain companionship by doubling up. Income maintenance eligibility rules that encourage such economies of scale would simultaneously relieve housing shortages, reduce poverty, and ease the troubles of transition singles. Specifically, in defining poverty thresholds for income-tested benefits, typical government programmes consider essential money needs in terms of the variations in size of families, but ignore equally important variations in time pressures. If two marginally poor 'broken' families with children join together to increase their resources and save time by sharing household tasks, they are sometimes treated by government eligibility rules as one unit and benefits are sharply reduced—a clear disincentive to joint household formation. If many single adults with children cannot command market wages high enough to escape poverty without outside income or without joining up with other adults, the government should provide maximum flexibility in income maintenance rules affecting household formation (Vickery, 1977). As we have seen, the size of the transition-single population is no longer trivial.

WORK AND THE WORKPLACE AS SOURCES OF MASS DISCONTENT*

If there is any theme that recurrently dominates debate about the quality of life, it is that the mass of modern citizens are increasingly alienated from their work; if they are not deeply discontented about particular jobs and occupations, then they are estranged from ever-more technocratic, bureaucratic, centralized workplaces. In turn, the combination of alienation from work and advances in real income produces a leisure- or consumer-oriented society characterized by the decline of the 'work ethic', a general withdrawal from work, and an intensified search for substitute leisure commitments.

This picture of work and its discontents misses most of what is going on. It is also ahistorical; it does not capture what is new about modern work. Work is now a social problem for four reasons, none of them unique to any 'post-industrial' era.

First, every society defines work as a central obligation for most of the population, but in modern society some people cannot obtain enough of it. The existing skills and talents of the population never perfectly fit the demands of the technology and the economy. The degree of incongruity between the cultural and genetic characteristics of the human material and the work roles to be performed is greatest in rich countries where occupations are numerous, specialized, and subject to rapid change. At any given time many adults are incapable of working or cannot find work; they must be trained or retrained, or the work or its location must be changed to fit their capabilities, or they must be otherwise taken care of.

Second, employers and officials often feel that their subordinates are not doing enough work or good enough work. Hardworking portions of the population sometimes complain that others are lazy. A typical finding: in a recent survey of 563 members of the American Management Association, 79 per cent agreed that 'the nation's productivity is suffering because the traditional American work ethic has eroded'; about a third of 69 union leaders agreed (Kanter, 1978, 56). To put this eternal complaint in historical perspective consider this preamble to a 1495 statute regulating hours; it is Parliament speaking: 'Diverse artificers and labourers...waste much part of the day...

---

*This section draws on my research of the 1960's, especially Wilensky (1960, 1961, 1966). A careful review of research done since my own, which is generally consistent with my conclusions about work in America, is Kanter (1978).

in late coming unto their work, early departing therefrom, long sitting at their breakfast, at their dinner and noon-meat, and long time of sleeping afternoon' (11 Henry VII c. 22). Whatever the trend in work performance from the fifteenth to the twentieth centuries, ruling elites have grumbled about the decline in the masses' zest for work for a very long time.

The third reason work is now seen as a social problem is that many people are discontented with the work they do. That may also have been true—even more true—in the period of early industrialization. What is new to our time is that the average worker is now enfranchised, literate, and organized into unions or professional associations. Further, an army of social critics (to which I myself belong)—intellectuals, experts, and journalists—join workers in giving the discontents wider circulation and greater credence. Similarly, the diffuse demand for participatory democracy—a contemporary version of an older demand for economic democracy—is mainly a product of changes in the organizational and political machinery for raising consciousness among activists and ideologues. It is not, I think, a reflection of large transformations in how masses of employees feel about workplaces.

The final reason that work is now defined as a social problem is that lack of work or alienation from it can place a heavy hand on the quality of life. Attitudes and practices developed in one sphere can spill over into another sphere—killing time at work can lead to killing time in leisure, and apathy in the workplace can become apathy in politics. Again, we do not know whether the long arm of the job has become more or less obtrusive in the rest of life, but there is no doubt that among substantial populations there is a tight link between work, careers, and leisure styles.

An elaboration of my skeptical stance may help.

The modern propensity to work

The leisure-oriented society is a mirage. Despite talk of the decline of the 'work ethic' and in the face of affluence for the majority, *modern populations remain busy—with some groups becoming busier while others are condemned to forced leisure*.

The average man's gain in leisure has been exaggerated by the selective comparison of gross daily or weekly averages in working hours with those of the 'take-off' period of rapid economic growth in England, France, and America —a time of brutal schedules and conditions (Wilensky, 1961). Estimates of annual and lifetime leisure and comparisons with earlier times suggest a different picture. The skilled urban worker has now achieved the position of his thirteenth-century counterpart, whose long workday, seasonally varied, was offset by many holidays, rest periods, and long vacations as well as work stoppages due to natural causes or external events. Annual hours of work now, as then, remain in the range 1900–2500. Moreover, since the mid-1930's workers in the US have taken productivity gains almost wholly in income rather than partly in leisure (Lebergott, 1968, 105), although their European counterparts have split the gains between income and leisure.

People in the upper strata have lost out. Even though their work lives are shorter and their vacations longer than those of lower strata, they work many hours, week after week—sometimes reaching a truly startling lifetime total. Top leaders in political and economic life, in the military establishment, education, the arts, and entertainment show a marked preference for income over leisure. At less exalted levels, millions of ambitious men adopt a similar way of life. Considering both 'moonlighting' (holding more than one job) and all the hours worked on the main job, there is some evidence of a slowly growing minority of the male urban labour force in America who usually work 55 hours a week or more.

How about women who, after all, have the most apparent choice in the matter? I have already mentioned a soaring rate of non-agricultural labour force participation among women, common to all rich countries. This figure, of course, excludes the work of home and family. It seems plain that emancipation, while it has released women for the labour market, has not to an equal extent released them from housewifery. Studies of the weekly round of women report a range of averages of 50 to 80 hours a week in housework, child care, and paid labour. Although men are beginning to share these tasks a bit more, when a woman with a child takes a job today, she typically is adding her work week to a 30- or 40-hour 'homemaking' minimum (Wilensky, 1968; Meissner et al., 1975).

On balance, the female 'work week' may be as long as it was a century ago, and pace-setting elites, the main carriers of cultural traditions and values, have probably increased their time at work.

It is not so much the general level of economic activity that has changed in the modern era as its distribution and the meaning vested in it.

People without jobs: clues to the primordial meaning and function of work

If a man's ties to work are so tenuous and his changes of job and employer so frequent and unpredictable that he never feels he has a job he can call his own, it does not make sense to speak of his work and its discontents. The central fact of his work experience is job chaos—the lack of any stable work milieu, organizational context, or career to which he can respond in a cheerful or alienated way. Such is the condition of marginal workers in every advanced country. There is a kind of forced withdrawal from work among (1) the involuntarily retired, (2) the intermittently unemployed, (3) the chronically unemployed and underemployed—three segments of the population that are increasing in numbers.

While women, especially up to the age 54 of or so, have increased their labour force participation, there has been since 1890 a decrease in the labour force participation rates of men in Great Britain, Canada, Germany, New Zealand, and the United States. Men aged 65 and older have reduced their participation rates far more than any other age category, mainly because of declining opportunity. Reduced opportunity is a function chiefly of educational and occupational obsolescence and the decline of 'old men's jobs' in proportion to the number of old men (Wilensky, 1966, 127–128). This premature retirement of the aged has recently accelerated in every rich country plagued by persistent and increasing unemployment and low growth rates (Fisher, 1978).

Do older workers retire not only because they lack opportunity but because they prefer leisure? The evidence, while not conclusive, points (as in the past) to ill-health as the main reason for 'voluntary' retirement and the desire for income as the main reason for staying on full-time. There are some national variations: a three-country survey done in 1962 concludes that given sufficient retirement income, more American retirees say that retirement is a desirable state than Danish or British retirees. But only about a quarter of the recent American retirees in that study said that they had retired because they did not want to work any longer (Shanas et al., 1968, 326). There are also obvious variations by type of work: male blue-collar workers with terrible jobs prefer retirement if they can afford it (cf. Sheppard and Herrick, 1972, 51–52).

It is possible that the aged can be coaxed into retirement by generous pensions, but as yet early retirement is typically a product of compulsion; it is the result of employer preferences for younger married workers and middle-aged women, and of government attempts to increase job opportunities for the unemployed young, women, and minorities, whose past and present disadvantages are now viewed as an urgent political problem (cf. Fisher, 1978, 4).

Indeed, the new 'class' struggle may take the form of growing bitterness among three populations competing for more work: (1) unemployed and underemployed young together with most working women; (2) middle-aged men and women who have established themselves in stable careers or secure jobs; and (3) older workers who want to stay on or who, if they are going to be tossed on the scrap heap, demand preretirement pensions, preferential unemployment benefits and tax treatment, and more liberal disability benefits with medical blessing in doubtful cases.

In short, men and women who have gained most 'leisure' need and want more work. An old paradox has become more prominent: those whose productivity is highest will work longer hours to support the forced leisure of people rendered obsolete by the activities of long-hours men and women.

These extremes of deprivation—the unemployed or underemployed young and the prematurely retired—dramatize the meaning and function of work for everyone. One of the most consistent findings in research on work is that people deprived of work are most isolated socially and most disturbed psychologically —in a word, demoralized (Bakke, 1935; Zawadski and Lazarsfeld, 1935;

Wilensky, 1966, 130). In rich countries of the modern era, work, whether it is becoming more or less central as a source of personal identity and social solidarity, still remains a necessary condition for drawing the individual into the mainstream of social life; it remains a symbol of one's place among the living.

Work alienation, indifference, and attachment

How about the meaning and function of work in the great majority of modern countries—the men and women whose information, opportunity, motivation, skill, and education enable them to find a solid place in the economy?

Since there are many useful reviews of findings on job satisfaction and discontent (e.g. Herzberg *et al.*, 1957; Wilensky, 1966; Kanter, 1978), I shall here emphasize a theme I still find absent from this literature. The most significant meanings of work are enchored in *a social context* (the nature of the work role, workplace, and community, and the place of work in the daily round), *the identity of the person* (does the work affirm the self or deny it?), and *the life cycle* (his time perspective and stage in the family cycle and his career, if any). The study of job satisfactions apart from these social and psychological roots is superficial.

If we draw on classic discussions of work alienation from Marx to such neo-Freudians as Erich Fromm we can define work alienation as the feeling that the routine enactment of the obligations and rights of one's work role is incongruent with one's prized self-image. For example, the kind of fellow I am at my best is not the kind of fellow I am obliged to be as assembler in a work crew.

To measure work alienation we must first measure prized self-image, the central attributes of self-concept to which strong positive feelings are attached. Then we must relate attributes of a specific role (recurrent behaviour which expresses the rights and duties of a social position) to these central attributes of self. We may speak of the person whose work role poorly fits his prized self-image as work-alienated.

In a study of 1156 employed men aged 21–55 in various occupational groups and strata in the Detroit area (Wilensky, 1966, 140–148), based on long interviews in 1960, we measured five attributes of self-image which could be most clearly validated or violated by the work role: sociable, intelligent, conscientious (competent, efficient), independent-autonomous, and ambitious. Later in these interviews, we covered six features of the work situation that could be related to these attributes of self-image. The match in Table 1 was made in constructing an index. If a man's friends think of him as a 'good mixer' and it would make a difference to him if they did not, and if, further, his job affords a good chance for sociability and it would make a difference to him if it did not, the fit is good and he receives a point for 'attached'. On the other hand, if sociability is part of his prized self-image, the job blocks it, and that bothers him, he receives a point for 'alienated'. Any other combination scores 'indifferent'. (A man who is indifferent

Table 1 Features of work situation related to attributes of self-image

Attribute of prized self-image (both perceived and valued)	Attribute of work situation (both perceived and valued)
Sociable	Can talk sociably on the job at least four or five times a day
Intelligent	Plenty of chance to use own judgement
Conscientious (competent, efficient) —person who believes that if a thing is worth doing, it is worth doing right	Chance to do work well—do a good, careful job Chance to do the things you are best at—use the kinds of skills you have
Independent—a man who will not hesitate to go it alone when he thinks he should	(For those with a boss) Boss not always breathing down your neck—not watched too closely
Ambitious—person who tries hard to get ahead	Good chance for promotion where you work

may complain about one or another condition of work, but such gripes are unrelated to major attributes of his better self.) Or take intelligence: the alienated man is saying, in effect, (1) 'I am reasonably intelligent and it's important to me that I be seen that way'; (2) 'Going through these motions on the job is a dumb show and any strong moron could do it'; (3) 'What is a guy like me doing here?'

By these stringent measures, relating work role to prized self-image, the incidence of alienation is low: only 177 of our 1156 employed men score 'alienated' on even one of the six possible attributes of the work situation; only 51 are alienated on two or more attributes, eleven on three or more.

In a multiple classification analysis, the best independent predictors of work alienation are (1) a work situation and organizational setting that provide little discretion in pace and schedule, and a tall hierarchy above (low freedom, high pressure), (2) a career which has been blocked and chaotic, and (3) a stage in the life cycle that puts on the squeeze (the measure combines 'large numbers of children living at home' with 'low amount of savings and investments'). Strong work attachment has similar but not identical roots; it is most frequent among men of medium to high status, 30 to 39 years old, whose careers have been orderly and whose present jobs provide much opportunity for both sociable talk and getting ahead of the work-load. (The causes of alienation need not be the causes of low attachment. For instance, blocked mobility, life cycle squeeze, and a large number of superior levels of authority foster alienation, but their absence does not assure strong attachment. Furthermore, restricted sociability on the job is apparently not a source of alienation, but plentiful sociability is a source of attachment.)

Obviously, work alienation may be more widespread than this strict measure indicates. Many aspects of male identity (such as masculinity) were not tapped, although it is possible that work situations can confirm or deny them.

Despite its limits, this index of alienation has the great merit of relevance to the classic discussions of work alienation in the social sciences. It is a useful device for linking social structure to the social self. I am inclined to take the amount of alienation uncovered as the minimum that exists, to attach weight to the differences among groups variously situated as to work and career, and to say that the results reflect a generally effective system of placement—such that most people either adjust their identity to the demands of the role (they acquire the proper 'occupational personality') or shift out of those roles that tend to punish them.

The principal finding is that the vast majority of the 'middle mass' (lower middle class and upper working class) and almost a majority of the engineers— swiftly growing categories of the labour force—are generally indifferent to work in the precise sense that their jobs neither confirm their prized self-image nor deny it for most of the attributes analysed. In the middle mass, more than one in five of the young white-collar men and one in three of the older blue-collar men score indifferent on *all* attributes.

Populations excluded from these samples—the lower half of the working class, the very young, men over 55, and women of any age—have less opportunity to become attached to work; their indifference would surely be more widespread.

From these data and from my interpretation of subsequent research in America using a variety of general measures of job satisfaction, I would venture the guess that the vast majority of Americans are 'playing it cool', neither strongly wedded to the job nor feeling it to be an intense threat to their identity.

The social critic might now say, 'OK, so the mass of men and women are not alienated from work, only indifferent to it; and they continue to prefer income to leisure. Is this not the triumph of the idols of consumption, the victory of consumerism?' Perhaps. But then we should not be preoccupied with 'work alienation'; we should instead debate the gains and costs of the middle-class package, the home and its appliances, the car, the colour television, the holiday cottage, and the modest luxuries to which the masses aspire.

My point is this: the work-alienated are a small minority compared with men and women without enough work of any kind. Further, it is likely that mass discontent is rooted in only moderate measure in the immediate work situation. Few people remain in one line of work, let alone one job, for their entire working lives. The average American male will hold at least a dozen jobs in a 46-year working life, most of them in quite different occupations and industries (Wilensky, 1960); and each of those jobs has a somewhat different mix of freedom and pressure (pacing, scheduling, sociability), status and authority, income and security; the dozen jobs will encompass diverse organizational settings. Why should we expect sources of alienation in the workplace to remain steady over all the jobs of the worklife?

Work alienation, workplaces, and participatory democracy

If the immediate work situation is not a major cause of widespread discontent, perhaps the structure of the workplace is. One thing is sure: there has been a recent revival of nineteenth-century demands for industrial democracy. The dominant theme of this revival is that the typical modern workplace is too big, too bureaucratic, too authoritarian, too technocratic, too centralized; that most employees work in such places; and that the modern workplace is a source of deep dissatisfaction with life and work (cf. Herbst, 1976; Thorsrud, 1976).

Sweden and Norway's remarkable new laws on the work environment and participation in decision-making are partly a product of these ideas. And in several rich countries 'decentralization' of industry, labour, and government is being sold as a kind of patent medicine—good for what ails you.

There is no doubt that many employees evidence a desire to participate in decisions that affect their interests. But that can mean the straight trade union protections, including crucial issues of health and safety, not broader participation in management. And, again, we must not mistake pockets of alienation for the general condition; or huge bureaucratic-technocratic-centralized organizations for the typical work environment. Nor can we safely assume that participatory democracy is an urgent demand of the average rank and file citizen or that, when tried, it leads to major improvements in either life satisfaction or the quality of life.

Three cautionary reminders may be a healthy corrective for the current enthusiasms: most people do not work in big bureaucratic, centralized organizations; 'bureaucratic-technocratic' is not the same as 'centralized'; and participation by subordinates in managerial decision-making, like other organizational arrangements, has costs as well as benefits.

First, in the United States, supposedly the ultimate in large-scale organization, most work does not take place in large bureaucratic organizations. Both production and employment in the 'post-industrial society' are supposed to be dominated by the 'service sector'; and it is quite true that economic development has everywhere moved more of the labour force into 'tertiary' occupations and industries. Where do people work in that expanding sector? Using 1958 data, Fuchs (1968) shows that the typical firm is small, owner-managed, and often non-corporate. In number of employees the typical workplace is small to medium sized—a sharp contrast to the older manufacturing sector. Using 1972 data, we can see that no matter how we view it, the picture remains much the same, the main shift occurring not from small firms to big firms, but from tiny firms to small firms. For instance, in 1958 in wholesale trade, retail trade, and miscellaneous services (which account for fully half of employment in the service sector) half the jobs were in companies with fewer than twenty workers; in finance, insurance, and real estate 41 per cent of the jobs were in such tiny firms. By 1972 these figures were down somewhat, but the heavy concentration remained in firms with fewer than 100 employees (wholesale trade, 77 per cent; miscellaneous services, 64 per cent; retail trade, 57 per cent; finance, insurance, and real estate, 54 per cent). Drawing the line at 'fewer than 500 employees' (medium size?), the concentration of service employees remains overwhelming; from 92 per cent of all workers in wholesale trade to 64 per cent in retail trade work in such firms. Contrast manufacturing: the percentage of workers in firms with fewer than 500 employees is only 29 (United States Bureau of the Census, 1972b, Table 9; 1972a, Table 1c).

When we discuss health and education we think of the huge medical complex and the factory-like central-city school, but most hospitals, clinics, and private schools and colleges remain small to medium sized (cf. Fuchs, 1968, 190). When we consider government, the gargantuan Pentagon and the Department of Health, Education and Welfare readily come to mind, but if we look at the swiftest growing part of government, local government, about half the employees work in units of fewer than 500 (Fuchs, 1968, 190). Add to all this a substantial minority of the labour force which moves in and out of self-employment (Wilensky, 1966, 113–114), and the picture is complete. Whether small is beautiful or not, a growing fraction of working Americans find themselves in small to medium-sized workplaces.

If we are looking for the typical workplace of modern society, however, we will find significant variation by country, reflecting the international division of labour. While the USA has become a kind of service centre, the Federal Republic of Germany has become the manufacturing centre of Europe. Thus, a larger proportion of Germans than Americans are employed in big hierarchical firms.

Not only is there immense diversity in the size of workplaces within and among rich countries, but also, and more important, there is immense variation in the degree to which organizational structures of the same size resemble the stereotypes of 'bureaucratic, technocratic, and centralized'. Scholars and administrators who wish to increase worker participation and enhance the work environment often confuse a bureaucratic form (specialized positions arranged in a hierarchy with activities governed by formal rules), on the one hand, with centralization of authority, on the other hand. And they view bureaucracy, the rise of the expert, and centralization alike as enemies of industrial democracy and meaningful work.

Let us concede that bureaucratic organizations have become more numerous in the past century or so; and that experts—people of specialized knowledge and skill—have become more influential in policy decisions in organizations both large and small, centralized and decentralized. At some extreme, there may even be a strong correlation among these attributes of structure: the Pentagon is bureaucratic and centralized; it is also loaded with staff experts. And it is not exactly a model of worker participation (although many people find their work in that huge defence apparatus quite challenging).

1. Bureaucratic versus technocratic

Complex organizations with many specialized roles do seem to have more people of specialized knowledge and skill on their staffs. But that very fact leads towards some de-emphasis of hierarchy and a decline in the rigid application of formal rule. Even the most monolithic industrial and political organizations are forced to supplement coercion with persuasion and manipulation and to attend to the problems of morale and motivation. This is especially true when they confront skilled workers at every level and it is most evident when persons in these categories are in short supply. The argument is both familiar and accurate: some tasks cannot be mastered without the development of more or less autonomous groups—crafts, professions, scientific disciplines.

The most severe test of this debureaucratization theme is the modern military establishment. In order to coordinate specialized units the traditional army sets up a command structure in which SOP (standing operating procedures), spit and polish, close-order drill—the mechanical assimilation of the army way—is the norm. Yet, contemporary armies in many modern countries have drastically changed in response to more sophisticated technology and missions and more educated, skilled recruits who expand the middle layers of the hierarchy. For two or three decades most military establishments have emphasized group initiative, informal out-of-channels briefings, democratic leadership styles, and the training mission rather than Tayloristic work organization. These shifts in organizational structure are reflected in a reduction of differences in rank; even the uniforms and the food look more alike (cf. Janowitz, 1960).

If the army has been debureaucratizing, then most industrial, professional, and government organizations facing the same requirements have surely shifted in the same direction—a trend that began long before the contemporary movements for participatory democracy.

2. Bureaucracy versus centralization versus worker participation

Again, they vary independently and have variable effects on job discontent. The central headquarters of a non-bureaucratic organization may delegate much authority to local units while the local leaders exercise tight control within their jurisdiction. Some of the least bureaucratic and most decentralized unions in the building trades in the US, for instance, are run like dictatorships.

Yet the craft jobs of these skilled workers typically provide considerable control over pace, schedule, or tools and techniques, and are quite gratifying—in the absence of participation in either managerial decisions or their union decisions. Conversely, a moderately bureaucratic and centralized health or welfare agency may provide considerable opportunity for participation for its numerous white-collar and professional employees; their unions may be more democratic and participatory than those of the building craftsmen. Yet the combination of bureaucracy, centralization, and participation may have little to do with job satisfaction. Some white-collar jobs are wholly programmed, others leave much room for judgement. Such variations in 'freedom' can overcome whatever good or bad effects the organizational structure may have.

In short, the decentralization of governments and economic organizations alike may have no close connection with either 'rule by rules' or worker autonomy, job satisfaction, and participation.

3. The benefits of bureaucracy

While debureaucratization has been a long-term trend, modern workplaces do retain many elements of hierarchy, specialization, and governance by formal rule. Aside from the obvious gains in control and efficiency, there are equally obvious gains in justice as well as worker morale, security, and job satisfaction.

Hierarchy may mean timidity, conservatism, and buck-passing if everyone is afraid of the boss, but it also means long lines of promotions and more stable careers. Specialized work may encourage trained incapacity, vested interests, and empire building; but it also fosters the full use of talents, knowledge, and skills, while providing niches for those with less skill. Impersonal rules may encourage red tape and technicism (rules become ends in themselves), but they also deter arbitrary decisions. Formal rules in selection, promotion, work-load, transfers, hiring, firing, discipline, and rewards increase fairness and justice. Formal rules of succession minimize insecurity when there is turnover at the top; specific, contractual obligations and spheres of authority limit the individual's subjection to authority.

As in all organizational arrangements there are trade-offs: a loss here; a gain there. It is by no means certain that the trend towards debureaucratization is without its costs.

4. The mixed blessings of decentralization

From Left and Right alike one hears proposals for decentralization, usually combined with attacks on bureaucracy and technocrats. No problem in organizational and political theory is more complex than the issue of 'decentralization'. The decentralization of the state, of diverse institutional spheres (polity, economy, religion, intellectual life, mass entertainment), and of diverse public services (health, safety, education, welfare) produce diverse results. Further, there are various kinds of decentralization—of authority, of records, of location, of loyalty, of channels of communication—each independent of the others, each with its own gains and costs, depending upon the purpose. Nevertheless, in the context of general demands for decentralization, one observation can provide the necessary caution: countries and institutions facing the most intractable problems are especially attracted to the slogans of 'decentralization' and 'participation'. The Italians, who somehow, in the phrase of Di Palma, 'survive without governing', face the near collapse of most public services, as well as the worst problem of youth unemployment; they are decentralizing by region. Some years ago, Mayor Lindsay of New York City, confronting nearly unmanageable racial conflict, bought the idea of decentralizing the school system, thereby accelerating its decline. And the British, at the height of their troubles some years ago, with a serious paralysis at the centre, produced partly by a fragmented and decentralized labour movement, were going for 'devolution'. In each case, decentralization complicates the planning essential for the management of a modern political economy.* When the problems seem insoluble, the central authority says to the locality, 'Look, you people down there. You feel we've been swarming all over you. Why don't you participate?'

In short, decentralization often represents merely an abandonment of responsibility at the centre to make decisions best made at the centre. Further, although advocates of decentralization often couple it with ideologies of worker participation in management, the two do not necessarily go together; as we have seen, a local unit of a national organization can be a tiny tyranny—decentralized but non-participatory.

5. The gains and costs of participation

In considering the participation of subordinates in managerial decision-making as a means of improving the quality of life or enhancing life satisfaction, we need to ask, 'What exactly is the problem for which participation is the solution?' From the great system builders of the early nineteenth century, such as Fourier and Saint-Simon, to today's architects of the Swedish and Norwegian laws on participation in decision-making, the advocates of worker participation have invoked a variety of goals to be pursued, areas or topics

---

*The decentralized socialism of Yugoslavia may be another example of an ideology poorly serving the needs of a modern economy. In this mecca of decentralization and workers' councils, the power of the self-governed communes and enterprises to defy any wage–price freeze or rollback or any effort to limit credit is astounding. The Yugoslavs, however, have a more forceful reason for decentralization: the geographical segregation of so many warring ethnic-linguistic groups, none so small that it can be ignored, makes the necessary central controls far more hazardous than they are in better integrated, richer countries. In fact, in several rich democracies, the centralized structures of autonomous labour, employer, and professional associations bargaining at the top under the auspices of moderately centralized governments have engaged in effective economic and social planning, thereby dampening social cleavages. Thus, Belgium and Holland, with their deep social cleavages, can achieve much the same consensus as Austria or Sweden, with their greater homogeneity and simpler party structures. (For detailed discussion of the issue of decentralization of governments and economic organizations see Wilensky, 1976, 21–47.)

for decision, and channels for action. In a careful review of evidence on types and effects of modern participation, Kenneth Walker (1974) uncovered six broad aims:

(a) *Defend and promote workers' interests* A goal of the workers' control movements—Anarcho-Syndicalists, Guild Socialists—and of labour unions.

(b) *Extend democracy to the workplace* Either distribute power more equally and handle conflicts of interest more democratically within all organizations, union, or management; or achieve harmony by eliminating bosses and employers. Some advocates of industrial democracy, among them the self-management theorists of Yugoslavia, also assume that participation at work will foster political participation away from work.

(c) *Reduce alienation and promote personal fulfilment* This aim derives from the literature reviewed above and assumes that modern workplaces are now dehumanized and regimented.

(d) *Utilize human resources more effectively* Derives from 'managerial sociology' or the 'human relations in industry' movement. Assumes that participation increases efficiency by tapping subordinates' ideas and improving upward communications; by inspiring harder, more rational work, more acceptance of decisions, and a reduction of labour disputes; and by spurring management to action.

(e) *Encourage cooperative attitudes and reduce industrial conflict* Derives from Catholicism, company unionism, and paternalism and typically assumes a harmony of interests in a plant community or the desirability of achieving that condition.

(f) *Mobilize workers for the solution of social or community problems and the administration of the welfare state.*

Here, again, the programmes pursuing these goals encounter several universal limits. I mention them not to argue that participation by subordinates in managerial decision is impossible but to emphasize the need for clarity about the conditions under which participation of subordinates in managerial decisions is least likely to achieve these goals.

(a) Participation can be a brake on efficiency when the need for speed is great and the costs in time and effort are prohibitive. Although management fears of such losses are typically exaggerated, there are many decisions in which the participative process paralyses decisions without achieving any of its goals.

(b) Participation can be ineffective when the relevant skills are lacking, particularly on decisions requiring knowledge of the particular organization and its environment or on technical or financial matters. In socialist and non-socialist countries alike participation through workers' councils or similar channels typically does not change the relative power of managers and experts *vis-à-vis* workers. Whatever the formal arrangements, the engineers, technicians, and managers in command of essential information tend to come out on top. In the extreme case, where the aim is to involve everyone, the least expert—younger workers, unskilled or less experienced workers and less educated workers—remain on the outside, just as they do without any restructuring of industry. (cf. Zupanov, 1973; Strauss and Rosenstein, 1970; and Sturmthal, 1964.)

(c)   Where participation requires that power be moved as close to the work situation as possible—the shop floor, the office desk—it threatens the functions of centralized bargaining, especially the capacity of top union leaders to cope with wage-push inflation. To defend workers' interests by increasing local autonomy is to lessen the chance of improving their real income through industry-wide or national collective bargaining agreements. (cf. Sturmthal, 1977.)

For my purpose of exploring the possibilities of participatory democracy for reducing alienation or mass discontent, these limitations are important. Where the promise of participation is not fulfilled—where workers' expectations for more power, income, autonomy, security, or improvements in the working environment are raised and then shattered—then alienation increases, management resistance hardens, and conflict intensifies. If I am right that most workers are not alienated in the first place, merely indifferent; if the studies that show apathy towards participation among non-participants and frustration among participants with high expectations are accurate (Walker, 1974, 28; and Tannenbaum *et al.*, 1974), we cannot look to this development for a major change in the quality of everyday life.

Under some conditions in some places, one or another goal of participation has been achieved. The most severe limit is not the costs of participation, for with experience these can be reduced; nor is it the lack of relevant skills, for with intense training and long experience, the untapped talents of non-participants can be developed. The commanding limitation is that in the long run a sense of participation that is unrelated to a continual harvest of real benefits, a sense of community that is illusory, will be revealed as fake and inspire more alienation than we see now.

INTERLOCKING CYCLES OF FAMILY, WORK, AND PARTICIPATION

If mass discontent is not rooted in the disintegration of the family, in the new leisure, in the work milieu, or in bureaucratic, technocratic, centralized workplaces—what are its roots? The morale or life satisfaction of the vast majority of modern men and women is shaped by normal strains of family transitions as they are intensified or lessened by variations in taxes, debt, and real income as these, in turn, affect the balance between aspirations and rewards.

'Life cycle squeeze' and the morale curve

From a review of research using age or life cycle variables and from social-psychological theory about the effects of imbalance between aspirations and rewards, in an early paper (Wilensky, 1961) I inferred a hypothetical morale curve for the general male population of modern society. I located stages of the life cycle where people experience least job satisfaction, lowest participation in community life, greatest financial and family burdens, and greatest psychological tension—a condition of 'life cycle squeeze'.

The essence of my theory is that job satisfaction and, indeed, life satisfaction are

> a function of disparity between rewards (what we get in income and job status) and aspirations and/or expectations (what we want in goods and services and job status); both pay-off and demand are likely to show a chronology linked to family life cycle and work history. Leaving aside the college crowd and the unusually ambitious, the young man fresh from high school, for a few years at least, finds himself with a happy combination of modest aspirations, limited responsibilities, and an income that seems large.
>
> A sharp change occurs, however, when home and children come into focus. As family pressures mount, the demand for credit in the product market and income in the labour market begin their swift ascent. The appetite for consumer durables and the demand for money and job security reach a peak in the 30's among married men with children....
>
> But the peak in actual income and security is seldom reached in this critical period.... For the manual worker, who is most subject to insta-bility of employment, seniority protection is as yet weak, and for all categories the period of maximum economic rewards comes later. A working wife is one solution, but the double-earner pattern is least fre-quent among the very families that feel squeezed—young couples with children at home.... The result: a morale trough which lasts until job aspirations and family pressures decline, rewards increase, or both. When children leave home and debts are paid off, job morale, indeed all satisfactions unconnected with child-rearing, should climb. Later, with retirement impending, the morale curve will vary, depending...upon type of career and strength of work commitment, but a final sag in morale seems most frequent. (Wilensky, 1961, 228–229)

The general hypothesis, pictured in Figure 1, is that points of maximum 'life cycle squeeze', and hence low morale, occur on average among couples

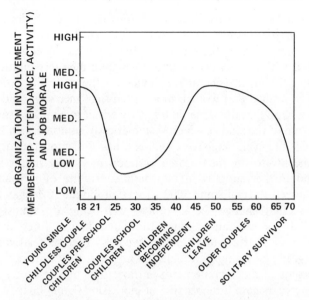

Figure 1 Hypothetical picture of the participation and morale curve for the general population of an urban-industrial society. Inferred from existing data for the United States on variations by family life cycle and/or age in economic rewards and aspirations, consumer behaviour and aspirations, and participation in formal organizations. Sources cited in Wilensky, 1961, ch. 8. Think of 'high' as a man who loves his work, belongs to a union or professional association, a church, and three or four other organizations, is active in them and enjoys them. Think of 'low' as a man who is unemployed, involuntarily retired, or work-alienated, and who belongs to nothing
Chart from Wilensky, 1962, 922

with preschool children, older couples, especially those prematurely retired, and solitary survivors.

The idea of interlocking cycles of family life, work, consumption, social participation, and morale is complex and yet parsimonious. It enabled me to reinterpret contradictory results of studies of job satisfaction—studies that ignored massive forces off the job that determined responses to work, whatever the alienating or non-alienating character of that work. It very likely can explain recent findings on age or life cycle differences in general life satisfaction, income dynamics, and cynicism about government. Campbell, Converse, and Rodgers (1976) investigated the general life satisfaction of a 1971 sample of over 2000 Americans aged 18 years and older. Their findings by stage in family life cycle match closely the morale curve of Figure 1. The most satisfied are young married couples without children; the least satisfied are married couples with preschool children, the widowed, and the divorced or separated. Although women in these 'happiness' studies are typically equally satisfied or more satisfied with the quality of their lives than men (see citations in Estes and Wilensky, 1978), in general they evidence the same life cycle curves as men. It can be argued that women more often than men say—and even feel— that they are 'happy' at the same time as they admit to clinically suspect symptoms. But none of the studies which systematically compare men and women, controlling for life cycle stage (or even age), has so demonstrated.

If we concentrate on the income component of the interlocking cycles idea, we find further support in two detailed studies of income dynamics. A five-year panel study of some 5000 American families (Morgan et al., 1974, 37–79) shows that changes in a family's well-being are almost exclusively rooted in changes in family composition and labour force participation; that young people starting new families typically become relatively worse off (compared with young singles or childless couples, they evidence slower rates of improvement in an 'income/needs' ratio); that people moving into their prime earning years gain little because of increasing family financial pressures; but that, again, the economic base for improved morale is strongest for the middle-aged. After the age of 40 or so the head of a household starts to see more improvement in the family purse as children begin to leave the home and in many cases the spouse is freed of home responsibilities and gets a job. Retirement, the authors find, means a drop in income with no proportionate decrease in needs. Analysing 1960 census data on earnings patterns by age and type of family separately, Oppenheimer (1974) adds an important elaboration: the imbalance between income and family needs varies only moderately by occupational group and category. For instance, 'no matter how their economic fates subsequently diverge, low earnings were characteristic of most young men whatever their occupational group' (p. 235). Only in very high-level professional, managerial, and sales occupations—a small minority of the labour force—do average earnings peak when family income needs are peaking.

Of course, in several rich countries, including Sweden, the rising level of unemployment and under-employment among young people is now intensifying their normal economic squeeze and related discontent.

Finally, if we consider political stance—an aspect of life more remote from the family and its earnings—we see a similar curve. 'Trust in government' has been least among American men and women over the age of 50; within the context of a decade's slide in confidence in government institutions among the general population, older persons have been the most cynical and estranged in every election since 1958, followed closely in 1964 and 1972 by the youngest age category studied (21–24 years). On the whole, people in their middle years have been and remain the most optimistic and trusting about Washington, DC (Miller, Brown, and Raine, 1973).

In short, the life cycle squeeze hypothesis can embrace a wide range of behaviour and attitudes, from the most personal satisfaction with the most local institutions (e.g. marriage and the family) to the most impersonal response to the most distant symbols (e.g. national politics).

Recently, we applied this hypothesis to a sample of 73 employed and 157 unemployed professionals in the San Francisco Bay area. We excluded the divorced, the separated, and the singles over 30 who had never married. We interviewed them in 1971–1973. Using an index of emotional stress (validated by independent clinical judgements) and an index of economic deprivation, we found that unemployed professionals experiencing high levels of financial stress fit the morale curve of the general population. Morale drops among couples with very young school-age children and among solitary survivors. These hard-pressed unemployed professionals display a sense of relief when children leave. For the continuously employed professionals, however, and, most surprising, even for unemployed professionals experiencing little or no financial stress, the morale curve is smoothed out; they show more balance between rewards and aspirations over the life cycle than most Americans; their morale stays high even after losing the spouse. The study suggests that the advantage of highly educated professionals in a solid economic position—having a professional identity embedded in a social network—functions as a buffer against social insecurity which, in turn, protects them from the intense psychological strains typical of the rest of the population. Employed or unemployed, they are cushioned against the standard shocks both by their privileged positions and by their anticipations for the future—in other words by the personal continuity afforded by a life plan (Estes and Wilensky, 1978).

Subjective and objective well-being

We are now in a position to resolve the puzzle that appears in many of the papers of this symposium—the recurrent finding in several countries that subjective life satisfaction or sense of well-being is more or less unrelated to objective conditions or the level of living (cf. Allardt, 1977; Inglehart, 1977).

To deal with each major pattern of behaviour—family, work, consumption, and community participation—separately is to ignore their interaction over the life cycle. When we focus on these interlocking cycles of 'career' (work and its rewards), consumption (and related debt), family life, and participation as they vary by group over time, we find that the objective conditions of living are closely connected with a variety of measures of life satisfaction and discontent. To understand the connections, however, we need a sense of the flow of time not only in the structure of societies but in the biographies of persons variously located.

Where does this leave the idea that there has been a major shift in values that accounts for the discontents of the young? A typical example is Inglehart's argument that, far from reflecting the normal strain of a life cycle transition, the young are expressing the new 'post-materialist', 'post-industrial' values of self-expression, personal freedom, creativity, self-actualization, and participatory democracy. The acquisitive, materialistic values of the past, embraced by their more established seniors, will fade away as this new political generation raised in the affluence of the postwar era grows older and comes to power.

The theme is familiar from a spate of counter-cultural books of the 1960's. But Inglehart bases his assertions on empirical data—a series of surveys conducted between 1970 and 1973 in ten European countries and the USA. Unfortunately, both the measures used and the lack of relevant data on stages in the family life cycle make it impossible to test the political generation virsus life cycle stage idea. However, even the age differences in values in Inglehart's data do not support the counter-cultural argument. Leaving aside some weaknesses in measurement,* here are the main findings:

1. The proportion of Post-Materialists is higher in all nations among younger, more educated respondents. Young university graduates are most post-materialist of all.
2. However, Materialists outnumber Post-Materialists in every birth cohort in every nation except the 19–28-year-olds in Belgium (Table 2-2).
3. The Materialists as a fraction of every nation are far more prominent than Post-Materialists—from about two Materialists for one Post-Materialist in Belgium to about six to one in Denmark (Table 2-3). The mean proportion of Materialists across eleven nations is 34.5 per cent; the proportion of Post-Materialists is 10.5 per cent; the rest are mixed.

In fact, as Inglehart's tables show, the issues that excite Western publics are overwhelmingly economic performance and political order. Asked in 1973 to choose the first and second most important of a list of twelve goals, the populations of these eleven nations ranked fighting rising prices as the leading goal, with economic growth and economic stability close by. Fighting crime and maintaining order were also typically near the top. In the aggregate, no post-material goal ranked higher than third in any of the eleven nations; the mean rating of 'more say on the job', the most popular post-industrial goal, was only sixth; the mean ratings of 'a less impersonal society' and 'more

---

*The respondents were asked to select two 'most desirable to you' items: maintaining order in the nation, giving the people more say in political decisions, fighting rising prices, protecting freedom of speech. Respondents who chose both 'more say' and 'free speech' are termed Post-Materialist; those who chose both 'maintaining order' and 'fighting rising prices' are labelled 'Materialist'. Surely, some of the respondents might expect that their government could at once protect free speech and fight inflation—which may be one reason that about half the sample are mixed types. Because the fraction of white-collar respondents is unreasonably high in France, West Germany, Italy, and Holland, sampling error may have created a strong bias towards the middle class and therefore exaggerated the post-materialist consciousness of these countries.

say in government' were similarly low (Table 2-6). Here, then, are further clues that, relative to the older issues, participatory democracy is not an urgent mass demand.

Summary and implications

Subjective satisfactions and discontents are anchored in changes in family composition, consumption pressures, job patterns, income flows, and debt loads as they interact and vary over the life cycle. The imbalance between aspirations and rewards is most oppressive among transition singles, young couples with preschool children, and the aged, especially solitary survivors. However, as one would expect, the small minority of more affluent, secure, and educated elites, blessed with challenging careers, evidence a higher level of morale over the life cycle and a somewhat different morale curve. Elites and masses alike are thus responding to objective life circumstances most of the time.

Public policies can ease the strains reflected in the morale curve. Regarding the family, Sweden is apparently the world beater not only in income equality (Wilensky, 1978) but in equality between the sexes. What I would advocate in the USA is already law in Sweden: every child has a right to a place in a day-care centre (although the queues are still long), men and women alike are entitled to parental leaves and some days off for the care of sick children, health insurance pays for abortions, and so on. That few fathers take advantage of any of these rights, that most working women remain in traditional women's jobs (nurturant, subordinate, expressive), and almost half are in part-time jobs is testimony to the strength of traditional definitions of sex roles. Whatever the shift in role behaviour, it would be fascinating to know whether Swedish public policies have begun to ease the life cycle strains I have emphasized in this paper. We lack the cross-national studies of life satisfaction necessary to link variations in public policies to life cycle stresses. The best comparative study of general life satisfaction shows substantial differences among cross-sectional samples in the nine EEC countries studied in 1976. On various measures, Denmark and the Netherlands lead in average satisfaction while France and Italy are at the bottom. Where life satisfaction was lowest, feelings of social injustice were strongest. Although Sweden was not included, its social policies and outcomes are closer to those of egalitarian Denmark and Holland than to those of France and Italy. Crude age breakdowns, however, do not permit inferences about family life cycle variations (Commission of the European Communities, 1977, 46–54).

Anything that reduces family strain and increases family resources at transition stages will make people feel better about their work. To cope with pockets of work alienation rooted in the immediate job (and not outside work) we do not require a major reorganization in the technical and social organization of work. All the students of work reform represented in this book agree that high-pressure, low-freedom jobs at the extreme are alienating, even hazardous to health. On this point, the reviews of evidence by Kahn, Broadbent, Karasek, and Edgren are consistent with the careful experimental research by Franken-haeuser. I would merely add that most of the changes in the work environment necessary to overcome these extreme conditions are at once undramatic and cost effective. For instance, the benefits of increased worker control over the workpace can often be achieved with minor redesigning of jobs and shifts in the flow of work or further mechanization to eliminate the most dehumanizing jobs. If we concentrate on those aspects of the work environment that are most damaging—high-pressure jobs with no control over workpace, workplaces with deafening noise and unusual danger—substantial improvements can be made without a massive reorganization of the economy or a grand-scale programme of worker participation on product mix, product design, plant location, investment policy, and the like, whatever the merits of such measures for other purposes. What is required is continued government, union, and management action on issues of health and safety and a gradual phasing out of high-pressure, machine-paced work, an elimination of remaining remnants of the old-fashioned assembly line depicted in Charlie Chaplin's *Modern Times*.

Adopting the working life perspective of this paper, assuming that most leisure is forced leisure and people want more work, the appropriate line of public policy is an active labour-market policy to improve the opportunities and reduce the insecurities of the young, the women, the older workers, the handicapped, and the guest workers; some hard thought about alternative work schedules ('flexitime', creating more part-time jobs, both permanent and temporary) and second careers (e.g. 'cyclical life plans' with breaks in mid-career with older and younger workers filling in); and, most difficult of all, a combination of improved prospects for the young, generous pensions for the old, and reduced compulsion for older workers to retire.

About participatory democracy: I leave it to my Swedish and Norwegian colleagues to predict whether their new arrangements for decision-making in industry will ultimately be a threat or a help to their greatest achievement—an unusual combination of centralized economic and social planning (the consensus-making machinery of Harpsund democracy), a civilized welfare state, and a high level of individual freedom.

REFERENCES

Allardt, E. (1977). On the relationship between objective and subjective predicaments, Research Report No. 16, Research Group for Comparative Sociology, University of Helsinki.
Bakke, E. W. (1935). *The Unemployed Man*, Dutton, New York.

Bane, M. J. (1976). *Here to Stay: American Families in the Twentieth Century*, Basic Books, New York.

Bell, D. (1973). *The Coming of Post-Industrial Society: A Venture in Social Forecasting*, Basic Books, New York.

Bell, D. (1976). *The Cultural Contradictions of Capitalism*, Basic Books, New York.

Campbell, A., Converse, P. E., and Rodgers, W. L. (1976). *The Quality of American Life: Perceptions, Evaluations, and Satisfactions*, Russell Sage Foundation, New York.

Commission of the European Communities (1977). The perception of poverty in Europe, EEC, Brussels.

Davis, F. (1971). *On Youth Subcultures: The Hippie Variant*, General Learning Press, Morristown, N. J.

Davis, N. Z. (1976). 'Women's history' in transition: The European case, *Feminist Studies*, **3**, 83–103.

Estes, R., and Willensky, H. L. (1978). Life cycle squeeze and the morale curve, *Social Problems*, **25**, 277–292.

Fisher, P. (1978). The Social Security crisis: An international dilemma, *Aging and Work: Journal on Age, Work, and Retirement* (formerly *Industrial Gerontology*), **1**, 1–14.

Fuchs, V. R. (1968). *The Service Economy*, National Bureau of Economic Research, New York.

Galbraith, J. K. (1967). *The New Industrial State*, Houghton Mifflin, Boston, Mass.

Herbst, P. C. (1976). *Alternatives to Hierarchies*, Martinus Nijhoff, Leiden, Holland.

Herzberg, E., Mausner, B., Peterson, R. O., and Capwell, D. F. (1957). *Job Attitudes: Review of Research and Opinion*, Psychological Service of Pittsburgh, Pittsburgh, Press.

Inglehart, R. (1977). *The Silent Revolution: Changing Values and Political Styles Among Western Publics*, Princeton University Press, Princeton, N. J.

Janowitz, M. (1960). *The Professional Soldier, A Social and Political Portrait*, Free Press, New York.

Kanter, R. M. (1978). Work in a new America, *Daedalus*, **107**, 47–78.

Lebergott, S. (1968). Labor force and employment trends, in *Indicators of Social Change Concepts and Measurement*, ed. E. B. Sheldon and G. S. Hollister, Russell Sage Foundation, New York, 97–143.

Maccoby, E. E. (1978). Current changes in the family and their impact upon the socialization of children, in *Major Social Issues: A Multidisciplinary View*, Ed. J. Milton Yinger and S. J. Cutler, Free Press, New York, 195–207.

Marsh, A. (1975). The 'silent revolution', value priorities and the quality of life in Britain, *American Political Science Review*, **69**, 21–30.

Mason, K. O., Czajka, J. C., and Arber, S. (1976). Change in U.S. women's sex-role attitudes, *American Sociological Review*, **41**, 573–596.

Meissner, M., Humphreys, E. W., Meis, S. M., and Schiew, W. J. (1975). No exit for wives: Sexual division of labour and the cumulation of household demands, *Canadian Review of Sociology and Anthropology*, **12**, 424–39.

Miller, A. H., Brown, T. A., and Raine, A. S. (1973). Social conflict and political estrangement 1958–1972, unpublished paper presented at the Annual Meeting of the Midwest Political Science Association, Chicago.

Morgan, J. N., Dickinson, K., Dickinson, J., Benus, J., Duncan, G. (1974). *Five Thousand American Families: Patterns of Economic Progress*, Vol. 1, Institute of Social Research, University of Michigan, Ann Arbor.

Nye, F. I., and Hoffman, L. (1963). *The Employed Mother in America*, Rand McNally, Chicago.

Ogburn, W. F., and Nimkoff, M. F. (1955). *Technology and the Changing Family*, Houghton Mifflin, Boston, Mass.

Oppenheimer, V. K. (1974). 'The life cycle squeeze: The interaction of men's occupational and family life cycles, *Demography*, **11**, 227–246.

Scott, J. W., and Tilly, L. A. (1975). Women's work and the family in nineteenth-century Europe, *Comparative Studies in Society and History*, **17**, 36–64.

Shanas, E., Townsend, P., Wedderbush, D., Früs, H., Milhøj, P., and Stehouwer, J. (1968). *Old People in Three Industrial Societies*, Routledge and Kegan Paul, New York.

Sheppard, H. L., and Herrick, N. Q. (1972). *Where Have all the Robots Gone? Worker Dissatisfaction in the '70s*, Free Press, New York.

Steiner, G. A. (1963). *The People Look at Television*, Knopf, New York.

Strauss, G., and Rosenstein, E. (1970). Workers participation: A critical view, *Industrial Relations*, **9**, 197–214.

Sturmthal, A. F. (1964). *Workers Councils: A study of Workplace Organization on Both Sides of the Iron Curtain*, Harvard University Press, Cambridge, Mass.

Sturmthal, A. F. (1977). Unions and industrial democracy, *Annals*, **434**, 12–21.

Tannenbaum, A. S. Kavčič, B., Rosner, M., Vianello, M. and Wieser, G. (1974). *Hierarchy in Organizations: An International Comparison*, Jossey-Bass, San Francisco.

Thorsrud, E. (1976). Perspectives on the quality of working life in Scandinavia, Research Series No. 8, International Institute of Labor Studies, Geneva.

Turner, R. H. (1976). The real self: From institution to impulse, *American Journal of Sociology*, **81**, 989–1016.

United Nations (1954) (1960) (1966) (1971) (1975). *Demographic Yearbook*, New York.

United States Bureau of the Census, Department of Commerce (1972a). *County Business Patterns*, Government Printing Office, Washington, DC.

United States Bureau of the Census, Department of Commerce (1972b), *Enterprise Statistics*, Government Printing Office, Washington, DC.

Veroff, J., and Feld, S. (1970). *Marriage and Work in America*, Van Nostrand Reinhold, New York.

Vickery, C. (1977). The time-poor: A new book at poverty, *Journal of Human Resources*, **12**, 27–48.

Walker, K. F. (1974). Workers participation: Problems, practice, and prospects, *Bulletin of the International Institute for Labour Studies*, **12**, 3–35.

Wilensky, H. L. (1960). Work, careers, and social integration, *International Social Science Journal*, **12**, 543–560.

Wilensky, H. L. (1961). Life cycle, work situation, and participation in formal associations, in *Aging and Leisure*, ed. R. Kleemeier, Oxford University, New York, 213–242.

Wilensky, H. L. (1962). Life cycle, work situation, and social participation, in *Social and Psychological Aspects of Aging*, ed. C. Tibbitts and W. Donahue, Columbia University Press, New York, 919–930.

Wilensky, H. L. (1964). Mass society and mass culture: Interdependence or independence? *American Sociological Review*, **29**, 173–197.

Wilensky, H. L. (1966). Work as a social problem, in *Social Problems*, ed. H. S. Becker, Wiley, New York, 117–166.

Wilensky, H. L. (1968). Women's work: Economic growth, ideology, structure, *Industrial Relations*, **7**, 235–248.

Wilensky, H. L. (1976). The 'new corporatism', centralization, and the welfare state, *Professional Papers in Contemporary Political Sociology*, Sage, London, and Beverly Hills, Calif.

Wilensky, H. L. (1978). The political economy of income distribution: Issues in the analysis of government approaches to the reduction of inequality, in *Major Social Issues: A Multidisciplinary View*, ed. J. Milton Yinger and S. J. Cutler, Free Press, New York.

Wilensky, H. L., and Lebeaux, C. N. (1958). *Industrial Society and Social Welfare*, Russell

Sage Foundation, New York. Enlarged paperback edition, Free Press–Macmillan, New York (1965).

Zawadski, B., and Lazarsfeld, P. (1935). The psychological consequences of unemployment, *Journal of Social Psychology*, **6**, 224–251.

Zupanov, J. (1973). Structural conditions for employees' participation, in *Industrial Democracy: Industrial Relations and Human Resources*, ed. C. P. Thakur and K. C. Sehti, Shri Ram Centre for Industrial Relations and Human Resources, New Delhi.

Discussant's Comments

TORE BROWALDH

A patient was once told by his psychoanalyst: 'Don't you worry. You have no inferiority complex. You just are inferior.'

This anecdote sums up my feelings after having studied the three papers submitted to this seminar and listened to the introductory remarks of Erik Allardt, Marianne Frankenhaeuser, and Harold Wilensky. I have learned so much from reading them. And I feel even more strongly that my own contribution to this seminar is indeed very shallow.

PROBLEMS OF DEFINITION

The term 'quality of life' has a sponge-like character, soaking up so many different elements, from better environment, less urban congestion, safety in the streets, and reduced crime rates to a society where plastic gadgets and competition are eliminated and we have reached a zero-growth economy. To many the good life is a state of mind, not measurable by objective facts. In a way this is the approach we in Sweden use in respect of illness. If you feel ill, you are ill, irrespective of whether or not there are objectively established symptoms. From this point of view I am impressed by Professor Frankenhaeuser's psychological research. Here we have hard facts. I do hope her methods will be applied more widely, because they allow us to measure the individual's reaction to certain elements in our society which threaten the quality of life. We find significantly higher adrenaline excretion in the high-risk groups on the assembly line and among the commuters who were in the more crowded parts of the train. This research in building a bridge between Professor Allardt's objective and subjective measures.

INTERACTION BETWEEN INDIVIDUAL AND SOCIETY

The main problem, however, is not one of definition. Rather it is to understand the intricate relationship between the individual's concept of what constitutes a good quality of life, the valuations of his local community, and the ambitions and beliefs of the modern institutions which influence his pattern of behaviour and his life-style: mass media, political elites and other ideological groups, trade unions, etc. Here we find a complicated feedback process, full of contradictions.

Let me illustrate a few of these.

In our society we have a built-in mechanism that is bound to create discontent about life. I am alluding to Professor Wilensky's theory that there is a contrast between our material wishes and needs, and our disappointments when it comes to satisfying them. This gap is enhanced by several phenomena. First, we have the constant stimulation of our desires by advertising. Secondly, there is information obtained through television and other media about other countries, about patterns of consumption of different groups in society, and about the behaviour of our new heroes, pop stars and athletes. Thirdly, we must not underestimate the impact of politics, where the party apparatus makes election promises which are not always kept. The individual is every day led up to the Mountain of Temptation and shown the glories of the material world—only to be let down when he is confronted with harsh reality.

Let me illustrate our dilemma from another angle. Trade unions demand higher wages, voters egged on by politicians expect continuous reform. We want to give away 1 per cent of our GNP to developing nations and still keep the right to spend $900 million net on charter travel to other parts of the world.

Sweden is a small country, where cost per working hour is higher than in competitor countries. A higher standard of living and new reforms, therefore, depend on our ability to absorb new techniques, to find more efficient ways of producing our traditional export goods, to innovate.

This means frequent changes in the organization of work and often a speeding up of the working pace, creating grievances and stress.

There is little understanding among the ordinary people that by aiming too high in respect of social reforms and private consumption we condemn ourselves to a higher pace of work, thus creating working conditions which limit or even reduce our quality of life. We are living on a social lie. I have an intuitive feeling that the continuous bombardment of advertising, information, and election promises makes it very difficult to eliminate the belief that society is qualitatively bad. If a specific grievance is taken care of, for instance by creating a better environment, building more day-nurseries, etc., most people will not feel differently. They will find new arguments for their underlying feeling, which is an undefined malaise about life in our society.

OTHER CAUSES OF MALAISE

If you try to analyse this malaise, there are several other strands.

First, we have the trend towards larger and more anonymous institutions. In industry the number of mergers has increased. The tax structure and political decisions favour the large units and make life difficult for small, family-owned industries. Trade unions have a preference for the large, stable corporations. It is much easier to deal with Volvo, Atlas Copco, and LM Ericsson than with 20000 small companies which are difficult to control regarding wages and working conditions.

Our popular movements show the same tendencies. The trade union central organization (LO) is reducing the number of unions. The savings banks 20 years ago numbered 530 and are now around 200. The cooperatives are closing down several thousands of their local shops and concentrating their resources on supermarkets and department stores.

Our municipalities are showing the same trend. Twenty years ago, Sweden had 2500 urban and rural districts. Now there are only 277. Twenty years ago urban and rural authorities were governed by 240000 elected citizens. The number is now about one-tenth of this figure. Schools, universities, and hospitals are also smitten by this 'gigantomania'.

This development emphasizes the individual's feeling of helplessness; the distance to the decision-makers is growing. There is a feeling that the anonymous group of bureaucrats in private industry, in trade unions, and in government administration is determining more and more. The extension of computer registers, the possibilities of coordinated runs of these registers have emphasized the feeling of being at the mercy of big government in both the private and public sector.

A certain apathy as regards politics is part of the picture. Once every three years a citizen has the right to vote for a list of candidates, the selection of whom he has not influenced, and express his preferences for a particular party's programme, a package of which he may dislike certain proposals and support others. Social, economic, and technological development complicates most political issues and gives the private citizen an impression of being outside the political debate.

THE QUALITY OF LIFE AND WORKING CONDITIONS

To some extent economic growth stems from the simple experience that production in large plants is more efficient than in small workshops. But we have also discovered that economy of scale is not always beneficial. Symptoms of a new type of industrial illness have appeared. Robots and machines, designed to eliminate physical labour and strain, have turned out to create psychological stress. Reactions to these new working conditions show up in increased labour turnover, apathy, and absenteeism.

Volvo has attempted to cope with this problem in a new way. To quote its president, P.G. Gyllenhammar: 'An assembly line is essentially a set of conveyors going through a warehouse full of materials. The materials are the focus of the system, not the employees. People are constantly having to run after their work as it moves past their stations.' Volvo started with the idea that perhaps people could do a better job if the product stood still and they could work on it, concentrating on their work. So Volvo developed industrial carriers at their Kalmar factory, each one carrying a single product. The carriers move according to the wishes of the workers. The employees are brought together in a working group, while in an assembly line situation they are physically isolated from each other.

The result of this new approach to car production has been higher job satisfaction, high productivity, and lower absenteeism. The other side of the coin is that the Kalmar plant represents an expensive capital investment.

In this connection I would like to relate a case from my years as executive vice president at the Swedish Employers' Confederation. In the south of Sweden two industrial plants employing female workers were neighbours. One of them had no difficulties in recruiting women—in spite of the fact that wages were significantly lower than at the other factory—and job satisfaction was markedly higher. The explanation was simply that the plant with lower wages was in the pharmaceutical industry, where the female workers wore linen frocks in gay colours and cleanliness was of the essence. Production in the other plant was dirty and the noise level high. Obviously what we call inner environment plays just as important a role for the quality of life as the wages.

CHANGING ATTITUDES

The connection between the individual's work effort and the functioning of society is made weaker. Employment is not looked upon as necessary because of what you accomplish, but because it gives you a job and an income. The closing down of a plant is opposed because job opportunities are reduced, irrespective of whether the end-product is necessary or useful to society. It is from this point of view rather significant that a proposal in January 1977 to reduce the number of prisoners caused a trade union leader to fight the project because of the dismissal of prison guards that was implied!

The pattern of consumption accentuates the isolation that is evident in working life. Many people have their own house and a summer cottage, a car or a boat, possessions that focus on the small group and the family. Television as a means of communication replaces direct contacts outside the family. You are together with your possessions and not with your friends, you take care of your gadgets instead of attending to your fellow beings.

The very low productivity within the service sector results in higher price increases for services than for products. This leads to a changeover to 'do-it-yourself' when it comes to simpler tasks like painting, woodwork, repairs, etc., once more focusing the individual on his possessions.

Human relationships are weakened, individual contacts become sporadic and superficial, without personal engagement. The feeling of affinity and mutual dependence evaporates, except when there is a crisis or when you want to defend yourself against the decisions of trade union or management bosses.

If I were a pessimist, I could outline a rather frightening scenario: the problems of fellowship and everyday existence are solved by mechanical and bureaucratic methods attacking the symptoms, not the causes. When school problems accumulate more (school) welfare officers and observation clinics are engaged. The local authority has family counsellors and the doctor has psycho-drugs. The helping hand of the friendly neighbourhood, the mutual care of the small community is replaced by paid administrators who by their situation feel their power over the individual.

TO SUMMARIZE

A sense of belonging must be part of the good life. But this is hard to achieve in modern society, which is dominated by the large corporation, the bureaucratic state, the congested urban areas, and the growing network of large institutions as, for instance, trade unions and the mass media.

Modern man runs the risk of becoming maladjusted. He is confronted by the centralized power structure and feels discontent *vis-à-vis* dominant bureaucracies, anonymity, and lack of comprehension. The individual's safety valve is the private sphere, his home and family. He carries in his mind a yearning for some ideal, for a way in which to construct meanings and values for his life.

But as his ideals are vague they also appear elusive. He pursues an absolute quality of life—and what he does in fact achieve is a series of relative successes in his working life, in his relations with other people, in his economic standard. And a relative success often seems to be a failure for the individual.

In the field of government administration it should be the aim to close the gap between the individual and the big bureaucracy, to protect and actively to foster the creation of intermediate structures in the neighbourhood, more cohesive groups in places of work and recreation.

A FOOTNOTE

Since 6 August 1945, when humanity with bewildering suddenness was thrown into the Atomic Age, we have seemed compelled to exclude from our quality of life definition the feeling of relative safety—we now have the power to turn our planet into a nova, an exploding star. I have often asked myself to what extent the fact that mankind has to live with the idea of its death as a species instead of individual death explains the malaise we find today.

Working Life
Edited by B. Gardell and G. Johansson
© 1981 John Wiley & Sons Ltd

Chairman's Concluding Remarks

DAVID HAMBURG

Let me now exercise the chairman's prerogative to add a few remarks that I hope will tend to be integrative in character, and also to add a little more information on health which is my primary field. I see a number of scientific clues in these papers and in this discussion regarding the effects of working life on health—both physical and mental health—which I regard as a continuum. Marianne Frankenhaeuser's paper provides a valuable point of departure, because I think some convergences in the evidence of various workers are highlighted by her analysis. She examines psychobiological responses in the work environment that are of interest in relation to disease processes over the long term. She finds that the responses most suspect with regard to possible health-damaging effects occur under conditions of (a) overload, (b) under-utilization, and (c) lack of control over one's own situation, a recurrent theme in this symposium. She is concerned with chronic effects of the work environment on health as are Kahn and Broadbent. She finds that coping is facilitated by at least two major considerations: (1) a moderately varied flow of stimuli and events; (2) psychologically meaningful work. This latter concept has embedded in it a number of interesting implications: (1) the work makes sense to the worker; (2) it is capable of some anticipation, a point emphasized by the Dohrenwends and others; (3) it contributes to self-esteem; and (4) it may have social significance, a point emphasized by Broadbent. Next, she emphasizes in coping the opportunity to exercise personal control over situational factors, a point emphasized also by the Dohrenwends. For Frankenhaeuser, this is a key to coping, viz. control over one's own situational factors in order to regulate the stimulus input. Broadbent emphasized this issue in respect to self-pacing being preferable to machine-pacing.

A point mentioned by Frankenhaeuser that deserves more attention than we are able to give it here is the restriction of movement, a point which I suspect has much physiological significance. Finally, she calls attention to issues of vigilance and responsibility—in which I suspect there is an optimal range. Some have pointed out that a sense of responsibility is important in worker satisfaction and may well relate in desirable ways to physiological responses. On the other hand, we have heard cases of excessive response in hyper-vigilance and the burdens of heavy responsibility. So there may well be optimal ranges. A particularly interesting point is that she refers to limits of adaptability and our 'old biological construction', an extremely important point. Her findings relate to the extension of earlier adaptive modes in human evolution and to some evolutionary novelties. In a moment I would like to try to put the issues we are discussing in evolutionary perspective. She and Kahn talk about the productive system of industrial times as greatly enhancing material welfare but also having harmful side-effects by analogy with medication. Any good drug has desirable effects but also, particularly over long periods of time, is likely to have side-effects that are unanticipated and sometimes harmful. It is particularly striking that she effectively undertakes an integration not only of psychology and biology in laboratory research, but also of laboratory and field studies with Gardell. Levi, who is here today, has also worked effectively in this integration of laboratory and field studies. Kahn's paper delineates the importance of these approaches, particularly the field experiment for analysis of public policy options.

Frankenhaeuser calls attention to the slow 'unwinding' after work overload; Gardell and Kahn also call attention to this phenomenon. She points out the great individual differences in magnitude and, particularly, duration of these stress responses, a point also made by Broadbent. Here we are beginning—only beginning—to understand the genetic influences on individual differences in endocrine responses and autonomic responses to stress. This linkage led me some years ago to propose an integrated behaviour–endocrine–genetic approach to stress responses. At Stanford at the present time, genetic factors determining individual differences in the response of the adrenal medulla to stress are being analysed by Ciaranello and Barchas. Similar considerations apply to the adrenal cortex and the thyroid.

In addition, she calls attention to environmental influences that bear upon these individual differences in response to stress—for example, the rapid recovery in her subjects after a vacation. It would be helpful to gather extensive data on effects of vacation or respite from pressures, particularly psychophysiological data. Such data would have a bearing on social policy. Are there in fact health benefits of mandated, paid vacations? It is a very important issue that is raised by her findings.

Frankenhaeuser, Kahn, Broadbent, Gardell, and Eketorp call attention to the need and possibilities for adapting technology to human psychobiology. I see a point of convergence also in the great emphasis given to the pervasive influence of solidarity and interpersonal relationships in the work situation (and elsewhere) referred to by Wilensky, Kahn, Dohrenwend, Allardt, Broadbent, and Palme.

Now let me try to put these problems into an evolutionary perspective. We are dealing here with problems and opportunities of incredible recency, if we keep in mind the time-scale of evolution. For millions of years, the work pattern, if I may put it that way, of the higher non-human primates (such as chimpanzees) and the hunting-and-gathering societies of our ancestors, involved several hours a day in the food quest. These groups ranged over several miles per day in a pattern which has remarkable consistency over many generations of our remote ancestors—with emphasis on the gathering of food-stuffs by females and emphasis on hunting by males. A great deal of physical activity was built into the food quest. These patterns of intensive activity were punctuated throughout the day, particularly at midday, by periods of rest. This is the characteristic 'work' pattern of the vast majority of the simple societies (of the order of fifty members) of the non-human primates which most resemble the human species—and also the hunting-and gathering societies that are definitely human. These millions of years were crucially formative for the biology of the human species, and the environment which we take to be natural in the late twentieth century is a very recent environmental transformation. It is a moment of evolutionary time, even if we confine the time-scale to mammalian evolution. So there is a sense in which we are dealing with ancient man in the twentieth century—ancient man biologically in terms of the forces through which natural selection shaped the human organism over an exceedingly long time. Frankenhaeuser raises a deep question about the fit of that organism with its present and very new environment. For any species, some patterns of be-haviour are easy to learn, some difficult, and some impossible. Although it is true that the human brain is enormously plastic, some behaviours are difficult to learn, some are learnable but difficult to sustain over time, and some are achieved only at high costs. This fundamental issue Frankenhaeuser is high-lighting for us. Our species has moved rapidly to take advantage of technological opportunities and their concomitant material benefits to undertake patterns of behaviour which are sometimes achieved only at high costs in terms of psycho-biology. The technology-driven transformation of the human environment, occurring since the industrial revolution and mainly in the past century, has produced many great social changes. These stimulating and baffling changes include the scale of society, the complexity of society, and the heterogeneity of society. Our life is now quite different from the small face-to-face groups of about fifty people which characterized the millions of years during which our ancestors were evolving into the present species, only a matter of some thou-sands of years ago. The drastic technological changes have rapidly brought about the most widely ramifying social changes, and the erosion of traditional institutions and guidelines for behaviour. All this leaves us in great perplexity: what to believe, how to be useful, what is worthwhile, how to ensure the attach-ments that have been part of our biology through evolution, how to make the environment reasonably predictable, how to reconcile achievement and eco-nomic productivity in competitive individuality on the one hand with coopera-tion and mutual accommodation on the other. These are great dilemmas, dilemmas which in large part have been created by the exceedingly rapid, in evolutionary terms, transformation of the environment which man has made.

One of these great transitions is the creation of a new chemical environment.

Now, what do I mean by that? In general, the health of populations requires us to examine radically new developments in human history, and one of these is the exposure to a much wider variety of chemicals in food and medicine and cosmetics and industry than ever before. This is mainly a post-Second World War development. The exposure has gone up in a way unprecedented in the history of the human species and probably of any species. We have only the faintest idea of how well we are adapted to these new molecules—or old molecules in new amounts. Are we ingesting, breathing, touching, handling substances that increase our susceptibility to a variety of diseases? There are thousands of new compounds that have come into common use since the Second World War. If there are toxic effects, one would usually expect a long lag time—20 to 30 years. So it is only now that our methods would permit us to detect for example, carcinogenic effects of compounds in the workplace or elsewhere. Unless the effects are overwhelming, which they rarely are, they are hard to detect with epidemiologic methods in human populations. The effects are usually subtle and chronic. They bear scrutiny.

In the United States, for example, between 500 and 1000 new compounds come into significant use each year. These are mostly compounds which the human species has never 'seen' before. We know little about how many of them may be toxic, how many of them may be highly beneficial, how many of them are essentially neutral with respect to health as they are commonly used. The problem is complicated by the fact that we know little about interactions of risks. Exposure to asbestos is risky by itself, but for heavy smokers it is much more risky. There may be many other interactions of this sort. It would be very helpful if we could identify genetic characteristics of those people who are especially vulnerable, because we could then focus preventive interventions on the high-risk individuals.

The great dilemma of the new chemical environment is that the risks are intimately bound up with advantages for future welfare. Both are embedded in dynamic technological innovation. The quality of life may be greatly enhanced —e.g. by synthetic penicillin. Some hazardous substances of the modern work-place offer encouraging lessons. One is vinyl chloride. The basic discoveries in animals and humans, the regulatory response, and the industrial changes to provide safety all have been made in this decade. Other cases may be more difficult. Much controversy revolves round the assumption that industrial corrections will usually be very expensive. Research will require strengthening to sort out major from minor risks, and to find ways to minimize exposure to high-risk substances. There are special dilemmas connected with the workplace as one segment of the new chemical environment. In the workplace, certain characteristics tend to occur: (1) high levels of exposure; (2) long durations of exposure; (3) the exposure of women of childbearing age. Small molecules of many kinds pass the placenta readily and so an upsurge of research on possible pregnancy exposures is now under way.

A five-year study by Rose and colleagues (1978) has just been completed on the biology and psychology of stress among air-traffic controllers. This is a difficult and taxing occupation, chronically stressful by its very nature in the light of present demands and technology. When the data become fully available, the study will deserve our careful attention. Preliminary results suggest that the air-traffic controllers, as compared with carefully matched workers in the airline industry, are at elevated risks for hypertension. There appears to be some elevations of risk also (though less striking) for alcohol-related difficulty, peptic ulcer, and perhaps diabetes. This study is especially interesting because it also gets at underlying biological processes involved in the production of disease, and may therefore increase our chance of intervening preventively in due course.

Now I would like to make a concluding comment which is the essence of what I would like to leave in your minds. In work as in other aspects of our lives, the health of our population is related to the enormous transition that our species has brought about since the industrial revolution and especially in the twentieth century. In a mere moment of evolutionary time, we have drastically transformed the world of our ancestors. The rapid population growth in most of the world, urbanization with its difficult ramifications, environmental damage and resource depletion, the risks of weapons technology and new patterns of disease—all these are largely products of changes that have occurred only in the most recent phase of human evolution. We have changed our diet, our activity patterns, our technology, the substances of daily use and exposure, our patterns of reproductive activity, and our patterns of tension relief and human relationships. Many of these changes are truly epochal in character, laden with new benefits and new risks; and most of the long-term consequences are poorly understood from a scientific point of view. Natural selection has shaped our ancestors over millions of years in ways that suited earlier environments, not necessarily the very different circumstances of our present life. We simply do not know how well we are suited biologically or behaviourally to the world our species has so rapidly made. This situation should provide a powerful stimulus for the life sciences, broadly defined, biological and behavioural sciences. We need a wider spectrum of research than ever before to meet these unprecedented problems, including the health problems. We are now entering an era in health of testing the extent to which the methods of science can be brought to bear over the entire range of factors that determine the health of the public—not only through medical care but also through the way we manage our personal behaviour patterns such as smoking and alcohol intake; and the way we manage our changing environment. Surely the modern work environment represents one of the most drastic transformations any species has ever brought about in so short a time. Its consequences, planned and unplanned, witting and unwitting, beneficial and adverse, deserve a higher priority in the science of the future than they have had in the past.

REFERENCES

Rose, R. M., Jenkins, C. D., and Hurst, M. W. (1978). *Air Traffic Controller Health Change Study: A Prospective Investigation of Physical, Psychological and Work-related Changes*. A report to the Federal Aviation Administration on research performed under Contract No. DOT-FA73WA-3211.

Part 5

The Role of Social Science in Working Life Policy

Working Life
Edited by B. Gardell and G. Johansson
© 1981 John Wiley & Sons Ltd

Chairman's Note of Introduction

ALBERT B. CHERNS

I have had the opportunity now to read and think about the papers prepared by Dahlström, Podgòrecki, and Thorsrud. These three thoughtful papers raise many questions, not all of which it will be possible to discuss in the time that we have available. I have, however, picked out some themes to which I think we might profitably give consideration.

First, there is the question: who can and who should have a 'working life policy'? It is easy, of course, to assume that it is in the province of government to have a policy for so global a topic. However, not the least of the virtues of the papers that we have before us is the emphasis that is put either explicitly or implicitly on the understanding that there are others besides government who will, and should, have a working life policy. If I may diverge for a minute from the themes in the papers, I would say that one of the most important virtues of a society that is both truly democratic and truly liberal is that it can provide the space within which individuals and groups can have and pursue policy. But, as we are reminded by all three of our contributors, a policy must be based on good information, and good information requires research. Who, then, should be the 'owner' of research? This is a question to which we shall have to return.

Returning to our theme, it seems to me that not only government, but political parties, unions, and employers' associations all can, and should, have a working life policy. One of the questions which is raised in the papers is 'To what extent can and should social scientists have a working life policy?'; and I would add, 'To what extent can individual workers have a policy for their own working lives?'

It is appropriate that the topic chosen for this symposium should focus on the quality of working life. This is not only because much significant work has been done in this country, and in this university, and in this department, but because it is becoming one of the central issues of our time. The quality of working life is a very significant part of the quality of life as a whole. Papers in other sessions have demonstrated this truth and explored the significance of the conditions of working life for health, mental health, and leisure. It is also important because the content of jobs is central to the distribution of social, political, and economic resources. In a recent publication on 'Social Equality' addressed by the Scientific Council for Government Policy to the Council of Ministers of the

281

Netherlands, job content is identified as the point of maximum leverage in the distribution of such resources. A third reason is that the quality of working life, and in particular job content, is a major element in the distribution of power within and among the institutions involved. And, finally, because in the way we look at the quality of working life we reveal our basic theories and assumptions about the nature of man and the nature of society.

THE ROLE OF THE SOCIAL SCIENCES

The three papers bring out several important roles that the social sciences play with regard to working life policy. First there is the function of the social sciences as a means of evaluating policy. This, of course, is of prime significance in Sweden, which as a society now possesses more comprehensive and more coherent policies for working life than any other, or, at any rate, any other of the societies that we could describe as 'capitalist' or 'mixed economies'. The social sciences provide essential tools for evaluating the policy as a whole and the many policies that go to make it up. But Dahlström draws our attention to the issue of whose policy should be taken as the starting-point for the social scientist. He reminds us that traditionally the social scientist has provided the tools for those who can afford to buy them, and that this in the past has meant government and the employer.

The second role is that of the social sciences as a vehicle for raising consciousness. In this capacity the social scientist has contributed along the whole range, from what might hopefully be described as 'pure' education to more or less naked propaganda. In whichever form, this represents a degree of committed action on the part of the social scientist. Perhaps the most interesting feature that is drawn to our attention is the contribution of action research to the learning process as a whole, and to conscience-raising in particular. This theme is implicit both in Thorsrud's and Dahlström's papers.

Podgòrecki explores a more traditional role for the social sciences, as generators of theory, concepts, and data, and he points particularly to the political implications of these traditional functions and reminds us that all research is a political act.

Finally, these papers tackle the question of evolving a strategy for the social sciences themselves. Not the least valuable element in Thorsrud's paper is his exploration of the possibilities of the democratization of research. Underlying this, of course, is the notion that the services of the social sciences should be available much more widely than the traditional research model permits. He is opposed to the model of the social scientist as expert, and here I think there is a potential conflict between his approach and that of Podgòrecki. If we look back on the other roles of the social sciences that I have drawn from the papers, we may see that in some of these the expert model may well have some appropriateness.

There are some other major issues which are touched on in the papers which seem to me to hold within them some of the keys to the ever-nagging problem of diffusion and implementation. I should like to pick out three, all of which are touched on by Dahlström. First he appositely questions the model of efficiency applied to work organizations. This is a favourite theme of my own. So long as organizations can rate as 'efficient' or 'profitable' through the flagrant misuse of social resources, particularly human resources, we shall bang our heads against self-imposed constraints. It simply should not be possible for organizations to make profits or their equivalent by returning less to the community than they take from it. But this theme is too wide for me to explore further here. Closely allied with it is Dahlström's preference for an orientation towards the 'macro' level of analysis and action. Since most of the social scientists who know what they are talking about in this field have engaged in explorations within organizations, it is not surprising that much of the most influential and practically useful work has been of a 'micro' character; but without attention to the 'macro', implementation will be limited and diffusion no better than chancy. The last of these issues to which Dahlström draws attention is the tendency for research to favour the forces of centralization. More than the democratization of research offered by action research will be needed to counter this trend.

The agenda before us is essentially one concerned with the appropriate institutional bases for the various social science roles. I do not see any possibility of constructing just one type of institution which would be capable of undertaking these different functions. On the other hand, a dispersal of these functions, each to one kind of institution, would lead only to fragmentation and dissipation of our own limited resources. The new unit established here can be but one of a network of institutions. The implication I draw from these papers, as well as from other experience, is that much attention needs to be given to the establishment and maintenance of a network, but usually, because this is everyone's job, it is nobody's, and no-one sets aside resources for this purpose. Perhaps this new institution can be innovative in this as in so many other respects.

Working Life
Edited by B. Gardell and G. Johansson
© 1981 John Wiley & Sons Ltd

The Role of Social Science in Working Life Policy: The Case of Postwar Sweden*

EDMUND DAHLSTRÖM

INTRODUCTION

The following analysis forms part of a larger project about the relationship of practitioners and social scientists in the process of creating knowledge within certain sectors (policy areas). The working life sector is one of three selected areas. Consumer protection and consumption comprise the second area, and the third consists of higher education and research.

Even a rather superficial look at the working life sector presents some interesting features, seen institutionally. It is an area in which the state or central government restricts its influence in favour of recognized and institutionalized bargaining parties. Although the parties are admittedly fitted into a frame that is upheld by the political system, the effect of this arrangement is to acknowledge them the right to decide by themselves on the formulation of joint rules by way of central contracts. This pattern may be seen in part as a typical characteristic of the Swedish scene.

Working life policy here refers to the type of policy which seeks to 'steer' (i.e. direct, manage, govern, and control) conditions and activities at factories, offices, shops, and other workplaces. It is a policy pursued at central and local level. The central level is concerned with legislative enactments in fields such as the right of association and labour law, rules and ordinances for occupational safety and the working environment, contracts between the labour market parties, etc. At local level the focus is on managerial planning and decisions on production and product development, personnel policy, supervisory practices, local contracts, the policy of plant-affiliated union branches, decisions taken by joint representative bodies, etc. Working life policy may be seen as one part of policy towards the employment sector, where the other large part consists of labour market policy. The latter aspect is beyond the scope of this paper and as such will not be treated in the present context.

---

*This is a revised and shortened version of a paper in Swedish: 'Samhällsvetenskapens roll i arbetslivspolitik'.

Science and research will be used here in a limited sense to refer to such advancement of the frontiers of knowledge as is made by scientists and researchers who are employed with scientifically researching institutions. This knowledge creation process must accordingly be distinguished from the *practical knowledge creation* which the practitioners evolve in their planning, policy formation, and decision-making. Here, of course, there are mixtures of these two forms which may be hard to classify, e.g. investigative bodies that function as consultants, or research experts attached to larger firms or companies. The practical search for knowledge leads at best to reliable cognition that we can call *tried and tested experience*.

Research and development (R&D) is a term that is customarily used to refer to that knowledge-developing activity which leads up to change. This concept has its roots in ways of thinking about natural science and technology which have proceeded from a centre–periphery model or from notions of linear diffusion. Basic research provides an information base that is elaborated by applied or target-oriented research and is passed on to development work, production layout, and marketing. This model has been criticized for its technical research component. Total doubt has often been cast on the model for its social science research component. According to the latter critique, basic knowledge proceeds from familiarity with the local scene and this local knowledge creation underlies

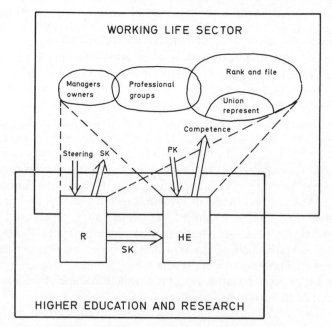

Figure 1 The technocratic model for knowledge development.
(R = research, HE = higher education, SK = scientific knowledge, PK = practical knowledge)

that social science research which brings together and integrates local bits of knowledge into a more general corpus. One model for research development would be interactive and is termed 'periphery–centre–periphery'.

Scientific institutions are often tied to institutions for higher education and to special professions, monopolizing corresponding knowledge and job areas, e.g. different types of technicians or economists. Research (R), higher education (HE), and professional organizations tend to be tied to each other as indicated in Figure 1. The professions have tended to have closer contact with management than with, for example, the blue-collar unions. In Sweden, however, they have had their own unions, and unionization and professionalization have coincided. Manager-owners and professional groups have had a strong influence on knowledge development, have steered research and the practical knowledge for education and research, and have been the main receivers of research findings. Scientific knowledge has been an important source of power for both management and professional groups. This model may therefore be seen as *technocratic* as it strengthens *the resoures of the experts*.

It is customary to analyse politics with reference to means and ends. I am going to look at working life policy on the basis of three goals which may now be regarded as central in the public debate on this policy: efficiency, satisfaction, and co-determination (participation in decision-making). The last goal may well be said to be the most controversial one. Our subject-matter will, therefore, be arranged in the following order: efficient organization of production, satisfactory working environment, and co-determination or industrial democracy. In the final section I shall take up the problem of local and central knowledge development and the organization of research against that background.

EFFICIENT ORGANIZATION OF PRODUCTION

Industrial growth during the postwar period has been marked by intensive efforts to rationalize economic activities with the aid of research. The rationalization has been steered by thinking in terms of profit maximization and rates of return on capital investment. In pursuit of these goals the employers have been able to count on receiving major support from the employee organizations and the trade unions, notably as manifested in central contracts on time and motion studies and cost reduction programmes (Dahlström, 1977). The lion's share of R&D devoted to rationalization has had a technical bias. More recent developments have incorporated cognitions emanating from managerial economics and the behavioural sciences, though on a much more modest scale.

All concrete organization of production builds upon ideas of organization irrespective of whether these are expressly stated or not, or whether they can be based on science and tried and tested experience or the latter only. Organization theory in the field of production life harbours notions of things that are calculated to promote efficiency in various respects.

One consequence of intensified rationalization in the business world has been to try to anchor more and more of the organization theories in R&D. However, the incremental translation of organization theory into scientific practice should be seen as an interplay between prevalent 'organization thinking', practically steered knowledge development, and scientific knowledge development. The given politico-economic frame and the existing production structure have imposed action and notion limits on scientific thought. To all intents and purposes, *classical management theory* can be seen as a codification of the existing administrative systems. Organization theory in the science domain has very much come to reflect prevailing notions and power relationships, and sometimes it has taken on a legitimizing function for existing structures.

Postwar technical research up to the late 1960s tied into a mode of thinking about organization theory that has been popularly known as 'scientific management'. This philosophy is of long standing, having evolved in factories under the aegis of technicians in an atmosphere of free enterprise and faith in the achievement potentials of an efficiently run engineering technique which looks upon human beings as workhorses (Braverman, 1974). Scientific management came to develop a system of principles for efficient organization of production. Efficiency was promoted by carrying to great lengths a division of labour with short operating cycles, a meticulously standardized and regimented work process, a system of payment for work by results, and a transfer of intellectual tasks from manual workers to white-collar specialists (supervisors, foremen, planners, timekeepers, inspectors, etc.). As seen by the manual labourers, this method of organizing work resulted in its systematic impoverishment so that there was less variety; the prospects for exercising influence over one's own work, the degree of skills required, and opportunities for learning on the job diminished; and the pressure to keep pace with work performance to earn the desired rate of pay became higher.

When trying to explore the postwar ideas of organization, we run into difficulties having to do with the lack of consensus between scholars as to schools of organization and the meaning and importance that should be ascribed to their theories. There is little agreement among theorists on how to classify organizational theories. To my mind this is due to the fact that organizational theory implies a considerable amount of political-ethical presumptions. As long as these are not made explicit, it is difficult to understand the theories and relate them to each other. Different organizational theories seem to emphasize different aspects (Abrahamsson, 1975).

There have been some interesting changes in organizational theory since World War II, and these seem to indicate changes in practical thinking and organizational structure, but the relationships between theory, practical thinking, and organizational structure are complicated. The older models of organizational thinking tend to conceive a rather mechanical relation between decision and execution, superiors and subordinates, and decision-making and performance, with some kind of direct steering of the rank and file (operatives) either in the form of strict supervision, machine-pacing, or payment by results (e.g. in the form of piecework). The older models also implied a static conception, assuming a rather permanent environment and goal structure. The later models are more open, there is less of structured and rigid permanent hierarchies and central regulations, and more of participation, flexibility, autonomy of local echelons and rank and file as well as more of intercommunication, cooperation, and mutual decision-making (Burns and Stalker, 1972; Rice and Bishoprid, 1971; Abrahamsson, 1975, 81f. and 110f.).

Other social science approaches displayed a somewhat greater independence of employer interests and to some extent became a source of criticism levelled at the prevailing conditions in working life. That observation holds true of the research which unfolded under the aegis of the behavioural sciences. This research came to be dominated by the *human relations school*, which stressed the importance of needs satisfaction, group formation in connection with work, democratic line supervision, good communications, the establishment of bodies for joint consultation between superiors and subordinates, the importance of education and training, positive in lieu of negative productivity incentives, etc. These ideas aroused keen interest both in employer and employee quarters. Employers saw this knowledge as an instrument for overcoming troublesome personnel problems such as employee turnover, absenteeism, insufficient motivation, and so on. The labour movement was interested in improving people's conditions and well-being at the workplace. These thoughts will be discussed in the following section.

Research into working life tied into personnel administration by making rational arrangements for the recruitment, induction, training promotion, transfer, self-development, and retirement of personnel. This was seen both as promoting efficiency and workforce satisfaction provided it was conducted on the basis of behavioural science know-how. Institutions for training in personnel administration were established with employer support and trade union approval. Psychologists, bringing to bear their skills in differential psychology and testing methodology, played an important role in this course of events. Human relations ideas struck sympathetic chords in university departments of business administration, psychology and sociology, as well as in those institutions, both public and private, which catered to the business world with their consulting and training services in personnel administration. The Swedish Council for Personnel Administration and foremen-training bodies aspired in their educational programmes to instil greater awareness of group-dynamic relationships (i.e. in small groups) and of a more democratic and considerate line supervision.

The postwar period has witnessed a change of sorts in the superior–subordinate relationship. We can see it in the current buzzword terminology, which speaks of 'co-worker' instead of 'subordinate'. This change may be seen in the context of changes in relations generally; the higher standard of living, the greater social security, the strong status of the trade unions, democracy's growing pervasiveness, expansion of the school system, changed relations between generations and between parents and children. The personally authoritarian flavour of everyday life has visibly diminished. No one stands any longer with cap in hand, titles are going through the window, and the 'du' reform (people calling each other by their Christian names) has been implemented. It seems utterly impossible to pinpoint exactly what role social science research has played in this development. The human relations school of the research community formed an integral part of the postwar effort to change workplaces, a change that eventually branched out into many other life areas. It can be said to have reinforced tendencies that were already on the go.

As far as can be judged, the ideas of the human relations school did not have a direct effect on the organization of production. The personnel specialists, who in part were carriers of that school's ideas, did not wield any greater influence over the design of the production organization. In that arena it was the technicians who had their way and their ranks accorded priority to the premisses of 'scientific management' throughout the period ending with the late 1960s. The actual design imparted to the cost reduction and time and motion study programmes produces readings which clearly favour the scientific management school (Dahlström, 1956). One can see the evidence up to his period in the constantly growing volume of piecework and in the increased close control and division of labour which characterized newer work forms, at least at intermediate levels of mechanization. Up to the 1970s the technician-led R&D in the production life area was screened off from the then existing body of critical social science research.

In the 1950s and 1960s Trist and Emery developed the idea of *combining technical with social knowledge* to develop a production process that was better geared to human needs and at the same time functioned efficiently (the socio-technical school). These ideas were transmitted to and practised in Norway, with Einar Thorsrud as charismatic leader. A pilot scheme jointly sponsored by the industrial relations parties was started there in 1967 and gradually took shape in a number of model experiments (Thorsrud and Emery, 1969; Gullowsen, 1975).

Concurrent with the 1966 revision of the works council agreement, the labour market parties formed an industrial relations group, known as the Development Council for Collaboration Questions (URAF), to foster joint consultations at workplaces. URAF started a pilot scheme which emphasized *socio-technical experimentation* (Lennerlöf, 1976; Björk, Hansson, and Hellberg, 1973; Björk, 1976; Stymne, 1976). Its philosophy and procedure were strongly influenced by the socio-technical school. It wanted to give the employees greater influence over the work process on the shop-floor. Production teams known as 'self-governing groups' were formed at workplaces; these groups assumed certain responsibilities and the members had their work tasks enlarged. At one workplace 'bossless' groups were formed. As in the Norwegian experiments, the researchers were active consultants who cooperated with joint representative groups. The results have been rather exhaustively documented in a series of reports and in a series of summarizing books. To judge from this material the experiments achieved varying degrees of success; they ran into snags which made it hard for the bargaining parties to agree on remuneration systems and the like. The diffusion effect seems to have been slight and the scheme was deemed among employers and unions alike to have been at least a partial failure. However, this assessment should be seen in the light of a disappointment that all parties have felt over URAF's activities and generally over the joint consultation system.

Experiments with self-governing groups or production teams, as well as with increased co-determination for the employees, have taken place at the same time in the central government sector under the auspices of the Industrial Democracy Delegation. Although experiments mounted at a state-owned tobacco plant have achieved some success, the scheme does not appear to have caused ripples with any major diffusion effects (Andersson, 1976).

As far as we can see, the research helped the trade unionists to crystallize their demands for another type of work structure that would afford greater scope for the individual's influence over work and a more meaningful job. The union congresses clearly spelled out these demands in 1970 and 1971 (LO, 1971; SAMKO, 1970; 1971; Gardell, 1976; SAMKO, 1976). They surfaced anew in 1976 in a fully-fledged form and are to be found in the demands made by the top-level wage-earner organizations for a new co-determination agreement.

Coextensive with the union-formulated demands for more self-governing and meaningful jobs, the business world teamed up with the technical department of SAF (the Swedish Employers' Confederation) to run a development project that directly sprang from the socio-technical ideas. The work that has been linked to SAF's technical department is poorly documented and it is hard to know what the department itself has initiated and what has been initiated locally (SAF, 1974). The general strategy has been presented in a programme statement, which attaches primary weight to initiation and implementation at the local workplaces. The development work has been carried on locally under joint representative auspices with an active role played by technicians, many of whom are middle managers. It is with these technicians that SAF's technical department has maintained liaison. The services of foreign consultants have been engaged. As a corollary of the emphasis put on practical and local initiatives there has been deliberate avoidance of more 'autonomous' research workers and social scientists. According to information provided by SAF, several hundred firms have conducted development work and the technical department has rendered continuous, on the spot assistance to some ten experimental firms. As criteria for considering an experiment to have been successful, the approaches adopted must have led to observable and reasonably significant changes, top management and the union leaders must have found the approaches to have fared well, and they must be convinced that it is worth going ahead and the firm must become so interested in the new ideas that their further in-house development will progress spontaneously.

Many question marks start to pile up when it comes to taking a position on what the experiments with 'new work forms' have led to. Here one is reduced to using the statements made by top managers and union officials, and there is no more detailed control of what has happened—for instance, of what the experiments have denoted for long-term efficiency in various respects and of what they have led to as regards job satisfaction. Because many changes have been implemented, it is hard to say what any one change such as the remuneration system—has entailed for other changes. All the firms accounted for in the reports have succeeded, which means that no mention is made of how many firms have failed. The presentations of successful cases are couched in terms which will attract publicity, and there is little control. Possibly important consequences are glossed or passed over—for instance, those having to do with the possibility that production teams may expel less 'efficient' workers or that the grouping in smaller units may reduce solidarity between employees. What is missing in the first place is a more penetrating analysis of the processes bound up with changes and work performance, e.g. of what may lie behind a certain productivity change.

That the socio-technical ideas have then, looked interesting and been tapped by practitioners should be seen against societal changes of the kind that to some extent have rendered older organizational forms obsolete. The heightened aspirations of men and women, the demand for greater flexibility in organizational structure, the tendency towards economic concentration, the increased product variation with demands for another type of steering, new technical aids which create opportunities for new solutions—all these factors are involved, not to mention others.

SATISFACTION AND THE WORKING ENVIRONMENT

The decade following World War II was marked by a keen interest in harnessing scientific methods to study the human condition. This can be seen as a manifestation of the buoyant optimism associated with scientific progress in those days, an attitude that was strongly influenced by American thought. Perhaps the most eloquent expression of this attitude was that of sociologist George Lundberg in his book, *Can Science Save Us?* There was no end to possibilities for solving the problems of work; all that was necessary was to make investigations of workplaces to find out what life was like for people in their daily rounds. Employers and unions both became interested in such research. The labour movement underlined the importance of using science to solve the problems of society. For instance, the use-science philosophy strongly imbued the cultural programme that the Swedish labour movement put forward in 1952 (SDP, 1952). Before then the problems of 'worker joy' (work satisfaction) had been taken up at length in conferences and books (Karlbom, 1949; Vestlund, 1949). Some American studies of working life problems were discussed, notably the studies done at Western Electric. The postwar era bore a strong stamp of American influence.

The interest in studying and improving the human condition was focused on the satisfaction of needs. Sociologists were engaged to study needs satisfaction and productivity, with use made of questionnaires and observations to find out how needs satisfaction correlated with productivity (Segerstedt and Lundquist, 1952; 1955; Dahlström, 1954; Pfannenstill, 1955; Törnqvist, 1956).

Several sociological studies were made of working life which took up different aspects. Consistent interest was shown in studying, first, how job satisfaction was affected by various circumstances in the form of personal rewards from work, e.g. the wages paid, the job's characteristics, type of supervision, and relations with workmates; and second, how the degree of satisfaction affected the relations to other factors such as class identifications, conflict attitude, productivity, absenteeism, propensity to quit, etc. Satisfaction came to be perceived as a crucial factor for many attitudes and actions. This point of view can be seen in comparison with the human relations school described in the previous section and whose ideas were rather widely held among behavioural scientists. Dissatisfaction could disrupt performance in many ways, e.g. by lowering productivity or producing conflicts and aggressiveness (according to the frustration-aggression theory). It could, therefore, be considered important to study satisfaction even though satisfaction as such was not always accorded such great value in its own right. For the employers the analysis of satisfaction offered an avenue to the solution of personnel problems such as employee turnover.

The interest in questionnaire-based surveys and in satisfaction came to be relayed by experts and consultants in personnel administration. They took over and developed interview and questionnaire studies at workplaces as a part of their consulting assignments. Very few of these studies have been publicly released. Their results and uses are kept in strict confidence as classified material. They were carried out in the 1970s on a big scale by organizations like the Swedish Institute for Public Opinion Research (SIFO) and the Swedish Council for Personnel Administration.

The studies of satisfaction with work had general and local recipients. On the general plane they led to a discussion about how to go about shaping the conditions of work so as to achieve maximum satisfaction for the employees. However, it is hard to pan these earlier studies for any across the board conclusions as to what was most important for well-being at the workplace. The studies tended to point up the social relations, with special emphasis on the relations to workmates.

The other general problem issue in these studies had to do with how job satisfaction reacted on other factors such as productivity, mobility, and absenteeism. As noted above, the human relations school had tended to stress the crucial importance of satisfaction for productivity, etc. The studies lent no support to the assumptions of simpler connections between satisfaction and productivity.

The questionnaire surveys not only shed light on these general connections, they also provided information about the local scene. It is possible that their greatest importance was that they furnished both management and union officials with intelligence on a number of disamenities that could be remedied locally. When questionnaire surveys were later used in the consultation, it is likely that the local recipient took on greater importance. The consultants would make known what the employees thought about different conditions, and these viewpoints would be central to the underpinning of discussions and the taking of measures.

However, investigations of employee satisfaction did show certain general patterns with regard to its distribution. Satisfaction tended to be greater for people who enjoyed a higher degree of autonomy in their work (Blauner, 1964; Etzioni, 1975, 223ff.). At the same time more sophisticated methods were developed to bring out different aspects of satisfaction, in order to tie in with international studies (Hertzberg, Mausner, and Synderman, 1959; Blauner, 1964; Gardell, 1971). A component was distinguished which was connected with a positive feeling of work enjoyment ('craft pride') and which pertained to more fundamental characteristics of the job, e.g. the control exercised over own work. Another component referred to work factors that are more external or physical. The application of improved techniques to the study of the objective factors in work made it feasible to relate the enjoyment of work to rather definite factors which had to do with the individual's degree of freedom and control on the job. This research directly supported those ideas of the socio-technical school that were touched upon in the previous section. The enjoyment of work meant that the job had a self-motivating character. 'Stimulating work' came to mean work that was both satisfying and self-motivating.

The sociological analysis of job satisfaction has emphasized two basic aspects: the historical increase of people's aspirations and the fundamental societal perspectives. The report on technological change and work adjustment that was submitted to the 1966 LO congress explicitly stressed the importance of aspiration levels for subjective satisfaction and of applying a non-alienated view to work (Dahlström et al., 1966). Both aspects came in for strong emphasis in the further pursuit of research into man in working life that was mentioned earlier in this paper.

The working life crisis which erupted in the late 1960s (specifically, the walk-out at the Kiruna iron mines in December 1969) came to underline the historical relativity of job satisfaction as subjectively perceived. Writers, journalists, and others began to describe the negative sides of working life, in particular for manual workers. The workers themselves reacted by staging wildcat strikes. Much of the new criticism aimed its fire at the working life research which had been pursued: labour science was accused of not paying sufficient attention to the unsatisfactory conditions which prevailed and of not having helped to raise consciousness about these disamenities. On the contrary, labour science was alleged to have joined a plot designed to cover up the disamenities and to defend that *status quo*—for instance, by presenting the results of satisfaction studies in which most of the employees said they got along fine with conditions at the workplace.

The 1970s witnessed an increasingly conscious view of working life with demands imposed not only on the health—promoting design of the physical factors but also on making the *psychosocial factors* promote a better social life on and off the job. A recently enacted law, the Work Environment Act, which came into force on 1 January, 1978, has put flesh on the bones of this trend.

The labour-science research has created a body of evidence on which to base standardized requirements to be met by conditions at the workplace. Bertil Gardell has sought to summarize conclusions as to which characteristics of industrial work are associated with psychosocial problems so serious that they should be avoided in future (Gardell, 1976):

—machine-paced work,
—standardized motion patterns,
—working methods and tools predetermined down to the last nut and bolt,
—constant repetition of short-cycle operations,
—unremitting necessity to pay superficial attention, especially in combination with closely controlled work pace,
—combination of foregoing work characteristics with payment by results,
—lack of opportunities for social contact during work,
—authoritarian supervisory practices.

Social science research has induced the legislators to specify the direction that improved standards in the psychosocial area should take. The commission of inquiry which drafted the working environment law made frequent reference to voluminous social science documentation.

It will be interesting to see how the 'knowledge problem' is going to be solved in this area and what role researchers and experts will play. There is *one route by way of expert assessment*, similar to the physician's role, which builds upon the inputs of local experts, and a more *pragmatic, political route* which, by invoking the co-determination law (Democracy at Work Act) and other laws, leaves it to the wage-earners as practitioners to pass judgement without the benefit of local expertise. In the latter case more of the background for making much assessments will be provided by tried and tested experience than by science. It stands to reason that research in this area is generally needed and it is also likely that such research will have a consciousness-raising effect; the ecological research based on the natural sciences has made the workers aware that the physical environment is fraught with hazards.

CO-DETERMINATION AND INDUSTRIAL DEMOCRACY

The Swedish society has long had powerful wage earner organizations. Employees have been enabled to exercise influence through their trade unions and the established system of collective bargaining. A rather high degree of 'self-policing' has ensued from the reaching of central agreements or contracts between the labour market parties. Up to the 1970s the unions confined their right to participate in decision-making ('co-determination') to setting the terms of employment. Even before then the unions had dissociated themselves from assuming responsibility for managerial decisions. They restricted their local influence to accepted bargaining relations and joint representative bodies with advisory powers (works councils, i.e. committees consisting of persons representing company management and workers, both blue-collar and white-collar).

Social scientists have devoted research to the bargaining system and labour market parties generally, from which it follows that the system's principal structure and functions are well-known. Studies of how the system operates locally have been few in number (Edlund, 1967; Ekeberg and Lanz, 1968; Hart and von Otter, 1970). The activities of local bodies for joint consultation have been monitored by centrally investigative bodies composed of the bargaining parties. These central joint representative groups have made studies based on data furnished by the members of local, joint representative bodies, the subject-matter of which has pertained to frequency of attendance at meetings, the items of business transacted, and value ratings made by the members. Some in-depth studies have also been made.

The overall impression left by these studies may be summarized as follows (Dahlström, 1956). Bodies for joint consultation have exercised rather marginal influence over the decisions taken. More important questions have been taken up via the direct bargaining route. Information has been presented at the meetings of these bodies, but it has been hard to pass this information further along. A gap has yawned between the regular membership of joint consultation bodies and the people they represent. A number of experiences gained in bigger companies were put on record, with particular mention of one coordinating body which after investigating production departments came up with results in the form of improved working conditions and better cooperation. Examples were also given of joint consultation bodies which blocked the treatment of unresolved problems, made it harder for the union to press ahead with bargaining, and absorbed valuable chunks of management time (Dahlström et al., 1971; Kronlund et al., 1973).

Up to 1966 both the labour movement and the research community showed only slight interest in consultation and co-determination. When the labour market parties got together in the mid-1960s to negotiate a new works council agreement, several studies got under way (Rehnman, 1965). The employers based their investigation on analyses by business economists which sought to show that if the existing 'balance of interests' in firms were upset due to increased employee influence, the firms would 'run aground'. This line of argumentation was refuted by sociologists (Schiller, 1973). The subsequent agreement did not lead to any significant change; indeed, the difficulties attending these negotiations swung the unions around to thinking that from now on they would try to get what they wanted from legislation and not from collective bargaining. The 1966 revision generated the pilot scheme, URAF, mentioned in the previous section (p. 290).

In 1966 the government constituted a delegation to mount experiments with most extensive industrial democracy in state-owned companies (företagsde-mokratidelegationen, FÖDD). Different kinds of experimentation were set in train with their focus on cooperation groups, self-governing groups (production teams), decentralization of responsibilities, and change of remuneration systems (FÖDD, 1971). The experts serving with this delegation were an active lot and they made stimulating contributions to the general discussion (Karlsson, 1969; Hammarström, 1973). In 1969 a delegation for administrative democracy (DEFF) was constituted. Made up of persons representing the state and the main organizations of state employees, DEFF was mandated to commence experiments in different areas. A state of the art analysis was made of various government agencies selected for these experiments. The agencies had set up decision-making bodies empowered to take decisions on matters of personnel policy (DEFF, 1976). Half the members of these decision-making bodies were appointed by the staff unions.

The growing unrest in the Swedish labour market which surfaced in the second half of the 1960s, when wildcat strikes occurred on a big scale, came to have great bearing on the molding of public opinion and debate. Analyses of the causes of these strikes were perhaps the most significant contributions that social science rendered to the reforms which followed (Dahlström et al., 1971). The origin of the strikes was seen in relation to existing labour-law frameworks. Jurisprudential and general history analyses of the origin and structure labour law proved to be of importance in this context. To illustrate, jurisprudential analyses showed how the Labour Court's earlier judgements, which confirmed paragraph 32, i.e. the right of employers to hire and dismiss workers and to direct and allocate work, rested on political grounds and that the legal experts here took a political stance (Geijer and Schmidt, 1958; Schmidt,

1969). Jurisprudential studies of contentious issues in litigation showed that the system has not been particularly sensitive to the employee side of the dispute (Edlund, 1967). Several sociological briefs drove home the thesis that the eruption of wildcat strikes must be seen in the light of the then existing balance of power, which was titled in favour of the employers at the local level due to the operation of paragraph 32, existing restrictions on strike and look-outs, priority given to the employers' interpretation, and defective knowledge resources in the employee camp (Korpi, 1971). The studies that social scientists made of the growing tendency to resort to 'labour shedding' and of the process of dividing manpower into two teams, 'A' (first-rate) and 'B' (second-rate), nourished demands for increased security of employment and for influence over hiring and firing practices. Shortcomings in the job world were also exposed by the Low Incomes Commission.

The role played by research in the course of events which led up to the labour-law reforms is hard to clarify. Research was instrumental in showing that the earlier system of works councils did not signify any real commitment to industrial democracy. It also contributed to identifying some of the factors that engendered unrest and discontent at the workplaces, pointing out that not a few of the difficulties were caused by existing labour law. There is reason here to go back to the research, mentioned in the previous section, into the impoverishment of work and the system of piece rates. The pilot scheme of experiment can hardly be said to have created a data base on which to build the later reforms. On the other hand, perhaps those experts and researchers who took part in the pilot scheme helped to enliven the discussion about industrial democracy. References are made to the scheme in official investigations and congress statements. Summing up, it may well be said that the researchers have played a less significant role here than in other processes of change in the area of working life, e.g. with respect to the new work forms or the development of labour market policy.

CURRENT PROBLEMS OF RESEARCH POLICY

The labour-law reforms have ridden on the crest of a wave of increased interest in working life problems and have also increased the interest in working life research. The advent of a Working Life Centre and the new programme written for the Work Safety Fund have heightened the relevance of the research policy debate in this area (PUFRA, 1978).

The enactment of the labour-law reforms along with the establishment of the Working Life Centre and the new programme responsibility vested in the Work Environment Fund has been motivated by a balance of power rationale. In cognizance of the growing power that the trade unions are going to wield, which will put it on a par with that wielded by the employers, a demand for cognitive symmetry has been put on record. In that way the emphasis on co-determination can be given an *ex parte* interpretation, i.e. it is meant to strengthen the corpus of knowledge commanded by the employees. But it can also mean that cooperation is being emphasized, that co-determination is a matter to be realized under joint auspices, and that the development of knowledge shall serve both parties. This ambiguity has become apparent in the course of discussion.

The employers have enjoyed a stronger position in the creation of knowledge both locally and centrally. This has been due to the *stamp of secrecy* imposed on conditions at workplaces, i.e. all material on working life is classified information. The manager-cum-employer has stood guard anxiously to make sure that any know-how of importance to his competitors does not leak out. The in-plant work of technical development and research has been the employer's exclusive domain. In so far as the generation of knowledge has been research it has formed an integral part of the company's capital investment activity and as such has become a managerial concern falling outside the sphere in which the unions could bargain and consult. When, during the postwar period, a body of social science research grew up alongside the technical and working life research, and in so doing came into touch with the employees through interviews, observations, and other fieldwork, another attitude gradually emerged. Since the employees were affected by this research, it was reasonable and even necessary to inform them about it and somehow gain their assent. The present course of events has moved towards pursuing more and more of the local, societal research under joint representative auspices. But the initiative and the steering has tilted more often than not towards the employer side.

According to one study of working life research, quite a few projects have had to be aborted owing to employer resistance; moreover, research reports have been prevented from circulating, sometimes with the consent of local union representatives (Berglind, Gardell, and Korpi, in press). There are examples where the Work Environment Fund has voted funds to finance projects that were subsequently aborted because the local employers refused to let the researchers inside the factory gates.

The demand to gain *admission* to the workplace for research has become a cardinal issue and has been taken up by the Labour Law Committee (Labour Law Committee, 1977). A law authorizing persons to enter workplaces for research purposes has been proposed by this committee's employee representatives. If the unions have given the go-ahead to a specific project, the employers must not be allowed to refuse the researchers admission. The employer representatives on the committee have contended that matters connected with such on the spot research should be regulated by contract between employers and wage earner organizations.

According to the government bill, the development of knowledge that is to be channelled through the Work Environment Fund and the Working Life

Centre must be practically oriented. The crux here is how to go about achieving this aim where the organization of research is concerned. In the first place, it involves the question of overall steering by practitioners of research in the working life area; in the second place, it involves the question of *ex parte* constraint. The discussion has roughly drawn the following distinctions: *monopartite research*, i.e. where projects are steered by and oriented towards one industrial relations party; *multipartite research*, where projects are oriented to several parties; and *party unconstrained* research, which is not oriented to any party. To all intents and purposes the latter type can be thought of as tying into a traditional basic research design, where the researcher pursues his studies on the basis of his intradisciplinary reasons. It has been questioned whether the strong emphasis on party orientation, irrespective of whether monopartite or multipartite research is involved, might not lead to the ultimate demise of that working life research which is not thus constrained.

The steering problem is closely bound up with the coordination problem. To what extent should coordination of research within one area be aspired to, and of what is this to consist? To illustrate, the Working Life Centre is supposed to be a coordinator, with communication being paramount, i.e. to support documentation within the area so that research will be accessible to the researchers and practitioners concerned, to see that the wishes of practitioners are channelled to researchers, and to put researchers in touch with practitioners. Conferences, periodicals, and series of reports are vehicles for the communicative coordination. But how far does one go from there to try to bring about integration in thinking, concordance, theoretical-practical focusing, etc.? This question has come to the fore with the emergence of many projects intended to shed light on the function and effects of the work reforms. The coordination requirement has had to do with such things as different types of problems and different branches of industry. Attention has also been called to the gains that stand to be made from amalgamating the various research projects provided certain data are collected, e.g. the findings of field surveys or questionnaire-based polls, or information is exchanged bilaterally in cases where the projects are partially overlapping. Further coordination is to be discussed at later conferences. There are some risks in carrying coordination to too great lengths, as when one tries to target all research projects much too narrowly.

Working life research in its more practical and mission-oriented form has actualized a type of research that is vaguely called *action research*. This term has as many meanings as it has users. Action research has often meant a locally anchored research where the investigator, working with local practitioners, joins a project aimed at making changes and is in on analysing and somehow evaluating these changes. Since it is the local practitioners who wield the power, the researcher's degree of activity will be circumscribed by the local power relationships. Mention was made earlier of two strategies used in local knowledge development. The URAF experiments were characterized by relatively active researchers who in some sense pressed for the adoption of changes in consultation with joint representative groups, obviously with the acquiescence of top management. The technical department's strategy seems to have allotted to the central experts a more cautious role, and its analyses have played up the significance of local initiative in the development of new work processes and played down the importance of central experts. Moreover, much is made of the point that this is not a matter of research but of development only. The problems of action research lead up to the vital questions of how *centre* and *periphery* stand *vis-à-vis* the creation of knowledge, and how research stands *vis-à-vis* practical knowledge creation.

The technical research has been decisive for the job world. Much of the process of creating knowledge about production forms and work forms has come under the influence of technical thinking. Frequent use has been made of a centre periphery model or linear diffusion model of R & D on the technical–natural science side. Starting out from the basics of fundamental research at the centre, the road leads to applied research and from there to development work, which is often thought of as taking place locally, i.e. on the periphery. The merits of this model have also been discussed for technical research. It seems even more problematical for social science research.

If technical – natural science research demonstrates that certain processes can be used to make this or that product, or that the manufacturing process generates substances posing a specific medical hazard, then this knowledge has a validity for local situations.

Societal knowledge is apparently incapable of being brought out in the same way through rarefied studies in laboratories at central level. We cannot invoke experimental studies, say of leadership patterns, to find interconnections which lend themselves intact to application to working life with its enormous variation. Knowledge development presupposes that we study the local scene. It is not until a local case has been tested and has produced the desired outcome that it can 'set a paradigm' and start to diffuse. Societal knowledge builds upon a knowledge of everyday life and the commonplace. These local circumstances furnish the base for building up a corpus of more general knowledge.

For local practitioners the local scene will always lie closest to their hearts. For them it suffices to have the local factors speak in favour of a solution, which then generates its own momentum for taking action to realize that solution. The question of whether the solution is universally valid becomes a secondary issue of greater interest to other practitioners in other local circumstances. The researchers will interest themselves in the generalizability, and as such will play a particularly strategic role in the diffusion process itself. In any event the local study does not get past cognitive development at the societal level.

Obviously, there are cognitions of importance for working life which do not have the local character here indicated. This certainly holds for societal conditions of the kind which extend beyond workplaces and which are bound up with broader processes and structures, e.g. labour market conditions, legislation, and other political and economic factors. They interest central practitioners.

The question of whether a centralistic bias is not built into the organization of research is one that carries equal force for the job world. Research is organized in line with central principles in order to arrive at general cognitions. At a rule these cognitions are centralistically addressed to society's inner sanctum, i.e. to persons who wield power and command resources. The research community will usually take less interest in the local recipients, i.e. in persons on the periphery of society or in those who have less power and resources. The centre–periphery model taken from sociology of knowledge theory is of relevance to the political-sociological model of centre and periphery. The political-sociological model has riveted its attention on information-knowledge, culture as an instrument of power and as resource. Galtung, who has developed the centre–periphery theory, shows that research is clearly a centre-strengthening force in society and a vehicle for the centre's hegemony (Galtung, 1977a).

As used here, the term 'centre' alludes to holders of power and as such encompasses persons who are custodians of capital, administration, and knowledge. The sectoral research is built up everywhere after the same centralistic patterns, and this observation also holds for the organization of the Working Life Centre.

Perhaps the importance of knowledge for the local practitioners in their consciousness-raising and local development activities has been underestimated. The cognitive-developing resources deserve a better job being made of diffusion. The research findings would then be circulated as an integral part of this diffusion process. The local units would be better equipped with local resources for cognitive development in order to receive general cognitions and develop local ones.

To a great extent the process of change in the body politic has been fuelled centrally via governmental intervention and legislation, and a great deal of the reform activity has been built up centrally. This process has been bound up with the immense power wielded by capital and market mechanisms at the local level, which has sometimes made it difficult to mobilize local branches of the labour movement. The trade union movement is characterized by centralization and concentration. Sometimes it has been easier to uphold democracy at central than at local level. The co-determination issue has been fuelled by a centralistic strategy, which makes it only natural to want to impart a centralistic structure to the cognitive development as well. This centralistic build-up of the production of knowledge may come to work at cross purposes with local initiatives and local mobilization. As the wage earners acquire greater influence locally, so too will they experience a greater need to participate in the local cognitive development in order to strengthen their awareness and autonomy.

The traditional technocratic model for research and higher education was

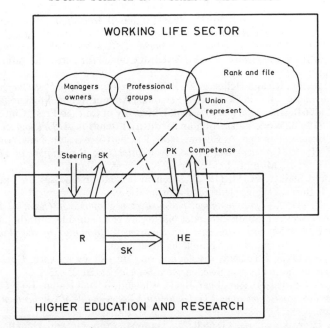

Figure 2 The democratic model for knowledge development.
(R = research, HE = higher education, SK = scientific knowledge, PK = practical knowledge)

presented in the first section of this paper (Figure 1). The above mentioned criticism points to the revised, democratic model presented in Figure 2 where Research is steered by broader groups, is built on broader practical knowledge from broader groups, and is addressed to broader strata; and where Higher Education is built upon practical knowledge from broader areas, is influenced by broader groups, and spreads its competence to broader strata. This would imply a successive weakening of professional domains.

This paper has dealt with several knowledge areas the professionalization of which may be questioned, e.g. job safety and job design, socio-technical planning and personnel management. Today the union movement attempts to mobilize its members on these issues as a preparation for the new labour laws that invite the rank and file to take a more participatory role in working life.

REFERENCES

Abrahamsson, B. (1975). *Organisationsteori. Om byråkrati, administration och självstyre (Organizational Theory. On Bureaucracy, Administration, and Autonomy)*, AWE/ GEBERS, Stockholm.
Andersson, B. (1976). Företagsdemokrati vid tobaksfabriken i Arvika. En utvärdering (Industrial democracy in the tobacco factory at Arvika. An evaluation), mimeo, Ministry of Industry, Stockholm.

304   WORKING LIFE

Berglind, H., Gardell, B., and Korpi, W. (eds) (in press). *Arbetslivsforskningens handlings-utrymme (Limitations to Research in Working Life)*, Tiden/Folksam, Stockholm.

Björk, L. (1976). *Människor, grupper och parter i förändringsarbete (Human Beings, Groups, and Parties in Reform Work)*. Swedish Council for Personnel Administration, Stockholm.

Björk, L., Hansson, R., and Hellberg, P. (1973). *Ökat inflytande i jobbet (Increased Industrial Democracy)*, Swedish Council for Personnel Administration, Stockholm.

Blauner, R. (1964). *Alienation and Freedom*, University of Chicago Press, Chicago.

Blauner, R. (1969). Work satisfaction and industrial trends in *A Sociological Reader on Complex Organizations*, ed. A. Etzioni, Holt, Rinehart & Winston, New York, 223ff.

Braverman, H. (1974). *Labor and Monopoly Capital. The Degradation of Work in the Twentieth Century*, Monthly Review Press, New York.

Burns, T., and Stalker, G. M. (1972). Mechanistic and organic systems, in *Industrial Man*, ed. T. Burns, Penguin, Harmondsworth, Middx.

Dahlström, E. (1954). *Tjänstemannen, näringslivet och samhället (Salaried Employees, Industry and Society)*. Studieförbundet Näringsliv och Samhälle, Stockholm.

Dahlström, E. (1956). *Information på arbetsplatsen (Information at the Work Place)*, Studieförbundet Näringsliv och Samhälle, Stockholm.

Dahlström, E. (1977). Efficiency, satisfaction and democracy in work. Conceptions of industrial relations in post war Sweden, *Acta Sociologica*, 20, 25–53.

Dahlström, E., Gardell, B., Rundblad, B. G., Wingård, B., and Hallin, T. (1966). *Teknisk förändring och arbetsanpassning (Technological Change and Work Adjustment)*, Prisma, Stockholm.

Dahlström, E., Eriksson, K., Gardell, B., Hammarström, O., and Hammarström, R. (1971). *LKAB och demokratin (The LKAB Company and Democracy)*, Prisma, Stockholm.

DEFF's report series, especially von Otter, C. (1976). Försök med förvaltningsdemokrati—en utvärdering av de anställdas delaktighet och inflytande (Attempts at civil service democracy), Report no. 9, *Medbeslutande i statsförvaltningen*, DEFF's slutrapport (final report).

Edlund, S. (1967). *Tvisteförhandlingar på arbetsmarknaden. En rättslig studie av två riksavtal i tillämpning (Negotiation Procedures in Labour Disputes. The Functioning of Two National Collective Agreements—a Study from the Legal Horizon)*, P. A. Nordstedt & Söners Förlag, Stockholm.

Ekeberg, L-O., and Lanz, S. W. (1968). *Blue-collar Workers' Participation in Management in Sweden*, RATI, Stockholm.

Etzioni, A. (1975). *A comparative Analysis of Complex Organizations*, New York, Free Press.

FÖDD. (1971–1973). Reports from the Committee on Industrial Democracy, Stockholm (in Swedish).

Galtung, J. (1977a). *Hvordan skal det gå med Norge? (What will Happen to Norway?)*, Gyldendal Norsk Forlag, Oslo, 241ff.

Galtung, J. (1977b). *Methodology and Ideology*, vol. on theory and methods of social research, Christian Ejlers, Köpenhamn, chs 3 and 4.

Gardell, B. (1971). *Produktionsteknik och arbetsglädje (Production Technology and Work Satisfaction)*, Swedish Council for Personnel Administration, Stockholm.

Gardell, B. (1976). *Rapport i psykosociala frågor (Report on Psychosocial Issues)*, Swedish Government Official Reports (SOU), Stockholm, 3, especially 79ff.

Geijer, L., and Schmidt, F. (1958). *Arbetsgivare och företagsledare i domarsäte (Employers and managers as judges)*, Gleerup, Lund.

Gullowsen, J. (1975). *Arbeidervilkår (Workers' Conditions)*, Forlaget Tanum-Norli A/S, Oslo.

Hammarström, O. (1973). *Handbook i företagsdemokrati för löntagare (Employees' Handbook of Industrial Democracy)*, Prisma, Stockholm.

Hart, H., and von Otter, C. (1970). Lokal lönebildning, mimeo, Department of Sociology, University of Gothenburg, Sweden.

Herzberg, F., Mausner, B., and Snyderman, B. (1959). *Motivation to Work*, Wiley, New York.

Information och samråd (1965). Swedish Employers' Confederation, Stockholm.

Karlbom, T. (1949). *Blodprov på arbetsglädje (Blood Tests as Indicators of Work Satisfaction)*, Tiden, Stockholm.

Karlsson, L. E. (1969). *Demokrati på arbetsplaster (Democracy at Places of Work)*, Prisma, Stockholm.

Kockumsrapporten (1970). Prisma, Stockholm, 73–74.

Korpi, W. (1970). *Varför strejkar arbetarna? (Why do the Workers Go on Strike?)*, Tiden, Stockholm.

Korpi, W. (1971). Om maktförhållandena och motsättningar mellan parterna på arbetsmarknaden (On power relations and conflicts in the Swedish labour market), in *Arbetslivet i kris och förvandling (Working Life in Crisis and Change)*, Rabén & Sjögren, Stockholm.

Kronlund, J., Carlsson, J., Jensen, I.-L., and Sundström-Frisk, C. (1973). *Demokrati utan makt. LKAB efter strejken (Democracy without Power. The LKAB Company after the Strike)*, Prisma, Stockholm.

Labour Law Committee (1977). Fackliga förtroendemän, möten på betald arbetstid och arbetslivsforskning. Delbetänkande av nya arbetsrättskommittén (Union officials, meetings during working hours, and working life research), Publication nr DSA 1977, **4**, Department of Labour, Stockholm.

Lennerlöf, L. (1976). *Arbetsledning (Work Supervision)*, Swedish Council for Personnel Administration, Stockholm.

LO (1971). *Demokrati i företagen (Democracy in Companies)*, Swedish Confederation of Trade Unions, Stockholm.

LO (1976). *Solidariskt medbestämmande (Co-determination)*, Swedish Confederation of Trade Unions, Stockholm.

Pfannenstill, B. (1955). *Begreppet arbetstrivsel—belyst genom en sociologisk fältundersökning av gruvarbetare: nordvästra Skåne (The Concept of Work Satisfaction—A Sociological Field Study of Miners)*, Gleerup, Lund.

PUFRA. (1978). *Medbestämmande och arbetsliv (Co-determination and Working Life)*, Report 1978, **2**, Work Environment Fund, Stockholm.

Rehnman, E. (1965). *Företagsdemokrati och företagsorganisation (Industrial Democracy and Industrial Organization)*, Swedish Employers' Confederation, Stockholm.

Rice, G. H., and Bishoprid, E. W. (1971). *Conceptual Models of Organization*, Appleton-Century-Croft, New York.

SAF (1974). *Nya arbetsformer (New Work Organization)*, Swedish Employers' Confederation, Stockholm.

SAF (1977). *Nya fabriker (New factories)*, Swedish Employers' Confederation, Stockholm.

Samarbete i framtidens företag (1965). *(Cooperation in Future Enterprises)*, Swedish Employers' Confederation, Stockholm.

SAMKO (1970 and 1971). Reports, Swedish Confederation of Salaried Employees (TCO), Stockholm.

SAMKO (1976). *Villkor i arbete—en skrift om personalpolitik (Working Conditions)*, Swedish Confederation of Salaried Employees (TCO), Stockholm.

Schiller, B. (1973). LO, Paragraf 32 och företagsdemokratien (Swedish Confederation of Trade Unions, management prerogatives, and industrial democracy), in *Tvärsnitt,* published in commemoration of the 75th Anniversary of the Swedish Confederation of Trade Unions.

Schmidt, F. (1969). *Kollektiv arbetsrätt (Collective Labour Law)*, P. A. Norstedt & Söners Förlag, Stockholm.

SDP (1952). *Människan och nutiden (Man and Contemporary Times)*, Social Democratic Party programme for culture, Tiden, Stockholm.

Segerstedt, T., and Lundquist, A. (1952). *Människan i industrisamhället (Man in Industrial Society)*, Part I (Working Life), Studieförbundet Näringsliv och Samhälle, Stockholm.

Segerstedt, T., and Lundquist, A. (1955). *Människan i industrisamhället, del II—Fritidsliv—Samhällsiv* (Man and Industrial Society, Part II Leisure—Societal Life). Studieförbundet Näringsliv och Samhälle, Stockholm.

Stymne, B. (1976). *Att organisera för medbestämmande (Organization for Co-determination)*, Swedish Council for Personnel Administration, Stockholm.

Swedish Metal Workers' Confederation (1969). Vilda strejker (Illegal strikes), mimeo.

Therborn, G. (1970). *Hamnarbetarstrejken 1969 och LKAB-strejken (The Dockers' and the Miners' Strikes)*, Zenith, Stockholm.

Thorsrud, E., and Emery, F. E. (1969). *Mot en ny bedriftsorganisasjon (Towards a New Company Organization)*, Tanum, Oslo.

Törnqvist, K. (1956). *Trivsel och konflikt i arbetslivet (Satisfaction and Conflict in Working Life)*, KF: s Bokförlag, Stockholm.

Vestlund, G. (1949). *Arbetsglädjens problem (Problems of Work Satisfaction)*, Industries Upplysningstjänst, Brevskolan, Stockholm.

Working Life
Edited by B. Gardell and G. Johansson
© 1981 John Wiley & Sons Ltd

Pathology of Institutions and Organizations versus 'Quality of Working Life'

ADAM PODGÒRECKI

Much may be said in abstract terms about the notion of quality of life. One can go further and may analyse the main definitions of this term, then specify subdivisions (such as quality of manual working life), take into consideration its specific meanings coined by various scholars, analyse how they are perceived by different social strata, and so on. In this paper we leave aside those reflections and take into consideration the relationship between the pathology of institutions and the quality of working life, assuming that the term 'quality of working life' is given its commonsense meaning.

Before this analysis is presented, let us state a premise which has an important bearing upon the whole concept of the quality of working life. It says *that the quality of working life depends less on the subjective evaluation of our own life than on seemingly neutral, but in fact quite often dysfunctional, networks of formal and informal entanglements which surround us in our everyday work.* Thus there is a need to develop those criteria which make it possible to identify the main dysfunctionalities of institutions and organizations. In this context we may note that the main thrust of present studies in the area of pathology and criminology is oriented towards individual or group deviance. Thus the essential problem of institutional deviance is neglected if not entirely overlooked. Leaving aside the interesting question of the genetic reasons for this, it seems advisable to propose a tentative set (a decalogue) of criteria for diagnosing the pathological structure or development of a given institution or organization. Some of these criteria refer to systematic observations or the administrative and managerial process, while others are directly derived from some main theoretical sociological concepts. Nevertheless, they can all be used as diagnostic tools in the analysis of social situations and processes occurring within institutions and organizations.

1. The first and essential criterion of the pathology of institutions or organizations is the inadequacy of their formal (or informal) structure to achieve goals which are set for them. Inadequacy of this type may be due to their designers' lack of ability in using the formal or informal tools in designing institu-

tions, or to their deliberate use of mystifying symbols to conceal the way in which they really work.

2. People who are unaware of the goals of their organizations and of the relationship to those goals of the means they are employing, who do not have reliable information about what is going on in their own (or related) sections of the whole working unit, who are not told the outcomes (immediate or long-term, direct or remote) of what they do and are in the dark about their future prospects, experience frustration and conflict, vertical towards superiors, or longitudinal towards each other.

3. Unclear standards for promotion or ones which operate on multiple criteria based on profession, membership of cliques, or party affiliation, for example, indicate organizational pathology or deviance. Characteristic symptoms are disappointed expectations, widespread feelings of injustice manifesting themselves in gossip, stress, envy, and other hindrances to coopera-tive behaviour.

4. Indolent management is a well-recognized disease of institutions or organizations, but has been analysed mainly from the point of view of their inefficiency and inability to achieve desired goals. However, dysfunctional management through the creation and constant reinforcement of a negatively working subculture substantially influences the atmosphere of the workplace.

5. Ritualism may be regarded as another criterion of the pathology of the life of organizations and institutions. Although ritual constitutes the most essential elements of the existence of some institutions (the Church, some spheres of university college life, some social clubs, for example), ritualism often binds working and social interrelations among co-workers in a way which not only hinders the accomplishment of the institutionally designed goals but may petrify and freeze the informal bonds existing among them. Ritualism is closely related to formalism. However, while ritualism emphasizes reliance on sacred procedure, formalism (needed when justice is based on im-personal rules), if translated into a virtue in itself, may contaminate the essence of organizational and institutional interrelations. Formalism then becomes less a functional restriction on arbitrary official governance than a strict imposition of the impersonally reified behaviour patterns upon cooperating working units.

6. Absence of formal rewards—or an unjust lack of balance between positive and negative sanctions—may restrain the creative initiatives which otherwise could emerge under the conditions of greater social visibility of distribution of these rewards. Formal (or informal) rewards tend to satisfy more when they are given in public. This may be due not just to human vanity but to the inherent (socialized by the community) imperatives of an intuitive sense of justice.

7. An underdeveloped network of social bonds (infrastructure) within an organization or institution may deprive its employees of the sense of mutual

care, trust, and community friendliness. The importance of these types of informal links inside institutions and organizations is constantly growing, since their members start to treat these organizations and institutions as their 'second home'. The steadily disappearing, traditionally entangled neighbourhoods and extended family bonds seem in this way to re-emerge on the level of the organizationally designed and structured working life conditions.

8. On the other hand, an overgrown network of informal social ties may shift the emphasis away from orientation towards the task and the solution of working problems and into personally tied and emotionally and socially absorbing activities. These activities may then emerge as the main goal of the growing infrastructure, thus overshadowing the orientation towards institutional or organizational goals. In consequence co-workers may establish a tendency to use their institutional working networks as elements to create new types of 'life nests' and 'pockets'. Indeed, in 'unhealthy' (for example, totalitarian) social systems these 'nests' or 'pockets' may constitute the only 'perversely' safe escape from the oppression of officially organized life.

9. In some situations these 'nests' or 'pockets' lose their originally designed task-oriented characteristics and are transferred into bodies which utilize existing working conditions for the achievement of new objectives defined by the bodies themselves. Thus institutional resources are utilized in the interest of those who have succeeded in grasping the control of these potentialities.

10. The penultimate criterion may be understood as a specific case of another, more general one, often described as 'goal displacement'. Informal networks may transform the means to an end into an (autotelic) and in itself. Remedies, solutions to specific problems, become ends in themselves, long surviving the problems that gave rise to them. The original aims are consigned to oblivion.

Much of the existing work in this area holds that the main thrust of the diagnosis of the quality of working life should be directed towards the measurement of people's subjective evaluations of their own lives. In contrast our thesis is that such a diagnosis should be directed towards institutional structures which link together stations–positions existing inside the complicated structure of modern societies. But these institutions, being politically and economically shaped, have a powerful, vested interest in presenting themselves as neutral. Their beneficiaries will be both strongly tempted and well placed to destroy the instruments of any diagnosis which is critical of, and unmasks, the real outcomes of these institutions.

These considerations support the thesis that the quality of working life may be better grasped through the specific mirror of its negative, deviant vision. If this is correct, then the deviance of institutional life should be studied in a more exhaustive manner. As we have said, levels of aspirations, the fulfilment of needs, the directions of desires or expectations have been until now the main target of studies of the quality of working life. Yet they cannot advance an objective criterion: so-called 'primitive' man could be more satisfied with his life conditions than the greedy *nouveau riche*. The pathology of institutionalized or organized life, not seen hitherto as an essential factor influencing the evaluation of the quality of life should receive more detailed scrutiny, though it shapes the working life in a structured, spuriously neutral, but essential way. What makes the situation more complicated is that the recognition of the real social situation also depends on the diagnostic tools which are at the disposal of specialists. A photograph is determined less by its objective than by the way it is taken. Even properly designed and produced scientific instruments are useless or even counter-effective, if social and political conditions do not create an atmosphere in which they can operate. So how can they be protected against political pressures not only from government or powerful corporate bodies but also from power-mongers within the social science community without then becoming the instruments of one ideological strand within the social science web?

The task of eludication of the quality of life (and in particular the quality of working life) is thus very closely tied to the problem of social values. The possible contribution of practical social sciences (sociotechnics or social engineering) to improve this quality is, therefore, highly complex. So, on the basis of the existing studies of the quality of working life, the following issues should be treated as especially important:

1. The assessment and measurement of subjective evaluation of the quality of working life by those who belong to the social stratum whose working life is being assessed.

2. Comparative analysis of working life styles typical for these social strata which are under inquiry.

3. Analysis of a complicated set of reified factors which affect the evaluation of the quality of life. These are regarded by the public as neutral ones, especially when they are linked to such obvious assets as refrigerators, telephones, housing, etc., and so do not appear to be structured by subjectively perceived 'patterns' or 'styles of life'.

4. Methodological evaluation of those behaviour patterns that appear to be regarded as objective since the subjective usually appear in the form of objective features.

As has been said, the above-mentioned issues are already recognized as the essential areas of inquiry in the study of working life. It is interesting that all of them deal with the sphere of values which is more or less hidden behind various external manifestations. But let us stress again that the central topic of consideration on working life conditions should be:

5. The analysis of complex institutional structures which present themselves as neutral—being hidden behind established, formalized, thus seemingly

impersonal, appearances. They profoundly determine the quality of social working life. This is because the institutions and organizations create a bridge between the world of subjective, individual values and the modern world of industrialized, urbanized, anomic, alienated, non-natural, external entities which surrounded the individual.

If these issues constitute the kernel of the problem of the quality of working life, then their *subjective evaluation* emerges as the axis of the whole analysis.

This, in effect, drastically narrows the role of practical social sciences. Instead of making direct recommendations to improve the quality of working life, these sciences seem only to be able to provide suggestions of an indirect type. So, since these sciences are supposed to use the accepted values of a social stratum as data which are 'given', and since these sciences do not have their own capacity to pronounce which values are right or proper, then their role should be mainly understood as the disclosure and elucidation of the hierarchy of accepted values, and the advising of the organizers of working life on how to implement those values which have already been accepted. As a metaphor, we may say that the practical social sciences do not produce diamonds but, by working on those which are available, transform them into brilliant.

If this assessment of the role of the practical social sciences is correct, then it is quite clear why the analysis of the pathology of institutions and organizations is a primary one: it may provide the instruments needed to unmask dysfunctional formal structures and also, possibly, to suggest desired designs for the quality of life for relevant working groups.

This task is no easy one, for the individual who is living in the modern world perceives the realm of institutions and organizations as an environment which is given, obvious, natural, anything but a man-made one. A person who enters it does not question, in principle, its intrinsic arrangements, he does not challenge the basic assumptions according to which it is constructed; he does not deny its validity. Rather, he tries to understand it, to single out its elements, to grasp the complicated mechanisms of its operation, to penetrate it—in short, to find the best ways to adjust himself to it. There is, of course, a relatively small proportion of people who consciously criticize and attack the underlying assumptions of the 'establishment'. Some express this type of criticism in the obvious rejection syndrome of 'drop-outs' from this 'establishment', or through its spurious rejection (which anyway gives them a wide social visiblity), they intend to manipulate this establishment in a more sophisticated and machiavellian way. Still, the average citizen of the world of institutions and organizations is characterized by an entirely different attitude. For him the world of institutions and organizations presents itself as natural as the jungle, the life in caves, the dangerous hunting, or the physical calamities of his prehistoric predecessor.

Norms generated in small groups—prohibitions regarding small insults, incestuous behaviour, lying, killing, theft of material goods—do not apply, as a rule, to the complicated structures of developed institutions and organizations. These have their own procedures, measures of expediency, specific subcultures, habits, mores, and rituals. The links between various effects of administrative behaviour and their bureaucratic causes are, as a rule, so remote, responsibilities are so divided, distortions of recommendations happen so often, anonymity of implementation is so well-guarded that the average member of an institution or organization is, even if he wishes to, unable to grasp the actual effects and moral values of his own participation extracted from the whole entanglements which are the dominant elements of institutional life. The 'well-rounded' individuum emerges as a net result of these socializing processes. If these expectations are deviant then the given individuum accordingly becomes deviant without even being aware of it. Here is the final trap. The type and quality of life provided in working organizations and institutions reproduce in their members their own arbitrarily designated patterns. This is why the analysis of the quality of working life must not be separated from the analysis of the deviancy of institutions and organizations and why the analysis should be, as much as possible, above the contradictory interpretations shaped by the political rationalizations already operating in the world of these organizations and institutions.

Working Life
Edited by B. Gardell and G. Johansson
© 1981 John Wiley & Sons Ltd

Policy-making as a Learning Process in Working Life

EINAR THORSRUD

THE BACKGROUND FOR SOCIAL SCIENCE INVOLVEMENT IN POLICY-MAKING

In the past, when social scientists were mainly occupied with the study of their own discipline and teaching a few students, there was little reason why they should be particularly concerned with policy-making. Nevertheless, some of them were interested in policy as a philosophical or as a social science problem and some of their ideas had a considerable impact upon contemporary society. Today, the reasons for concern are much stronger and partly of a different nature:

1. Policy-making in the government as well as the private sector is more and more based on social science. Consequently there is a need for better knowledge about policy-making as a research problem.
2. The social science institutions need better policies for their own sake, partly to maintain a proper relationship between themselves and other institutions using their knowledge and services, and partly to manage their own resources better as part of the scientific establishment. It seems hard to meet the first need without simultaneously working with the second one.

At the first international conference on social science policy (Cherns, *et al.*, 1972) there was little support for the opinion that scientists can 'stay clean' and only 'present the facts for the policy-makers'. Involvement in policy takes place at least in the choice between problem areas where one decides to work or not to work. An unrealistic dichotomy between research and policy often results in an 'uneasy partnership', most often with government as a dominating partner (Lyons, 1969). There was a great variation among conference members in their degree of willingness to take an active role in policy matters.

Bertrand de Jouvenel felt that 'the social sciences have proved far too conservative intellectually'. He referred to how 'the most careful study of past correlations could not predict, and cannot explain the upsurge of student

313

militancy that travelled out from Berkeley and reached such astounding importance in Europe in 1968'. He also recognized that 'changing the world as we see it
may be occasionally the work of some major social thinker, but mainly it is an
ongoing phenomenon, occurring outside our professional circles. . . .'. He
concluded by suggesting that we should 'shift our attention somewhat from the
reassuring lawfulness of averages to those small beginnings, of which some will
come to nothing and others will have great momentum'.

Eric Trist stated: 'We have insufficient theoretical background to solve
problems internally from our models because we must go into the field' to
determine our problems. He has worked out a differentiation of social science
institutions which would make them more able to control their own development and cooperation and also more efficient in accumulating knowledge as well
as using it:

Type A (profession based) research/service 'mix'; within user-organizations to
undertake work on immediate practical problems.

Type B (discipline based) research/teaching 'mix'; within universities, to
advance the frontiers of fundamental knowledge while ensuring its reproduction
in the next generation.

Type C (domain based) research/application 'mix'; intermediate bodies
between user-organizations and orthodox university departments. Their
primary task is research on the relations between men and their environments, and they contribute both to theoretical development and to the advancement of practice.

Andrew Shonfield put forward the main reasons for the particular role of
economics in policy formation. 'The first; that it operates within a comprehensive theoretical system which, at any rate in principle, purports to cover the
relationships between all relevant phenomena in its field of study. Second, that
it is measuring manageable aggregates of social data.' Many of the participants
in the conference accepted these reasons as valid, but they also pointed out the
trap that exists for any social science to distort the nature of a problem by
defining it by what can be measured as part of a preconceived theoretical model.
They seemed to agree that the suggestion to look at policy-making as a learning
process might be a way of avoiding this trap (Thorsrud, 1972). It might also be a
way of dealing simultaneously with the two types of policy problems:

—policy-making as research problem;
—policy-making as a professional problem which arises as soon as the social
  scientist gets involved in policy-making.

Social scientists in academic institutions have been much concerned with
research policy as a condition for research mobilization to improve policy-
making. In cruder terms this has usually meant making requests for research
money to be used according to the rather vague rules of the academic system,
mainly with reference to academic freedom and knowledge as a value in itself.

Quite often the critical role of the university in society is stressed. We shall return to this critical role.

If defined as a learning process, research policy is not a condition for getting involved, but rather the outcome of a stepwise development over time. The following steps can be identified:

(1) Problem identification and preliminary allocation of resources.
(2) Search for alternative problem-solving activities, building of trust between parties to be involved, and sharing of responsibilities and resources.
(3) Stepwise experimental change.
(4) Evaluation and diffusion of results (in the form of a framework for strategic decision-making).
(5) Re-allocation of resources to match emerging changes and selection of new participants for revised problem identification (1).

The parenthesis above: a framework for strategic decision-making is my preliminary definition of policy. In this context the definition of policy is less important than the clarification of necessary steps in policy-making, steps which represent conditions for policy-making. This statement about what is 'important' is obviously a value statement. My concern is primarily the building of maximum policy-making capacity into work organizations, rather than building the best possible data bank or the best possible model of policy-making. I do not underestimate the importance of these other tasks. They are closely related to what I have chosen as a primary task within the research domain where I am engaged.

SOME EXPERIENCES WITH POLICY-MAKING IN THE INDUSTRIAL DEMOCRACY PROGRAM IN NORWAY, 1963–1973

The first review of this kind was presented in 1970, at the conference mentioned above. It is now possible to make a second review.

The research domination of the first phase, when the demonstration projects were carried out (1963–1968), was probably unavoidable. It turned out to have serious negative consequences, particularly for the evaluation and diffusion phase. Nevertheless, the domination was relatively small as compared with similar projects elsewhere. We did discuss our own and alternative approaches with representative bodies at the shop floor level, at the company and local union level, and at the national employer–union level. In retrospect we can see that the open discussion we had on alternative models helped to reduce the research domination, or the domination of any other single party. This lesson was utilized in the shipping programme to be discussed later.

The methods of data-gathering were too conventional to avoid the model of 'the researchers know'. We used very little survey interviewing, or other semistandardized methods, but enough to create the impression that we would know 'what people felt'. We involved people at all levels in socio-technical analysis, but not enough in most cases to make them take over the ownership of the project and develop their own methods. When this happened our degree of ownership of a project was reduced immediately. Too late did we see that this could be part of our strategy.

We made continuous efforts to demonstrate that job design criteria, autonomous work groups, etc., were initial steps of a development process. But we were continuously confronted with the reaction that autonomous groups were goals and not, as we insisted, a condition for self-regulation in organizations.

The research domination would have increased further if the projects had been important as a basis for academic qualification. They were not at the time when the researchers were closely attached to them. The researchers' personal engagement in the projects was in some respects similar to what is well known in clinical practice. Dependency upon the specialist can easily prevent the 'patient' from standing on his own feet. Herbst (1976) has made a review of the projects as developments towards non-hierarchical forms of organization. His basic idea is that such developments are only possible if those involved are ready to shift their models of change as soon as new levels of development have been achieved. If not, encapsulation and stagnation will occur.

It was not until 1973–1974 that we found a way of avoiding the research domination by use of *participant design workshops*, originally developed in Australia (Emery and Thorsrud, 1976). The basic principles here were to insist that the company and the union agree on what problems to start working on and that they select a composite team to do the field analysis and development work, supported by other workshop groups and the researchers as resource people. From the workshop a wider network for the support of development projects could emerge. This sort of network will be discussed later.

The encapsulation of the experiments as 'foreign bodies' was partly created by the research domination in the demonstration projects, partly by the reactions of those surrounding the projects. Those inside the projects were often considered to be elite groups, although they were the people who had done the old jobs. It was thought that their reward for success was greater than that of those who followed and 'only did what had been done before'. This was not the reality because copying never worked. But those who were just observers of the experiments thought otherwise. The new concepts used by researchers contributed to their belief.

The word experiment labelled the projects as something not quite real. When the researchers learned how to reduce their 'ownership' the employers and the unions kept too much control in their headquarters.

In 1970 they set up their own national council to guide and, in fact, to control new projects. According to the strategy of diffusion we had initiated (the cascading effect in organizations), this was an important step towards institutionalization. Too late we learned that our models might have to change after each phase of learning (Herbst, 1976).

Perhaps the most serious form of encapsulation occurred because middle and top management as well as the local unions did not follow up the field projects with necessary changes in the supervisory system, in work planning, in wage systems, etc. The researchers could have achieved more in this respect, e.g. by insisting upon middle management restructuring when autonomous work groups had been established. Encapsulation would in one sense be reduced, but the result would also be that the projects remained research dominated. Sometimes the researchers would become the new specialists, closely related to middle management or union headquarters.

We learned too late that the projects implied frontal attacks on bureaucracy in enterprises and unions. We had not been prepared to protect them from the counterattacks that were bound to come. These attacks took two different forms: first, to withdraw necessary reinforcements, mainly higher level learning in new forms of work organization; secondly, the follow-up of initial changes in one part of an organization took too long to be realized in other parts. When unconventional work systems conflicted with bureaucratic ones, the 'wait and see attitude' would sooner or later put an end to diffusion. However, the survival rate of the encapsulated projects was still remarkable. This would have been even more so if we had learned early enough to use the bureaucratic counterattacks as effective cases for confrontation and clarification.

The 'harmony model' versus the 'conflict model' did not represent a problem in the projects, although it was made a point of major criticism, mainly by other social scientists with a strong political conviction. In fact we never participated in projects where a choice between these two models was made. In all the projects there were phases of harmony and phases of conflict following each other, depending on the actual conditions in the field sites and the companies.

One thing we learned too late was to take care to select the right type of issues for confrontation in the field sites. A 'good issue' would usually be one which demonstrated a clear choice between basically different principles of organization. At the same time it was necessary to have issues where those who took sides were forced to come out in the open and state their views. Views in this context meant basic values and ideas of alternative models of organization structure and of the process of change. Without confrontation it would usually be difficult to make a conscious evaluation and choice. To establish phases of development is to highlight critical events. Without critical events the learning which took place would not reach the level of policy-making.

Advocates of 'the conflict model' usually see the abolition of private ownership in firms as a basic condition for democratization of the workplace. They seem to overlook the fact that capital means something quite different in the mixed economy system practised in Norway from that in marxist theory. Secondly, they insist that their model of democratization of industry be used and not the ideas and values of those involved in the Industrial Democracy Program in Norway. Finally, they seem to take little interest in the fact that publicly owned and state-owned firms, as well as cooperatives, have been involved in the same type of projects aiming at workers' increased control over their workplace and employment situation. They have not done particularly well compared with firms in the private sector. This does not mean that open confrontation about investments and other economic issues are unimportant in developing new policies for the democratization of industry.

One type of confrontation was often avoided in the projects we are discussing in this paper, namely the one between the local and the national union bodies. In retrospect the reasons are obvious. The Norwegian Confederation of Trade Unions (LO) had not been successful in transferring responsibility for the projects to the national unions (metal, chemical, paper, etc.). Again, the 'sheltered experiment' was an unfortunate concept. When local unions needed their national headquarters to act, either to help sort out conflicts or to establish new types of agreements on wages, etc., one of two things happened. Either the issue was transferred to LO or the national union treated the issue as one which had to wait for the periodic bargaining to come up since usually a new principle had to be introduced. Again, bureaucracy had a good chance to take the wind out of the sails of projects which had not yet attained a level of consolidation. In one case a local union in the chemical industry went a long way towards introducing a new policy, namely 'the right to learn on the job' as a part of the labour contract. The national union had not been much involved. Later, national headquarters made no effort to protect and further utilize this achievement. Instead of having a constructive confrontation the local union 'was taught a lesson' for exceeding its power. The central union learned nothing, but maintained bureaucratic control.

The limited diffusion of new forms of work organization taking place in Norway after 1969, when the demonstration projects were over, is important in our context. Did this in fact mean that the projects were unsuitable as steps in policy-making as a learning process? To a certain extent this was so, for reasons indicated above. To some extent it was not so, because the demonstration projects initiated a great number of developments in enterprises which never started any projects. They just picked up whatever they could learn from the projects. Sometimes they learned that particular constraints had to be removed in order to create freedom for local developments. Typical constraints were centralized work planning, or traditional supervision, or specialist domination, or rigid work segmentation. Sometimes they learned to introduce autonomous work groups, project groups, or matrix organization. Sometimes they learned perhaps the most important lesson of all from the projects, namely how to build a self-governed development process for new forms of work organization.

Recently, when a new law on work environment was passed with the support of unions and employers' organizations, some of the principles from the projects were written into the law (job design criteria, local analysis, and learning activities). Many firms and unions have started organizational change programmes to put the law into practice.

In some cases there was local collaboration between enterprises, schools, and other institutions to support non-hierarchical forms of organization. The participant design workshops mentioned above did sometimes play a role in these developments; sometimes they started spontaneously, sometimes they were linked to the new regulations on work environment.

A special research and development programme started in the Norwegian merchant navy in 1968, and we shall analyse in some detail how the policy-making process took place in this case.

THE SHIPPING RESEARCH AND DEVELOPMENT PROGRAMME

The identification of problems was based on experiences in industry and elsewhere, which shipping companies, unions, and researchers could bring together for joint discussions on how to improve the *quality of working life* in the merchant navy. (This particular concept was not central but indicates the area of interest.) In fact, we were careful not to use any special names for the projects. To name a project is the first step towards assuming ownership. The point of departure could be seen as diffusion from the industrial democracy programme, but care was taken to avoid copying. Since industrial firms had started to move away from hierarchical forms of organization, the recruitment and training of sailors would be very difficult, unless the merchant navy moved in the same direction. Recruitment was rejected as too narrow a problem area for a project. Work organization on board, the 24-hour community at sea, and the careers of sailors were included. When different projects were set up it was not so easy to state their objectives as to see what they tried 'to move away from'. In fact, concepts like non-bureaucratic forms of work were used to indicate objectives. In retrospect we can see that this type of objective is the most realistic for policy-making in an unpredictable environment.

As a policy development group, the industry and the four unions, together with three government directorates, set up a so-called 'contact group'. There were several confrontations in this group about the policy implications of what the field experiments introduced in terms of new forms of work systems, career patterns, and life-style on board ship. Membership of the contact group varied over time and it became a centre for network building rather than a formal representative sanctioning body. Over the next six years some 25 key people in Norwegian shipping and related unions and other organizations were involved in 30 half-day or full-day meetings were they discussed in detail project plans and results. Over and over again union, employer, and government representatives stated that they had no authority to endorse new policies. Over and over they agreed that the local developments on the ships had to be supported because it would be the only way to get concrete evidence of which new policies could be formed. Gradually a policy-making process was in operation. The researchers were the first to admit that this was something the contact group members had not been prepared for. Nobody withdrew from the group because of this. The majority of the contact group members visited ships in foreign harbours to find out what was going on. In very few cases did they report back to the group a warning against continued local developments. In most cases they actually supported the maintenance of the momentum of decentralized activities.

Several confrontations took place in the contact group or between organizations outside the group meetings. The first ones occurred when staff alternated between deck and engine departments on the first project ship. The next one occurred when a common messroom and dayroom for the whole crew was introduced. Both confrontations resulted in compromises which meant that some ships would be allowed to try out the new systems while the majority of ships continued as before. There was a serious confrontation when one crew proposed to experiment with a varying size of crew during the year according to the work-load. The crew sent two spokesmen to the contact group, but they had to return to the ship and report that organizations ashore were not yet ready for this reform.

Another confrontation took place when a government commission was set up to revise seamen's training and proposed new career structure based on project ship experiences. Again a compromise was reached, in this case after three years and after the intervention of the Norwegian Parliament.

A major characteristic of the shipping project was that problems were identified by mixed groups of sailors, officers, researchers, and others at different levels on board ship and in shipping companies and related organizations. The contact group became an open forum for sanctioning and for confrontation and for the clarification of principles. Policy discussions started informally inside unions, companies, employers' organizations, and government bodies. But only one basic principle emerged during the early phase of the projects, namely to create freedom for local experimentation and to protect the developments until some concrete experience could be accumulated and evaluated. Perhaps without being aware of it, people in policy-making positions started to accept the need for a continuing learning process, which seemed necessary for any basic change in policy to become effective in day-to-day working life and in the institutions of shipping and seafaring.

The contact group soon accepted the need for the allocation of research money and other resources to be located on board some ships, in some companies, and in a research institute.

The search for alternative approaches was undertaken partly in the contact group, partly in the first shipping firm chosen for organizing the first field project. The firm selected a project group including two crew members of a new ship to be launched one year later. The project group visited industrial firms, unions, and others involved in similar projects and learned something about the alternative types of issues as well as different phases to be initiated. The top and middle management of the firm had several meetings, some with the researchers, to formulate what they called the objectives of the project and the constraints. The basic objectives were to create a more stimulating work situation at sea to release human resources, to improve work and ship culture, particularly through possibilities of learning, and finally to develop active adaptation among sailors, in the firm and in the shipping industry to meet technological, social, and economic changes. The special constraints mentioned were safety rules and other regulations, special transportation and operational conditions, and labour contracts which might have to be re-negotiated. During the work with these objectives, those who took part found that they had a mainly symbolic effect. It was agreed that a greater real effect was that one had to stop the centralization of control and the bureaucratization of work. Only a broad outline of alternative action programmes was agreed upon before the project group started its work on planning concrete changes. A general contract between the firm and the research institute outlined the resource allocation and the responsibility for the first action phase of the first project. The institute made it clear that the contract would be re-negotiated when evaluation of the first project had taken place. The concept 'earn the trust of other parties' was introduced. It can be seen clearly that this second phase of search and of sharing responsibility was initiated long before the first phase of problem identification had finished. The main reason for this overlap is that different people and groups get involved successively. Some have entered the next phase before the others are ready. This represents a basic problem of timing in project planning. The first project ship got into serious trouble when the last 15 to be recruited out of a total crew of 23 found that those recruited first had already worked out most of the project plans for the following six months. A serious confrontation took place and the programme moved back several steps before it could move forward again. On the other hand, how could recruitment on a voluntary basis take place before someone had made at least a sketch of what he was inviting people to take part in? The learning that took place during the confrontation was mainly what Emery (1977) has called parameters of improved communication, i.e. openness (no camouflage), basic similarity (equal human value), a mutually shared field of interest, and trust.

Two stepwise change programmes were carried out in different ships belonging to the same firm. There were several reasons for doing this. We had learned from the industrial projects that when one project in an organization started to move it was important to start one or two more. One out of two or three was bound to get into trouble which would take time to sort out. If too much time pressure existed, learning would not take root. It was better to shift attention to another project for a time. This also took some of the halo effect away from pioneers. In addition it was important to broaden experience before evaluation and diffusion started. The two ships represented different levels of technology and different new ideas of reorganization had to be tested. The second learned from the first but copying was not possible.

Evaluation and diffusion of results began when the first ship had been at sea for 14 months. At this time the plans for the second project ship were presented to the contact group. The group received progress reports every third month or so from the time the first ship sailed (after one and a half years of project preparation). At least three people who had sailed with the ship met the contact group and answered questions when reports were discussed. The contact group visited the ship. In a two-day evaluation meeting the major changes from traditional to new forms of work systems and ship culture were analysed and evaluated:

—from office centred to ship centred annual budgeting;
—from detailed to general ship–shore reports (75 per cent of standard reports dropped);
—from office controlled to ship controlled maintenance plans;
—from officer controlled to partly joint crew controlled work planning;
—from supervisory to group control of work quality;
—from office personnel management to ship management;
—from mono-role and closed careers at sea to multi-role and new sea–land careers. (There was only a small beginning in this direction);
—from segmented living territories to partly joint territories on board;
—from hierarchical information system to non-hierarchical;
—from segmented work and education to integrated work and learning (on this point much less was achieved than expected);
—from high level of turnover to majority of crew as 'permanent';
—from segmented departments to integrated departments (this was not successful in the middle level–junior officers–and less successful for deck crew than for engine).

The most important evaluation took place on board when, after one year, the crew decided they wanted to continue their new forms of work and life at sea. The firm made its overall evaluation clear by proposing a second and more advanced project. On the other hand, it was clear that it would be a long time before a new policy would penetrate all levels of the firm. The contact group made its evaluation on each major step of change mainly in the form of 'no objection to continued try-out'. The government authorities made two types of evaluation. On the one hand, they authorized new types of rules for training and size of crew and for the building of ships. The technology of ships was changed in many respects, particularly in terms of safety rules and in the improved standard and layout of cabins, common office and free-time areas, common mess- and dayroom, etc. On the other hand the Directorate of Shipping gave support to previous project crew members who joined project teams designing new ships.

This meant two things. First, that sailors were accepted as competent partners with a right to influence their future work environment. This is a parallel to what in 1974 was introduced in a new law on work environment in industry (Gustavsen, 1977). Secondly, the new participatory design process encouraged a flexible network of collaborative relations between organizations designing and building ships. Previously these organizations had worked as segmented bodies very much according to bureaucratic rules. Obviously a transfer in this direction will take a long time. We can see no way in which a policy change can be achieved before a stepwise learning, evaluation, and diffusion process has occurred based on concrete experience.

The diffusion from ship to ship and from firm to firm went on for some five years before a breakthrough could be expected. There are signs now that it is about to occur. Roggema and Hammarström (1975) and Herbst (1976) have analysed the conditions for this. One important sign is the one mentioned about the design of ships. Another is the new educational system to be introduced by Parliament in 1978. A third sign is that, after six years, the firm starting the first ship project has realized that most of its ships (total 45) are in fact working along the same lines as the two first project ships. Often the firm has stated this *to be* its policy, but only now, after six years of learning, it *is* policy. However, much is yet to be done before all the experiences turn into practical use and before most of the ships move on to new levels of development and thereby create the basis for new policies.

The most important event in the diffusion of new policy in Norwegian shipping took place three years after the first ship project had been evaluated. A suggestion came from one of the new project ships in a different firm that they would like to compare results and experiences with others. This ship had made a breakthrough in using work planning to create a learning community on board (Johansen, 1977). By this time a great number of project ships had been started with introductory training programmes run by the shipping industry confederation. Some key representatives from these ships and two of the researchers formed a kind of secretariat and a new type of conference was planned under the name of 'Ship meets Ship'. First, a shortlist of some ten 'leading ships' was circulated and eight agreed to send representatives. Then each ship agreed on what to put on the agenda for a week's conference, and selected relevant members at different levels to represent them. The shipping firms accepted the plan and did not interfere in the planning. The 'Ship meets Ship' has now been organized for the third time. It represents a network of development teams across different firms and unions. The centre of information shifts from group to group, from person to person according to what the primary task of the conference is. In all these meetings basic policy issues have been discussed, e.g. decentralized work planning which integrates work and learning, new manning systems based on multi-role, group work, and matrix organization, new career and wage systems facilitating shore to ship and ship to shore alternation. Unions, shipping firms, government agencies and the researchers are invited to join particular discussions but the 'Ship meets Ship' network is not controlled by specialists or by shore organizations. This type of network developed at the same time as a number of school projects in Norway faced problems of diffusion (Herbst, 1976). They had emerged from industrial projects but with less research domination, and single projects were encapsulated.

Re-allocation of development resources started to take place when the ownership of the projects moved from the researchers and the contact group to different ships in different firms. The research group changed from project-based to programme-based research after two years. During the first period the research staff consisted of two permanent institute members paid by government, and one senior and two junior project workers paid by the shipping industry. The institute offered to set up a five-year programme or to close the first project after feedback and evaluation of results. A programme was decided upon with a partly new content, concentrating on participatory ship design processes, decentralized work planning, development of matrix organizations, a new education and career system, and diffusion strategies.

In 1975 a confrontation occurred between the institute and the National Research Board. We offered to re-negotiate a new five-year programme with the Board—or to close the programme after feedback of results. Unions, government agencies, and others put pressure on the Research Board to continue, and budgets were granted. Two years later the department of shipping budgeted for two permanent members of the institute to work on the programme. The content has now shifted towards the family and community relations of seafarers. At the same time diffusion strategy, safety training as part of work planning, and educational and career changes are still important. The last 'Ship meets Ship' conference in 1978 gave strong support to the revised programme. At the same time it encouraged the research to be linked to new types of standard labour contracts regulating new forms of manning, work planning, and training on board new ships. The chairman of the 1978 conference was in 1975 the first of a series of sailor research fellows to work for 3–6 months at the institute. This captain has recently left the sea in order to join the naval research institute after a confrontation with his shipping firm because the stability of crew required to continue a new learning culture was not maintained. Regression in policy-making had taken place partly under pressure of the economic crisis in shipping. The first shipping firm to start project ships has confirmed its policy of democratizing its ship organization as a basis for surviving the crisis. The department of shipping and trade is soon to deliver a report to Parliament on democratization in the shipping industry. Two basic approaches are recommended: One is to introduce a new type of contract for employee representation on the boards of firms, another is to continue development work on board ships to improve day-to-day work, culture, and life at sea.

SOME CONCLUDING REMARKS

The most important experience gained from 15 years of involvement in development work and policy-making in industry, education, public administration, and shipping is reflected in the book called *People can do research* which we hope to publish shortly. It reports how groups of workers, managers, pupils, and others have carried out their research and development programmes. We have learned to fill quite new roles as researchers in a participatory learning process which I would call 'policy-making to democratize work'.

The democratization of research does not mean that everybody can decide everything in research irrespective of their competence or their work role. But it does mean that research will have to abolish its hierarchical form of organization and communication. And it does mean that social scientists are certainly not the only ones who can contribute to a research and development process, particularly when it is related to policy-making. In a world where youth cultures and women's cultures are likely to change important parts of society, it is time for the social sciences to stop and think before we continue to accumulate specialist power in our new profession.

Policy-making in the social sciences does not seem to occur as long as the academic institutions are separated from work life outside, from schools, hospitals, etc. I experienced a culture shock on returning to university after ten years of involvement outside. It is indeed shocking to see how policy problems are handled—or rather how they are not handled because administrative problems and power games are given priority in decision-making and policy-making bodies. The new representative bodies where students are supposed to have influence have not changed this situation. I see no way out of this deadlock unless students, teachers, and researchers establish network relations to outside institutions of work, welfare, education, and public administration. These relations must be based on concrete collaboration rather than the abstract exchange of information. (Nothing seems less efficient in changing research policy than research policy committees.)

As long as the university seems unable to change its policies in relation to the outside world, and to sort out internal relations, what is now called the critical role of the university is most likely to be perceived as hypocrisy.

When involving the social sciences in policy-making as a learning process, the first step may be to identify basically different types of research. To do this we have to get off our hobby-horses, which are often called research models, and take a real look at what we actually do when we do research. Herbst (1976) has suggested a classification, presented in Figure 1 and Table 1. What is our relationship with those with whom we interact? Do we treat them as objects or do we have collaborative relations? In what ways do our research methods function as media which structure our thinking and our relations?

At least if we do research in working life we have to accept that the rules of the game are slowly changing. To participate in this change is perhaps a fruitful way of getting involved in social science policy-making as a learning process.

REFERENCES

Cherns, A. B., Sinclair, R., and Jenkins, W. I. (eds) (1972). *Social Science and Government*, Tavistock, London.

Emery, F. (1977). Parameters of improved industrial communication, *National Labour Institute Bul.* (6), New Delhi.

Emery, F. E., and Thorsrud, E. (1976). *Democracy at Work*, Nijhoff, Leiden.

Gustavsen, B. (1977). Legal regulation of jobs and work organization, *National Labour Institute Bul.* (1), New Delhi.

Herbst, P. G. (1976). *Alternatives to Hierarchies*, Nijhoff, Leiden.

Johansen, R. (1977). Changes in work planning increase shipboard democracy, *National Labour Institute Bul.*, (1), New Delhi.

Lyons, G. M. (1969). *The Uneasy Partnership*, Russel Sage Foundation, New York.

Roggema, J., and Hammarström, N. K. (1975). *Nye Orgaisasjonsformer till sjøs (New Forms of Organization at Sea)*, Tanum, Oslo.

Roggema, J., and Thorsrud, E. (1975). *Et Skip i Utvikling (A ship in Development)*, Tanum, Oslo.

Thorsrud, E. (1972). Policy making as a learning process, in *Social Science and Government*, ed. A. B. Cherns, R. Sinclair, and W. I. Jenkins, Tavistock, London.

APPENDIX

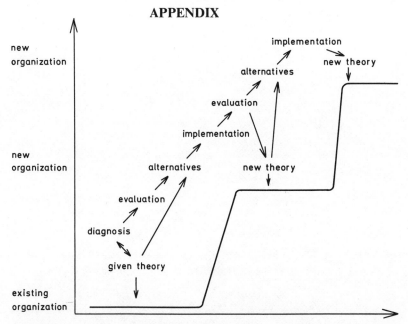

Figure 1 Phases in action research contain basic and applied research as part components in a different form and context (Herbst, 1976) Reproduced by permission of H. E. Stenfert Kroese

Table 1   Types of social research

Research relationship	Product	General type of research
Researcher-object	*The product is a theory.* The data and those from whom the data are obtained are looked at as dispensable after use. The theory is assumed to retain eternal validity.	Basic research
Researcher-client	*The product is a new system.* The theory is given in advance and does not basically change as a result of research.	Applied research
Collaborative researcher-organization relationship. Research capacity is gradually built into the organization as a necessary condition for a self-maintaining learning process	*The product is a new process.* 1. The theory about the existing organization will no longer be relevant after the new type of organization has been established. 2. The new organization is a point of departure for exploring further developmental possibilities (Figure 1).	Action research

Source: Herbst, 1976, Epilogue.

Working Life
Edited by B. Gardell and G. Johansson
© 1981 John Wiley & Sons Ltd

Discussant's Comments

BJØRN GUSTAVSEN

The purpose of this contribution is to discuss some aspects of the relationships between research and reform in working life—what role must research play in order to contribute significantly to such reforms?

The following remarks will have to be rather brief. They will, furthermore, emerge from one particular point of view: the position of action research as it has been developed at the Work Research Institute in Oslo over the years. We do not claim originality on all points; rather the reverse: as you will see, our meta-scientific position actually corresponds rather closely to points of view quite common in contemporary debates on meta-scientific issues. What I believe we might claim some credit for, however, is to have taken the points beyond the level of general declarations, and turned them into a reasonably consistent 'praxis'. For this reason our research position is argued not only in terms of the theory of science but also in terms of what types of transactions with researchers are meaningful *to other people*—those still commonly referred to as 'respondents'.

The social sciences have generally tended to take some basic assumptions as given, such as:

—It is possible to generate autonomous knowledge about social and human phenomena—what we get to know in particular settings can be abstracted from these settings and given a life of its own as 'kept knowledge' within a community of researchers.
—The knowledge is organizable: of particular importance is the belief that it can be brought into some sort of hierarchical form. It is, for example, possible to distinguish between insights on the basis of level of generality and to order insights according to this.
—The knowledge is cumulative: as project follows upon project we get to know more and more and eventually today's knowledge gaps will be filled by secure insights enabling us to take stands on all those issues on which today we must postpone judgement.
—'Scientific' knowledge in itself generates sufficient conditions for the definition of new research problems and projects. We do not have to take stands on extra-scientific issues (unless we want to) to be able to proceed with our

329

work, and we can consequently claim 'objectivity' in relation to social and political issues.

If theses such as these are taken as points of departure certain consequences follow in terms of the way research in organized and performed. One example is the answer often given by social scientists when they are approached for help in the solution of practical problems: 'Sorry, we do not yet know enough to take a stand—so rather than ask us questions you should give us money for more research.' Another example of the typical exercises are the efforts at generalizing research results far beyond the setting from which they actually emerge. How many times have we, for example, been confronted with a 'new theory of job satisfaction' based on interviews with 250 employees in a company in a town in the Middle West, USA? A further example: it is still hard to find a paper not stressing the 'need for further theoretical development', probably caused by the feeling that our knowledge is not so well ordered as it should be, combined with the thesis that we are about to make a significant breakthrough.

Emerging from theses such as the ones mentioned are also particular views on the informal social organization among researchers. As pointed out by Herbst (1974) there is a relationship between maps of knowledge and the social structure among the bearers of this knowledge. If we believe that social science knowledge can be cast into a well-ordered hierarchy, contributions to the top of this structure tend to be acclaimed as the most significant and important. As most researchers want to be significant and important, this means that a lot of effort is channelled into the top of such a presumed hierarchy of theories and insights. As these elements at the top tend to be very general and very abstract, the efforts of those who want to join this discussion tend to take on the same characteristics. This concentration on abstract and general issues has a further problematic consequence: the emergence of informal but none the less important hierarchical control relationships within the social science community. Those whose contributions to the top of the hierarchy happen to catch on each time tend to become focal points of interest for other social scientists and, through this, to exert a lot of influence. Gouldner (1971) gives an excellent description of how Parsons came to play such a role not only in American, but also in large parts of European social science. While on the subject of Gouldner, by the way, I think he overlooks a rather basic point in his otherwise excellent book: he seems to see the struggle between Parsonian functionalism and marxism as the dynamic force in sociological development. I believe that both paradigms are vehicles for cultural imperialism and their problem is how to get rid of them—not necessarily as sources of ideas, or inspiration, if one is so inclined, but as sources of social control.

Some of the theses presented above have been attacked from some quarters throughout the whole lifetime of the social sciences. The last one, particularly—

the belief that it is possible to avoid taking stands on questions of politics and values—has been under heavy and concentrated fire more than once. Some of the other beliefs, however, seem to have escaped more slightly. This might be owing to various reasons, for instance that some of the main critics of the 'non-political' character of Western social science have themselves shared some of the other beliefs, like, for example, the marxists who seem to share the thesis that it is possible to generate a closed system of autonomous knowledge for the interpretation of social phenomena. On the other hand, the view that social science knowledge is not very liable to organization, that it is open-ended and continuously developing and changing, has also been expressed now and then through the years, e.g. by Weber in his treatise on Roscher and Knies (Weber, 1975; see also foreword by Oakes).

I will not make the point that there is no truth whatever in the previously mentioned beliefs. This would obviously be something of an overstatement. Neither will it be argued that the consequences drawn are completely without reason. It is, however, unnecessary to put forward such a claim to argue the case for an important *redirection of efforts* within the social sciences, towards a more action-oriented type of research that we will return to presently. In this context we will take as a point of departure that such theses are highly problematic, and that it is equally valid to describe the social sciences as confronting the following situation:

—The knowledge we generate will rarely give a full and total insight into whatever phenomenon we study. Rather, what we can gain is partial insight; an insight covering certain aspects.
—From this it usually follows that the knowledge is not liable to far-reaching organization.
—The possibilities for abstracting something that can be put into use generally out of particular research situations—bound in time and space as they are—are at least more limited than generally believed (up to now.)
—The knowledge we generate is not necessarily cumulative: social systems change and develop, and as they do so the knowledge necessary for understanding them must also of necessity change.

If we accept theses like these as a point of departure for research, what consequences will follow?

A main point is that if the insights we can contribute to a situation are limited and partial, then it will obviously not be possible for us to 'take over' as masters of understanding and decisions. The option is instead between either withdrawing or *entering into a collaborative relationship with someone else* whose knowledge and insight can *supplement* our own. Withdrawal would be a feasible policy if we could return tomorrow on a surer footing. This, however, is rarely the case. We must, therefore, if we want to play any role of significance at all, choose the option of entering into relationships with other people.

From entering into such a relationship, a new set of conditions emerge. We might, as researchers, be interested in 'descriptions', in 'understanding', in 'contributing to the knowledge about', or whatever the introductory phraseology of social science studies might be. Other people, however, rarely share such a research interest. Their primary problem is usually how *to act*; how to develop their relationships with each other and with the technical tools they apply. Some counterparts can sometimes utilize descriptions—e.g. in the form of conventional research reports—to form an action basis for themselves. This will probably be the case for people in the higher echelons of organizations rich in resources. For other people—e.g. factory workers—this will rarely be the case. A joint venture between them and researchers will then of necessity have to include us taking part in the practical solutions to problems. Only through this can a relationship be established that is meaningful also *to the other party*.

It follows that the type of research tactics favoured by, for example, the ethnomethodologists (Garfinkel, 1967) will be inappropriate, even though it is a form of action-oriented research that we can, in certain respects, be in agreement with. Great fun though it might be to report on how the social structure of a factory was brought down through the researcher playing a series of sprightly practical jokes on the foremen and shop stewards, such behaviour on the part of the researcher would hardly constitute the basis for fruitful collaboration. One might even go a step further and guess that the repercussions for the researcher might be even more heavy. Consequently, we find few examples of ethnomethodologists—or similarly oriented researchers—entering factories.

If we want to act together with other people, we will soon discover that it will not be possible to separate the contributions of the researcher from the contributions of other actors. The different contributions will enter into a developmental relationship with each other, generating an end-product that is more than the sum of the original inputs. At least, this is how a fruitful collaborative relationship should be, and if we, as researchers, to be able to delimit our responsibility, insist on giving only a 'definable' contribution, then we destroy the possibilities for development to take place. What we have to do is to enter into a *dialogue* where the dialogue itself aims at producing new insights—an approach commonly believed to have been advocated by a relatively early student of human and social issues: Socrates.

If we believe that collaborative efforts with other people to solve problems is a core element in research activities, then further consequences follow.

Firstly, research is a process that takes time. Hit and run research (e.g. as based on three contacts with the field: when permission to interview is sought, when the questionnaires are handed out, and when the report is delivered—

each step, by the way, usually more strained than the last) is no laudable form. Instead, the researcher has to guarantee presence as long as there might be any need to call him or her in.

Secondly, the necessary research competence must be present at the contact point in the field. Because the transactions with other people are generative efforts and not simply the 'application' of something given from outside, those researchers who are to play a role must be present. In other words, a hierarchical distinction between masters back home in their offices (or at international conferences) and assistants out in the field is not feasible, at least not as the main pattern. The same can be said about the use of high-status advisors who are themselves not part of the field situation. Those in the field must obviously draw upon whatever knowledge the social sciences have to offer—however limited it might sometimes be—but this must be done on the basis of felt needs in the field situation and not on the basis of established social links and dependencies.

We can generalize this by saying that hierarchical research organization—however the hierarchy is defined, be it formally or informally, within the individual institution or across institutional boundaries—is at best a difficult construction. What must consequently be sought are decentralized patterns of research organization.

We must, furthermore, bring the counterparts of the collaborative relationship into the picture when research is to be *evaluated*. It will be detrimental to the emergence of socially relevant action research to leave evaluations completely in the hands of other academics—as the case usually is today.

The realization that 'users' ought to exert some influence over research is a main reason for ongoing changes in research organization in all the Scandinavian countries. As work research is concerned, management have to a large extent been among the users for a long period, and have developed various channels of influence in relation to research. Of a more recent date is the role the trade unions, public administrators, and politicians are given in the governing bodies of research. This is, of course, all to the good, but must not overshadow the fact that adequate influence is not exerted primarily in boards and committees but through the concrete, daily collaboration that is the core of action research. Even though it is clear that the unions must be represented if one is to have central boards and councils at all, we must not be led to believe that putting as many union representatives as possible into as many boards and councils as possible is equal to 'worker controlled research'. Channelling other people's influence into boards and councils only, can actually lead to even more centralization than we already have in research and research policy, and consequently to reduced possibilities for influence from those who are directly concerned by the research.

Further points could be added. However, as the time for this contribution is limited, I will have to stop the listing of points here. In putting forward

requirements like these, I have also put forward what I believe to be basic requirements for research that is to give significant contributions to developments in working life. I would like to stress, though, that I do not suggest that
developmental field work is the *only* legitimate research activity. My argument
is that this must be the starting-point—the foundation of research. Many have
looked for a foundation in terms of *insights*—I believe it more relevant to
define this foundation in terms of *necessary social relationships* ensuring us
anchorage in real life. Having established such a basis, however, that brings
us into a set of basic contact relationships, we can proceed to let other types
of research grow from these. For instance, surveys clarify certain issues, if
we have already established a politically relevant conceptual framework and a
social setting in terms of, for example, trade union contacts that can ensure
that the research has meaning to other people.

As best as we can, we try to develop the Work Research Institute along
such lines as indicated here. We believe it to be the only basically sound approach to the utilization of research for reform in working life. We will, on
the other hand, not claim unlimited success; the path we have chosen is not
an easy one and it is still in need of considerable development.

This being the anniversary of a university—albeit a university that includes
some of the most meaningful and important work research done in Scandinavia
—I will make a few comments concerning universities in general. Except for a
few individuals, they have not favoured the type of research orientation advocated here. We have, admittedly, some traditions of university-based action
research. Again with a few exceptions, these actions seem mostly to be 'raids'.
Every now and then the researchers throw themselves into the field; relatively
soon, however, they start trickling back to the university to perform the more
agreeable tasks of writing and thinking. This does not constitute *permanent
action* and the action will, I believe, have to be permanent—or, to use another
phrase, institutionalized in the characteristics of the research organization.

The development of action-oriented social research, that can contribute
in a concrete way to the posing and solving of problems in society, constitutes
an *organizational* challenge more than anything else. Establishing so-called
'applied' non-university institutions does not automatically solve the problem—sometimes rather the opposite, because they are often founded on the
belief that there is knowledge that is 'present' independently of the 'application process' itself. One overlooks, in other words, that even the most 'applied of all applied' institutes has to generate knowledge and has to have
sufficient resources to learn from its own fieldwork. The only basically valid
solution, as I see it at the moment, to the generation of a relevant type of
research, will be cross-institutional research programmes where people from
different institutions join each other in action programmes and work together
in the field, each drawing upon his or her particular background as a resource
in the joint effort. By background is not only meant knowledge, but also

institutional conditions. It is, for example, clear that the concept of freedom of research is also of basic importance to field-oriented research. University-based research will be closer to such a concept and its meaning in various contexts than will research in non-university-based institutions. One major contribution, then, from university-based research to a joint effort, can be in the definition and guarding of the freedom of research.

REFERENCES

Garfinkel, H. (1967). *Studies in Ethnomethodology*, Prentice-Hall, Englewood Cliffs, NJ.
Gouldner, A. (1971). *The Coming Crisis of Western Sociology*, Heinemann, London.
Herbst, P. G. (1974). *Socio-technical Design. Strategies in Multi-disciplinary Research*, Tavistock, London.
Weber, M. (1975). *Roscher and Knies: The Logical Problems of Historical Economics*. Macmillan, London.

Index

337